LOUIS-FERDINAND CÉLINE

LOUIS-FERDINAND CÉLINE

JOURNEYS TO THE EXTREME

DAMIAN CATANI

REAKTION BOOKS

Published by Reaktion Books Ltd
Unit 32, Waterside
44–48 Wharf Road
London N1 7UX, UK
www.reaktionbooks.co.uk

First published 2021

Printed and bound in Great Britain by TJ Books Ltd, Padstow, Cornwall

A catalogue record for this book is available from the British Library

ISBN 978 1 78914 467 3

CONTENTS

Louis-Ferdinand Céline, *c.* 1934.

Introduction

Between 1926 and 1932, Elizabeth Craig, a striking American dancer, was the lover and confidante of Louis Destouches, a medical doctor who worked for the League of Nations. At that time, neither of them could have imagined that he was on the cusp of becoming the famous author Louis-Ferdinand Céline. Many years later, she vividly recalled an incident that could easily have featured in one of his novels:

> One evening in Holland he took me to a certain street where these young women were selling their beautiful children. They'd walk up and down the street with their children, then hand the child to a customer, always a man [. . .] The man would give the mother a dollar bill and both the mother and child would go in. He would do whatever he pleased with the child. Louis would ask me:
>
> – You see how vicious life is?
>
> – It can't be all over the world like that, maybe it's just the Dutch who like that kind of thing.
>
> – No, it goes on in Paris too, but not quite in the same way.
>
> – Why don't you do something about it? If you think it's so terrible, why don't you try to make it illegal?
>
> – Oh, but it is illegal. They could get in bad trouble if caught, but on certain streets you can walk up and down and the gendarme or policemen will look the other way.[1]

This was all too much for the well-brought-up young lady to bear. She questioned why they were even looking, especially if he was not willing to do anything about it. Céline, however, refused to budge: '– I just wanted you to know. You who think that everybody is so beautiful and nice, that life is so simple, that all you have to do is have a happy attitude and life will be a beautiful journey.'[2]

When we read Céline, we are frequently placed in the same uncomfortable position as he put Elizabeth Craig, whose bubble of middle-class privilege he was determined to burst. He wants us to know, just as he wants her to know, that far from being a 'beautiful journey', life, as he observes in his debut novel, is a 'journey to the end of the night'. Just like its title, the book immediately grabs our attention, never to relinquish it. It drags us, often against our will, into the darkest corners of the human psyche, confronting us with the ugliest unspoken truths, which we would much prefer to keep at arm's length. The much-discussed 'shock value' of Céline's novels is a means to an end, rather than an end in itself. Its purpose is to awaken our social conscience by confronting us with the full spectrum of human injustice and the stark realization that we are often powerless in the face of suffering.

This powerlessness is especially felt by those at the bottom of the social ladder, with whose dire circumstances Céline became all too familiar. His life, in many ways, was a moral education on the plight of the underdog. As a soldier who was badly injured in the trenches, a supervisor in the colonial plantations of Africa and, later, a doctor who did his daily rounds in Paris slums at the height of the Depression, he saw ordinary people systematically being trampled underfoot, as the indifferent authorities stood idly by. His works seethe with anger and exasperation at this cynical exploitation of the little man. Yet as with life itself, they catch us by surprise by salvaging unexpected nuggets of comedy gold from even the most hopeless situations. At its best, Céline's prose is charged with an almost unbearable tension, like a finely tuned violin whose strings threaten to break at any given moment. It excels in walking that tightrope between the tragic and the comic by employing a style that repels us with its visceral, hard-hitting depiction of reality, while at the same time drawing us in with a coruscating black humour that generates outrageous moments of unexpected hilarity at the sheer absurdity of man's fate.

By striking the right balance between despair and happiness, Céline's novels succeed where his life often failed. They can be considered journeys to the extreme in their willingness to tackle taboo subjects and push stylistic boundaries to the limit with their satirical use of slang and disruption of narrative flow, which, even today, still irk some traditionalists.

From *Death on Credit* onwards, Céline's boldest and most contentious stylistic departure was his increasing use of ellipses, which he referred to as 'les trois points' ('three dots'). In this book, where three dots appear in quotations from Céline's novels and letters, these are his own, unless they are in square brackets, in which case they indicate a deliberate elision on my part.

But the moral and aesthetic risks of Céline's journeys are handsomely rewarded by their destination: few can match Céline's searingly honest account of the injustice of war and social oppression. In the early 1930s, he was heralded as the voice of the people. But from 1937 onwards, the anti-war stance of his fiction that had earned him such praise and admiration began to take him in a more sinister direction. The laudable pacifism of his novels became distorted by the hateful bigotry of his pamphlets. What was previously a justified satire of military and institutional authority turned into an irrational zealous crusade against the Jews, whom he wrongly blamed for trying to wage another war on Hitler. Céline was in grave danger of trading his humane literary transgressiveness for a hateful political extremism. He foolishly took his eye off the ball by cutting off the supply line that had made him such a great writer: his own inner life. Instead of mining the rich seam of his personal experiences to delve deep into the human condition, he succumbed to the external distractions of fascism, by advocating a French alliance with Hitler as the only way to avoid a new war. It would be a long road back for Céline to regain the trust and esteem of the public and critics who had once embraced him. He spent the 1950s clawing his way back into their affections by turning inwards once again and making himself – and not politics – the primary source of his writing.

It is not as if Céline's life was dull and lacking in incident. He had no shortage of exciting raw material on which to draw. Born Louis Ferdinand Auguste Destouches in the Paris suburb of Courbevoie, on 27 May 1894, he would become a jeweller's apprentice, soldier in a cavalry regiment, war invalid, trader on an African cocoa plantation, doctor, globetrotting head of the hygiene section in the League of Nations, acclaimed novelist, polemicist, fugitive, political prisoner, social pariah and eccentric recluse. As an adolescent, he already felt different from the herd. Acutely self-conscious about his limited schooling, he was driven by an insatiable desire to expand his intellectual horizons. His rebellious streak emanated, in part, from his social unease at coming from a lower-middle-class background. His sympathies naturally lay with the working-class poor, rather than the bourgeoisie, in whose presence he never felt entirely comfortable. This resentment can partly be attributed to his disgust at the moral hypocrisy of his own parents' bourgeois pretensions. Nothing was more galling to Céline than phoniness and 'keeping up appearances'. Time and again, his novels deploy his exceptional powers of observation to peel away the multiple layers of man's duplicity and self-righteousness.

As we shall discover, however, his penetrating insights into human psychology were the product of hard graft, as well as talent. Each of Céline's eight finished novels underwent a painstaking process that he called 'transposition': the meticulous reworking, through the creative filter of his imagination, of events or characters that were taken directly from his life. His works can be categorized as semi-autobiographical: they are a unique hybrid of fact and fiction, in which one or other aspect is given greater prominence, depending on the novel in question. Yet the curious reader who approaches Céline for the first time could be forgiven for thinking that he had only ever written the one novel: *Journey to the End of the Night* (*Voyage au bout de la nuit*).[3] The bulk of critical and public attention remains overwhelmingly focused on just this one work. There are several reasons for this. One is that this novel, together with his second novel *Death on Credit* (*Mort à credit*), remains untarnished by the fascist period of Céline's life and career. It pre-dates his antisemitic pamphlets by five years. Another is that this is the most stylistically 'accessible' of his novels. Though his 'spoken' writing style and his disruption of narrative rhythm were rightly heralded as bold and innovative at the time, his more radical break with literary language and tradition only truly began with the more difficult *Death on Credit* in 1936. There is also the recent revival of interest in *Journey* as a novel about the First World War.[4]

This is not to say that the attention and praise lavished on *Journey* is unwarranted. It remains one of the most important novels of the twentieth century and is firmly enshrined as a timeless classic. In a survey conducted of 6,000 French television viewers in December 2014, asking them to name one book that had changed their lives, *Journey* ranked number three, behind only Antoine de Saint-Exupéry's *The Little Prince* and Albert Camus' *The Outsider*.[5] *Journey* also remains, by far, the most translated of Céline's works, the majority of his Anglo-American readership, for instance, having first encountered him via either John Marks's initial translation of 1933, or Ralph Manheim's significantly better 1966 translation.

But this extensive focus on *Journey* has created a rather narrow and lopsided view of Céline with respect to his literary output as a whole. This book aims to redress this imbalance by casting the net wider than more specialized works of criticism to encompass his other, lesser-known novels.[6] These include not only the unfinished *Cannon Fodder* (*Casse-pipe*) and the (almost) completed volume of *Guignol's Band II* – published posthumously as *Pont de Londres* (London Bridge) in 1964 – but the unjustly neglected and least known of Céline's post-1945 novels, *Féerie pour une autre fois I* and *II* (published in English as *Fable for Another Time* and *Normance*). The latter two works can legitimately be regarded as the most stylistically innovative of all Céline's novels, even if they were poorly received at the time.

This book also takes a bird's-eye view of the wider literary landscape of which Céline was undoubtedly a part. For all its originality and brilliance, *Journey* was not written in a cultural vacuum. It shared the same basic literary impulses and thematic concerns as important works by other novelists from that era: André Malraux, Louis Guilloux and Jean Giono. Céline biographer and critic Henri Godard suggestively calls these writers *les romanciers de l'existentiel* ('the novelists of the existential').[7] The word 'existential' here refers neither to a particular school of writing, nor to philosopher Jean-Paul Sartre's abstract doctrine of existentialism, but to a collective literary reaction to a specific historical crisis – the First World War. So shaken were these writers by the war, which coincided with their impressionable adolescence or young adulthood, that they felt compelled to re-evaluate the human condition as a whole, by pouring out their anxieties onto the written page – Malraux's 1933 novel is even called *La Condition humaine* (The Human Condition). In this regard, they saw each other as kindred spirits: Malraux sent a signed copy of his novel to Céline and wrote an incisive article on Guilloux's *Black Blood* (1935), while Céline sent a signed copy of *Journey* to Guilloux.[8]

The shared existential crisis that the war provoked in these writers also prompted them to reconceptualize the novel as a genre. The previous, slightly older generation of writers – Marcel Proust, André Gide and François Mauriac – had experienced the war only *indirectly*, and thus not been affected by it to the same degree. Their literature remained focused on individual and selective concerns, since they felt no need to address collective problems that implicated mankind as a whole. They wrote about morality, family relations, struggles with sexuality and so forth, but without ever seeking to place them within a broader historical and socio-political framework. As critic Georges Henein commented at the time, 'Nothing seems indispensable to them, nothing seems urgent.'[9] Céline's generation was quite different:

> The proud solitude of the intellectual is slowly giving way to a fraternal solidarity that reconnects him to all living people who, like him, are in danger. This is no longer a trivial parlour game with no real future, but on the contrary an essential mission for which every thinker, every intelligent man, becomes responsible.[10]

By distancing themselves from their predecessors, Céline and his contemporaries also revived an intellectual tradition that could be traced back to the German philosophers Arthur Schopenhauer and Friedrich Nietzsche, French poet Charles Baudelaire and Austrian psychoanalyst Sigmund Freud: a loss of faith in Enlightenment optimism.[11] The First World War had shaken this belief in Enlightenment progress to its very foundations. Novelists were now keen to shine a spotlight on man's capacity for evil and his thirst for destruction.

If the broadening of discussion on Céline from *Journey* to his other novels and cultural influences is one aim of this book, another is to avoid being sucked into what I refer to as the 'Céline culture wars': the internecine battle, especially within France, over his exact place in the literary canon. The controversy primarily hinges on what to do about his antisemitism. Should this be used as a stick with which to beat his literature, or should it instead be condemned as something that is exclusive to his pamphlets, and hence not strictly relevant to our evaluation of his qualities as a novelist? There is no straightforward answer to this, but this book endeavours to strike a balance: to condemn the antisemitism, while acknowledging the greatness of the writer. It is my hope that an English-language biography affords me the necessary degree of critical distance from the heated debates in France to provide as objective an evaluation of Céline as is possible for someone with such a controversial reputation.

In so doing, I take my cue from the late, great American novelist Philip Roth, whose own masterpiece *Portnoy's Complaint* was influenced by Céline's *Death on Credit*. Commenting on Céline in 1984, Roth felt quite able to separate the man from the work, despite his own Jewish background:

> To tell you the truth, in France, my Proust is Céline! There's a very great writer. Even if his anti-Semitism made him an abject, intolerable person. To read him, I have to suspend my Jewish conscience, but I do it, because anti-Semitism isn't at the heart of his books, even *Castle to Castle*. Céline is a great liberator. I feel called by his voice.[12]

Today, there are many in France who would be appalled at Roth's sentiments, especially in light of the publisher Gallimard's recent proposal to republish Céline's antisemitic pamphlets. Those in favour of republication emphasize the need to get his antisemitism out into the open in a historically responsible way that highlights the harm it caused; those against say that this is both offensive to French Holocaust survivors and also plays into the hands of extremists, especially with the recent rise in antisemitism. This heightened sensitivity in France is understandable, given Céline's status as a major French author. What is at stake is not just *his* legacy, but that of the French literary canon as a whole. National hostility to the republication also taps into the growing phenomenon of 'cancel culture'. This term usually refers to social media campaigns that seek to deny a platform to controversial people of influence, including those in the arts.[13] 'Cancel culture' is not always restricted to the living. In the wake of the Black Lives Matter movement, Oriel College, Oxford, decided to remove a statue of Sir Cecil Rhodes that is displayed on its premises. This followed Oriel's resistance to a previous campaign to have it removed in 2016.[14] Rhodes was a historically significant figure who founded Rhodesia and the prestigious Rhodes Scholarship, but he was also a racist imperialist. Whatever we may think of particular examples, the questions they raise are often those, as we shall see later on, that have been asked of Céline himself. Is moral accountability more important than historical legacy and artistic accomplishment? Is it legitimate to tolerate both good *and* bad in the same person? Exactly *who* decides who should be 'cancelled' and is it acceptable to silence those who disagree with them? In July 2020, a group of 153 writers and intellectuals, including Noam Chomsky, J. K. Rowling and Salman Rushdie, signed a letter to *Harper's* magazine. They expressed concern that, in the otherwise welcome push for change (in this case, reform of the U.S. police and greater social inclusion), 'norms of open debate and toleration of differences' were being threatened by 'ideological conformity'.[15]

By writing a biography of Céline in English, I hope to avoid the potential pitfalls of 'cancel culture' by observing the specifically French phenomenon of the Céline culture wars from the perspective of an impartial outsider.[16] Moreover, this book also gives me a welcome opportunity to explore his largely positive reception in the Anglo-American world. The later chapters will show how American writers and intellectuals were among the first to campaign for Céline's amnesty and rehabilitation in 1946, when he was languishing in a Danish prison and considered *persona non grata* back home. American-Jewish academic Milton Hindus was such a champion of Céline that he even visited him in Denmark during his exile in 1948. Americans felt less caught up in the spirit of revenge against fascist collaborators that typified the purge or *épuration* in France. Céline's appeal to Americans was not just some passing fad, but spanned several generations. His anti-authoritarian depiction of the absurdity of violence found an especially captive audience among those who opposed the Vietnam War in the late 1960s. The publication of *Castle to Castle* (*D'un château l'autre*) in 1957, while ensuring Céline's literary comeback in France, was still greeted with considerable hostility by both the communists and the far Right. But the publication of Ralph Manheim's translation of this same novel in 1969 garnered almost universal praise in the United States, most reviewers showing themselves to be perfectly capable of separating the man from the author. At the height of the Cold War, civil unrest and the conflict in Vietnam, Frederic Morton wrote in *Nation*,

> Céline is not just a historical milestone . . . *Castle to Castle* proves how appallingly up-to-date its dead appalling author is; that – God help us! – he becomes more contemporary with every riot and each newly installed missile site . . . Céline's style consists of outcries and exclamations, groans and curses, all in white heat, separated by dots which like machine-gun bullets mow down even the mitigating orderliness of grammar . . . Céline has been buried for eight years now, but his shriek still hangs in the air, calling us, fiendishly, each by our own name.[17]

Dominick Abel of the *Chicago News* gushed,

> It is impossible to do justice to Céline in a few paragraphs, almost impossible to convey any idea of the searing, brutal power of this the first of the great black humourists . . . Céline catches you by the throat and rubs your face in the excrement of mankind. The experience is

> scarcely pleasant – who likes to be shown all the warts all the time? – but it is unforgettable and in a strange way cathartic and salutary.[18]

This latter quality is also noted by Erika Ostrovsky, herself a distinguished Céline critic, who highlights his 'mastery in creating one of the truly cathartic experiences of contemporary literature'.[19] Raymond A. Sokolov of *Newsweek* went even further, claiming that he 'may be the most influential writer of our time'.[20] Praise also came from the unlikeliest of quarters: *Christian Science Monitor* compared him favourably to one of the great canonical poets of the past: 'Though Dante is all-time world champion, the blackest of them all, few others can beat Céline in the blackness and intensity of his distaste for the human condition and with himself.'[21] *Playboy* praised the 'turbulent genius of those war years' and perspicaciously commends Céline's ability to move beyond his customary self-pity: 'in the final two-thirds of the novel, Céline transcends hysterical self-justification, transfiguring his sense of personal outrage into an eloquent eyewitness chronicle of inhumanity'.[22] Milton Hindus, despite his tricky encounter with Céline in 1948, aptly summarized his vast impact on the literature of the twentieth century, especially in the United States:

> As time goes by, it becomes clearer that, regardless of other intrinsic merits, Céline is the indispensable writer for an understanding of a good deal of the history of twentieth-century literature – not merely in France but around the world. Norman Mailer, Henry Miller, Joseph Heller, Markfield, Burroughs, Ginsberg, Sartre, Kerouac – the Existentialists, the Beats, the Angry Young Men, the fashionable 'school of Black Humor' – all seem to derive from or be related to him in one way or another, even when, as Bruce Jay Friedman confessed in *The Times* a couple of years ago, they have never directly read him.[23]

If Céline's popularity in the Anglo-American world is a central focus of this biography, this should not detract from his positive reception elsewhere. In a 2016 survey, Céline critic Régis Tettamanzi noted the proliferation of translations all over the world.[24] The Netherlands, Italy, Japan, the United States and Germany translated most of Céline's main works early on, subsequently publishing new translations of these same works, as well as his lesser-known works, such as his correspondence, plays, medical writings (his thesis on *Semmelweis*) and interviews. Examples include the new translation of the so-called 'German trilogy' into Italian (1994), the translation of his *Lettres à la N.R.F.* into Dutch (1996) and the edition of *Cahiers Céline 4* into German (1998). In 1994 Russia produced a new translation of *Journey* to replace Elsa Triolet's original version; Spain produced an updated translation of *Death on Credit* in 1987, as well as of *Rigadoon*, *Guignol's Band* and *Fable for Another Time* and *Normance* in the 1990s. *Journey*, *Death on Credit* and *Semmelweis* even exist in Catalan, as does *Journey* in Basque. Moreover, there are countries that have recently translated Céline for the first time: Ukraine (*Fable for Another Time* and *Normance* in 2003), South Korea (*Journey*, 2004) and even Brazil, which since 1994 has translated *Journey*, *Semmelweis* and *Castle to Castle* into Brazilian Portuguese.

If translations of his novels are in rude health, the relative scarcity of biographies on Céline is attributable in no small part to the particularly daunting challenge he poses: his reputation for racism and fascism precedes him, a fact that naturally predisposes us to see only his character flaws and hence to categorize him as an 'evil' human being with no redeeming qualities. An alternative approach, which was especially prevalent in the 1970s, is to evaluate Céline's conduct and character from a medical, rather than purely moral, standpoint. This entails examining his life through the prism of psychiatry, psychoanalysis and neuropathology in the hope of establishing whether or not his more reprehensible behaviour – both his racism and other negative traits – was not caused by some kind of personality disorder, mental illness or even his war injuries. The danger of such approaches, however, is that they allow us to let Céline off the hook for his racism, by exonerating him of personal responsibility for it. This is one reason why this biography eschews a purely psychiatric or psychoanalytical interpretation of his life. Another reason is that such approaches are often reductive and inconclusive because they force us artificially to fit his personality into a particular theoretical mould. Nevertheless, some awareness of Céline's psychological and medical profile is beneficial, if only to pre-empt the very opposite danger: making snap moral judgements about his character that completely dismiss the possibility that mental or physical trauma had an impact on his behaviour.

Which Céline: Writer or Madman?

The most comprehensive analysis of Céline from a pathological perspective has been provided by psychiatrist Isabelle Blondiaux.[25] Literary theorist and psychoanalyst Julia Kristeva's *Powers of Horror: An Essay on*

Abjection (1980) remains a seminal psychoanalytical study of Céline, but its primary focus on the abject lies outside the scope of this biography.[26] Blondiaux identifies, from a 'nosological' perspective ('nosology' meaning the classification of diseases), three personality traits in Céline that have elicited significant interest from literary critics and medical commentators: his paranoia, his neuro-psychic pathology (or war wounds) and his so-called 'mythomania'. Let us take each of these in turn. First, if there is some disagreement about the nature and extent of Céline's paranoia, all commentators agree that it never reached the point that he succumbed to it completely. The American Milton Hindus, Céline's staunch defender, intuitively surmised from his own encounter with the author that, although his behaviour was, at times, on the brink of madness, he never relinquished his self-control. Hindus pinpoints the hostility Bardamu feels from his fellow passengers on the ship the *Admiral Bragueton* in *Journey* as an example of Céline's persecution complex. Nevertheless, Hindus concludes that Céline's discernment and artistic powers allow him to keep his paranoia in check and merely use his reading public as a confessor.[27] Critic Albert Chesneau, in his psycho-critical study of the author, argues that Céline was 'circumstantially paranoid' ('paranoïaque de circonstance'); in other words, his paranoia was latent, traceable back to his childhood and emerged in his adulthood only intermittently, especially when he suffered a professional setback. Whenever he felt his *mythe personnel* ('personal myth') as a writer to be under threat, his paranoia would get the better of him, but he was mostly able to suppress it.[28] In his medical doctorate on Céline, Dominique Durette echoes Chesneau's opinion that Céline's paranoia was both circumstantial and reversible, and that it reached its height in the images of persecution in his antisemitic pamphlet *Trifles for a Massacre* (*Bagatelles pour un massacre*). Durette traces a trajectory in Céline's personal life that culminated in this persecution complex: initially, in his 1913 adolescent diaries, his proud character made him feel destined for an extraordinary life; his war wound the following year confirmed this belief; but his identification with the ostracized and persecuted subject of his 1924 medical thesis, Doctor Ignace Philippe Semmelweis, reinforced his complex, as did the rejection of his play *The Church* by his Jewish boss at the League of Nations, Ludwig Rachjman. The last straw for Céline was the hostile reception to his novel *Death on Credit*, the rejection of his ballets and imminent war. Writing an antisemitic pamphlet was thus his way of channelling his feelings of persecution into a reassuring explanation that gave them a broader coherence: he could blame all the ills of the world – decadence, dehumanization through mechanization, imminent warfare – on Jewish domination. Nevertheless, Durette shares Chesneau's belief that Céline's paranoia was never absolute or irreversible; otherwise, he would have become a fully fledged collaborator and not tried to distance himself from his 'delirium of persecution' after the war. To some degree, he 'simulated' his paranoia and took some pleasure in turning it into a kind of 'aesthetic delirium' that was a convenient device to justify his antisemitism in his pamphlets.[29] Hindus in the late 1940s and Chesneau and Durette in the early 1970s provided intriguing, but ultimately speculative, interpretations of this salient character trait in Céline.

More persuasive and precise is Jean-Claude Ollivier's assessment of Céline's paranoia. In his 1970 medical thesis, Ollivier categorizes Céline as a 'sensitive paranoid person' ('paranoïaque sensitif'), according to the typology of German psychiatrist Ernst Kretschmer. Céline combines the usual characteristics of the paranoid personality type – an exaggerated sense of self (pride and self-reliance), self-love, authoritarianism, intolerance of others, a rigid personality, mistrust and susceptibility – with other traits such as vulnerability, hypersensitivity, feeling tormented, dissatisfaction and emotional and depressive tendencies. Sensitive paranoid types such as Céline end up harming themselves more than they do others. Ollivier's reading is accurate, insofar as Céline managed to sabotage his own career with his antisemitic pamphlets and fascist sympathies, even if he did make something of a comeback in 1957. But of particular relevance to this biography is Ollivier's contention that Céline's writing was a form of catharsis that prevented his paranoia from degenerating into a psychotic pathology.[30] We shall discover the letters in which Céline reveals his profound need to *unburden* himself of his psychological traumas by writing his novels *Journey* and *Death on Credit*. As much as he found writing to be an agonizing and exhausting process, it was his emotional crutch: an essential form of therapy and self-preservation that he could not do without.

The 1970s' psychiatric and psychoanalytical studies of Céline's paranoia and its relationship to his antisemitism were largely speculative. More recently, there has been a shift towards a more empirical medical evaluation of his war wounds, the second category identified by Blondiaux. Suffice it to say that his injuries included radial paralysis to the nerve on his right arm, vertigo and tinnitus. A recent article attributes his tinnitus to two possible causes: a noise trauma or direct traumatism of the left petrous bone during the First World War, and

Ménière's disease.[31] Céline himself ascribes his symptoms to Ménière's disease in his novel *Fable for Another Time*: 'I vomit! . . . I buzz! . . . Vertigo! It's called Ménière's vertigo . . . The houses are spinning! And then! They rise!'[32] These debilitating symptoms also have a devastating psychological impact. This also begs the question, raised by Blondiaux, of whether or not a causal link can be established between Céline's psychological behaviour and his war wounds. Citing military psychiatrist Claude Barrois, she even wonders whether they were not responsible for the author's paranoia. Drawing on his own experience of treating traumatized soldiers, Barrois identified in his patients a persecution complex that is manifested internally as repeated nightmares and externally as the form of a threat, leading to social withdrawal and the phobia of interacting with others. Could Céline's own persecution complex have been caused by the trauma of the First World War?

Another related, but unresolved, question, which also pertains to present-day military conflicts, is whether or not Céline suffered from shell shock, or what today we would refer to as post-traumatic stress disorder (PTSD). A 2002 medical thesis argues that he did, despite scepticism from other commentators: 'None of the signs of war commotion, war emotion or hysteron-pithiasm, the three main clinical expressions of war psychoneuroses, are present in Céline's war experience.'[33] Nevertheless, critics and biographers overlook the obvious symptoms of PTSD that are displayed by Bardamu, Céline's semi-autobiographical first-person narrator in *Journey*. Without explicitly naming this condition, Céline evokes, in the most accurate and heart-wrenching terms, the recently demobilized Bardamu's flashbacks and mental breakdown that are triggered by a visit to a deserted funfair in Saint-Cloud with his American lover Lola. Bardamu's fragile state of mind first becomes apparent when he initially welcomes the sight of trees and then suddenly finds it deeply unsettling: 'Those trees are as vast and strong as dreams. But trees were something else I distrusted, ever since I'd been ambushed.'[34] When he and Lola then contemplate the funfair's shooting range, called the Gallery of Nations, the sight of the little figures that constitute targets becomes temporally confused in his mind with the real killing of the war:

> People had shot at those things for all they were worth, and now they were shooting at me, yesterday and tomorrow. 'They're shooting at me, too, Lola,' I cried. It slipped out of me. 'Let's be going!' she said . . . 'You're talking nonsense, Ferdinand, and we'll catch cold.'[35]

Once he and Lola retire to a nearby restaurant, the rows of diners are a further visual reminder of shooting targets, which cause him to have an uncontrollable panic attack:

> But we'd hardly sat down when the place struck me as monstrous. I got the idea that these people sitting in rows around us were waiting for bullets to be fired at them from all sides while they were eating. 'Get out!' I warned them. 'Beat it! They're going to shoot! They're going to kill you! The whole lot of you!'[36]

The onlookers show little sympathy, some of them calling him an 'anarchist', while others 'thought I was just syphilitic and severely insane'.[37] Bardamu then comments on the moral absurdity of war, since he is considered mad for not wanting to fight, while those who do are deemed to be sane: 'They consequently wanted me to be locked up until the war was over or at least for several months, because they, who claimed to be sane and in their right minds, wanted to take care of me while they carried on the war all by themselves.'[38] Despite a lack of concrete evidence to show that Céline himself suffered from PTSD, this passage certainly indicates his keen interest in the topic, even before the medical community had studied it properly or given it a more precise clinical name. Moreover, Lola's insensitivity and the unsympathetic reaction of the diners show just how misunderstood this condition was at the time. Bardamu's suffering is caused not just by the condition itself, but by the uncaring attitude it elicits in others.

Let us now turn to the third personality trait identified by Blondiaux, Céline's 'mythomania', or what his biographer François Gibault has called his *fantaisie affabulatrice*, or 'storytelling fantasy'.[39] Examples abound of Céline exaggerating, or even completely inventing stories about his own life: his false claim that he suffered a head wound in the First World War, resulting in unintentional trepination; that he met Emperor Franz Ferdinand in Nice in 1911; that he worked for four years in the Detroit Ford factory (he, in fact, only visited it once); writing that he was a lieutenant on his first marriage certificate in 1915, when he was actually only a *maréchal des logis* ('non-commissioned officer'). These are by no means isolated examples. If commentators all agree that this mythomania existed, they disagree on how it should be judged. If we make a moral judgement, then Céline is a liar, thereby further reinforcing our negative assessment of him as a racist, pro-fascist; if we regard it as a charming eccentricity, a colourful aspect of his personality, then this is merely an extension of his talents as a writer with a fertile imagination. This is certainly how his lover Elizabeth Craig fondly recalled it.[40] But if we diagnose his mythomania as a personality disorder, a psychiatric problem, then this paradoxically weakens the hypothesis that he was paranoid: there is a significant element of enjoyment and playfulness in mythomania that is completely at odds with the more reactive suffering that is associated with paranoia. Since it is hard to ignore Céline's paranoid behaviour, it is perfectly plausible to regard his mythomania as an essentially harmless manifestation of an overactive imagination that sometimes blurred the boundaries between his fictional universe and his lived reality.[41]

The conclusions to be drawn from the various 'pathological', as opposed to moral, interpretations of Céline are as follows: he was quite badly affected by his war wounds – notably his tinnitus and vertigo; writing was his cathartic way of managing his paranoia; he was familiar enough with PTSD to be able to describe its symptoms in his fiction; and above all, there are no medical grounds to excuse or provide mitigation for his antisemitism. Despite the suggestion that paranoia can be induced by war trauma, he knew exactly what he was doing when he wrote his pamphlets (whether or not this was genuine or 'simulated' paranoia), since all commentators are unanimous that at no point did he ever relinquish his self-control and descend into psychosis.

Psychiatric and psychoanalytical theory can shed valuable light not only on Céline's personality and behaviour, but on his novels. This is because he *himself* took an active interest in this area. He was especially drawn to Freud, whom he read from the late 1920s, even meeting distinguished psychoanalyst Anny Reich in Prague in 1932. This coincided with the early stages of *Death on Credit*, in which Freud's presence can be felt in the storyline: in particular, in the adolescent narrator Ferdinand's obsession with sex (voyeurism and masturbation); and in the 'Oedipus complex', when he physically assaults his father, sides with his mother and then has a sexual relationship with another 'mother figure', the attractive Nora Merrywin. Freud's notion of the 'death drive' particularly resonated with Céline, who almost certainly read *Beyond the Pleasure Principle* (1920) and *Thoughts for the Times on War and Death* (1915). Both Freud and Céline independently made a connection between the First World War and man's horrifying capacity to kill: the psychoanalyst turned this into a theory, whereas the novelist gave it cathartic expression in *Journey*, based on his own, harrowing experience of the trenches.

If Freud's death drive only hovers over *Journey* and *Death on Credit*, it is explicitly mentioned, in Céline's 1933 lecture on Zola, as the cause of man's imminent political demise. The frequent presence of the word *rêve* ('dream') in *Journey* also suggests Céline's familiarity with Freud's *The Interpretation of Dreams* (1913).[42] In the end, his encounter with Freud benefitted his novels far more than it did his own mental health, since he never underwent psychoanalysis himself. As for Freud, he was far less taken with Céline's work than Céline was with his, since he struggled to read *Journey,* finding it too nihilistic.[43]

Freud is not alone in confusing Céline's pessimism with nihilism. As I endeavour to show in this book, Céline – his inexcusable pamphlets aside – was far too sensitive to human suffering to be a nihilist. His compassionate side first emerged in his childhood, when he realized he wanted to become a doctor. In a revealing interview with journalist Jacques Darribehaude shortly before he died, Céline explained his attraction to medicine as a caring profession that was far more enticing than the career in jewellery his mother had envisaged for him: 'They wanted to turn me into a buyer! A vendor for a department store!'[44] To the young Céline, the doctor who came to treat his limping mother possessed a 'magical' altruistic power that was completely alien to the commercial world of his parents: 'I saw a miraculous bloke, who cured people, who did astonishing things with a body that did not want to walk. I found that amazing. He seemed very knowledgeable. I found him, absolutely, to be like a magician.'[45]

Céline lamented that his parents' universe was one of 'frenetic acceptance'. He was frustrated not just by their obsession with money, but by their unjustified reverence for those who had it. As a seamstress, his mother's entire livelihood depended on wealthy clients, so she refused to criticize the rich and stoically accepted her lot in life: 'My mother always said to me: "You little wretch, if you didn't have rich people, if there were no rich people, we wouldn't have anything to eat. You see, rich people have responsibilities . . ."'[46]

If medicine represented a potential escape route from commerce, a career as a writer was not even remotely on his radar. From a purely literary standpoint, however, these two professions would turn out to be mutually beneficial. The semi-autobiographical, first-person narrator in several of his novels, especially *Journey* and *Castle to Castle*, is afforded a privileged perspective by virtue of his profession as a doctor. As a medic, he is able to move seamlessly through different social spaces, observe many more people at close quarters than the average citizen, and hence has a unique insight into their inner lives. The doctor–narrator thus enhances Céline's ability to write socially informed novels. But so far as his public image was concerned, combining the roles of doctor and writer often proved tiresome to Céline. The success of *Journey* was entirely unexpected. As he told the journalist Madeleine Chapsal of *L'Express* in the notorious 1957 interview that launched his comeback novel,

> When the book came out, I was pissed off. Céline is my mother's name. I thought I would fly under the radar. I thought I'd make money for the flat, take a step back from it all and carry on with medicine. But I was discovered by a journal called *Cyrano*, which eventually tracked me down after looking for me. From that moment onwards, life became impossible. Medical life that is . . .[47]

Céline's first publisher, the Belgian Robert Denoël, cleverly exploited this image of the 'humble doctor' and 'reluctant author': the writer whose sympathy with the underdog is attested by his tireless treatment of patients in a downtrodden Paris suburb. Céline was only too happy to play along with this strategy of semi-anonymity that paradoxically piqued public interest, in a way that is not dissimilar to the Italian writer Elena Ferrante, author of *My Brilliant Friend*, who also writes under a pseudonym and refuses to reveal her true identity. If, contrary to Ferrante, Céline did allow his true identity to be revealed, he did so in a tightly controlled way, and shunned the limelight as much as he could, especially after the bitter experience of not receiving the Goncourt Prize in 1933. His early interviews, as we shall see, generally portray him as a dapper young man of exemplary character, dressed in his white doctor's coat, conscientiously going about his medical business. In his spare time, he was able to cultivate a loyal circle of bohemian and artistic friends and made Montmartre the hub of his active social life.

When he returned from exile to France in 1951, however, Céline was a shadow of his former self. The well-dressed, handsome, sociable doctor and writer of the 1930s was now a hunched, frail and dishevelled social pariah who rarely ventured out of his house in Meudon, where he lived with his much younger third wife Lucette. It became something of a Mecca for literary admirers, but few were invited in. To a certain extent, this aloof and misanthropic image was one that Céline deliberately cultivated, in the manner that contemporary French novelist Michel

Houellebecq does today. Photographs and television footage of Céline from the late 1950s reinforce this perception of a scruffy, bad-tempered old man. As Lucette later recalled,

> When the journalists started making their way to Meudon to visit the monster, he hammed it up, he gave them their money's worth. He was playing a part, becoming a caricature of himself. They believed him, and he was delighted. As in ancient Rome, in the arena with the lions, people came for blood. So that is what he gave them.[48]

The 1957 interview with *L'Express* is a prime example of this. The role he plays is no longer that of the humble doctor and defender of the poor, but that of the 'grumpy old man', who rails against the demise of the novel, which has been hastened by a public that now prefers superficial pursuits:

> The public is interested in cars, alcohol and holidays . . . Today Balzac is not read to learn about what a country doctor is, or a miser. You can find that in newspapers, weekly magazines. Young girls learn about life in weeklies and at the cinema. So what the hell can a book do? Before you learnt about life in a book. That's why young girls were not allowed to read novels.[49]

Céline now regards even his own early literary success as a curse. He expresses his exasperation at the continued admiration for *Journey*, whose style he considers to be dated: 'Yes, there too, they piss me off. In "Journey", I still make certain concessions to literature, to "proper literature". You still find erudite sentences. To my way of thinking, from the technical point of view, it's a bit dated.'[50]

This statement is both honest and disingenuous: honest because, as the following chapters will show, he gradually honed his oral style of writing with each new novel; and disingenuous because, by downplaying the literary importance of *Journey*, he enhances, by implication, the value of his forthcoming novel. Even more disingenuous – and typically provocative – is his claim not to care what the public think of his books: 'I do not write for anybody. That is the worst possible thing, to stoop that low. One writes as an end in itself.'[51] When Chapsal reminds him that he directly addresses his readers in his new novel and then apologizes for forgetting them, he replies,

> That's just a thing I do. In truth, I hold them in contempt. What they think and what they don't think . . . If you start worrying about what they think, you have to deal with readers, the reader, that takes the biscuit! No, I don't need that, he reads, so be it, he doesn't like it, too bad![52]

He claims to publicize his work only because it pays the bills:

> I talk about it because I would quite like an advance from Gallimard [his publisher]. I talk about it because it's commerce, that I have to pay this horrible house, which is hideously expensive, where I do the vacuuming and tiling myself, as well as the cooking and everything else.[53]

This was far from true, since he and Lucette could afford a cleaner and were hardly penniless. Nor can he resist playing the martyr card – the self-pity that was so typical of his later years – by reminding his readers of the hostility he faced in 1944: 'I had absolutely no desire to go to Sigmaringen [the seat of the Vichy government in 1944–5]. Only, in Paris people wanted to gouge my eyes out. To kill me. I got caught up in a whirlwind.'[54] Céline was, in fact, very much the orchestrator of his own downfall and could easily have avoided this whirlwind had he chosen to do so. Nevertheless, as we will see, it is a testament to his perseverance and talent that, despite his declining health, he was able to claw his way back to literary fame in the last four years of his life, when he published the German trilogy of *Castle to Castle*, *North* (*Nord*) and *Rigadoon* (*Rigodon*), which rank among his finest works.

In writing this biography, I have been conscious of my debt to previous ones: not only to Henri Godard's 2011 biography (which has since been supplemented with addenda), but to those of Frédéric Vitoux, François Gibault and Pascal Fouché. Vitoux offers valuable witness accounts from Céline's widow Lucette Destouches, who died in 2019 at the astonishing age of 107; Gibault's exhaustive three-volume work, albeit dated in places, is especially insightful on Céline's childhood and upbringing; and Fouché offers a succinct synopsis of his life, supplemented by a rich source of photographs, as well as a shrewd analysis of his cultural legacy. But the constant influx of new sources – particularly the discovery of previously unpublished letters – means that some of these biographies need updating. The monthly journal *Le Bulletin célinien* has proved especially informative on the so-called Goncourt scandal of 1933 (when Céline was controversially refused the prestigious literary prize), Céline's stay in Sigmaringen in 1944 and early 1945, and the recent debate over the proposed republication of the pamphlets. The research archives of IMEC in Normandy have been a veritable treasure trove, not only for images of the author and his circle, but for Anglo-American journal and newspaper reviews of his novels, as well as his relationship to the publisher who 'discovered' him, the Belgian Robert Denoël.

All of these sources are like pieces of a jigsaw that have enabled me to build as balanced and detailed a picture as is possible of this highly complex man and his work. For all the controversy surrounding him, however, there is one thing about Céline that is beyond dispute and which we are about to discover in the following pages: his extraordinary ability to write.

one

A Petit-bourgeois Childhood

Louis Ferdinand Auguste Destouches was born at around 4 p.m. on 27 May 1894, on the modest first floor of 11, rampe du Pont, above his mother's fashion and undergarment (*modes et lingeries*) shop in the Paris suburb of Courbevoie, on the banks of the Seine. He was the only son of Marguerite Destouches (née Guillou), a seamstress, and Fernand Destouches, an insurance clerk. Shortly after their marriage, the headstrong young woman decided to strike out on her own, rather than continuing to work as a humble employee in her mother's lace shop in rue de Provence, in central Paris. Her newborn son was baptized the day after his birth and swiftly packed off to live with a wet nurse in the healthy country air of Yonne, since Marguerite was worried she had contracted tuberculosis. After one year there, he spent the following two years with a second wet nurse in Puteaux, his very first memory, according to his novel *Death on Credit*:[1] 'From the garden of the nurse's place in Puteaux you could look down over the whole of Paris. When Papa came to see me, the wind ruffled his moustache. That's my earliest memory.'[2]

Thus was forged the future writer's predilection for living in places with splendid views of Paris: between 1929 and 1944, his elevated Montmartre residence overlooked the entire city, as did his house in the suburb of Meudon on the banks of the Seine, where he spent his last years, from 1951 to 1961. But as a young child, his family was forced to relocate from the periphery back to the centre: the embarrassing failure of Marguerite's business meant that she had to swallow her pride and resume working for her mother. The Destouches moved first to 19, rue Babylone, in the 7th arrondissement, opposite the religious order of the Missions étrangères de Paris, where the young Louis was struck by the loud bells that called the priests to prayer; and then to the more peaceful sanctuary of rue Ganneron in the 18th arrondissement. Finally, in the summer of 1899, just after Louis' fifth birthday, the young family settled down at 64, passage Choiseul, a commercial arcade in the vibrant Opéra district, where his mother once again became the proprietor of her own, and this time more successful, lace shop.[3]

Céline thus barely got to know Courbevoie at all. But this did not prevent him, as an adult, from endowing his birthplace with considerable symbolic significance: specifically, in relation to his class, literary career and social outlook. The *banlieue* (suburb) perfectly encapsulated the ambivalence of his background. Just as Courbevoie was situated 'in between' the city and the countryside, so too Céline was born into the petit bourgeoisie, the 'intermediate' class, that was neither the proletariat nor the bourgeoisie. His mother had risen from her *paysan* (peasant) roots to the role of seamstress and shopkeeper, thanks to her own mother's lace shop and business acumen; his father was born into a bourgeois background, but stuck in a dead-end job he considered to be beneath him: that of a lowly paid insurance clerk. Thus Céline's upwardly mobile mother and professionally unfulfilled father had strong bourgeois *aspirations*, even though their socio-economic status was lower middle class. They were obsessed with keeping up appearances, a habit that Céline grew to despise and mercilessly satirized in his writings. His parents' self-righteous obsession with seeming better off than they actually were was a greater source of unhappiness to them than economic hardship itself. As he would reveal in an interview years later, 'It was poverty . . . harder than poverty because with poverty, you can let yourself go, but there it was poverty that was kept under wraps, that type of dignified poverty is awful.'[4] The brutal honesty that became a hallmark of Céline's writing thus originates, at least in part, from his exasperation with his parents' social hypocrisy. That which they desperately sought to hide – social and economic hardship and personal failings – he was only too eager to expose.

Courbevoie was, moreover, an apt reflection of his status as a literary 'outsider'. Its location on the edge of the capital reinforced the myth that he was an anti-establishment writer, who was very much on the fringes of the Parisian metropolitan and intellectual elite. This image proved especially useful from 1945 onwards, when his plummeting popularity as a fascist sympathizer prompted him to construct a narrative of victimhood, in which he portrayed himself as an unjustly persecuted author.

Céline and his parents.

Finally, Courbevoie represented his profound ambivalence towards modernity. At the time of his birth, it was undergoing the uneasy transition from an agrarian economy to urban industrialization. Once a bucolic village that comprised fields, rural footpaths and eighteenth-century houses, it was rapidly being taken over by factories that manufactured Dion-Bouton motorcars, Guerlain beauty products and Carmelite Melissa water.[5] Increasingly reachable by rail since 1839 and with an ever-expanding river port, Courbevoie was no longer the gateway to the countryside, but rapidly becoming engulfed by metropolitan Paris. Today it has become almost indistinguishable from nearby Neuilly and the commercial district of La Défense. Céline readily identified Courbevoie's *paysan* past with a wholesome authentic 'Frenchness', a quality that he also associated with his fellow Courbevoie native, the famous actress Arletty, whom he first befriended in 1941.[6] 'I am a native, a "Fellegh" [nationalist rebel] of the *banlieue*,' he proudly reminisced about his birthplace, in April 1956.[7]

Céline's romanticization and mythologization of Courbevoie is in stark contrast to his caricatural and earthy depiction of his relatives in his 'coming of age' novel, *Death on Credit* (1936). This frequently shows them – especially his father – in an exaggerated or unflattering light, often, as we shall see, for the purposes of dramatic effect and social critique. The novel's family portrait is largely consistent with that provided by his childhood correspondence and photographs. Viewed together, these three sources offer a detailed and mainly accurate picture of his upbringing, and share a common leitmotif: the young Louis felt suffocated by his loving but overprotective parents. This stemmed, in large part, from their own unfulfilled social ambitions, which they projected onto their only son, for whom they nurtured high hopes. Their stifling influence was, in part, counterbalanced by two other close relatives: his maternal grandmother, Céline Guillou, the inspiration behind his pen name, 'Céline', and whose death, in December 1904, greatly affected him; and his maternal uncle, Louis Guillou, who served as a surrogate father figure. These were the only family members who managed to relieve him of at least some of the oppressive burden of parental expectation.

His father, Fernand Destouches, was born into a bourgeois family in Le Havre in 1865, the son of an eminent and sea-loving professor of rhetoric, who died aged only 38, leaving behind a widow, four sons and a daughter. He was sent, aged eighteen, to the prestigious Lycée Condorcet in Paris, where his professor of literature was Maxime Gaucher, who would also teach none other than Marcel Proust, the novelist whom Fernand's son would later seek to rival and challenge. However, Fernand left school in 1885 without even completing his *baccalauréat* (the qualification obtained at the end of secondary school). He thus had to abandon his ambition to become a ship's captain and signed up instead for the artillery for five years. He would continue to wear a sailor's cap in his leisure time as a reminder of his maritime passion. In *Death on Credit*, Céline attributes much of Fernand's difficult personality to his frustration at not pursuing a career at sea: 'My father wasn't an easy man to get along with. When he wasn't in his office he always wore a cap, the nautical kind. It had always been his dream to be captain of an ocean liner. That dream made him mighty bitter.'[8] By the time he was discharged from the artillery, aged 24, and needing to make a living, Fernand reluctantly joined Le Phénix insurance brokers as a lowly clerk, where he would remain for 33 years, from 1890 to 1923. He was only promoted to 'deputy head of section' (*sous-chef de service*) the year before he was forced to retire from hypertension, aged 58. His office headquarters in rue Lafayette were a short distance from Céline Guillou's lace shop in rue de Provence, and this is where he courted her daughter Marguerite, much to her mother's disapproval.[9] The shrewd, hard-working businesswoman, who was from hardy Breton peasant stock, may have been from a lower class than Fernand, but she took a dim view of an impecunious, dilettantish bourgeois suitor with limited career prospects.[10] Nevertheless, he was undeterred and married Marguerite in the suburb of Asnières on 8 July 1893, despite having a net worth of only 500 francs, compared to her 8,000 francs.[11]

In attendance were Marguerite's brother and Fernand's new brother-in-law, Louis Guillou, who was to become the sympathetic Uncle Édouard in *Death on Credit*. Married but childless, Louis would prove to be a more successful, generous and understanding male role model to his nephew than Fernand. Adept in business, like his mother, and in tune with the modern world, he ran a lucrative raincoat store in rue Lafayette.[12] The proud owner of a motorcar, he would regularly whisk the young Louis away from the claustrophobic passage Choiseul to the country house he rented in Ablons. Detested by Auguste (the fictional name Céline gave to Fernand in the novel), it is Édouard, as we shall see, who rescues his nephew from his father's wrath, by proposing the study visit to England and finding him apprenticeships.

Fernand felt overshadowed not just by his in-laws, but by his own ancestors and relations. In 1794 his thrice-married great-grandfather, Thomas Théodore Des Touches, had emerged from the Terror as a prominent Republican, rising from the status of *écuyer du roi* (king's squire) to senior administrator of the department of Morbihan.[13] And Fernand's

The Destouches and Guillou families, *c.* 1895. To the left: Marguerite Destouches (née Guillou) carrying Louis. To the right: her mother Céline Guillou, her brother Louis and Fernand Destouches.

own father, the professor of rhetoric, was a revered and distinguished family member. Céline himself proudly refers to the literary legacy his paternal grandfather has handed down to him, in the prologue to his novel *Guignol's Band*:

> Got to admit to you about my grandfather, named Auguste Destouches, he went in for rhetoric, was even professor of it at the lycée in Le Havre, and was brilliant at it, around 1855 [. . .] He won all the medals of the French Academy.
>
> I keep them with strong emotion.[14]

If Fernand failed to measure up to his father, he was also far less successful than his older brother Georges, whose promotion to secretary general of the Faculty of Medicine in Paris in 1906, a post he retained until his retirement in 1926, earned him a handsome 7,000 francs a year. Fernand would use Georges' influence to help Louis (such as when Louis was injured in 1914), but he deeply resented Georges' career advancement as a freemason, which created jealousy and tension between the two sides of the family.[15] Georges was the kind of self-important authority figure who was the perfect target for his nephew's satirical gifts: in *Death on Credit*, he is portrayed as the dull freemason Uncle Antoine, who works, until his death from cancer, in the Office of Weights and Measures, and whose wife is a young woman from Statistics.

None of the other Destouches siblings were as successful as Georges, but they still led more interesting lives than Fernand. Fernand's second brother, René, was an eccentric who allegedly fell off a cliff while walking. He was secretary to the president of Crédit Lyonnais, *barnum* (circus showman) at the 1900 Universal Exhibition and employee of the Compagnie des télégraphes. Céline was close to René's daughter, his cousin Christiane.[16] In *Death on Credit*, René becomes Uncle Rodolphe, a maverick drifter, who lives in train stations, is a 'troubadour' at one of the stalls of the Universal Exhibition, and one day runs away with the circus never to be seen again. Céline was always drawn to non-conformists such as him, which included his other uncle, Charles, the third of the Destouches brothers, who is sympathetically portrayed as Arthur in the same novel: 'he lived like a real bohemian.'[17] Charles had various jobs: salesman in the Printemps and Bon Marché department stores, draftsman for confection catalogues and a *ponceur de broderie* (embroidery sander).[18] The one Destouches daughter, and Céline's favourite aunt, was

Amélie, who became Tante Hélène in *Death on Credit*. A talented pianist, Amélie married a rich Romanian aristocrat, Zenon Zawirski, and opened a music school in Bucharest, where she taught the piano. After she had been widowed, she spent her last days in a hospice in Angers, to which Céline sent her a luxury edition of his novel, before she died in 1950. As Tante Hélène, she is glamourized into a sexually emancipated woman who elopes to Russia, where she is killed by an officer's bullets.[19]

In *Death on Credit*, the fictional father Auguste is a true-to-life but exaggerated version of Fernand.[20] There is his bourgeois sense of superiority, especially over his wife's non-bourgeois family; his intellectual pretensions; his 'mythomania', or exaggerated storytelling; the blaming of his failures on Jews and freemasons (Auguste, like Fernand, reads the far-Right journal *La Patrie*); his grudge-bearing self-pity; artistic leanings (Céline's father drew cartoons for *Le Charivari*); and a nostalgia and love for the sea.[21] Céline openly acknowledges that he inherited his love of the ocean from his father – it is one of their few shared bonds – but gently mocks Auguste's antisemitism, without acknowledging his own. Fernand's prejudices were typical of the 'anti-dreyfusards' of the 1890s. Alfred Dreyfus, a Jewish captain in the French army, was wrongfully arrested on suspicion of spying for the Germans. French society at that time became bitterly divided into the pro- and anti-Dreyfus camps, bringing antisemitic sentiments to the fore. The one aspect of Fernand's personality, Henri Godard maintains, that is probably exaggerated is his temper, and this is because it plays both a comical and allegorical role in the novel.[22]

Clémence, the fictional version of his mother, is also broadly similar to the real Marguerite Guillou. Her name in the novel is probably inspired by the playwright Pierre Corneille's tragedy *Cinna ou la clémence d'Auguste* (Cinna or the Clemency of Caesar Augustus, 1642), thereby alluding to her 'tragic' status as a long-suffering spouse, mother and daughter.[23] Clémence's atrophied leg and limp in the novel borrow directly from Marguerite's real-life disability from childhood polio. But so, too, does her indefatigable energy for work, her resigned attitude to hardship, her acceptance of the social order, her incarnation of the values of her petit bourgeois background, her consciousness of having married 'up', socially, if not economically, to a more educated man who did not belong to the world of commerce. Having gained a foothold on the social ladder, she wanted her only child to climb the next rung by securing a position in the international jewellery trade with a prestigious clientele. Céline would later comment that his mother's personality was close to his own: a workaholic who was conscientious to the point of anxiety and found it difficult to enjoy life: 'I inherited from her that bizarre temperament that consists in not deriving pleasure from anything, nothing at all.'[24] His third wife, Lucette, would later add that Marguerite was a pious, devoted and hard-working woman, whose only fault was her 'excessive volubility'.[25]

Céline's family thus consisted of an assortment of characters whose intertwined lives and clashing personalities inject considerable drama and tragicomedy into his novel. But they also offer a window into a particular historical era: the so-called Belle Époque, the period from the 1880s to 1914. Céline's narrator and alter ego Ferdinand undergoes an awkward transition from infancy to adolescence that closely mirrors the rapid evolution of France itself from its nineteenth-century rural and artisan values to twentieth-century urban industrial modernity. Céline's novel is thus as much a social allegory as it is a coming-of-age tale; his own struggles, and those of his family, are those of the petit bourgeoisie – the forgotten class – who desperately seek to keep pace with this new modernity and way of life. In this regard, Céline's novel sets the bar very high: it overturns deeply entrenched assumptions about the Belle Époque as a golden age of unprecedented economic, cultural and national prosperity and progress that came to an end only because of the outbreak of the First World War in August 1914. His powerful counter-narrative shows that this era was prosperous for only a small elite, from which Céline's family and social class were completely excluded: as the petit bourgeois community of small shopkeepers who struggled to make ends meet, they fell through the cracks. And this counter-narrative is as much literary as it is historical, for it challenges Marcel Proust's depiction, in his novel *In Search of Lost Time* (*À la Recherche du temps perdu*), of this very same historical period, but from the more privileged viewpoint of the affluent upper bourgeoisie and aristocracy of western Paris. Having invested such high hopes in his novel, it is little wonder, as we shall see in Chapter Four, that Céline took its failure so badly.

If Proust's literary landscape is made up of elegant salons in the plush *hôtels particuliers* of western Paris that regularly host piano recitals and erudite discussions, Céline's world is far grittier and dominated by the hustle and bustle of the passage Bérénisas, the fictional name he gave to the passage Choiseul in the 2nd arrondissement, in the capital's Opéra district. This Second Empire, nineteenth-century arcade and its environs dominated his life between the ages of five and thirteen. The claustrophobic enclave – which still exists to this day – was populated almost exclusively by the petit bourgeois class of *petits commerçants*, or small shopkeepers. The very architecture of the arcade was an apt reflection of their social outlook and especially that of Louis's parents: 'keeping up appearances'. If the rows of respectable shopfronts, including the prestigious publisher Alphonse Lemerre, were presentable enough to entice a transient bourgeois clientele, the living quarters were grim and hidden from view: located above the premises, they were not only cramped, but reached by a narrow, winding staircase that led to a top floor that was almost completely deprived of light and air. In the summers, the stench of dog urine and the gas lamps made the air particularly difficult to breathe, especially with the glass dome that encased the arcade from above. Little wonder, as Godard suggests, that once he was an established author, Céline hankered after more light and airy residences that were located in the *hauteurs de Paris* ('Paris heights') in Montmartre, and the banks of the Seine, in Courbevoie.[26]

The young Louis had only been living in the passage Choiseul for about a year, when he was taken to visit the 1900 World Exhibition in Paris. This was France's opportunity to showcase to the world not only her economic prosperity as a major colonial power, but her scientific, technological and cultural advancements. The exhibition made France, as cultural historian Michel Winock aptly puts it, 'the window to the modern world' ('la vitrine du monde moderne').[27] There is no question, as historians have shown, that there was much for France to be proud of at this time. By the turn of the century, she had turned a stagnant agrarian and artisan economy into a large-scale industrialized one that had narrowed the gap with her mighty imperial rival, Great Britain.[28] By 1914 France was the biggest exporter of cars in the world, and the manufacturers Renault and Peugeot, the tyre manufacturer Michelin, not to mention the aviator Louis Blériot, the Cornu helicopter and the Bréguet-Richet gyroplane, placed her at the forefront of the transport revolution.[29] She was also one of the leading pioneers in metallurgy, armaments, engineering and chemistry, culminating in Marie Curie's two Nobel Prizes. Communications were vastly improved by the telegraph and the telephone, with 3,000 users in Paris by 1900.[30] The Lumière brothers had pioneered an exciting new medium – film – that would completely revolutionize the entertainment industry. This led to a cinema boom, spearheaded by Gaumont and Pathé, and the opening of no fewer than 37 cinema halls in Paris alone by 1914.[31]

Thus when the young Louis Destouches actually attended the 1900 exhibition as a starry-eyed six-year-old, he had every reason to share in this collective sense of wonder, pride and celebration. But writing with hindsight, as an adult author, he looks back on this major historical moment as something of a false dawn, a rather overblown and ostentatious sham. Yes, the exhibition was an awe-inspiring visual spectacle, but to what extent did it *really* reflect an improvement in the lives of ordinary people? His narrative provides two contrasting viewpoints on the exhibition from the two family members who least get on: his sceptical maternal grandmother, who sees the exhibition as wasteful and unnecessary, and her son-in-law, young Ferdinand's father, who regards it as a welcome distraction from the monotony of his daily life and a way to satiate his intellectual curiosity and love of storytelling. Owing to her hard-working, thrifty *paysan* roots, his grandmother warns that the exhibition is the road to perdition that will lead honest, hard-working people astray, and leave behind (rather like the modern-day Olympics) excess clutter, obsolete landmarks and epidemics spread by the influx of foreigners:

> Grandma had her doubts about the forthcoming World Fair. The last one in '82 hadn't done anything but screw up small business by making a lot of damn fools spend their money in the wrong way. After all that ballyhoo, all that fuss and bother, there was nothing left but two or three empty lots and a pile of rubbish so disgusting-looking that even twenty years later nobody was willing to take away . . . not to mention the two epidemics that the Iroquois, the blue, the yellow and the brown savages had brought over. The new world Fair was bound to be even worse. There was sure to be cholera. Grandma was positive.[32]

After initial reservations, his father is a complete convert to the exhibition: 'To everybody's surprise he was delighted . . . Pleased, happy, like a kid who's been to fairyland.'[33] Once Auguste obtains free tickets from his brother Rodolphe (based on Céline's real-life uncle René, who worked there), he uses the exhibition as a pretext to show off his erudition to his son and wife about the various countries, civilizations and inventions that are on display:

> We went to see the natives . . . We saw only one, behind a fence, he was boiling himself an egg. He wasn't looking at us, he had his back

> turned. It was quiet there, so my father started gabbing again with lots of animation, trying to enlighten us about the curious customs of tropical countries.[34]

Céline subtly satirizes the whole enterprise as a rather showy and patronizing display of colonialism. Not only is the native not remotely interested in the exhibition, but he is hostile, completely ignoring Auguste's speech: 'He wasn't able to finish, the Negro was fed up too. He spat in our direction and disappeared into his cabin.'[35] Indeed, the Céline who reminisces as an adult about the child that he once was, rather leans towards the scepticism of his grandmother, instead of the intellectualizing of his father, since he views the displays as impressive, but wasteful: 'Two rows of enormous cakes, fantastic cream puffs, full of balconies crammed with gypsies swathed in flags, music and millions of little light bulbs that were still lit in broad daylight. That was wasteful. Grandma was right.'[36]

As for Auguste, however, his love of pontificating and showing off his knowledge is not confined to the exhibition itself; it also offers him the opportunity to recount his visit to the neighbours in the passage Bérénisas, who have been unable to attend it. He is perfectly prepared to embellish reality, since this boosts his ego and makes his wife proud that she has married an educated man:

> Papa told them the story with thousands of details . . . some of them true . . . and others not so accurate . . . My mother was happy, it had been worth it . . . for once, Auguste was being really appreciated . . . She was mighty proud for his sake . . . He puffed himself up . . . he laid it on thick . . . She knew he was telling fairy tales . . . but that's what it is to be an educated man . . . She hadn't suffered for nothing . . . The man she had given herself to was somebody . . . A thinker . . . There was no denying it. All those poor bastards sat there with their tongues hanging out . . . Pure admiration.[37]

So far as we know, Auguste's 'mythomania', or propensity to tell tall tales and exaggerate the truth when it suited him, was a characteristic of Céline's real father and one, as we have already seen in relation to Courbevoie, that was inherited by the author himself.

But as Céline critic and biographer Frédéric Vitoux has perceptively noted, the use of language by Céline's various characters – whether excessive, or more restrained – is a direct reflection of their personality type, and by extension, of their ability to cope with reality. Verbose characters, such as Auguste, who are prone to embellishing the truth, are individuals who are *unable* to face reality; their profound sense of dissatisfaction with their own lives is so acute as to make language and storytelling their only escape route from it.[38] Rather than confront it head-on, they transform reality into fantasy. As we have already seen, Auguste (and the real-life Fernand Destouches) was an educated bourgeois man who was deeply frustrated by his job and felt intellectually unfulfilled.

At the opposite end of the spectrum are those characters, such as Grandmother Caroline (or Céline Guillou, in real life) and his Uncle Édouard (Louis Guillou), whom Vitoux calls *les silencieux* (the silent ones). They may not say much, but *what* they say counts – it is a mark of their lucidity and firm grasp of reality, of their ability to see things for what they are:

> There is a minority of individuals who . . . know to be wary of the illustrious and damaging impact of language. These are the 'silent ones' of this fictional universe, whose decision not to speak is entirely commensurate with their lucidity. These are the clairvoyants of this world of suffering, those who are arguably the most unhappy owing to their accurate outlook on sorrows and torments, but at the same time the chosen few who, by seeing the world for what it is, acquire, by virtue of its real miseries, the possible remedies to its genuine afflictions.[39]

If Fernand's fantastical retelling of the exhibition to his fellow shopkeepers is the mark of a personality type whose excessive use of language deflects, rather than confronts, reality, it also draws attention to an inconvenient truth: the glorious Belle Époque of the bourgeoisie that is incarnated in the international exhibition excludes whole swathes of French society. Those who cannot obtain tickets are also those to whom this world of inexorable progress and affluence is completely alien. Auguste's account of the exhibition may well be overblown, but to the majority of his neighbours who could not attend it, it is the nearest they will ever get to partaking of the prosperity it represents.

This is not to say that the passage remained completely untouched by the Belle Époque, as Ferdinand is quick to acknowledge, upon his return from studying in England:

> In the Passage des Bérénisas, in all the shop windows, a lot of changes had taken place while I was gone . . . They were going in for the 'modern style' with lilac and orange tints . . . Convolvulus and orange were all the rage . . . They climbed up the windows . . . done up into carved moulding . . . Two perfume stores and a gramophone shop opened . . . There were still the same pictures outside our theatre, the Plush Barn . . . the same posters in the stage entrance . . . They were still playing Miss Heylett and still with the same tenor – Pitaluga . . . He had a heavenly voice, every Sunday he bowled over his female admirers in the Elevation at Notre-Dame-des Victoires . . . For twelve months every shop in the Passage was talking about the way this Pitaluga sang 'Minuit Chrétien' at Saint-Eustache on Christmas! . . .[40]

He observes the beautiful, floral mouldings of the 'modern style', or 'art nouveau' that marked the turn of the twentieth century, as well as the elegance of the perfume stores and the exciting novelty of the gramophone shop. But he is far more inclined to celebrate the *continuity* from the previous century, than the changes of the new one: especially, the live performances of Pitaluga, a popular late nineteenth-century singer.

This is a timely reminder that the district where Céline grew up was not only commercial, but steeped in popular culture. It was the heartland of the *opérettes*, *opéras comiques* and *opéras légers*, all variants on the genre of the 'light opera' that was launched in the late nineteenth century to great acclaim by Jacques Offenbach, who was very much admired by Céline, despite the composer's Jewish origins. The young Louis grew up surrounded by his music, together with that of the other exponents of the genre, such as Antoine Adam, André Messager, Robert Planquette and Charles Lecocq. Céline's mother's boutique in the passage Choiseul was directly opposite the artists' entrance of the Théâtre des Bouffes-Parisiens, also known as the Salle Choiseul, which was opened by Offenbach himself in 1855. The equally famous Salle Favart was a stone's throw away, as were the venues Les Variétés, L'Apollo and the Théâtre de la Renaissance. The colourful posters on the walls, the crowds of people that poured in and out of the performances, the popular lyrical arias and the names of singers were as much a part of the young Louis' daily backdrop as the hubbub of commercial activity. This whole tradition illustrates a particularly intensive moment of literary creativity in France, which Céline attributed to French *génie* (genius) and would unfortunately turn into a racial category in his pamphlets. But the lightness and exuberance that characterize these *opérettes* were something that directly fed into his development of a more lively and emotive literary style.

The second musical genre that dominated the district and era in which Céline grew up also had an impact on his literature: popular songs held a democratic counter-cultural appeal. They were a catalyst for his spontaneous, 'anti-academic' style of writing, which sought to break the Proustian mould of erudite and highly constructed sentences. As early as 1907, he mentions his love of the song 'Ma Tonkinoise', a huge hit the previous year. In subsequent works, especially *Fable for Another Time*, he would frequently mention popular genres: traditional, children's, military, drinking, revolutionary and sentimental songs. In the mid-1930s, when he was writing *Death on Credit*, he tried both to record existing songs and write his own. He tried to get the realist singer Marianne Oswald to record and sing 'Katika la putain' ('Katika the whore'), but the project never materialized.[41]

It is precisely this joyful and emotionally charged tradition of popular culture – songs and light operas – that Céline feels is threatened by the arrival of an impersonal and rational modernity. He is not opposed to all that is new as a matter of principle, so long as the communal ties to the rich and authentic heritage he knew as a boy are not severed forever. For instance, he recognizes that while the replacement of gas by electricity will finally get rid of the unbearable stench in the arcade, there is also the danger that the arcade could be destroyed and replaced altogether:

> There was talk of installing electricity in all the shops in the Passage! Then they'd get rid of the gas that started whistling at four o'clock in the afternoon from three hundred and twenty jets . . . it stank so bad in that confined space (added to the urine from the dogs, which were getting to be more and more plentiful . . .) that at about seven o'clock some of the lady customers began to feel faint . . . There was even talk of tearing us down completely, of dismantling the whole gallery! Of removing our big glass roof and building a street eighty feet wide where we were living . . . My oh my! But the rumours weren't very serious, actually it was poppycock, prison gossip. We were prisoners in a glass cage and prisoners we would always be![42]

Céline expresses via his narrator, Ferdinand, not only his own fears, but those of the entire community in which he grew up, a community that perceives its entire identity to be under threat.

This change is mirrored by Ferdinand's equally awkward transition from boyhood to adolescence. His return from England and arrival in the renovated arcade coincides with everyone remarking how much he has grown: 'All the neighbours in the Passage were flabbergasted at the dimensions I had assumed . . .'[43] This is typical of the novel as a whole: the individual's body acts as a barometer for his or her economic fortunes or misfortunes. No better is this illustrated than when Ferdinand's long-suffering mother – Clémence in the novel – is forced to venture out by foot to the suburbs in Chatou, carrying a 20-kilogram (44 lb) bag to sell her lace to customers, because her small shop is struggling to compete with the new factories. When she returns, her feet and legs are in absolute agony, a pain that is accentuated by her atrophied limb. The lower middle class's struggle to adapt to this new modernity is reflected viscerally via *physical* suffering: 'she couldn't stand up, her face was ravaged with the pain in her leg. She whined like a dog and lay all twisted on the linoleum . . .'[44]

This close link between physical and economic decline is also reflected in the novel's title. Its literal meaning refers to the commercial term – frequently used in the nineteenth century – that the buyer acquires the possession of goods 'on credit' (*à crédit*), before they have been paid. But it also has a more metaphorical meaning: namely, that it is an inherent biological law that there is no life without death. Therefore, the notion of 'death on credit' implies that life is a progressive payment by each individual of the death that he carries within him from birth.[45] It is no coincidence that the dominant lexical fields in the novel are those pertaining to money and commerce (*aubert, se beurrer, banquer, biffeton, bourre, bulle, credo, décher, douiller, flouze, fourguer*), which are often used in conjunction with verbs that designate talking, often in a business context (*bavacher, baver, bavocher, bavoucher, jaboter, jacter, jaspiner, mouffeter, parlocheur, tanner*). Céline draws on a rich lexicon of Parisian slang from that era, for which no precise equivalent words exist in English. To these can be added the multiple words used to describe the human body, whether in relation to death (*calencher, crever, crounir, estourbir*), eating and drinking (*becter, becqueter, brifer, carne, cacher, s'entonner, licher, rempiffrer*) – and the sex act or genitalia (*astiquer, biroute, bistoquette, bourrer, branlocher, burne, copeau, croquette, englander, (se) farcir, miser, motte, panais, peau de zébi, queue, rotoplots, tringler*).[46] Those critics who, at the time, dismissed this slang as evidence of the author's vulgarity and scatological desire to shock overlook its deeper psychological relevance: the fact that so many competing words exist to express such a small number of irreducibly human urges and fears reinforces the novel's message that life, at its core, is a desperate struggle for survival.

As for the link between physical and economic decline, for many in society, this is exacerbated by modernity. To the bourgeoisie, this modernity is synonymous with Belle Époque prosperity, whereas to the petit bourgeoisie, it usually spells financial hardship. No more is this illustrated than when the young Ferdinand hits his father Auguste over the head with a typewriter, following a bitter row. The typewriter, like the gramophone, or electricity, is a symbol of technological progress and an improved standard of living – an improvement, that is, for the bourgeoisie, but not for an ageing and lowly insurance clerk, like Auguste. In a long and pompous letter to his son, while Ferdinand is away studying in England, Auguste complains not only of his lack of discipline and progress in English, but of the hardships he himself is facing in his insurance office. He has been supplanted by younger, more ambitious colleagues, so to make ends meet, he is being forced to type at home:

> On the off chance, in a last impulse of self-defence, I have undertaken (a desperate measure) the task of learning to operate a typewriter, outside the office of course, taking advantage of the little time I can spare from deliveries and errands for the shop. We have rented the machine (an American make) for several months (one more expense). But here again I harbor no illusions! . . . At my age, as you can well imagine it is not easy to assimilate so novel a technique, new methods, new habits, new ways of thinking![47]

Modernity – epitomized here by a typewriter from America – merely exacerbates, rather than alleviates, his pre-existing social frustrations and professional disappointments. The typewriter was also seen as an instrument to be operated by women, thus adding to the degradation of Auguste's situation. This contrasts markedly with his brother-in-law, Édouard, who is closely based on Louis' real uncle, Louis Guillou. Édouard's ability to adapt to the modern world and his successful business as a patented inventor and vendor of bicycle pumps, mean that he is far more level-headed and comfortable in his own skin than Auguste. Quite apart from his lucid grasp of reality, he incarnates, like Louis' grandmother, the second personality trait of the *silencieux*: empathy.

Both Édouard and Grandmother Caroline adopt a nurturing and understanding attitude towards Ferdinand, which is far more productive than the pushy and overbearing approach of Auguste and Clémence. They give the boy the freedom to develop and express himself at his own pace. Contrary to Auguste, Édouard does not tax his nephew with 'heavy' and serious subjects, but discusses boxing, his inventions and tools. What little he does teach him is of a practical nature that smooths his passage from boyhood to manhood: for instance, how to shave. Édouard thus shows a sensitivity to his nephew's needs that the boy finds both touching and disconcerting. During the six weeks he lives with his uncle, he is afforded an unprecedented freedom which has the paradoxical effect of pricking his conscience and getting him to take personal responsibility for his own life. No longer does he automatically rebel against his parents' excessive discipline and formality by being wilfully lazy and irresponsible. For instance, he decides, off his own bat, to do the dishes. This emphasis on learning for himself rather than being spoon-fed is entirely in keeping with Céline's auto-didactic leanings.

Édouard thus represents, as Vitoux aptly puts it, 'the silence of certain characters, who refuse to impose lies on others or even a well-intentioned, but inhibiting or moralising word.' This provides Ferdinand with 'an immense sense of calm, a space that is propitious for personal reflection'.[48]

Until her death in 1904, this same nurturing and comforting presence in shaping his view of the world is provided by Grandmother Caroline, who secretly buys Ferdinand illustrated comic books, much to the disapproval of his father:

> On the way home she'd stop at the corner of our Passage and buy me a copy of *Illustrated Adventure Stories* from the newspaper woman with the charcoal foot-warmer. She'd hide it for me in her panties, under her three thick petticoats. My father didn't like me to read such hogwash. He claimed it corrupted you, that it didn't prepare you for life, that I'd do better to learn the alphabet out of something serious.[49]

Apart from the adventure stories, Louis' bond with his grandmother was further reinforced by their shared love of popular culture. It was she, and not his parents, who took him to exciting and fun shows. In later interviews, he fondly reminisced how at the Robert Houdin (now the Musée Grévin), he would climb with his grandmother into a large shell (*obus*) for a simulated voyage to the moon.[50] She also took him to see Harry Houdini, Robert Houdin's admirer, at the Olympia in 1901, as he recalls in his later novel *Castle to Castle*, as well as to the Hippodrome on place Clichy, to see the horse and chariot races, and the Cirque d'Hiver (winter circus) and the Théâtre du Châtelet.[51]

Both Ferdinand's Uncle Édouard and Grandmother Caroline are thus a breath of fresh air after Auguste's pompous formality and emphasis on academic learning, which is frequently peppered with Latin quotations. What is more, they represent an equanimity and patience with the young boy that contrasts markedly with his father's temper tantrums, in which he sometimes dispenses with propriety and formal rhetoric altogether and unleashes a torrent of abuse on his son. One day, Ferdinand is sent by his mother to do some food shopping, only to return home late, drunk, penniless and without the food, which he has shamelessly squandered or bartered in exchange for alcohol. For Auguste, this is the last straw, his son's intolerable behaviour becoming the focal point for all his pent-up frustration at his dire social and economic situation. He thus launches into an expletive-laden rant:

> Suffering arsehole Christ Almighty! My poor dear, what did we do to produce such vermin? As corrupt as three dozen jailbirds! . . . Profligate! Scoundrel! Idler! And then some! He's calamity personified! Good for nothing except to rob us and clean us out! A pestilence! Gouge us without mercy! . . . That's all his gratitude! For a whole life of sacrifice! Two lives of torment! We're nothing but a couple of old fools![52]

The real Fernand Destouches is unlikely to have used such language, so in this regard, Auguste departs significantly from biographical fact. But Céline includes such exaggerated episodes for comic effect, and to demonstrate his aversion towards pompous academic rhetoric and preference for the greater emotional authenticity of an oral vernacular language, which as we shall see, he wishes to revive from the Renaissance.

To sum up, the young Louis' education is shaped by two opposing camps, each with its very distinctive approach to life. There are his sanctimonious petit bourgeois parents, who impose a rigidly formal learning on the boy that reflects his mother's social ambition and his father's bourgeois intellectual snobbery. There is also the more informal attitude of his grandmother and uncle, which, on the contrary, encouraged him to discover the world for himself, to enjoy learning for its own sake, and to remain grounded in the authenticity of popular culture. These clashing world views explain not only much of *Death on Credit*'s dramatic tension, but the psychological origins of his novels as a whole. Their irreverence, individualism and anti-authoritarianism are an act of rebellion – both conscious and unconscious – against the suffocating conventionality of his parents. Moreover, his father's death in March 1932 gave him the freedom to portray him in a more caricatural way than if he had still been alive, as well as refresh his memory about his childhood, probably because it gave him access to childhood letters that he had not seen for years.[53]

Yet as much as he resented the pedagogical formality of bourgeois education, Céline saw his lack of schooling as a shortcoming. He attended school only between 1900 and 1907: four and a half years at the communal school in square Louvois, one and a half years in a religious school in the same district and the remainder in another state school, on rue d'Argenteuil.[54] He did not take his *baccalauréat* until many years later, stopping his studies once he had passed his *certificat d'études*, at his first attempt, in June 1907. Once again, the reason was his parents, who had a very clear idea of the career their son should pursue: working as representative for an international jewellery company. This career required not a *baccalauréat*, but apprenticeships. This explains the emergence of Louis the autodidact and independent thinker who wanted to compensate, *by dint of his own efforts*, for his lack of secondary education. He would read voraciously in the few spare hours at his disposal, without the slightest encouragement or guidance from anyone:

> While I was working like a slave, at my parent's, or for my bosses, I used my pocket-money to get hold of the secondary school syllabuses, the books; I would swot up in the corners, my eyes exhausted and burning from a lack of sleep. Everything was lodged into my head, Latin, Greek, maths, history. This lasted years. Nobody encouraged me, or told me how I was doing.[55]

In these troubled teenage years, Louis primarily satiated his thirst for knowledge through two periodicals: *Je sais tout* and *Lecture pour tous*. They allowed certain ideas – both good and bad – to percolate into his consciousness. Examples of the former are references in May 1909 to the 'martyrs of science', which included Philippe Semmelweis, on whom

Céline would later write his medical thesis, in 1924, and Pliny the Elder, whom he mentions in his novel *Fable for Another Time*. Examples of the latter, however, were the colonialist and racist ideology that was variously directed at the Far East, Africa and Jews.[56]

Yet for all his complaints about having to study all by himself, the young Louis was still afforded unique opportunities that most lower-middle-class French boys in the early twentieth century could only dream of: the experience of learning a foreign language abroad. Since the plan was for him to work in the international jewellery trade, his parents felt it necessary for him to have a working knowledge of the two other major European languages at the time. This is why, once their financial circumstances improved following the death of his grandmother in 1904, Louis was sent first to Germany, in 1907–8, and second to England, in 1908–9.

Here, *Death on Credit* is just as instructive for what it *excludes* from his post-school education, as it is for what it includes. No mention is made of studying in Germany, yet a significant portion of the novel is devoted to England. The likely reasons for this are twofold. First, a French novelist writing in 1936 who showed any kind of fondness for or familiarity with Germany, when the threat of Nazi invasion was looming, ran the risk of alienating his French readers. If, as we shall see in Chapter Five, his pamphlets advocated, for pragmatic political reasons, a Franco-German alliance, Céline preferred to keep his novels as a space for stylistic experimentation and a social satire of his past, rather than for ideological comment on current affairs. Second, Céline was much more of an Anglophile than he was a Germanophile: arguably, his favourite author was Shakespeare, and he spent one of the happiest years of his life in London in 1915, recuperating from the trenches. And his love of England was further confirmed when he paid homage to London in his later novels *Guignol's Band I* and *II*.

Nevertheless, his experience of Germany at the time was largely a happy and productive one. Since he does not mention Germany in *Death on Credit*, our main source of information about this period – when he was aged thirteen and fourteen – comes from his earliest surviving letters, written primarily to his parents. They reveal a fascinating tension between the innocent, happy-go-lucky, obedient child who has yet to rebel against his parents, and the developing adult who is beginning to question and even mock authority and the status quo. In other words, the demands of filial duty and convention vie with that emerging spirit of irreverence that set the tone for his later fiction. Many letters still show Louis the child: an energetic, affectionate, studious, sociable boy who loves outdoor activities, such as sailing in his boat Le Tom on the river Seine at Ablons. He reassures his parents that he is studying hard, improving his piano playing and dutifully writing to his uncles and aunts. One of his favourite phrases, to placate his anxious parents, was 'il ne faut pas vous faire de bile': 'you musn't get worked up'.[57]

Such is the tone of the letters he sent from Diepholz and Karlsruhe, where he studied in 1907 and 1908. By all accounts, his time at Diepholz, with his host family, Herr and Frau Schmidt, was a happy one, even if this small town on the banks of the Hunte, near Hanover, was unremarkable and known primarily for making cigars.[58] Despite his reservations about Frau Schmidt, whom he considered moody and taciturn, he was evidently very fond of her husband, Hugo Schmidt, a science teacher and the headmaster at the local school attended by Louis. The feeling was mutual, since Hugo Schmidt encouraged Louis in his study of German, regularly writing positive progress reports to his parents and ensuring he was kept occupied with healthy outdoor pursuits such as cycling, ice-skating, swimming and walking. He severely reprimanded his pupils for teasing this young French visitor, whom he considered to be hard-working, pleasant and intelligent. As a dutiful son, Louis was all too aware of the sacrifices his parents had made for him, even telling them to refrain from buying him a violin or a boat. He was happy to earn extra pocket money by giving French lessons to one of his teachers, performing little electrical experiments for the inhabitants of Diepholz and showing films with a cinema projector offered to him by his uncle Édouard.[59]

His filial duty and gratitude are given fulsome expression in the New Year's wishes he sends to his parents at the end of 1907:

> I wish you everlasting good health, I thank you with all my heart for the sacrifices you have borne for my future. But believe me that I will not be an ingrate and that later on you will have good reason to be happy about the major sacrifices you are making for me mummy and daddy.[60]

The obsequious and obedient tone suggests an eagerness to please his morally conventional parents. But we also begin to see glimpses of the writer he would become: specifically, in his use of an irreverent, satirical tone that incisively questions authority and refuses to take things at face value. Every so often, he rails against the polite conventions of letter-writing to reveal his sharp eye for social observation. Recounting his attendance of the 'feast of Sedan' to celebrate the Prussian victory against the French on 2 September 1870, for instance, he pokes gentle fun, albeit in faulty German, at the military hats and patriotic chants in praise of the Kaiser:

> There on the main square the town authorities were parading with ridiculously tall small caps: it was hilarious . . . The biggest drag was that after the patriotic speech by the prefect, everybody shouted 'es lebe Kaiser' [*sic*], while waving their hat. To avoid looking ridiculous, I did as they did and shouted 'Long Live the Kaiser' [. . .] I did not go to school as it was the feast of Sedan. Out of 'patriotic respect' I did not go, but I regret it because cakes were being handed out.[61]

At the age of fourteen, Louis was already questioning the value of military patriotism, thereby prefiguring his anti-war stance of *Journey to the End of the Night*. The seeds of his future pacifism are also evident, when he reflects on the bullying he suffered at the hands of German pupils. This expands into his more general concern with a mounting nationalism he discerns among the younger German generation, as opposed to their elders, who had known the Franco-Prussian War:

> I am starting to make some observations and this is the conclusion I have drawn . . . that is, that the new German generation is far more patriotic than the old one that witnessed the war and its horrors. What is more, they do not spare me any cruelty.[62]

These social observations are accompanied by early indications of another of his stylistic traits: his black humour. To give just one example, when Herr Schmidt's mother comes to babysit her grandchildren in their parents' absence, she is described in less than flattering terms as 'a really decent woman, but ugly, ugly . . . like ten times worse than Mère Gaudolot [a neighbour]. Imagine a little old woman as ugly as the 7 deadly sins, her skin as wrinkled as drumskin.'[63]

The letters from Diepholz, then, exhibit his nascent talent for subversion and observation, which was no doubt a reaction to the excessive formality of his parents. And sure enough, once he returned to France for Easter 1908, his father made him sit an oral and written exam in German. It exposed grammatical deficiencies, which meant that he was sent for a second language study visit to Germany in September, this time in Karlsruhe, with a new host family: the Biltroffs.[64] The husband, Rudolf Biltroff, was everything Hugo Schmidt was not: a strict disciplinarian, who ran the boarding house with a rod of iron, and whose wife was scarcely more welcoming, given her previous bad experiences with ill-disciplined French boarders. Although he enjoyed lengthy bike rides with Herr Biltroff's sixteen-year-old son, two other German-language students and a young Italian, Herr Biltroff was rather critical in his letters to Fernand Destouches about Louis' slow progress in German and lax attitude to work.[65] Louis himself was not happy with the state of his lodgings and requested to change bedrooms. It was with some relief that he returned to the passage Choiseul on 28 December 1908, via Strasbourg.

If he omits Germany from his novel, this is not the case for the next two phases of Céline's life, which comprise the bulk of his teenage years, from the age of fourteen to almost eighteen: his study trip to England from February to November 1909, and the four apprenticeships he undertook between January 1910 and May 1912. However, these episodes are not recounted exactly as they happened, but undergo chronological changes and fictional embellishments. These modifications are not some whimsical flight of fancy on Céline's part that undermines the autobiographical premise of *Death on Credit*. Rather, they act as a reminder that his novel is not just an autobiography, but an exploration of a new literary style. Thus his novel draws *primarily* on his childhood experiences, but these experiences are transposed, through the prism of his imagination, into a new type of literary language. The change in chronology reflects what Godard refers to as Céline's 'discontinuous' style: his shift towards a narrative technique that recounts key events from his life not in the order in which they happened, but *the (dis)order in which he remembers them*. This gives the impression of spontaneity and authenticity, since memory does not operate in a rationally structured and linear way.[66] Moreover, adolescence is fertile ground for Céline's comic style. Its traditional associations with rebelliousness on the one hand and awkwardness and naivety on the other, mean that he is able to place his alter ego Ferdinand in compromising and farcical situations that are the direct result of his 'difficult' teenage years. Having known nothing until then, other than smothering parental love, he is completely unprepared for the ruthless, dog-eat-dog world of commerce, where he also encounters the opposite sex for the very first time. As a sexually eager but inexperienced adolescent, he lacks both the discipline and the savvy to avoid awkward situations that land him in all sorts of trouble. His clumsy attempts to extricate himself from these situations are what generate much of the novel's risqué and bittersweet humour. Finally, by inserting the England episode *after* the apprenticeships rather than before them, Céline was able to inject into his novel a dose of drama that was simply lacking in real life.

The banal facts are that on 22 February 1909, Fernand Destouches accompanied his son to England on the ferry. Now that he had learned German, studying English was the logical next step for Louis' future career in the international jewellery trade. He initially attended the University School in Rochester, which proved to be a disaster. Louis complained vociferously to his parents about the lack and quality of the food, the poor teaching and the headmaster and his wife: 'I don't like Mr. Tonkin very much, Mrs. Tonkin even less so.'[67] Within less than a month, he was moved to Pierremont Hall in Broadstairs, which was far more comfortable, agreeable and well run, Louis frequently praising this establishment in his letters. Mr and Mrs Farnfield, who ran the school, were friendly and accommodating, and Louis made rapid progress in English under their tutelage. Sporting activities such as football, golf (which he hated) and athletics were encouraged, as was piano playing, which he was taught by Mrs Farnfield.

In the novel, however, his study trip to England is introduced into the narrative in far more dramatic fashion: it is proposed *in extremis*

Facade of Pierremont Hall, Broadstairs, Kent, where Céline went to school, March–November 1909.

The dining hall at Pierremont Hall.

as the only possible course of action, following Ferdinand's two disastrous apprenticeships in Paris. He is sacked first, from the cloth-maker Berlope for misbehaviour and a poor attitude, and second, from the jeweller Gorloge, for stealing a precious jewel. So mortified are his parents at this dent to their social reputation that his father flies into a rage, to which Ferdinand retaliates by smashing him over the head with the typewriter. Only *then* does Édouard suggest sending his errant nephew to England to set him on the right path, and to wait until the domestic storm passes.

The Berlope and Gorloge episodes are loosely based on the three apprenticeships Louis really did undertake in Paris. Between January and August 1910, he was apprenticed to Raimon, a wealthy cloth merchant with outlets in Lyon, Saint-Étienne, London and New York.[68] Next, he was a jeweller's apprentice at Robert in the elegant rue Royale, until April 1911. His work certificate commended him for his honesty and the quality and precision of his work.[69] Gibault speculates that his stint with Robert may have been cut short by a minor scandal in which he obtained money from a certain client, Madame Guerraz, in exchange for sexual favours. In his third apprenticeship, with Henri Wagner, Louis delivered jewels to wealthy clients, but appears to have misplaced two Lalique hatpins worth 180 francs the pair and a walking stick worth 95 francs, both of which had to be compensated by his father.[70] Thus, despite a couple of minor blots on his copybook, he came through his apprenticeships without any major problems.

However, the novel cleverly turns Louis' minor misdemeanours into major scandals, which are not only uproariously funny, but prick the bubble of respectability that is so precious to Ferdinand's parents. Céline's comic imagination transforms his own, real-life teenage encounter with Madame Guarraz at the jeweller Robert and his loss of the Lalique hairpins from Wagner into Madame Gorloge's sexual seduction of Ferdinand. This is part of a plan, deliberately hatched with her lover, her husband's brutish employee Antoine, to steal the hairpins from Ferdinand's pockets, during intercourse. The preamble to this episode plays on a cliché of male adolescence: sexual frustration. Ferdinand and his fellow teenage assistant Robert make a habit of spying on Madame Gorloge through a peephole, where they see her removing her underwear in the toilet and also making vigorous love to Antoine: 'It was a good place . . . ringside . . . You could see the whole bed . . . we couldn't miss a trick . . .'[71] Thus, when the time comes for her to seduce Ferdinand, he is mere putty in her hands, and succumbs to his teenage lust: 'I played the ardent lover, I climbed, I squeezed, I grunted . . .'[72] Try as he might to explain to his parents that he has been duped, they refuse to listen, so exasperated are they by his incorrigible lack of discipline, which they consider to be the ultimate social disgrace. His parents are once again exposed for being more concerned with their 'respectable' reputation, than with their son's happiness: 'Ah, be still, you little wretch! . . . You don't realize how you're hurting us! . . .'[73]

As for the apprenticeship with Berlope, this is a similarly bawdy and comic portrayal of adolescent sexual awakening (such as when Ferdinand sneakily takes a break from his work to masturbate in the toilets), with an underlying social satire of the exploitative nature of apprenticeships at that time. Around 1910, child labour laws were not what they are today, and teenage apprentices such as the young Louis Destouches would typically be ordered to work long, gruelling hours with little or no pay.[74] His time at Berlope is thus depicted in a less-than-flattering light: his supervisor, M. Lavelongue, is constantly on his back and regularly reports back to his parents that Ferdinand is doing badly, while the other apprentices spread malicious rumours about him. Apprenticeships are depicted as a Darwinian struggle for survival, in which desperate young apprentices will go to any lengths to rise up the greasy pole, even if that means bad-mouthing their rivals. This was based on the young Louis' own unpleasant experiences. His thirst for knowledge and frustration at his lack of schooling meant that he would steal away an hour here or there to read, and even avoid taking public transport to make his deliveries, spending the money he had been given on books instead. Consequently, some of the working-class apprentices regarded him as an aloof snob, which did not help him fit in. The apprenticeships are thus a baptism of fire: the naive adolescent is thrust head-first into a world of adult cynicism, hypocrisy and one-upmanship. And the loss of his sexual innocence is a metaphor for the irrevocable loss of his childhood innocence.

Ferdinand's study trip to England similarly allows Céline to mine the rich seam of adolescent rebellion and awkwardness to portray him in compromising and comical situations. But it does so in a way that also draws subtle parallels between Ferdinand's lack of familiarity with the English language and Céline's own tentative forays into a new style of writing. The adult author's search for literary innovation is thus mapped onto his teenage protagonist's own journey of self-discovery. Just like his apprenticeships, Ferdinand's novelistic portrayal of his English sojourn is more dramatic and comical than what the young Louis actually experienced. To begin with, he attends only one school – Meanwell College – and not two. Second, his whole trip is presented as his first real taste of freedom from his parents and an opportunity to stand on his own two feet. If Fernand personally accompanied Louis all the way to England, in *Death on Credit* Ferdinand's parents merely escort him to the Gare du Nord in Paris in a scene of emotional and farcical farewells. There is thus a significant element in the novel of 'when the cat's away the mice will play.' No sooner has he landed in England, than he has a fumbling encounter with a fellow teenaged food vendor called Gwendoline, before he even arrives at his new school. The school itself, like the first school Louis actually attended, University School, is in Rochester and on a hill overlooking the port. But its name, Meanwell College, is obviously satirical. Not only does it contain the adjective 'mean', which reinforces the mounting economic difficulties it faces, but the term to 'mean well' sums up the good but ultimately futile intentions of its owners: Mr Merrywin, and his beautiful young wife Nora Merrywin, who quickly becomes the latest object of Ferdinand's adolescent sexual fantasies.

The attractive and graceful Nora, whose piano playing enchants Ferdinand, was almost certainly modelled on the musical Elizabeth Farnfield, the headmaster's wife in the school in Broadstairs, as well as the pianist Lucienne Delforges, with whom Céline was having an affair while writing his novel in 1935. This is a perfect example of his method of literary transposition: Nora is neither a real person, nor is she completely invented from scratch. Instead, she is a hybrid of autobiography and fiction and of two different people he successively met both as a child and as an adult. Her character is the result of imaginative reconstruction that allows him to mould her into an important symbolic figure in his novel. The first role she fulfils is that of the other female characters the teenaged Ferdinand has encountered thus far, the object of sexual fantasy: 'I'd never seen Nora dressed in a light colour, a tight-fitting blouse, pink satin ... It brought her tits right out ... The movement of her hips was terrific too ... The way they swayed, the mystery of the arse ...'[75] The second is that of a patient, maternal figure who encourages the reluctant Ferdinand to study and to learn, even though he is deeply reluctant to do so.

To the young Ferdinand, Nora's marriage to the much older and unattractive Mr Merrywin is an enigma. Both sexually and emotionally speaking, she embodies perfection, whereas her husband is a repellent and weak figure. Worse still, he reminds Ferdinand of the dry academic teaching he abhors, and which he associates with the bourgeois formality of his father Auguste:

> He wrote whole sentences on the blackboard in capital letters ... easy to decipher ... and the translation underneath ... The kids repeated them altogether, in chorus ... in cadence ... over and over ... I opened my mouth wide ... I pretended something was coming ... I was waiting for something to come out ... Nothing came out ... Not a syllable ...[76]

This points to the recurrent leitmotif of Ferdinand's stay: his refusal to speak English, purely in order to spite his father. This is the ultimate act of adolescent rebellion. Whereas Nora's attempts to get him to talk at least involve a gentle coaxing that he appreciates, her husband, Mr Merrywin, gets deeply frustrated and commits the ultimate act of betrayal by expressing his concerns about Ferdinand in a letter to his father Auguste. The ferocity of his father's response in three angry letters ('stupid, bristling with threats, bloodcurdling oaths, insults in Greek and Latin, warnings, prospective punishments, selected anathemas, infinite grief ... My conduct was diabolical!'), not only strengthens Ferdinand's resolve not to speak English, but alienates him from Mr Merrywin altogether: 'I locked myself in my silence, I was very angry with him.'[77]

Nora, by contrast, represents a sensual and lively connection to language. When she reads an illustrated book to Ferdinand and Jongkind, a fellow pupil who is mentally disabled, she brings the story to life: 'I could see the princes, the upraised lances, the knights . . . the purple, the greens, the scarlets, all the armour studded with rubies . . .'[78] He is, naturally, attracted to her, but Céline subtly turns Ferdinand's adolescent fantasy into a self-reflection on his own literary style. Because he can barely understand a word of English, when he listens to her speak, he concentrates not on its meaning, but on the musical and sensual qualities of the language: 'I listened to her like a song . . . Her voice was like the rest of her, enchanting gentleness . . . What interested me in her English was the music, the way it danced in and out of the firelight [. . .] I was letting myself be bewitched.'[79] These are precisely the qualities of language Céline tried to bring to life as a writer. He cleverly turns his coming-of-age story into a commentary on his own evolution as a novelist.

Indeed, there is another occasion in which Céline makes a subtle connection between England as a place of childhood memory and England as a pretext for exploring his literary style as an adult. This is the episode when Ferdinand and his parents cross the Channel by ferry, in a farcically ill-conceived attempt to sell their wares on the country's southern coast. In a comical slapstick scene, a real feast of scatological humour, all of the ship's passengers violently succumb to seasickness and thus start vomiting uncontrollably. When a woman unintentionally throws up all over Ferdinand because of the wind, he decides to retaliate by vomiting back onto her. Her husband and Ferdinand's father try to separate them: 'All of a sudden she turns her head back into the wind . . . The whole stew that's been gurgling in her mouth catches me full in the face . . . My teeth are full of it, beans, tomatoes . . .'[80] As exaggerated as it seems, this scene is partly rooted in biographical experience. Contrary to the novel, Louis made two trips from England to France by ferry during his study year, in May and August 1909. But both the letters in which he recounts his crossing of the Channel similarly refer to seasickness in the most graphic terms. The first letter describes him vomiting all over a priest: 'The wind blew everything onto a clergyman's robe'; the second recounts a young girl being sick all over *him*: 'a young girl who was next to me lets out a real sauce onto my yellow boots.'[81] Just like the letters from Diepholz, we can see the early seeds of Céline's gift for satire and sharp social observation.

But this vomiting scene has cultural as well as a biographical resonance. For it distinctly recalls Renaissance author François Rabelais' hyperbolic, scatological depictions of the body. Rabelais, as the critic Mikhail Bakhtin has shown, reversed the linguistic and social hierarchy by shifting his focus 'downwards' to 'the lower bodily strata': excrement, guts, blood and urine. His use of the vernacular was intended to upset the established order.[82] This dimension of human experience had been excluded from literature since the Renaissance. As Céline made clear in a 1957 article, Rabelais has unceremoniously been dislodged from the French canon:

> To tell the truth, Rabelais's gamble didn't pay off. He didn't succeed. What he wanted was a language for everyone, an authentic one. He wanted to make language democratic, a real battle. He was against the Sorbonne, the scholars and all that. The Establishment, the king, Church, style, he was against them.[83]

Today's French, according to Céline, is not Rabelais' legacy, but Jacques Amyot's, the translator of Plutarch, and the founder of a stilted academic style that has endlessly been reproduced ever since, including in journalism:

> No, he wasn't the winner. It was Amyot. The translator of Plutarch: in the following centuries he had much more success than Rabelais. We're still living off him and his language today. Rabelais had tried to introduce spoken language into written language: a stalemate. Whereas Amyot, people now continue to want Amyot, the academic style. That is just writing sh . t: stale language.[84]

Amyot's stylistic victory over Rabelais has led to the pejorative adjective 'rabelaisean', with its vulgar connotations:

> French has always been a vulgar language, since its birth at the Verdun treaty. Only nobody wants to accept that and Rabelais continues to be treated with disdain. 'Ah! that's Rabelaisian!' people sometimes say. That means: be careful, that thing is not refined, it lacks politeness. And the name of one of our greatest writers has been used to make a defamatory adjective. Outrageous![85]

Céline identifies in Rabelais an unjustly neglected great writer who embraced, rather than rejected, popular culture. He embodies a forgotten oral, vernacular literary tradition that has been suppressed by the academic style of writing. Just like the popular songs and lyrical *opérettes*

Céline heard in the Passage Choiseul as a child, Rabelais represents that authenticity and raw emotion that he would like to reintroduce into literature.

Aside from its positive recuperation of the 'rabelaisean' style, this episode once again dramatizes, in a tragicomic vein, the petit bourgeois obsession with 'keeping up appearances'. Auguste gives a far-fetched account of the trip to England to the neighbours of the passage Choiseul, just as he did when he told them about his visit to the Exposition Universelle of 1900. Only this time, he tells the story not only to impress them but because he is too ashamed to admit the truth – that the trip was a complete disaster and they managed to sell nothing:

> Now it was over, he stopped at nothing, he gave them all the wonders they could ask for . . . He shot off his mouth like a machine-gun . . . Mama didn't contradict him . . . She was always happy to see him triumph . . . 'Isn't that right, Clémence' he'd ask her when his story was getting a bit too tall . . . She nodded, she backed up everything he said . . . Of course she knew he was overdoing it, but it gave him pleasure! . . .[86]

When asked by the optician from number 37 whether they had made it to London, he embellishes the trip with the story of a dramatic shipwreck:

> Soon word got around that we'd been in a big shipwreck . . . that the women had been landed on the cliffs with a cable . . . He made it up as he went along . . . And the way we'd gone roaming around London with the other survivors . . . mostly foreigners! He stopped at nothing! . . . He even imitated their accents.[87]

For all of Auguste's flaws, Céline does not present him in a purely negative light, for this episode demonstrates his gift as a raconteur and hence the 'oral' power of language, that same spontaneous and emotive language that Céline himself was trying to reinject back into literature.

If Louis Destouches' visits to northern Europe feature prominently in *Death on Credit*, his one visit to southern Europe as a teenager is not included at all. This was his fourth, and most prestigious, apprenticeship, which was undertaken in Nice, with the highly reputable international jewellers Lacloche Frères. Valued at 6 million francs, with stores in Paris, London, Madrid, Aix-les-Bains, Saint-Sébastien, Biarritz and Nice, they counted three royal households among their clientele.[88] Working for Lacloche exposed him to a world he could scarcely have imagined existed: that of the well-heeled foreign aristocracy who came to winter in Nice and flaunt their wealth. This was the crème de la crème of Belle Époque high society. It is scarcely surprising that Louis' exposure to such a world of luxury should have been excluded from *Death on Credit*, for it would have completely contradicted the novel's tone and social theme: that of a struggling class – the petit bourgeoisie – that did not share in the spoils and riches of the Belle Époque.

Although no letters from this period survive, Céline fondly recalls his time in Nice in his pamphlet *Trifles for a Massacre* (*Bagatelles pour un massacre*), in which he paints a nostalgia-filled portrait of economic extravagance and sexual hedonism. Lacloche is given the Jewish name Ben-Corème, without being subjected to that pamphlet's usual horrific antisemitic slurs, which suggests the adult Céline's fond recollection of a happy time working for a fair employer. Ben-Corème (or Lacloche) entrusted Louis with two tasks: to deliver highly precious jewels to the luxury residences of aristocratic clients, and to spy on these clients to prevent them from shoplifting. Céline paints an almost Dickensian portrait of a poor, honest boy working himself to the bone to indulge the whims of a decadent and less-than-honest ruling class. He is paid 55 francs a month (in reality, it was 150) to trudge up the Mont Boron hill every day, wearing out the soles of his shoes, which his employer dutifully replaces every two weeks: 'My parents, who were so poor, yet so scrupulously honest, had sworn on their life, that I would not steal a penny . . . that I could be trusted with treasures. In fact, I was frequently entrusted with them – these were not idle words.' He carries boxes overflowing with jewels to palatial residences

> for the 'stylish ladies' to choose from . . . the most famous kept women of the era . . . to pander to the whims of a 'high life' clientele, the most extravagant in Europe, the most capricious 'members of the club', the Queens of the Boudoir. In my pockets, which were sealed by a safety pin, I would carry in just one day more riches than a Spanish galleon returning from Peru.[89]

His second task was to spy on potential shoplifters from the back shop.[90] The main culprits are Italians and Slavs, especially the elegant Russian female aristocrats:

> I knew all the thieves [. . .] I could see it coming . . . As it happened . . . Psss! Where it was slipped into the sleeve. I went 'tap-tap-tap'! three little knocks on my door. . . That was the arrangement with Ben Corème . . . The matter was always handled without a hitch, never a scandal.[91]

It was perhaps these types of incident that inspired one of those rare moments in *Death on Credit* when Ferdinand is exposed to the world of high society Paris. His mother is trying to woo a very wealthy client, Madame Pinaise, a beautiful aristocrat who lives in a luxury residence across from the Solférino bridge. Ferdinand is shocked to see her stealing a handkerchief from the pile of merchandise his mother, Clémence, is desperately trying to sell: 'A flash! I see her . . . Mme. Pinaise . . . She's swiped a handkerchief. It's disappeared between her tits.'[92] The stranglehold the aristocracy exerts over small shopkeepers such as Clémence is emphasized by her refusal to report Madame Pinaise, for fear of losing customers and her reputation: 'If I had taken it away from her, we'd have lost her as a customer! . . . And all her friends too! . . . There would have been a scandal!'[93]

When he recalls his time in Nice, he places greater emphasis on the sexual perks of his apprenticeship than on class injustice. He indulges in the same adolescent sexual voyeurism as when he spies on Madame Gorloge in *Death on Credit*:

> I can't complain, my role had its perks . . . benefits . . . when they were beautiful, the clients . . . sitting down . . . swishing . . . they hit me hard . . . I looked at their legs. I was transfixed. Ah! The curve of the thighs . . . I didn't jerk myself off [. . .] My puberty was great, a fantastic orgy of sex. It didn't prevent me from being honest and scrupulously vigilant.[94]

Céline's exposure to the aristocracy natural triggered his mythomania: that tendency he inherited from his father to embellish, or even invent, particular episodes of his life for effect. In a 1916 letter to his childhood friend Simone Saintu, he boasts that he identified an elegant, elderly gentleman sitting on a bench on the promenades des Anglais as the Emperor Franz Josef.[95] The emperor declined the young Louis' request to sign his card, saying that it was the only one he possessed. Instead, he gave the embarrassed Louis his own card, which said, 'F. J. Habsburg, Emperor of Austria'. Although the emperor looked 'hideously old' ('atrocement vieux'), Louis recalls with admiration, 'from that day on the prestige of ancient monarchs shot up in my estimations as much as that of the jewellery trade plummeted.' Gibault rightly contests the historical veracity of this account, but it is another example of Céline's 'them-and-us' mentality: the gulf he acknowledges between those with 'old money' and the aspirational petit bourgeoisie to which he belonged.[96]

His pamphlet's satire of the aristocracy extends to its mental deficiencies and frivolous detachment from historical reality, as epitomized by the tsar's uncle, another alleged client of Lacloche: 'He was at least two metres tall. It was he, this giant, who ultimately lost the war and the Russian armies. Ah! I could already have warned them in 1910 that they were going to lose everything . . . He never did know what he wanted . . .'[97] Extravagant, impatient and clumsy, the tsar's uncle breezes into the store, demanding to purchase a bracelet for a lady. He then stuffs his overcoat pockets full of bracelets and diamond-encrusted cigarette cases. He bangs his head on the door as he leaves, despite Ben-Corème's warning. When he decides to come back in, he bangs his head again: 'He is about to come back into the boutique . . . Bamm! He bangs his nut again! He holds his head in both hands . . . He takes a step back . . .'[98]

He then dismissively asks for the bill to be sent to his nephew in Saint Petersburg. The uncle's detachment from reality reaches its nadir when his palace is transformed into a psychiatric institution: 'Events have conspired since 18 to make his grand palace on the Neva the "Brain Institute" For the Study of Psychic Phenomena.'[99]

Yet for all that he viciously satirized the aristocracy as a mature writer in 1937, back in 1911, the young and impressionable Louis Destouches was undeniably attracted to its opulent lifestyle and the exclusive world it inhabited. Much to his parents' consternation, he was dazzled by the glitz of the Côte d'Azur and lived well beyond his means. This was no doubt, in part, a reaction to his strict and spartan upbringing, in which luxuries were very much frowned upon. A despairing Fernand Destouches documented Louis' spending spree in his accounts. From January to March 1912, Louis got through no less than 954 francs, when his wage with Lacloche was only 450 francs, in addition to 180 francs pocket money. Even allowing for his board and lodging of only seven francs a day with M. and Mme Carpatti, at 5, rue du Congrès, he was clearly overspending.[100] His money was primarily lavished on the popular culture he so loved – the cinema matinees and music hall shows of the Eldorado Casino in rue Pastorelli, where he saw light operas and stand-up comedians such as 'Polin' (Pierre Paul Marsalès), writer of 'Ma Tonkinoise'– as well as, in all probability, young women.[101] Fearing the worst, Fernand Destouches had armed his headstrong son with what nowadays would be called a sex manual, by syphilis specialist and member of the Académie de médecine Alfred Fournier, entitled *Pour nos fils quand ils auront 18 ans. Quelques conseils d'un médecin* (For Our Sons When They Turn 18).[102]

A draft letter written by Fernand to Lacloche, shortly after Louis' return from Nice, suggests that he had taken full advantage of his sojourn away from the passage Choiseul. In a deeply bombastic tone, Fernand apologizes profusely to Lacloche for not contacting him sooner about his son's progress, since Louis had only given his parents three days' notice about his departure from Nice. Fernand expresses his grave concerns about Louis' unruly behaviour and the squandering of his parents' hard-earned money:

> You will easily understand that it was not without a great deal of apprehension that I resigned myself to leaving entirely to his own devices and without the slightest monitoring a 17-year-old boy [whose] character was already very independent. Nevertheless, I was very conscious of the danger of seeing frittered away the moral and physical instruction we had, despite our modest means, so painstakingly instilled in him by dint of major financial sacrifices.[103]

Following Louis' indiscretions in Nice, his father administered some tough love by sending him on his military service in the prestigious barracks of Rambouillet, on the outskirts of Paris, in the 12ème régiment des cuirassiers. This was done on the understanding that he could resume his apprenticeship with Lacloche afterwards, an idea the jeweller welcomed, since his own son, who worked in the family business, was in exactly the same boat. If Louis was fascinated by military parades, he was far less keen on military service.[104] He was, therefore, in for a real shock. Rambouillet was an elite garrison known for its strict discipline and specialist cavalry unit.[105] Bullying and being subjected to verbal abuse by non-commissioned officers was part and parcel of the treatment meted out to the new recruits. Among them were Breton recruits, who barely spoke a word of French and considered Louis to be an aloof Parisian. Much of this coarse language, climate of bullying and the linguistic and social divisions finds its way into his unfinished black satire of the barracks, *Cannon Fodder* (*Casse-pipe*).[106]

Furthermore, without their son's knowledge, the Destouches requested regular reports from his superiors about Louis' discipline and progress. It is quite possible that Marguerite's relationship with rich clients in her lace shop helped them secure this special favour.[107] Despite this, for the first time in his life, Louis experienced genuine depression and homesickness, and even contemplated desertion.[108] He was completely unsuited to the cavalry: not only did he hate horses, but he had no aptitude for riding them, which evidently affected his morale. He suffered minor injury from falling off his horse and struggled mightily to pass this aspect of his training. No more strikingly is his troubled state of mind articulated than in his deeply introspective but little-read diary, the *Carnet du cuirassier Destouches* (Cavalryman Destouches's Notebook), one of the earliest examples of his nascent literary talent and acute powers of psychological analysis. Written in an aphoristic, unpunctuated style between November and December 1912, when he was at his lowest ebb, this rare glimpse into the young Louis' innermost thoughts, refreshingly stripped bare of the melodramatic rants and rhetorical flourishes that would characterize much of his later correspondence, shows him at a crossroads. Even before the trauma of war, we see a young man already asking himself remarkably mature and bold questions about the future direction of his life. He has a prescient, candid

Céline with horses, Rambouillet, *c.* 1913.

intuition that he will always be too proud to settle for the norm, even if this means experiencing great hardship as well as success:

> [But] what I want above all is to live a life full of incidents which I hope Providence will place along my path and not end up like so many who have plotted just the *one* amorphous continuous trajectory on one planet and in one life, unaware of any deviation that would allow them to gain a moral education.
>
> If I have to undergo major crises that life has in store for me maybe I will be less miserable than the next man because I want to know.
>
> In a nutshell I am proud is that a fault I don't think so and it will cause me problems or perhaps *Success*.[109]

We see Céline's conviction, both arrogant and legitimate, that he is different from the herd and hence destined for great things and unique experiences. But these hinge on his willingness to embrace, rather than avoid, the inevitable crises life will throw at him. Given his injury in 1914, his phenomenal literary success some twenty years later and subsequent exile, imprisonment and ostracization, his prediction that his future would be one long roller-coaster ride has more than a prophetic ring to it.

In his troubled mental state, his taste for retail therapy resurfaced. Twice he was reprimanded for his loose spending habits, the first time in May 1913. Captain Servat, who had lent him 15 francs, expressed his grave misgivings on 12 May that Louis had also borrowed 60 or 70 francs from his fellow soldiers. Unbeknownst to Louis, his parents visited Servat in secret to pay him 10 francs, which he then lent to Louis, pretending they had come from him. On 16 May, Servat wrote back saying,

> You do not have to keep it from Louis that I was the one who wrote to you but he does not know you came. I gave him the 10 francs you gave me, telling him that I was lending them to him. He still owes Bezard 5, Prunier 10, Clement 8,60. I do not think he wishes to tell you.[110]

Three months later, Servat informed Louis' parents that he had paid a visit to the passage Choiseul (but they were not in) to report that their son had once again got into debt, this time by ordering an expensive carpet. This not only was done against the express wishes of his superiors, but undermined Louis' authority over his own men, as a newly appointed brigadier.[111] Despite his indiscretions, he was promoted to this rank in early August 1913.

Captain Schneider makes it clear to the Destouches that, although he lent his personal support to their son's promotion, they should not indulge him in any way, since his discipline has become lax once again.[112] Despite Rambouillet's strict reputation, Céline was thus shown an uncommon degree of favouritism by his commanding officers, as a slightly exasperated letter from Lieutenant Colonel de Marcieu makes clear to his father, on 9 August 1913:

> We, and I in particular, have been extremely considerate and patient with your son! We looked upon his early impetuousness as the likely consequence of his youth and impressionable nature rather than an innately bad character, and so we turned a blind eye to it and allowed his true qualities to come to the fore and now he is brigadier, with his foot in the door; I have no doubt that he will now do his utmost to repay you for the refined education you have given him and us for the faith we have shown in his future.[113]

A further letter, this time from non-commissioned officer Roger Gorus to Fernand Destouches on 11 December 1913 reassures him that not only has his son split up with his *petite amie* (girlfriend), but his debt problems have been resolved and he has learnt his lesson, even though his pride has been hit hard: 'since this lesson has hit his ego hard, I think I can vouch for his good intentions.'[114] Louis' stint in the barracks was not entirely unproductive, for it helped forge his sympathy with the underdog. At one end of the social spectrum, his cavalry regiment was regularly asked to participate in the local stag hunts organized by Prince Orloff and the Duchesse d'Uzès; at the other end, he and his regiment were subjected to stone-throwing when they were sent to break up a strike on 1 May 1913 in the Pyramides district of Paris. He was shocked at the 'consent by the populace to live the life of a pig' and that 'the revolutionaries were often treated as hooligans, even by the populace'.[115] All in all, however, the barracks of Rambouillet represented the absolute low point of Louis' adolescence.

Up until that point, the single most devastating moment of Louis' life had been, without question, the death on 18 December 1904, when he was aged ten, of his beloved maternal grandmother, Céline Guillou. There is a deep personal resonance to her death that distinguishes it from

Céline in cavalry uniform, May 1914.

the other two deaths in the novel: that of Nora, who throws herself in the river, and of Courtial de Pereires, who shoots himself. Although both these deaths are tragic suicides, they are entirely the product of the author's imagination, which allowed him to reinforce the symbolic link in his novel between economic despair and physical decline. Nora's despair (aside from her shame of sleeping with Ferdinand) is that Meanwell College goes bankrupt, while Courtial's anguish is caused by the failure of his potato harvest and crippling gambling debts. But

Grandmother Caroline's death is much more poignant than the other two, because it is directly rooted in a heartfelt biographical experience. If the exact cause of Céline Guillou's death is unknown – in the novel, she catches a fatal chill while unblocking the drains of her tenants in Asnières in the middle of winter – what is certain is that she died prematurely, after a hard life. This is in keeping with the novel's title – 'death on credit' – since she dies as a result of menial work and economic activity.

The description of her death in *Death on Credit* ranks among the most moving in the whole of Céline. Despite spending most of his novel writing *against* Proust and his cossetted, privileged depiction of the Belle Époque, here he implicitly acknowledges him. Ferdinand, like the narrator of *The Guermantes Way* in *In Search of Lost Time*, is woken up to say goodbye to his grandmother for the last time.[116] He is ushered into her bedroom, once the doctor has left. Caroline's dying words have a poignancy, authenticity and unadorned simplicity to them that contrast with the pompous, moralistic remonstrations of his father. The young Louis is infinitely more receptive to his grandmother's simple wisdom than he is to the torrent of parental warnings he has become accustomed to receiving. Her death brings about an unexpected suspension of hostilities between the family members, a genuine spirit of forgiveness and solidarity that unites them in grief. And this cessation of petty squabbling is matched by the writer's deft reversal of his usual hyperbolic satire with a suggestive passage of beautifully delicate understatement:

> We closed the shop. We rolled down all the blinds . . . We felt kind of ashamed . . . Kind of guilty . . . We didn't dare to move, for fear of spoiling our grief . . . mama and all of us cried with our heads on the table . . . We weren't hungry . . . We didn't want anything . . . We didn't take up much room, but we'd like to have made ourselves even smaller . . . to apologize to somebody, to everybody . . . We forgave each other . . . We begged and promised to love each other . . . We were afraid of losing each other . . . for ever . . . like Caroline.[117]

The customary obsession with 'keeping up appearances' and carrying on with business as usual is replaced by a rare moment of authentic individual introspection, in which the shop is closed and the family retreat into it. Exceptionally, Ferdinand's parents do not try to hide their vulnerability. For once, presenting a respectable front to the outside world and pretending that all is well is not their priority. Stripped of all their usual affectations, they simply shrink into their shells inside the shop, now a nurturing womb-like space, rather than an outward-facing hub of commercial activity, and they confront their real feelings of hurt and numbing grief.

Caroline's passing is a double-edged sword. On one hand, it is a painful reminder that death is never far from the surface, infiltrating all aspects of our existence, in the guise of economic and physical decline, the latter symbolized by her daughter Clémence's throbbing leg. On the other hand, her passing is also a healing emotional balm: it possesses a noble innocence and moral dignity that elevates it – if only temporarily – above the trivial demands of petit bourgeois materialism and social affectation. Her slow, quiet demise, in the presence of loved ones who give her a dignified and deeply personal farewell, is in stark contrast to the absurdly barbaric, undignified and impersonal deaths that Louis Destouches would have to confront as soon as he was mobilized from the Rambouillet barracks and sent to Flanders, at the outbreak of the Great War in August 1914. His life would never be the same again.

two

War and Colonialism

If Rambouillet was a culture shock to Louis, then it was nothing compared to his horrific experience of the Great War. In the twelve and a half weeks between his mobilization on 1 August 1914 and his serious injury by shellfire in late October, he witnessed a carnage so utterly horrendous that it left permanent mental scars. As Véronique Robert-Chovin aptly puts it, he began the First World War as Louis Destouches and ended it as Louis-Ferdinand Céline.[1] This catalogue of horrors turned the naively optimistic boy into a profoundly traumatized and disillusioned young man. Despite months of intensive medical treatment, he never fully healed from the radial nerve paralysis to his right arm and was thus discharged with the status of war invalid, or *mutilé de guerre*. What his experience of battle lacked in duration, it more than made up for in its ferocity. Caught in the horrific bloodbath of the 1914 autumn campaign, he saw men fall like flies all around him, as his cavalry regiment, the 12ème cuirassiers, desperately strove to withstand wave after wave of German mortar and artillery fire. Having stared death squarely in the face, he became a staunch, lifelong pacifist.

It is no exaggeration to say that had it not been for the First World War, Céline may not have had a literary career at all, for his primary motivation for writing his first, groundbreaking novel, *Journey to the End of the Night* (1932), was to unburden himself of the trauma he had been carrying inside him for over fifteen years. His book was, therefore, primarily cathartic: a necessary release from the intolerable psychological nightmare he – as well as an entire generation of young men – had been unable to shake off for almost two decades. His compulsion to 'exorcize' the war is emphatically confirmed by a letter of 21 March 1930 to his friend and fellow war veteran Joseph Garcin: 'As you know, I'm writing a novel, a few personal experiences that need to be convincing on paper, the share of insanity, the hardship also, a huge undertaking... The war, first of all, on which everything hinges, and has to be exorcised.'[2] Thus was born the novel's first-person narrator Ferdinand Bardamu, Céline's satirical and semi-fictional alter ego, who is both a self-professed coward and an anti-hero. Contrary to his companion Ganate, Bardamu viciously debunks the official consensus that war is a form of morally heroic patriotic duty. Instead, he argues, it is an exercise in mass deception and hypocrisy by those in power, who cynically deploy jingoistic rhetoric to send society's underdogs to the front to fight on their behalf:

> Our masters have a fine time with beautiful pink and perfumed women on their laps. They send for us, we're brought up on deck. They put on their top hats and give us a big spiel like as follows: 'You no good swine! We're at war those stinkers in Country No. 2! We're going to board them and cut their livers out! Let's go! Let's go![3]

Yet Bardamu does not follow his own advice, since he himself becomes unwittingly caught up in this patriotic fervour. He decides to join up on a whim, when his curiosity is piqued by the seductive sight of a passing regiment headed by a colonel on horseback:

> But just then, who should come marching past the café where we're sitting but a regiment with the colonel up front on his horse, looking nice and friendly, a fine figure of a man! Enthusiasm lifted me to my feet.
>
> 'I'll just go and see if that's the way it is!' I sing out to Arthur, and off I go to enlist, on the double.[4]

Bardamu's initial dilemma – whether to embrace war as patriotic duty or denounce it as the cynical exploitation of the little man – gets to the heart of a long-standing historical debate: did the eagerness to fight extend to all Frenchmen, or was it merely confined to a small elite? The former view was taken as a given until the 1970s, largely on the basis of the 'national awakening' (*réveil national*) and spirit of revenge (*revanchisme*) that had gathered momentum since France's humiliation by the Germans in the Franco-Prussian War of 1870. Territorial skirmishes with Germany over Morocco in 1905 and 1911 only strengthened France's resolve to

Bardamu joins up. Woodcut illustration for *Voyage au bout de la nuit* by C. Serveau, Éditions Ferenczi (1935).

regain from her old enemy the lost territories of Alsace-Lorraine. She consolidated her imperial alliances with Russia and Great Britain to counter the threat of Germany. Thus the assassination of the Habsburg heir, Archduke Ferdinand, in Sarajevo on 28 June 1914 by a member of Young Bosnia, a revolutionary group allegedly opposed to Habsburg rule, was the pretext to go to war everyone in France had been waiting for. At its outbreak, the nationalist renewal prompted citizens of all stripes to set aside their social, political and spiritual differences to forge a 'sacred union' (*union sacrée*).

But in 1977 historian Jean-Jacques Becker questioned the assumption that everyone in France had been spoiling for a fight. Drawing on reports by prefects and schoolteachers, he showed that shock and consternation, rather than enthusiasm, were the predominant reactions in many parts of the country to news of mobilization. The more resolute mood that emerged around mid-August, when most of the men were sent to the front, had far less to do with Alsace-Lorraine and avenging 1870 than with a sense of duty to defend against an unjustified attack by a long-standing aggressor.[5] As for the so-called 'cult of heroism' surrounding the war, this was largely confined to the educated Parisian elite. The main, far-Right nationalist group, Action française, was primarily made up of an educated, urban elite seduced by the royalist rhetoric of Charles Maurras, a few artisans and office workers, but hardly any peasants or members of the working class.[6] Symptomatic of this upper-class bellicose nationalism was Agathon, the pseudonym employed by Alexis de Tarde and Henri Massis, two young, affluent nationalists who published a work in 1913 entitled *Les Jeunes gens d'aujourd'hui* (The Young People of Today). This was, by far, the most comprehensive survey conducted among young people on the eve of war about their nationalist sentiments. Based on a series of articles published in 1912 in *L'Opinion*, it was confined primarily to male students aged 18 to 25 in Paris. The conclusions drawn were that the current young generation had a 'taste for action' ('goût de l'action'), as opposed to the 'dilettantism and intellectualism of the previous generation' ('dilettantisme et à l'intellectualisme de la génération précédente'). It symbolized a 'French renaissance' characterized by 'patriotic faith' ('foi patriotique'), a taste for heroism, Catholic and moral renewal, the cult of Classical tradition and political realism.[7] This young male elite found in war 'an ideal of aesthetics, energy and strength' ('un idéal d'esthétique, d'énergie et de force'). As for the word 'war', it has 'suddenly regained prestige . . . War is above all in their eyes (young people) the occasion for the most noble of Roman virtues' ('a repris soudain prestige . . . La guerre est surtout à leurs yeux (les jeunes gens) l'occasion des plus nobles vertus romaines . . .').[8]

Bardamu's well-founded misgivings about a selfish, jingoistic elite that regards working-class soldiers as expendable reflects the post-war Céline's battle-weary and lower-middle-class pacifism, his angry reaction to the bellicose nationalism typified by Agathon. Nor, in August 1914, did the inexperienced cuirassier Destouches have anything remotely in common with the upper classes that idealized war. He was just another naive and depoliticized young man, a 'virgin of horror' ('puceau de l'horreur'), as the novel aptly calls the young soldiers, who fought out of a sense of duty, rather than conviction. On 1 August 1914, the cavalrymen of the 12ème cuirassiers departed from Rambouillet for the Woëvre, stopping first in Commercy, then Sorcy on the 2nd or 3rd, followed by Loupmont and Mesnil-sous-les-Côtes on the 11th. Having reached Moranville on 17 August, Louis Destouches wrote that fighting had begun and the battlefront was over 30 kilometres (18½ mi.) long.[9] His early letters from the front express the resigned pragmatism, rather than unequivocal enthusiasm, that Becker highlights as typical of the mood of the time:

> Morale is good, after the heart-wrenching goodbyes at Rambouillet. Everyone is heading for the unknown, albeit with butterflies in their stomach, which is giving the group a small flutter of excitement that is masking its quite legitimate apprehension. Nevertheless I am convinced that everyone will do their duty. My morale has never been better. The call for general mobilization will be made at 12 noon.[10]

This is not the idealistic patriotic fervour of Agathon, but a practical sense of moral duty tinged with understandable apprehensiveness about what is to come. Since the letters, unlike the novel, chart events in real time, before the actual fighting begins, they do not yet show any signs of Céline's later anti-authoritarianism but retain a faith in his superiors. On 2 August, at Sorcy in the Meuse, he mentions that a German soldier has been killed, just as he was about to blow up a lock. This reinforces his confidence of victory and he praises his officers: 'I believe we will be victorious, that would be very good because only indecisive victories lead to deaths [. . .] The officers are up to the task and the c'ptain is a model of calm.'[11] This desire to fight and prove his worth eventually leads him to kill a German officer in mid-September:

> At last I've got one!!!!!! Tonight we saw the Germans again close up. (We even killed one of them [. . .] I got a fine specimen!) whose military booklet I am sending you – all his gear is in the hearse – which I include here. He's from the Engineer Dragoons in Neustadt the country of brother Schmitt. He was killed by a peak shot to the neck. We still more or less march day and night without respite, only stopping for an hour here and there. [. . .] above all the crossing of the Meuse [. . .] is the most horrible spectacle I have ever contemplated. In the middle of the night, fifteen times I saw German pontoon engineers rebuilding the same bridge, as it was systematically being engulfed by our artillery. I believe that a major battle is imminent in which blood will not be haggled over. Let's go!!![12]

Here we begin to notice a change: his initial enthusiasm at killing the enemy (emphasized by the multiple exclamation marks) is superseded by his dawning realization that war is horrific. The 'official' version of war as a moral, patriotic duty is severely tested by the abominable spectacle of the carnage that unfolds before him. And there was no greater carnage than the systematic sabotage by the Allies of the bridges and tunnels of the river Meuse to halt a major German counter-offensive. General Joffre's plan to defeat the Germans by Christmas with a pre-emptive strike through the Ardennes had backfired. The Battle of the Frontiers (as the series of Allied defeats between 20 and 24 August are collectively known) meant that by the end of August, some 75,000 French soldiers had already died (27,000 of them on 22 August alone), and the total killed and wounded numbered 260,000, against much lighter German losses. Joffre reported on the 24th to his war minister that the general attack had failed, so the Allies had to revert to the defensive.[13] The German advance was eventually halted by the series of interconnected conflicts known as the Battle of the Marne between 5 and 9 September, a chilling prelude to the four-year stalemate of trench warfare that was to follow.

Thus, what Céline is reporting here, as events unfold before his very eyes, is fighting at its most intense, even hand-to-hand, during that frantic initial phase of the war when the Germans actually came closer to victory than at any other point. He is a victim of what the historian Lancelot Farrar has called the 'short-war illusion', the mistaken belief, held by all sides, that hostilities would be over by Christmas and normality would quickly resume. This catastrophic miscalculation was to shape not only Céline's psychological and literary outlook, but, as historian David Stevenson reminds us, the entire world order:

> Much of the historical significance of 1914 [. . .] lies in the very fact that the fighting was not over by Christmas. The repercussions included 8 million dead, and many times that number traumatised or maimed; as well as worldwide economic dislocation, both hyperinflation in the 1920s and the Great Depression in the 1930s being more or less direct results.[14]

Of all his disturbing letters sent from the front, none shows greater urgency than the one announcing his killing of the German soldier. An almost paralysing fear mingled with incipient trauma marks a major tipping point from his belief in the war, to revulsion at its horror: 'As I continue with this letter, battle is engaged in the vicinity of Bar le Duc. We are in reserve. Order given any minute now. Will be on horseback tonight ?!!!'[15] The letter ends with an incredibly poignant sentence that has been crossed out: 'I am very worried' ('Je suis très inquiet'). Both this erasure and the confused mingling of a question mark with exclamation marks indicate an emotional turmoil so acute as to be almost beyond words. Ironically, this has the stylistic quality of what he later called 'spoken emotion' and strove to put into his fiction.

The younger Destouches would require many weeks and months to comprehend the full implications of this carnage, whereas Céline the author, who writes with the benefit of hindsight, fiercely condemns war from the outset. The mature Céline is well aware that France's victory in November 1918 was a hollow one: being on the winning side did not make the sacrifice of French lives any more necessary or justifiable. Bardamu witnesses not only this senseless massacre, but the lack of compassion exhibited by those who give the orders:

> Under the colonel's withering look the wobbly messenger snapped to attention, pressing his little finger to the seam of his trousers as the occasion demanded. And so, he stood on the embankment, stiff as a board, swaying, the sweat running down his chin-strap; his jaws were trembling so hard that little abortive cries kept coming out of him, like a puppy dreaming. You couldn't make out whether he wanted to speak to us or whether he was crying.[16]

This is no longer the colonel on horseback whom Bardamu had admired in Place Clichy, the 'fine figure of a man' who was 'looking nice and friendly'. Rather this is a cold, stand-offish superior who strikes such fear into the messenger that he is reduced to a quivering wreck, and barely able to speak:

> The man finally managed to articulate a few words:
> 'Colonel, sir, Sergeant Barousse has been killed.'
> 'So what?'
> 'He was on his way to meet the bread wagon on the Etrapes road sir,'
> 'So what?'
> 'He was blown up by a shell!'
> 'So what, damn it!'
> 'That's what, colonel, sir.'
> 'Is that all?'
> 'Yes, sir, that's all, colonel, sir.'
> 'What about the bread?' The colonel asked.

> That was the end of the dialogue, because I remember distinctly, he barely had time to say 'What about the bread?' That was all. After that there was nothing but flame and noise. The kind of noise you wouldn't have thought possible. Our eyes, ears, nose and mouth were so full of noise that I thought it was all over and I'd turn into noise and flame myself.
>
> After a while the flame went away, the noise stayed in my head, and my arms and legs trembled as if somebody were shaking me from behind. My limbs seemed to be leaving me, but then in the end they stayed on. The smoke stung my eyes for a long time, and the prickly smell of powder and sulphur hung on, strong enough to kill all the fleas and bedbugs in the whole world.[17]

With visceral directness, Bardamu relays, in real time, the brutal death of the colonel and messenger by shellfire not through his intellect, but his sensory perception. He has no cognitive understanding of what has just happened; he merely experiences it as an assault on his senses that reduces him, as well as his fellow soldiers, to the powerless insignificance of insects.

As for the colonel's cold, robotic responses to the death of a fellow human being, this operates as a satire of war on several levels. There is the sheer insensitivity of the military hierarchy to the suffering of those under its command, a theme that has since been satirized in both novels and films ranging from Joseph Heller's *Catch-22*, and Stanley Kubrick's *Paths of Glory* and *Full Metal Jacket*, to the British comedy *Blackadder*. Moreover, the colonel's repetition of 'So what?' suggests that he belongs to a military tradition that has no time for emotions, but only the succinct and rapid delivery of facts to those he commands, a desire to 'spit it out, man'. Finally, war is implicitly portrayed as a source of such extreme duress, that it brings out man's animal instincts: the frantic quest for food that overrides any form of altruism. This explains why the colonel cares more about the bread than he does about Sergeant Barousse.

But this lack of altruism is not confined to the military hierarchy alone. Bardamu himself is actually *pleased* Barousse has died, since the latter had punished him for exceeding his food ration:

> I thought of Sergeant Barousse, who had just gone up in smoke like the man told us. That was good news. Great, I thought to myself.

> That makes one less stinker in the regiment! He wanted to have me court-martialled for a can of meat. 'To each his own war!' I said to myself.[18]

Bardamu may be separated from the colonel by military rank, but he shares his universal human instinct for survival.

And just as hunger is a great equalizer, so too is death. The shell that kills the lowly messenger and the colonel eradicates whatever difference in rank originally existed between them. Reinforcing this satire is the implicit debunking of the French Republican tenets of 'liberty, equality and fraternity', tenets which are not applied in life, but only in death. Only *after* they have been killed do the colonel and messenger embrace like brothers and reach an equality that did not exist when they were alive:

> As for the colonel, I didn't wish him any hard luck. But he was dead too. At first I didn't see him. The blast had carried him up the embankment and laid him down on his side, right in the arms of the dismounted cavalryman, the courier, who was finished too. They were embracing each other for the moment and for all eternity, but the cavalryman's head was gone, all he had was an opening at the top of the neck, with blood in it bubbling and glugging like jam in a kettle. The colonel's belly was wide open and he was making a nasty face about it. It must have hurt when it happened. Tough shit for him! If he'd got out when the shooting started it wouldn't have happened.
>
> All that tangled meat was bleeding profusely.[19]

This passage compels us as readers to acknowledge the plausibility of such apparently insensitive behaviour. Morally speaking, we have difficulty accepting that human selfishness, even when motivated by hunger, can take precedence over our altruistic sympathy for another person's death. And yet these frenzied examples of 'every man for himself' encapsulate the barbaric reality of war, which has nothing to do with the heroic notions of patriotic self-sacrifice that constitute military propaganda back home.

The constant lack of food was an all-too-present problem that crops up in many of Céline's letters from the front. On 17 September, he begs his parents to send him chocolate, as he can no longer stand the sight of meat: 'it is difficult to feed oneself, since I who have never liked meat can no longer stand it.'[20] And this revulsion to meat is transformed into one of his novel's most shockingly arresting descriptions. Against a deceptively peaceful and bucolic backdrop, the mutton and beef destined to feed the soldiers is a tangled mess of blood and guts, over which the men fight tooth and nail. Both its repulsiveness and the violence it elicits make this mountain of rotting meat almost identical to the piles of corpses strewn across the battlefield. Food and death thus become virtually indistinguishable:

> The meat for the whole regiment was being distributed in a summery field, shaded by cherry trees and parched by the August sun. On sacks and tent cloths spread out on the grass there were pounds and pounds of guts, chunks of white and yellow fat, disemboweled sheep with their organs every which way, oozing intricate little rivulets into the grass round about, a whole ox, split down the middle, hanging on a tree and four regimental butchers all hacking away at it, cursing and swearing and pulling off choice morsels. The squadrons were fighting tooth and nail over the innards, especially the kidneys, and all around them swarms of flies such as one sees on these occasions, as self-important and musical as little birds.[21]

Just when he thought the war could not get any worse, the horrific spectacle Céline witnesses on 26 October, the day before his serious injury, plumbs new depths of inhumanity: the massacre extends from armed soldiers to defenceless, innocent civilians, including a pregnant woman:

> I hope that we will be uncompromising and cease, after so much bloodshed, playing the knight, it's a role the Germans don't understand very well and those who will negotiate will only have to go and witness a little spectacle of the type we saw the day before yesterday at La Fosse, where a family of 14 people, defenceless civilians, were killed by *spears*, of whom the oldest grandmother was 78 years old and the youngest 15 days . . . and that's not counting the pregnant mother whose stomach the soldier had cut open.[22]

Was it Cuirassier Destouche's justifiable outrage that led to his serious injury at the end of October? Did it spur him into volunteering for a dangerous mission he could quite easily have avoided? The commonly accepted version of events is that between 25 and 28 October, his regiment was sent to bolster the left flank of the 66th infantry division, whose mission was to retake Poelkapelle in Flanders from the Germans along the western flank, while the 125th division was to attack from the east. A message had to be relayed between the two divisions through contested territory, to ensure a coordinated attack. Céline put himself forward to lead a small group of men on this dangerous mission. Having successfully delivered the message, he was almost home and dry, when, according to J. Schneider, the captain of his regiment, as told in a letter to Fernand Destouches on 30 October, at 18.00, Céline was hit by a bullet to the right arm.[23] He was subsequently transported by ambulance to Hazebrouck military hospital. A concerned Fernand Destouches anxiously relayed the nature of the injury to his brother Charles on 5 November: a gaping wound that was the result of a bullet that ricocheted into his right arm, fracturing a nerve.[24] Nevertheless, Gaël Richard points to some glaring discrepancies between the letters and Céline's medical dossier. The latter not only dates the injury to 25 and not 27 October, but specifies a *coup de sabre*, a 'sword wound', *in addition* to the bullet wound. It is quite possible that Céline was injured on 25 October, since an ambulance report from Ypres states that he and his men were evacuated to Hazebrouck hospital on 26 October.[25] However, the sword wound is far more doubtful, since it was subsequently added to his dossier, in different handwriting, over a year later, on 7 December 1915. Since he was about to be examined by a doctor in London, on behalf of the French recruitment office in Paris to confirm his definitive official status as a *réformé no. 2* (a soldier no longer fit to fight), and since an illustration of his heroic exploit had, in the meantime, appeared on the front cover of the patriotic journal *L'Illustré national* on 3 November showing him galloping on horseback and wielding a sword, it was necessary that his medical dossier conform to the 'version' of events portrayed by the press. That he received more than one wound is not impossible: in a letter to Fernand Destouches (5 November 1914), Houzet Boubers, a colleague of his in the Hazebrouck office of the *Phenix* insurance firm, refers to 'wounds' in the plural, *les plaies* (5 November 1914); moreover, in 1946, Céline claimed that prior to being hit by the stray bullet, he had injured his head after being thrown by a shell against a tree, which appears to be confirmed by a photo of him wearing a head bandage in Val-de-Grâce. However, as Richard, citing Jean Bastier, argues, Céline definitely could *not* have been injured by a sword: the battle raging around him consisted of mortar and machine gun fire, meaning that the enemy took shelter in their trenches. In such circumstances, it is unlikely that the Germans would have exposed themselves to shellfire to attack him with a sword. This was not the first time that Céline would indulge in some self-mythologizing.

Even so, if he exaggerated his injury, it was still bad enough to require serious medical attention and to elicit contrasting opinions from a whole panoply of experts. The following five months were instrumental in shaping his view of his future medical career in both positive and negative ways. His initial experiences at Hazebrouck hospital were hardly encouraging. The bullet in his arm was probably extracted by an inexperienced 35-year-old GP, Gabriel Senellart, on 28 and 29 October. Céline showed little faith in this novice, fearing the amputation of his arm, as suggested in a letter from his father to his Uncle Charles on 5 November.[26] That same day, Houzet, who visited Louis every day to keep his concerned parents abreast of his progress, reported that the doctor wanted Louis evacuated to Dunkirk hospital, where his arm would receive electroshock therapy.[27] On 1 December 1914, Louis was transferred to the Val-de-Grâce hospital in Dunkirk, after pressure exerted by his uncle Georges Destouches, secretary of the Faculty of Medicine at the University of Paris.[28]

At Val-de-Grâce, Céline's situation improved. He was officially presented and photographed with the prestigious Médaille militaire that

Céline (centre), Albert Milon (front left), Val de Grâce, December 1914.

had been awarded to him on 24 November by General Joffre himself. His parents glowed with pride, as they did about his appearance on the cover of *L'Illustré national*.[29] He also met Albert Milon, who was the inspiration for Bardamu's friend and fellow convalescing soldier Jean Voireuse in *Journey*. Not only was he from a humble background like Céline, but he had similarly suffered a serious bullet wound and lost the use of his left hand.[30] Greatly appreciated for his good humour, Milon would become one of Céline's regular correspondents when Céline was in London and Cameroon.[31]

Val-de-Grâce temporarily restored Céline's faith in the medical profession in the figure of 61-year-old Adolphe Jalaguier, an eminent doctor in charge of the serious casualties, who had distinguished himself in orthopaedics and paediatrics.[32] But his optimism was short-lived. Transferred to the auxiliary hospital at 121, boulevard Raspail in Paris between 27 and 31 December, Céline refused a second operation on his radial nerve by Dr Édouard le Bec. Shunted back and forth between various hospitals, he eventually ended up at Villejuif, at the Paul Brousse hospice, which was run by a forty-year-old Swiss oncologist and neurologist, the rising star Gustave Roussy, who was to inspire Dr Bestombes in *Journey*.[33] Highly ambitious and from a wealthy and influential background, he no doubt persuaded Céline, perhaps with the intervention of his Uncle Georges Destouches, to undergo a second operation to reduce the radial paralysis to his right arm, on 15 January 1915. This operation was carried out by the slightly older and equally promising Professeur Antonin Gosset. The operation to suture the radial nerve to Louis' right arm was both risky and innovative and seems to have contributed to scientific research.[34] Gosset himself was the first to carry out a nerve transplant between two people, and Céline acknowledged him in his thesis on Semmelweis in 1924.[35]

Céline's extensive medical records make no mention of his alleged cranial injury – a hole in the skull – which supposedly necessitated the insertion of a steel plate. This alleged injury was repeatedly mentioned not only by Céline himself, but by loyal friends and acquaintances such as Henri Mondor, Marcel Aymé, Evelyne Pollet and Milton Hindus.[36] It is far more likely that he suffered from Ménière's disease: a combination of partial deafness, vertigo, intolerable tinnitus and auditory hallucinations, all probably caused by his first war injury, in which he was flung into a tree by a shell attack. Indeed, as Robert-Chovin argues, this is almost certainly the injury to which he refers in a letter sent to his parents on

27 September: 'I've just experienced an emotional milestone [. . .] we were abundantly showered for 10 minutes by shells of all types of caliber [. . .] my hand was drenched in blood when I arrived.'[37] Céline himself refers to Ménière's in *Fable for Another Time* and provides a detailed self-diagnosis of his head and ear injuries in a document he drew up for his Danish lawyer Thord Mikkelsen on 30 November 1946.[38] He mentions enduring almost constant headaches, severe deafness, vertigo and permanent whistling in his left ear, ever since his first injury in 1914. The vertigo and tinnitus prevent him from sleeping more than six hours a night, symptoms for which head massages and daily doses of phenobarbitone and aspirin provide limited relief. These symptoms became more acute during his incarceration in Denmark.[39] In his fiction, such as in the opening chapter of *Death on Credit*, the adult narrator occasionally puts his affliction to creative use when he mentions the noises in his ears as a source of dreams: 'The fact is that in the days when I had that buzzing in both ears, even worse than now, and attacks of fever all day long, I wasn't half so gloomy . . . I had lovely dreams.'[40]

At the time, however, the medical priority was to treat his arm, not his head. He was transferred to the auxiliary hospital in Vanves, established in the Lycée Michelet, on 22 February 1915, where Doctor Laurens and his superior Doctor Moty reassessed the wound. He was granted leave on 7 March, on the proviso that he receive electroshock treatments until 27 March.[41] He was able to stay with his parents in rue Marsollier, where he was feted as a war hero by most, and aroused envy in others. For a while, he basked in this heroism, but soon came to reject it. Even though his arm was never the same, he took advantage of what Gibault calls this 'false gaiety', in which a strange carnival atmosphere reigned in Paris, while the war still raged on the front.[42]

If this gaiety was 'false', it is also because, despite appearances to the contrary, civilian life could be as ruthlessly self-interested and cruel as military conflict. Céline's novel devastatingly debunks the prevailing notion that the worst aspects of human behaviour are confined to the battlefield, whereas civilian life remains largely untouched by them. On the contrary, civilian life is merely a less extreme and more insidious version of the violence and Darwinian struggle for survival that take place on the front. Whether they work in commerce, the arts or even the medical profession, all citizens, in different ways, seek to profit as much as they can from the war and its victims. There is Madame Hérote, the cynical, sterile lingerie shop owner, who rents the back of her shop to strangers frantically seeking furtive sex: 'she levied a tithe on all sentimental transactions.'[43] She takes a perverse pleasure in bringing couples together and 'breaking them up by means of tale-telling, insinuations and out-and-out treachery'.[44] In so doing, she blatantly takes advantage of people's desperate search for happiness in the face of death: 'We went there to grope for our happiness, which all the world was threatening with the utmost ferocity.'[45] Then there is Bardamu's fleeting, unfaithful lover, the violinist Musyne, who obtains a 'certificate of heroism' signed by 'one of our glorious generals' for playing in the orchestra of the Theatre of the Armies and sleeping with the soldiers.[46] This certificate, in turn, makes her both musically and sexually alluring to some Argentinian soldiers: 'The poetry of heroism holds irresistible appeal for people who aren't involved in a war, especially when they're making piles of money out of one.'[47] Céline's satirical portrait of heroism as a highly valued sexual and artistic currency is by no means pure invention on his part. Celebrated actress Andrée Mégard, wife of Firmin Gémier, the director of the Théâtre Antoine in Paris, visited him in Val-de-Grâce hospital shortly before May 1915, accompanied by her friend Marie Samary. Mégard asked Samary's son, Charles Esquier from the Comédie-Française, to transpose Céline's exploits on the battlefield into a theatre monologue. He was sent the monologue in a letter, along with an invitation to attend the performance. He saw his story portrayed in overblown heroic terms that bore only a passing resemblance to the truth.[48] The monologue claims that the tendons of his right arm have been severed by a spear that rendered it useless – 'the hand is hanging, pathetic, shattered like a dying flower, whose stalk has been crushed' – and the myth that he used a sword is perpetuated by the closing line, 'I can still hold my sword with my left hand.'[49] Céline's exasperation with this type of hypocrisy was sufficient incentive for him to adapt the incident to his novel. One day, Bardamu is visited in hospital by a 'beautiful young actress from the Comédie' who 'questioned me about my feat of arms' and 'asked leave to have the most intense passages in my narrative framed in verse by a poet who happened to be one of her admirers'.[50] The poet in question, who, rather hypocritically, 'has been kept [. . .] out of the army' because he is 'frail', writes 'at the risk of his health and last spiritual energies' a 'rhymed narrative' called *The Moral Cannon of Our Victory*.[51] Needless to say, when he attends the recitation at the Comédie-Française with fellow patient Branledore, Bardamu's exploits are presented in far more heroic terms than even he had anticipated. This is due to a combination of the poet ('her poet was miles beyond me for fantasy') and Bardamu himself ('the poet was rendering a deed of awe-inspiring bravery that I had attributed to myself') being extremely liberal with the truth. To the ecstatic audience who 'clamoured for their hero' this does not matter, since 'Luckily, when it comes to heroism, people are willing to believe anything.'[52]

But military 'heroism' is exploited not just for triumphalist artistic propaganda, but in more subtle, pragmatic ways by those who are directly involved in the war themselves: soldiers and doctors. At Voireuse's instigation, he and Bardamu decide to make extra money by visiting the families of fallen soldiers to make them feel better with stories of their exploits, even if these are untrue:

> [W]e'll go and see a lady I know, her son was a buddy of mine, killed on the Meuse. I go and see his parents every week and tell them how their son was killed . . . They're rich . . . The mother gives me a hundred francs or so every time . . . They say it makes them happy . . . So . . .[53]

Even those who seem to be above moral criticism are not beyond exploiting military 'heroism' for selfish purposes: the eminent Professor Bestombes, 'our medical major with the beautiful eyes', uses his patients as human guinea pigs, to enhance his medical reputation:

> Would it interest you, Bardamu, [. . .] to know, that I shall be reading a paper on the fundamental characteristics of the human mind at the Society for Military Psychology tomorrow? [. . .] You see, Bardamu, the war, by providing us with such unprecedented means of trying men's nervous systems, has been a miraculous revealer of the human mind![54]

It is perhaps no coincidence that Bestombes is portrayed as an ambitious careerist, since, as we have seen, he was inspired by Gustave Roussy, the pioneering Swiss surgeon who pressured Céline into having a second operation on the radial nerve of his left arm.

But Céline presents the reader with an additional moral dilemma: are those who cynically distort the idea of heroism for their own opportunistic ends (economic, artistic, medical), despite knowing the harsh reality of war, any worse than those who are naive enough to believe that this heroism is sacrosanct? This dilemma is perfectly encapsulated by Bardamu's American girlfriend Lola, who completely romanticizes this notion of patriotic heroism:

> To Lola's way of thinking, France was some sort of chivalric being, not very defined in space or time, but at the moment dangerously wounded and for that reason very exciting. When anybody mentioned France to me, I immediately thought of my guts, so I wasn't nearly so open to patriotic ardour.[55]

Lola's idealization of patriotism is not actually altruistic, but *selfish*: it so excites her sexually, that she ends up cuckolding Bardamu with officers who are better decorated and hence more 'heroic' than him: 'Their competition was redoubtable, armed as they were with the seduction of their Legions of Honour.'[56] In the end, Céline intimates, whether they are cynically calculating or idealistically naive, every citizen is just as morally irresponsible and egotistical as the next, because none is prepared to denounce heroism as a dangerous myth behind which society hides in order to avoid facing the harsh reality of war.

All told, Céline's war experience and convalescence are not only thoroughly documented by letters and medical records, but satirically transposed with an admirably succinct psychological acuity and moral insight into fewer than a hundred pages of his novel. However, this cannot be said about his stay in London between May 1915 and May 1916, which remains partially shrouded in mystery and does not feature at all in his fiction until *Guignol's Band*. As one of many injured soldiers declared too unfit for combat, Céline was nevertheless still deemed useful to the war effort. Hence, on 6 May, no doubt because of his knowledge of English, he was appointed by the Grand Quartier général (G.Q.G.) as an auxiliary inspector in the military section of the Consulat général de France, 2e bureau, 51 Bedford Square in London.[57] This was a purely administrative role, a sedentary post to which his arm injury posed no obstacle. He arrived in London, via Folkestone, on 10 May. In the highly paranoid climate of espionage and counter-espionage, passport procedures had been tightened up on 3 March 1915. Additional requirements were now needed beyond the passport itself, which significantly increased the workload of the consulate: the interviewing of applicants, who had to provide valid reasons for travel, together with two photographs and stamps. As one of the auxiliary inspectors of the G.Q.G.,

Céline had to conduct these interviews under the overall authority of a military attaché of the embassy, Vicomte de la Panouse. In the spring of 1915, the workload was distributed among Captain Savy, a commissaire, an inspector from the civil police and four agents, most of whom had been injured in the war and were new to this role. Céline and Georges Geoffroy, his friend and flatmate in 71 Gower Street, were two of these.

Working in the passport office was certainly no sinecure. It was extremely chaotic and busy. Most travellers from Great Britain going to France transited through the capital. Every day the office at Bedford Square was mobbed from 7 a.m., two hours before the opening time, by over four hundred people demanding visas. From March 1915, overwhelmed by the new regulations, the embassy requested more staff, including Céline, to cope with the workload. In the following three months, 24,000 people, up to three hundred a day, were processed. An Anglo-French-Belgian conference of August 1915 further tightened up procedures, thereby adding to the workload. Applicants, who were fed up and angry at the long queues, demanded all sorts of special exemptions and permits.[58] Between April and August 1915, the military inspectors were able to arrest fourteen suspects with false or stolen passports.

The total mayhem of the passport office was rich source material for the slapstick scene in *Guignol's Band*, in which Ferdinand desperately tries to jump a ridiculously long queue in order to speak to the French consul. The comic effect is generated by the sharp contrast between the glacial pace at which the stuffy officials process the applications and the teeming, angry crowd of louse-ridden individuals from all four corners of the world, who are scrambling to get into the building:

> They all flock to the door every time it opens . . . it's a mixed sort of mob . . . they shove one another into the railings . . . they're all scraping away at the lice . . . digging at themselves . . . tickling . . . a hodge-podge . . . and cute specimens . . . big merchants and moujiks! . . . lots of all kinds . . .[59]

Claims later made by both Céline and Geoffroy that they were involved in espionage and even met famous spy Mata Hari in the Savoy Hotel, where she frequently stayed, have since been discredited. Céline's rank was far too junior to warrant his involvement in such missions.[60] Sex, not espionage, was an activity more in keeping with his character. Ambassador Paul Cambon expressed concern that his young male employees were far too easily distracted by *influences féminines* (feminine influences), a fact later confirmed by Céline's flatmate Geoffroy when reminiscing about their frequent escapades to Soho.[61] They would go to the music halls with kitchen staff as a way of getting in, where they would meet performers such as the then-famous Alice Delysia and Aimé Simon-Gérard at the Palace Theatre, which sparked Céline's lifelong interest in dancers. In Soho, they also frequented French pimps and their protégés, who were 'always willing to offer us dinner'. Céline's sexual escapades in the louche milieu of Soho's music hall and prostitution district of 1915–16 were further influences on the two volumes of *Guignol's Band*, inspiring, among others, the roguish pimp character Cascade. Further information about this world was later gleaned from Joseph Garcin, who had lived in London at the time, and Jean Cive, a prominent figure in the French prostitution racket in Soho, whom Céline met in the mid-1930s through his friend Henri Mahé.[62] Another major character in *Guignol's Band*, Sosthène, the eccentric performer who dressed in Chinese costumes, was based on the magician and illusionist Chung Ling Soo, who appeared on stage at the Empire at that time.[63]

However, Céline came crashing back down to earth when he was definitively discharged from the military. In a climate in which the desertion of French soldiers in London was rife, a number of commissions sought to clamp down on those young men like Céline, who were *réformés no. 2*, temporarily discharged or in the auxiliary services. They were either to be sent home, or back to the front, if deemed fighting fit. In London, Consul General de Coppet, who was responsible for decisions on staff and liaising with the recruitment office, discharged cuirassier Destouches on 2 September 1915, confirming his definitive discharge on 7 December, without a pension. Céline's precarious situation is humorously conveyed in the first volume of his novel *Guignol's Band*. After being informed of his discharge, Ferdinand exaggerates his 'heroic' military record to try to persuade the medical officer to let him back into the army: '"I killed twelve of 'em!" I raise the figure . . . "I killed a hundred! . . . It's not over! . . . I want to go back! I want to kill a thousand! I want to redeem my errors! . . ."'[64]

Little is known of the next five months of Céline's life in London, and especially about how he made ends meet. Once he left his lodgings at 71 Gower Street (following his departure from the passport office) and moved to 4 Leicester Street, he appears to have tried his hand at a variety of jobs: reading tarot cards, or working in an aircraft wing factory connected to Chung Ling Soo or in a London hospital at Mile End are all possibilities that have never fully been substantiated.[65] Did he receive help from the likes of Édouard Bénédictus, the inventor and friend who acted as a witness at his first wedding? Or from other contacts he had made in the scientific world mentioned in his letters from Africa?[66] *Guignol's Band* hints that drug trafficking and working as a pimp are two illegitimate professions that Céline may have dabbled in at the time.[67] If there is no evidence of the former, then he made a partial confession about the latter to Albert Paraz in 1948: 'I had everything to be a pimp. I turned people down in London. I could have been rich at 25 if I'd wanted to and considered a gentleman today.'[68] When Céline was working on *Journey*, Henri Mahé told him a story about how a prostitute had offered him money, to which he answered quite peremptorily, 'Having been injured in 14, I found myself in London, the 2nd office . . . I met a whore there . . . I married her . . . three days later I scarpered to Africa, in the middle of the rainforest . . . there you go!'[69] Céline's later novel, *Fable for Another time* (*Féerie pour une autre fois*) suggests he may have met the woman in question, Suzanne Nebout, in a louche Soho bar called the Ciros, where she and her sister were dancing to a sex-crazed male audience.[70] Born into an impecunious Parisian family in December 1891, her father remarried after her mother's death, and she gave birth to an illegitimate child aged only nineteen.[71] She went to join her older sister Henriette, who was living in London. How did Céline meet her? He himself remained coy on the subject, leaving only scraps of information through conversations with friends and occasional references peppered throughout his later novel. The names Marie Louise and Janine were probably stage names, as suggested by a letter to Georges Geoffroy on 27 October 1947.[72]

According to Lucette Destouches, Céline's third wife, Suzanne Nebout was 'more or less a dancer or night club employee'. He was in love with both Suzanne and her sister Henriette, but married Suzanne to make their residency in England more secure. They looked after him well, he lived in their milieu of pimps, and they offered to pay for his studies.[73] Suzanne almost certainly inspired Molly, the whore with the heart of gold in *Journey*, who develops a strong attachment to Bardamu in Detroit. She supports him financially, encourages him to leave the dehumanizing and soul-destroying work of the Ford car factory, buys him a 'four piece suit' and urges him to pursue more intellectually fulfilling work as a translator. Like Suzanne, Molly also has a sister.

The marriage took place on 19 January 1916 in the Saint Martin's registry office.[74] Even though marriage did not automatically qualify them for settled status, it did have the advantage of confirming Suzanne's and Céline's identity and domicile, which would allow them to gain rights as residents at a later date. Though the marriage was recognized by British law, it was not communicated to the French consul, which allowed Céline to marry Édith Follet in 1921.[75] Suzanne and Céline lived as man and wife for only a very brief time before he suddenly left London, departing for Cameroon on the HMS *Accra* from Liverpool on 10 May 1916, after a brief interlude in Paris. Why did Céline abandon his marriage and London so quickly? The theory of drug trafficking and illegal smuggling is too fanciful, but Richard points to two external pressures. The first, suggested by *Guignol's Band*, is that he was in trouble with the consulate and the British police. Cascade tells Ferdinand (Céline's semi-autobiographical narrator), 'They came looking for you too! [. . .] They want you at the Consulate! . . . Sure! Sure! . . . You can see why!'[76] This is plausible, given that in early 1916, the English press and public opinion were accusing French deserters of stealing English jobs.[77] The second external pressure on Céline may have been that his marriage with a young woman who had been part of the world of prostitution for two years got him into trouble with her protectors. One such protector was allegedly, according to Georges Geoffroy, an English colonel, who probably inspired Colonel J.F.C. O'Collogham in *Guignol's Band*.[78]

The theme of departing certainly influenced both *Journey* and *Guignol's Band*: Bardamu leaves Molly on a platform by boarding a train; Ferdinand was about to board the ship *Kong Hamsun*, without Virginie.[79] Bardamu expresses remorse about Molly. She tries in vain to keep him, but despite his love for her, he cannot fight his restlessness and heads back to Europe. Racked with guilt, he later writes to Molly repeatedly, but never receives an answer. We can almost hear Céline's apology to Suzanne when he confides in an intimate confessional mode,

> Good, admirable Molly, if she ever reads these lines in some place I never heard of, I want her to know that my feelings for her haven't changed, that I still love her and always will in my own way, that she can come here any time she pleases and share my bread and furtive destiny.[80]

Céline's guilt was no doubt exacerbated by Suzanne's tragic demise after he left her. She never heard from him again, at least according to her sister Henriette.[81] She went to his parents in rue Marsollier to inform them of the marriage.[82] It is possible that they bailed her out, because soon after her return to London in August 1916, she became the proprietress of a small Marylebone hotel at 44 Manchester Street, which she ran with her sister.[83] She eventually married a Swiss man, Jean Trichard, in Montreuil in August 1920, who agreed to adopt her young daughter. She stopped running the hotel in April 1921, and sold it when her health collapsed in the spring of 1922. After convalescing in the Netherlands and Germany, she died in the Luisenhospital, on 22 September 1922, before her 31st birthday, while Céline was sitting his medical exams in Rennes, completely oblivious to her fate.[84]

He was probably informed of Suzanne's unfortunate death by her sister Henriette, whom he met by chance, years later, just as he was about to leave Montmartre in June 1944. He recalls this chance meeting near his flat with great remorse and nostalgia in *Fable for Another Time* and also in a letter to Georges Geoffroy.[85] We will probably never know why exactly Céline abandoned his wife and her sister so seemingly callously, but *Fable for Another Time* suggests that his remorse was genuine and profound: 'I've committed only one crime in my life, only one real one . . . seeing as I left my little sisters-in-law, poor little girls, in November '17 . . .'[86]

The personal and professional failure of London explains why Céline sought a completely new challenge by going to Africa. He had already entertained with Albert Milon the idea of joining a Franco-Belgian expeditionary corps to the Congo when he first arrived in London in 1915.[87] Now that he was back in Paris, with no concrete plans, he jumped at the chance to earn good money as the supervisor of a cocoa plantation for the French colonialist forestry company Sangha-Oubangui. Having already acquired rubber plantations in the Congo, this expanding company was given a new concession in February 1916 in the newly French part of Cameroon.[88]

By signing a contract with Sangha-Oubangui, Céline became a small cog in the wheel of the colonial 'scramble for Africa' in Cameroon. Though far removed from the military conflict in Europe, the situation in Cameroon was a direct consequence of it. Following the outbreak of war in August 1914, the French and British had sent an expeditionary force to the German colony of the Cameroons, in order to reconquer the territory from their European enemy. By February 1916, this had been achieved, so in July that year, France and Britain agreed to divide the spoils between them, with the majority of the territory going to France. By signing up for one of the forty or so major colonial companies that had originally been created with the approval of the French parliament in 1889, Céline was actively participating in this latest phase of French overseas expansion. Following in the footsteps of Joseph Conrad, whose six months in the Congo in 1890 inspired his famous novella *Heart of Darkness*, Céline was similarly about to immerse himself in colonialist Africa, which would also lead to some of the most captivating pages of *Journey*.[89] At the time, however, writing a novel was the last thing on his mind: this trip was purely about adventure, a change of scene and making money.[90] It would prove to be one of the most psychologically and intellectually formative experiences of his entire life.

Following the arduous, disease-ridden crossing, Louis' first impression of Africa was that of the star-struck European who is intoxicated by its alluring exoticism. In a letter to his parents on 10 July, he writes with a lyrical celebration of nature that is reminiscent of Jean-Jacques Rousseau:

> I am for a moment, absolutely, exclusively, perfectly happy. The breeze reaches me from the horizon and sprinkles a dusting of golden sand over the thousand little white flowers that shake straightaway, in unison, like little flowers that are anxious about their corollas.[91]

Psychologically speaking, his initial enchantment with Africa as exotic 'Other' echoes his early enthusiasm for London in 1915: both were foreign climes that promised sanctuary from the trauma of war. But if the British capital had ensured (at least initially) his relatively smooth transition back into civilian life, his time in Cameroon was far more akin to shock therapy. The enticingly carefree world of Soho had allowed him to bask in sexual hedonism and drift from job to job. From the get-go, however, Cameroon imposed on him a far more stringent regime of self-reliance and self-discipline, an invigorating tonic that was dictated by the need to make a living in a punishing tropical climate. Céline, in other words, got far more independence and escapism than he bargained for, since he often had to work or travel alone in remote, dangerous locations. In a letter to his parents on 14 July 1916, he recognized just how much his life had changed since leaving the Rambouillet barracks a mere two years earlier:

> When this time two years ago, I was parading among so many people who are no longer with us, in that poor 12e regiment that now only exists as a memory, I had no inkling of all the events that would follow and especially that I would find myself in Bikomimbo 48 months later.[92]

His job as supervisor of the cocoa plantation in Bikomimbo, though adventurous, was risky and arduous, especially during the first three months of his ten-month stay in Cameroon (the remaining seven, he was able to remain in Bikomimbo).[93] During that time, he would travel upriver for three days to Dikipar along the Campo, the river that marks the border between Cameroon and Portuguese Guinea. Accompanying him was twenty canoes' full of cargo. Once in Dikipar, he would spend a week with 1,200 indigenous workers, picking and gathering cocoa on an enormous plantation left by the Germans. This cocoa would then be packed and expedited to the coast, from where it would travel to Duala by steamship. With his porters, provisions, fold-down bed and rifle, he would then venture further inland to Spanish Guinea, the Upper Congo and the mountains towards Chad, where he would sell his cargo at a high price and, on his way back, buy precious goods such as ivory for a bargain. He would sometimes spend two or three weeks without seeing a fellow European, sleeping in indigenous huts with 'my rifle in my arms for all eventualities'.[94]

If his letters to his parents typically assured them of his moral and financial responsibility, they also underlined that, without self-reliance and self-discipline, survival in the Dark Continent – especially when faced with solitude – was simply impossible:

> Up until now I had a very poor understanding of what isolation means, since civilized life hardly allows for it, if at all. It is rational that in normal life, we are heavily reliant on one another. Even under fire, I had not experienced this sensation, so difficult at first, of feeling alone, absolutely alone and of knowing and realizing quite clearly that whatever happens, you have yourself, and only yourself, to rely on. This is an obstacle you have to overcome as soon as possible, which can be vanquished only with a certain energy.[95]

Céline encountered the epitome of stoicism in the face of adversity in a Parisian artilleryman called Harte, who manned a forgotten outpost some ten days' distance from the coast and five days by road to his nearest neighbour, a missionary in Upper Congo. Ever since the Germans were driven out, Harte had stayed put, awaiting orders that never arrived, while the other men and horses had succumbed to sleeping sickness or other tropical diseases. Harte was 'resistant to death in whatever form it takes' ('réfractaire à la mort sous quelque forme elle se présente'), having buried all the remaining men. His past was mysterious, 'an ill-defined profession' ('une profession mal définie'), but he had fought in a regiment in France before being transferred to Colonial Artillery regiment. Vice had given his face a 'vindictive ugliness, accentuated by two small, black, wicked bright eyes' ('laideur vindicative, accentuée par deux yeux, petits, noirs, méchants et vifs') and fever a 'yellowish patina, on that ravaged, emaciated and bloodless face' ('patine jaunâtre, sur ce visage ravagé, maigre exsangue').[96]

Céline's new life of survival against the odds led him to make an important distinction, in a letter to his father, between two types of colonialists and colonies: the *côtiers*, or coastal inhabitants, and the *broussards* or 'bush-men'. He identifies with the latter. Those who live on the coast are like soldiers on the front – exposed to the constant threat of death – and those who inhabit the bush are the soldiers *behind* the front, who are removed from direct danger. The *côtiers*, who are well known in France, live in the large coastal towns 'in close proximity to the aperitifs, brothels and hospitals' ('à proximité des apéritifs, des bordels et des hôpitaux') and are characterized by 'their habitual drunkenness, debauchery and the fanciful stories they tell' ('leur ivresse habituelle, leurs débauches et les histoires fantasmagoriques qu'ils racontent').[97] These are habits they have picked up from their predecessors and which they subsequently pass on to the new arrivals. Those most susceptible to this debauched lifestyle have fled lives in Europe that were 'limited and poor' ('étroite et besogneuse'). They descend into alcoholism and try to stave off fever with copious amounts of quinine, reassured by the close proximity of the hospital and doctors to cure them if their health declines too much – only by then, it is too late:

> [. . .] it is already too late, all the medicines have no impact on an intoxicated organism, as the old saying goes, 'he has been hit by the bamboo stick'.
>
> ([. . .] il est déjà trop tard, toutes les médications restent sans effets sur un organisme intoxiqué, selon l'expression coûtumière 'il a reçu le coup de bambou'.)[98]

The second type of colonialist, with whom Céline explicitly identifies, is the *broussard*. He not only learns to be self-reliant by living alone in the bush (like Harte), but scrupulously avoids alcohol and sex, as he knows that each of the *côtier*'s habits of 'Intemperance, Debauchery, all manner of Excesses' ('l'Intempérance, la Débauche, les Excès d'un ordre quelconque'), 'opens the door towards Death, against which he will have repeatedly to struggle all on his own' ('ouvrent [. . .] une porte à la Mort contre laquelle il devra seul et par ses propres moyens, lutter et lutter encore'). Céline claims that 33 per cent of the *côtiers* who live in the large coastal towns die, whereas the *broussards* almost always survive. They are also strikingly different in dress and appearance. Whereas the *côtier* has an 'unhealthy' olive complexion, 'an unsettling look' ('l'œil trouble') and is 'lanky, scruffy, unkempt, repulsive' ('dégingandé, débraillé, peu soigné, répugnant'), the *broussard*, the 'real colonialist' ('vrai colonial') is well turned out, clean, clean-shaven, bronzed and European-looking, with arched eyebrows. His smart outfit, including his tie, commands the respect of the indigenous population and hence guarantees his safety. Céline ironically cites Livingstone as an example of the disciplined *broussard*, who only contracted fever on the one occasion he forgot to shave. Finally, the *côtier*'s tastes are predictably 'exotic': if he makes it back to Europe, he 'walks only on tiger skins, and his walls are bedecked with troubling and unclean fetishes' ('ne pose les pieds que sur des peaux de tigres, et ses murs sont garnis d'inquiétants et malpropres fétiches'). The *broussard*, on the other hand, has more sober and restrained tastes: 'he professes a particular cult for Linoleum and freshly toned engravings' ('il professe un culte particulier pour le Linoleum et les gravures aux tons frais').[99]

Such detailed, caustic descriptions anticipate both the best and the worst of Céline's later writings: they show his great flair not only for characterization and sharp social observation in his novels, but for reductive stereotyping in his pamphlets. In the main, however, the mediocre, diseased and debauched *côtiers* provide a rich seam for his magisterial satire of colonialism in *Journey*. Aside from the obvious thematic parallels between the letters and the novel – Doulala, Campo and Bikomimbo become Fort-Gono, Topo and Bikomimbo, and the Compagnie Sangha-Oubangui is renamed the Compagnie Pordurière, a likely scatological allusion to *par derrière* (from behind) – there are also crucial differences. The letters, via the figure of the *broussard*, still retain faith in a 'responsible', 'disciplined' and productive model of colonialism. This is the model that Céline himself followed and jauntily offered to his friend Albert Milon, when he tried to persuade Milon to join him in his colonial adventure.[100]

Despite the crushing heat, mosquitoes, illness and solitude, Céline used his time in Cameroon far more profitably than in London. He comes across as optimistic, dynamic and eager to learn, as opposed to the Bardamu of the novel, who is lethargic, pessimistic, ill-disciplined and just happy to survive. Nowhere in the novel, for instance, do we get a glimpse of Céline the intellectually curious autodidact, who enthusiastically conducts scientific and medical experiments and devours new works of philosophy and literature he has requested from home. He experiments with atoxyl injections to combat sleeping sickness, studies vegetable and animal toxins under the microscope and tries to 'do good' ('faire du bien') by treating the locals with medicines from his own pharmacy.[101] He even observes the behaviour of female scorpions, who kill the males after mating, with a magnifying glass.[102]

His mind at this time is bubbling with all sorts of ideas, some of which would later find a positive outlet in his fiction. He is particularly struck, for instance, by the philosopher Henri Bergson's theory that man's 'qualitative' subjectivity is synonymous with a 'spontaneity and freedom' ('spontanéité et liberté') that is absent from his more conventional 'quantitative' approach to reality. It is not hard to see a connection here with Céline's own later conception of an emotionally spontaneous style of writing that is filtered through the privileged lens of a first-person narrator.[103]

The novel, on the other hand, offers a scathing indictment of colonialism as a doomed enterprise and of colonialists, with rare exceptions, as society's forgotten 'losers'. Rather than working productively and resisting tropical disease, the new arrivals are quickly exploited and easy prey for an army of blood-sucking mosquitoes:

> Those half-baked little specimens had come to tropical Africa to offer their flesh, their blood, their lives, their youth, to their bosses, martyrs for twenty-two francs a day (minus deductions), and they were happy, yes happy, down to their last red corpuscle, for which ten million mosquitoes were lying in wait[.][104]

Many colourful examples abound of the disease-ridden and debauched *côtiers* and of their squandered energies. Fort-Gono, the main coastal town, is essentially a den of perdition: 'At nightfall the native hookers came out in strength, wending their way between the clouds of hungry mosquitoes, armed with yellow fever.'[105] To relieve boredom, the little clerks have 'fever contests', which consist in comparing thermometers to see who has the highest temperature.[106]

As for Bardamu, the only aspect of the *broussard* mentality he shares with Céline is a refusal to drink and smoke, much to the annoyance of the Company Director ('Such abstinence surprised him. In fact, he scowled').[107] Aside from that, he has far more in common with the passive resignation and indolence of the *côtier*.[108] Like the typical *côtier*, he views sickness and a stay in the hospital as a welcome respite from work and the harsh climate: 'The only really desirable spot I came across in the whole town was the hospital [. . .] my ambition was to be sick, plain sick.'[109] The novel thus bears no trace of the optimism, resolve and thirst for knowledge contained in the letters written over a decade earlier.

As for the Director, he personifies both the *côtier*'s unappealing physique and his vices of intemperance, debauchery and excess. He lives on top of a red cliff 'cavorting diabolically with his Negress under the tin roof with the ten thousand kilos of sunshine on it' and has a past 'as full of low dodges as a prison in a seaport town', and 'his face had the terrifying look of an undeniable murderer, or rather, to be fair, the look of a reckless man in a terrible hurry to get ahead.'[110] When writing these words, perhaps Céline was thinking of men such as Harte, or the disabused hotchpotch of colonialists he encountered in the isolated colonial outpost of Batanga: an American former soldier and amputee searching for gold mines, the sergeant in charge of this solitary outpost who is grateful for any company and a Portuguese missionary on his way back to Gabon. By day, they take shelter from the sun, while at dusk, they cool off in the sea and entertain each other with stories. The Portuguese missionary, a big-game hunter, recounts in 'a violent language and with a lilting Portuguese accent' how he had been forced to massacre monkeys who had sacrilegiously adopted the habit of bombarding him with coconuts during mass.[111] Everyone laughed, until the American cut everybody short by declaring that 'ever since the war – he never again killed monkeys, they looked too much like men, he said. Nobody said anything for the rest of the evening.'[112]

Thus the letters, like the novel, share a powerful leitmotif: war is an inescapable reality that lives on in the minds of those who have experienced it, even once they are far removed from the battlefield. Neither the Parisian Harte nor the American gold hunter are able, like Céline himself, to shake off a military past in Europe. The exception to this rule in the novel is General Tombat, who avidly follows the war in Europe, rather than seeking to forget about it. Tombat has offered his services to "Greater France" after his ear was split at Charleroi. Even long after the battle of Verdun, 'that epic battle was still on his mind', and he anticipates a French victory. Bardamu, echoing Céline's adverse reaction to the story of the monkeys, belongs to that majority of colonialists that does not wish to be reminded of the war, especially when they are so far away from it: 'It was so hot in the warehouse and France was so far away that we could have done without General Tombat's predictions.'[113] Both the letters and the novel thus depict war as a psychological trauma that follows its victims to the ends of the earth: even the most remote colonies.

The lingering mental scars left by the war forced Céline to reassess his view of human nature, politics and society. His letters to his parents, to Milon and especially to Simone Saintu show him grappling with pacifism as the only alternative to what he now begins to consider as hypocritical patriotism and obsolete political discourse. Several times he refers to France as a decadent and degenerate civilization that is stuck in the past and far too deferential to its ageing leaders. It lags behind more dynamic and younger civilizations, such as its ally Russia, which one day 'will also endure the weakening effects of decadence'.[114] And he anticipates his satire of French revolutionary values in *Journey* (the colonel and the messenger are locked into an embrace only *after* they have been blown up), by similarly denouncing French revolutionary egalitarianism as a failure in peacetime, but a success in wartime, because death is no respecter of social class: 'Had the bloodshed been carried out on a strictly egalitarian footing the doctor of science would have no more been spared than the last of the illiterates.'[115]

He especially fears for those demobilized soldiers returning to civilian life in this decadent society. Having developed a disdain for life and an indolence and a fondness for drink after long periods spent in the trenches awaiting death, they will have little incentive to reclaim those jobs taken by women in their absence, preferring instead to live on their pensions and war indemnities.[116]

This slightly self-righteous tableau of the lethargic, decadent soldier prefigures the more mature, literary depiction of the military 'rejects' in Fort-Gono. The disapproving tone of the letters has been replaced by the disabused empathy of the novelist. These forgotten 'fallen' soldiers wallow in sickness, vice and apathy, the very antithesis of those traditional patriotic notions of military valour and heroism:

> Most of the white conscripts were permanently in the hospital, sleeping off their malaria, riddled with parasites made to order for every nook and cranny in the body, whole squads stretched out flat between cigarettes and flies, masturbating under mouldy sheets, spinning endless yarns between fits of painstakingly provoked and coddled fever. Poor bastards, they were having a rough time, a pitiful crew in the soft half-grey light of the green shutters, re-enlisted men soon fallen from celebrity, side by side – the hospital was mixed – with civilians, all hunted men in flight from bosses and the bush.[117]

Deprived of its special privileges, the military is forced to mingle indiscriminately with civilians. Not only does Céline satirize the military as a 'fallen' institution, he once again emphasizes, as he does throughout the novel, that war pervades all facets of civilian life. In other words, human conflict is not merely confined to the officially sanctioned military battle in Europe, but extends to the more localized infighting and Darwinian struggle for survival that constantly takes place between the three layers of the colonialist hierarchy: soldiers, civil servants and traders:

> We always talked about the Governor, the focus of all our conversations; then we talked about possible and impossible swindles, and lastly about sex: the three colours of the colonial flag. The civil servants present made no bones about accusing the military of wallowing in peculation and abuse of authority, but the military paid them back in kind. The traders, for their part, regarded all these prebendaries as hypocritical impostors and bandits.[118]

Whether in a military or civilian context, the compulsion to fight is thus an intrinsic part of human nature.

Bardamu's bleak depiction of colonialism as an absurd, doomed enterprise made up of diseased, incompetent and egotistical individuals, most of whom are the forgotten outcasts of European society, reinforces Céline's reputation as a nihilistic writer, who views human nature as flawed and beyond redemption. But this would be to overlook those infrequent but touching moments of compassion in which he recognizes the best side of humanity.

In the remote outpost of Topo, Bardamu encounters the debauched and boorish Lieutenant Grappa, who enjoys meting out justice to the indigenous population, as well as his more reserved second in command, Sergeant Alcide: 'a good sort, obliging, generous and all' but 'crushed by his enormous resignation' at having been stuck in this thankless role for three years.[119] One evening, Bardamu stumbles upon a photograph of a young girl, 'a sweet little face with long curls', whom Alcide reluctantly confesses is Ginette, his orphaned ten-year-old niece.[120] Alcide has deliberately volunteered to stay an extra three years at the godforsaken outpost of Topo just so he can pay, with 'his meagre wages', for Ginette's convent school and medical treatment for infantile paralysis. Bardamu is so moved by Alcide's confession that he is filled with self-loathing ('Next to Alcide I was an impotent slob, boorish and vain') and total admiration at the sergeant's act of extreme altruism:

> With hardly a thought of what he was doing, he had consented to years of torture, to the crushing of his life in this torrid monotony for the sake of a little girl to whom he was vaguely related. Motivated by nothing but his good heart, he had set no conditions and asked nothing in return. To that little girl far away he was giving enough tenderness to make the whole world over, and he never showed it.[121]

Characters such as *Journey*'s Molly and Alcide elicit empathy from the reader because they show a more hopeful and compassionate side to Céline, one that rarely surfaces in his fiction, but was to find an outlet in the next phase of his existence: his medical vocation and work as a hygienist for the League of Nations.

three

Inventor and Doctor

Having fled the claustrophobic parental nest to savour the liberating expanse of the African bush, Céline's enforced repatriation back to France in May 1917 was something of an anticlimax. Like the returning prodigal son, he had to readjust to paternal authority. And this authority decreed that his future lay in the international jewellery trade with the Lacloche brothers. Now that injury, trauma, tropical disease and his short-lived first marriage were behind him, it was high time he got a proper job. But Céline was a risk-taker who lived in the moment and followed his instincts. So he dug his heels in and refused to play ball. As far as he was concerned, London and Africa had taught him far more than any jeweller ever could: how to fend for himself, circumvent danger and expand his intellectual horizons. Africa, in particular, had provided both the ultimate psychological test – learning how to survive in a hostile environment – and a powerful mental stimulant: days spent in solitary contemplation of its majestic beauty had sharpened his senses, awakened his curiosity and made him feel alive again.

Such daunting, but enriching, adventures were not readily available in the passage Choiseul. He had already crammed more memorable moments into his 23 years – some horrific, others exhilarating, but none of them dull – than most people would in an entire lifetime. Here was confirmation, if any were needed, of the self-diagnosis he had made four years earlier in the *Carnet du cuirassier Destouches* that he was 'different from the herd', and destined to follow his irrepressible wanderlust by living as many different experiences as possible. But this character trait, he would later acknowledge, was also his Achilles heel: if it made him stand out from the crowd, it also sabotaged his prospects of long-term happiness and stability. As we have seen, Céline's remorse at abandoning his first wife, Suzanne Nebout, is projected via Bardamu's similar guilt at his own incurably selfish restlessness. Molly, the kind-hearted woman who loves Bardamu unconditionally and could have made him happy, is the inevitable casualty, like Suzanne, of his stubborn refusal to settle down:

> I was afraid of hurting her. She understood and anticipated my concern. She was so nice that I finally told her about the mania that drove me to clear out of wherever I happened to be. She listened to me for days and days while I held forth, laying myself disgustingly bare, fighting with fantasies and points of pride, and she never lost patience, far from it.[1]

But in 1917, barely back from the tropics, and stuck in his parents' flat, Céline had little time for self-recrimination or regrets. He was too busy going stir crazy and wondering what to do next. It is doubtful, as some have suggested, that the Lacloches reneged on their promise to re-employ him on account of his arm injury. Far more likely is that Céline was the one who chose to avoid *them*. He had no desire to lead a regimented life of routine work in his home city and under the watchful gaze of his parents. He could easily have re-established contact before leaving for London in late 1914 or following his return to France in late 1915. But there is no evidence that he did so.[2] Perhaps he wanted to avoid the same fate as his father, who was now a disillusioned, frustrated man, after decades of being stuck in the same dead-end desk job that he hated.[3]

This is why Henri de Graffigny entered his life at exactly the right moment. Céline saw Graffigny as a kindred spirit: a larger-than-life eccentric (to this list could be added his future father-in-law Athanase Follet, the painter Henri Mahé and Paul Laffitte), whose energetic, rebellious streak appealed to Céline's own dynamic and contrarian personality. Graffigny's 'can-do' zest for life was the perfect antidote to his own father's gloomy defeatism. Céline met him through another charismatic non-conformist, Édouard Bénédictus, a friend and acquaintance from his London days, who had acted as witness to his short-lived marriage to Suzanne. Bénédictus was not only a multi-talented musician and composer (he had known Ravel), but a renowned chemist and physicist, who ventured into the decorative arts. This Jewish-born polymath, whom Céline described as a 'rocambolesque, cabalesque, hoaxer' ('rocambolesque, cabalesque, mystificateur,'), inspired the mystical inventor

Sosthène de Pereires in *Guignol's Band*, a zany character obsessed with Tibet, Hindu dances and Chinese costumes.[4]

One of several Jews who, ironically (given Céline's later anti-semitism), played a prominent role in Céline's life, Bénédictus was linked to Henri de Graffigny via their mutual employer Paul Laffitte, editor of the journal *La Sirène* (for whom established author Blaise Cendrars wrote and produced illustrations) and another, scientific journal, optimistically called *Eureka*. It was Bénédictus who recommended Céline to *Eureka* as a general dogsbody, proofreader and occasional translator (from French into English), in close collaboration with its major contributor and copy-editor from October 1917 to February 1918: Henri de Graffigny.[5] Though Céline, as Richard points out, was usually loath to divulge the identity of those who inspired his fictional characters, he made an exception for Graffigny: he provided the model for the flawed but likeable inventor Courtial de Pereires, for whose journal, *Le Génitron*, Ferdinand works in *Death on Credit*: 'Of course, Courtial is de Graffigny great inventor and prince of makeshift repairs – a genius impostor to whom I owe a lot as you know.'[6] A precocious autodidact, like Céline, Graffigny was a charismatic polymath. His aptitude for science, especially in the realm of electricity, became apparent from an early age, together with a gift for drawing and writing stories. In 1882 he published his first science-fiction adventure story, *De la Terre aux étoiles, voyage dans l'infini* (From the Earth to the Stars, Voyage into the Infinite), prefaced by his friend the astronomer and writer Camille Flammarion.[7] Between 1880 and 1888, Graffigny undertook no fewer than twenty hot-air balloon ascensions that clearly inspired the hilarious and hair-raising balloon flights Ferdinand undertakes with Courtial. He published over two hundred works on clocks, materials, cycling, automobiles, aeronautics and all types of electrical appliances. His *Dictionnaire des termes techniques employés dans les sciences et dans l'industrie* (Dictionary of Technical Terms Employed in Science and Industry), edited by Dunot and Pinat in 1906, comprised no fewer than 839 pages and 25,000 entries.[8] Selective translation of his works secured him an international reputation. If he was considered more a 'popularizer' of science than a pioneer, a few of his inventions, such as his electric car run by a chromic acid battery, caught the eye of respected peers such as Louis Figuier, a scientist, writer and professor at the École de pharmacie of Paris.[9]

Like Céline himself, however, Graffigny was prone to self-mythologizing. His name suggested aristocratic ancestry, but he was born Raoul Henri Clément Auguste Antoine Marquis in 1863, the son of an accountant. He simply chose the name of his modest birthplace, the village of Graffigny-Chemin, which bordered Haut-Marne and the Vosges.[10] Nor were the titles and qualifications he claimed to possess – civil engineer in 1896, aeronautical engineer in 1909, professor at the Institut électrotechnique in 1923, professor at the École du génie civil in 1926 – ever properly authenticated. He did, however, gain some success by writing futuristic novels inspired by Jules Verne: *Les Aventures extraordinaires d'un savant russe* (The Extraordinary Adventures of a Russian Scientist across the Solar System) was published in four volumes with his co-author Georges le Faure by Edinger in 1888. An astronomical novel, it was included at the Exposition Universelle of 1889.[11]

Thus Graffigny left a respectable scientific and literary legacy, despite being a bit of a charlatan. It was, above all, his larger-than-life personality that appealed to Céline the novelist: this eccentric 'nutty professor' required only minor tinkering and embellishment for him to become one of Céline's most memorable tragicomic creations. And if Céline transposed Graffigny's energetic quirkiness to Courtial, so too did the zany inventions in the journal *Eureka* provide inspiration for its novelistic counterpart *Le Génitron*. Among the inventions that recalled the contemporary spirit of Dada were shoes with interchangeable soles, white ink to mark black sheets and a vacuum cleaner designed specifically for automobiles.[12]

As with many great literary characters, Courtial represents a host of psychological and moral contradictions. On the one hand, he has an irrepressibly childlike enthusiasm for his inventions, which he eagerly transmits to the errant young Ferdinand through his genuine paternal concern for his education. Like Ferdinand's maternal Uncle Édouard, Courtial represents a surrogate father figure, whose relentless drive and zest for life stem from his anarchic individualism and insatiable curiosity. He is thus a refreshing antidote to the pompous, ultra-conventional Auguste, whose anger with the world stems from his own unfulfilled ambitions. Where the biological father projects his frustrations onto his son, whom he repeatedly admonishes as a lost cause, the more encouraging surrogate regards him as a rough diamond that is merely in need of polishing: 'You're not a bad kid, Ferdinand . . . your father's mistaken about you. You're unformed! Unformed, that's it! . . .'[13] This also reflects Courtial's wider pedagogical mission to make science accessible to the masses, in order to improve their lives. To that end, he rails against the prioritizing of profit over ideas, a murky practice backed by corrupt scientific institutions that plagiarize inventions such as his and distribute awards and honours on a purely ad hoc basis for self-serving, rather than meritocratic, ends.

Yet Courtial's staunch defence of ideas for their own sake is undermined by his hidden vices: adultery, gambling and alcohol. Ferdinand is frequently placed in the awkward position of having to place bets on horses on his behalf, as well as lying to customers, debtors and Courtial's long-suffering wife, as to his activities and whereabouts. His vices lead him into all sorts of financial scrapes, for which drastic – and invariably highly questionable – solutions need to be found. The most ingenious and comical of these is his scheme to entice aspiring scientific inventors to pay 'registration fees' to his journal for the sum of 52 francs, in exchange for the journal publicizing and endorsing their ideas.[14] Needless to say, a bevy of young hopefuls naively part with their hard-earned money, only to see little, if anything, to show for it in return. The at-once amused and exasperated Ferdinand has to act as a gatekeeper. It is he who has to deal with the furious complainants who come storming into the newspaper offices, while Courtial hides shiftily below a trap door. Ferdinand's tactic is to adopt a form of reverse psychology: to defuse the customer's anger by pretending to be even more infuriated with Courtial than he is:

> I amazed the lunatic by the virulence of my hatred for the loathsome Pereires . . . I took him every time in nothing flat . . . with my hair-raising insults! . . . In that province I was supreme! . . . I flayed him! I stigmatized him! I covered him with garbage, with pus! . . . That abject villain! That mountain of shit! Twenty times worse! A hundred times! A thousand times worse than the customer had ever thought on his own! . . .[15]

Once the coast is clear, Courtial re-emerges from under the trap door, expressing his deep gratitude to Ferdinand ('Ferdinand! You just saved my life . . .'), but seeking reassurance from his charge that he had only been pretending, that he did not really mean the horrible things he had said about him:

> But I do hope, Ferdinand, tell me now, that I haven't fallen as low as all that in your esteem? You'd tell me wouldn't you? You wouldn't hide it from me, would you? I'll explain my position if you want me

> too. Go ahead! . . . I do hope these little acts you put on have no effect on your feeling for me! That would be too dreadful! Your affection for me is unchanged? [16]

These are the tears of a clown. Courtial's comic exterior masks a deep-seated insecurity and constant need for approval. For all his eccentric and roguish charm, his frequent close shaves and his daring schemes, he is, deep down, a tragic figure: highly sensitive and unstable, riven by self-doubt and with a fragile, self-destructive ego.

Courtial's fall from grace, like Auguste's, is presented as the symptom of a wider historical crisis. The downfall of the petit-bourgeois artisan class extends to that of the individual free thinker. Courtial epitomizes the last in a long line of distinguished nineteenth-century positivists, such as Henri de Graffigny and his rival, the astronomer and early science-fiction author Camille Flammarion, who champion autonomous intellectual freedom and creativity. Courtial is thus a throwback to an era when progress was still the product of personal human endeavour, rather than impersonal commercial imperatives. In this regard, he is anticipated by Dr Baryton in *Journey to the End of the Night*, the head of the asylum in Vigny-sur-Seine, who similarly represents a dying breed of medical practitioner struggling in vain to stem the tide of an increasingly profit-driven world. As the city encroaches upon his peaceful suburb, his patients turn into avid consumers who demand the latest and most sophisticated devices to treat them:

> Those insatiable families were always demanding, always insisting on newer and newer methods of treatment, more electrical, more mysterious, more everything . . . The most recent, most impressive machines and contraptions. And he had to submit, on pain of being outdone by his competitors.[17]

Writing during the economically depressed 1930s, Céline is casting a wistful gaze back to his childhood and the prosperous years of the Belle Époque, when original thinkers such as Courtial de Pereires or Baryton still had the intellectual autonomy to improve society on their own terms, rather than caving in to the pressures of mass consumerism. Thus Courtial's precipitous downfall and horrific death – a more extreme version of Baryton's own descent into madness and abandonment of his practice – signal, at a deeper level, the extinction of the humanist individual in the face of a dehumanizing modernity.

Indeed, despite his flights of fancy and irresponsible attitude to money, Courtial has the social awareness to recognize that idealist lone wolves such as he is are an endangered species, so a more collectivist and traditionalist approach is needed to ensure their survival: 'The individual is washed up! . . . You won't get anything out of individuals! . . . It's to the family, Ferdinand, that we'll have to turn! Once and for all, to the family! Everything for and by the family!'[18] Hence his desire to embark on another hair-brained scheme that would kill two birds with one stone. The first is to create a socially utopian institution that would house, educate and transform underprivileged city children into model citizens. Dubbed the 'Renovated Familistery for the Creation of a New Race', this is modelled on the experimental school known as 'La Ruche' ('The Beehive'), conceived by the anarchist Sébastien Faure as a rural idyll against the encroaching forces of urban industrialization.[19] No longer contaminated by the unhealthy, polluted air of the cities, these deprived and sickly children would swiftly be transformed, under the guidance of Courtial and his wife, into vigorous and highly productive members of society, who apply the 'positivistic, zootechnic and horticultural' values they acquire.[20] But beneath this utopian rural idealism lies a more self-interested motive: to exploit these children's labour and the subsidies they attract to sell potatoes cultivated via electricity.

Both these events – the phalanstery and the 'radiotellurism', as Céline calls the cultivation of potatoes by electricity, were loosely inspired by the final years of Graffigny's life, which were spent in Septeuil, a small village of 867 inhabitants in Seine-et-Oise (the model of Blème-le-Petit in *Death on Credit*).[21] Reputed for its invigorating country air, it became, in the early twentieth century, a favoured spot for children's institutions and asylums, notably the foundation L. Bellan. George Duhamel devoted several pages to it in his *Géographie cordiale de l'Europe*.[22] It cannot have escaped Céline's attention that Graffigny and his wife intervened to look after several children when one such orphanage, the Contamine, housed in the château at Septeuil, closed in late 1921. When Céline and Lucette visited Septeuil just before the war, Céline may well have spotted a grocer's shop called 'Le Familistère'.[23] Aside from running this ill-fated orphanage, Graffigny really did attempt to grow potatoes via electroculture, a method he had already tried before the war in the Oise. However, contrary to the novel, he confines this agricultural experiment to his garden.

Needless to say, both the 'Familistery' and the radiotellurism end in disaster. Of the fifteen children – nine boys and six girls – three do not show up, and those that do are lazy and unruly rather than diligent and disciplined. The cost of supplies to feed growing children soon proves to be too much, so they quickly turn to theft, until they are eventually caught:

> We'd lost our authority. But those little tricks leave traces . . . two days later the cops came around asking for big Gustave and little Leone . . . They hauled them off to Beauvais . . . We couldn't protest . . . They'd got themselves pinched picking a billfold! . . .[24]

Far from becoming model citizens, the children, and even Courtial's wife, develop a reputation in the village for thieving. This incurs the wrath of its inhabitants, who throw stones through their windows in retaliation.[25] The rapid dwindling of supplies is exacerbated by the complete failure of the potato crop.

In an ironic twist of fate, reality was to catch up with fiction. Céline and his third wife Lucette visited Graffigny's widow shortly before the war (and hence after the publication of the novel). By then, she was bedridden and in need of money. She had agreed to be paid by the *assistance publique* (social welfare) to house and feed fifteen children, but she was unable to cope. The famished children pounced on the jam and cakes brought by Céline and Lucette, and the fields outside were strewn with their toys and little windmills. This was all that remained of the 'telluric potatoes'.[26] Graffigny died on 3 July 1934, though there is no evidence to suggest that he took his own life, as Courtial does in the novel.[27] His last two years had been spent as actively as ever, producing another novel, *Electropolis* (1933), and two pamphlets on aerial navigation and electricity.

Courtial's horrific death allows Céline the novelist to flex his imaginative muscles, departing from his more or less faithful transposition of Henri de Graffigny. In the grotesque evocations of Courtial's disfigured, bloodied corpse, the result of shooting himself through the mouth, one can perhaps detect the influence of Bruegel, the Flemish artist whose striking paintings of grotesque, distorted bodies Céline discovered in Vienna in late 1932:[28]

> The double barrel went in through his mouth and passed straight through his head . . . It was like a hash on a skewer . . . shreds, chunks and sauce . . . Big blood clots, patches of hair . . . He had no eyes at all. They'd blown out . . . His nose was wrong side out . . . nothing

> but a hole in his face . . . [. . .] The body bent crooked like a Z . . . the head impaled on a gun barrel . . . First you'd have to straighten him and get the gun out . . . His back was all bent, his arse was wedged between his heels . . .[29]

If modern society precipitates Courtial's dramatic death, its institutions are also woefully ill-equipped to deal with its aftermath. Man's impotence in the face of mortality is satirically laid bare by the police officers who bungle the investigation of Courtial's death and the even more inept clergy, which is represented by the mad eccentric, Father Fleury. The incoherent and dishevelled priest refuses to believe Courtial has taken his own life in the light of his spiritual teachings:

> 'The Director! . . . The Director! . . .' he started bellowing again . . . 'I've given all I had! . . .' And he went down on his knees again, he kissed his crucifix . . . He crossed himself a thousand times . . . He stayed there in an ecstasy . . . his arms stretched out on both sides . . . He made a crucifix of himself! . . .[30]

For all his official honours ('his whole soutane was full of orders and medals . . . and several Legions of Honour . . . '), the priest is nothing more than a ludicrously hyperbolic parody of Christ's crucifixion, and hence of the empty symbolism of Christian ritual.[31] The exasperated Ferdinand's decision to confront the raving Father Fleury with the harsh physical reality of Courtial's bloodied corpse pushes this parody to a grotesque extreme. The priest is so discombobulated by this horrific spectacle that he inexplicably plunges his hands into the bloodied corpse, extracting bits of blood, flesh and bone:

> He's in a frenzy! Stark-raving mad! He won't let me cover him! . . . He sticks his fingers into the wound . . . He plunges both hands into the meat . . . he digs into all the holes . . . He tears away at the soft edges! . . . He pokes around! . . . He gets stuck! . . . His wrist is caught in the bones! Crack! . . . He tugs . . . He struggles like he's in a trap . . . Some kind of pouch bursts! . . . The juice pours out! It gushes all over the place! All full of brains and blood! . . . Splashing! . . .[32]

This is an example of what Julia Kristeva, writing on Céline, defines as the 'abject': those borderline situations that we face as human subjects

– such as being confronted by a corpse – that threaten our very sense of identity.[33]

If the fictional Courtial's horrible death embodies the crisis of modernity, then the real-life Graffigny at least had some positive impact on Céline's life: he was the unwitting catalyst in launching his medical career. According to Céline's own version of events – yet another example of his self-mythologizing – a competition for scientific inventions had brought him and his mentor Graffigny to the office of 'an important man who had a professorship and was in charge of the école'.[34] When this eminent professor was temporarily called away to an adjacent office, Céline allegedly spotted on his desk a letter from the Rockefeller Foundation requesting help to recruit candidates for the fight against tuberculosis. Céline decided to steal the letter as proof of the professor's recommendation for the position. The more likely scenario, as Céline confirmed in his interview with Charles Chassé in 1933, is that he simply saw a small advert placed by the foundation seeking employees for its campaign against tuberculosis. As a newly demobilized soldier eager to find work, he blustered his way through the interview and despite his inexperience in public speaking, obtained the post, largely thanks to his fluency in English.[35]

His interviewer was probably Selskar M. Gunn, an American doctor of Irish extraction, who was to become another influential father figure in Céline's early career. A former professor of public health at MIT in Boston, Gunn was co-director with Livingston Farrand, president of the University of Colorado, of a commission funded by the Rockefeller Foundation for the prevention of tuberculosis in France. A philanthropic organization founded in 1913, this foundation sought to assist refugees, orphans and tuberculosis sufferers around the world. The anti-tuberculosis campaign in France was spearheaded, with the backing of the Red Cross, by the Duchess de Richelieu and ratified by the French government in January 1917.

As part of their initial training, in January 1918, Céline and his friend Alfred Milon, the fellow injured soldier he had befriended at Val-de-Grâce and whose services he also managed to enlist, joined a team put together by the commission. Its mission was to tour the department of l'Eure-et-Loire in Brittany and give educational talks to the public on the dangers of tuberculosis. The team's two main speakers were a feminist journalist, Alice La Mazière, and Alexandre Bruno, doctor at the Roosevelt Hospital in New York, who trained Céline in the art of

The puppet theatre of Henri de Graffigny (profile, third from right) as part of Rockefeller mission, 1918.

public speaking. As for Graffigny, he was asked to join the team as both a chauffeur and photographer.[36]

The period from 10 March to 10 December 1918 was crucial for Céline's linguistic and intellectual development. While the rest of Europe was fighting itself to a standstill, he was giving lectures, often to primary-school children, on the dangers of tuberculosis. The commission's propaganda campaign unequivocally denounced the disease as the 'enemy within' (*ennemi intérieur*) that killed one in eight French citizens. Considered just as threatening as the Germans, tuberculosis was condemned in terms that were no less jingoistic.[37] The lectures given to adults would typically conclude with a rallying call to Breton mothers,

Official welcome for Rockefeller mission, Rennes, March 1918. Louis Destouches (second from left), Docteur Athanase Follet (third), Professor Selskar Gunn (fifth), General d'Amade (ninth).

reminding them of their moral patriotic duty to nurture healthy children and do all in their power to protect them from this pernicious threat to the future prosperity of the nation.[38]

If his talks had to follow this standard, patriotic template (they were probably written by Alexandre Bruno), they still afforded Céline the opportunity to develop two of his typically *célinien* talents: his oral eloquence and his anarchical subversiveness. Regarding the former, in his 1933 interview with Charles Chassé, he recalled his nervousness – 'how I spluttered the first few times!' ('Ce que j'ai pu bafouiller les premières fois!') – upon giving the first lecture, on 13 March in the cinema Omnia in Rennes, with various American delegates in attendance, as well as prominent figures in Rennes, including the mayor, army generals, members of the clergy and Céline's future father-in-law Athanase Follet.[39] He need not have worried. *L'Ouest-Éclair* commended him for speaking with 'considerable knowledge of the topic and the cultured palate of the most eminent connoisseurs'.[40] Another local newspaper praised his second lecture, on 18 March (this time delivered to one hundred Rennes schoolboys), for eliciting enthusiastic applause from his audience, which expressed 'the interest he had shown in this exposé'.[41]

Céline, however, was incapable of adhering to convention for very long. Shortly after his death in 1961, one member of the audience recalled that 'carried away by his talent and verve', Céline at one point decided to stop talking about tuberculosis to offer his 'personal views' on current affairs. The respectable dignitaries were not amused. The clergy left discreetly, to be followed by the *préfet*, the American officers and the French generals.[42] But at least one attendee was captivated by Céline's lecture: Édith Follet, the impressionable and attractive eighteen-year-old daughter of Athanase Follet. Professor of clinical medicine at the University of Rennes, officier de la Légion d'honneur and a highly influential figure in Rennes, Follet was instrumental in bringing the Rockefeller commission to Brittany. He and his wife, the daughter of eminent surgeon Augustin Moravan, invited the Rockefeller delegation for a sumptuous dinner at their home, where Céline sat opposite Édith. Édith inadvertently played footsie with Céline, to which he wasted no time in responding. She soon fell under his spell, being seduced by his 'extraordinary eyes', whose shade of blue changed according to his mood.[43] Céline would soon find pretexts for calling in on the Follets, during which he would pass on secret notes to Édith via the sympathetic governess.

It is here that Céline does an unexpected U-turn. Having for so long resisted the life of conventional bourgeois respectability his parents had tried to foist upon him, he now – at least outwardly – embraced it both personally and professionally by asking for Édith's hand in marriage. Why the sudden change? Vitoux speculates that Céline was driven by love and impatience – impatience at consummating his relationship with a respectable young woman who had vowed to her mother to stay chaste until she was married.[44] As for Follet, he recognized Louis' charms, but wanted his daughter to marry someone respectable: hence the condition that he first complete his *baccalauréat*, as a stepping stone to medical studies.[45] Towards the end of his life, Céline recalled that the prospect of a medical career happily coincided with his long-held childhood ambition to become a doctor, whereas literature, at the time, held no appeal whatsoever:

> I had the medical vocation, whereas I did not have the literary vocation at all. I considered the literary profession as something completely grotesque, pretentious, stupid, which was not suited to me. Not serious, in other words . . . Whereas I always had the medical vocation . . . Oh, in a profound way . . . From my earliest childhood I found nothing more respectable than a doctor . . .[46]

Céline duly passed his *baccalauréat* with a 'merit' (*mention bien*) on 2 July 1919, before his marriage the following month on 10 August.[47] The following summer, two important things happened: on 9 June, Athanase Follet was elected into the Académie de médecine, and on 15 June, Édith gave birth to a daughter, Colette.[48] Céline proved to be a devoted father, who fretted over his daughter's health. He was now a big fish in the relatively small pond of Rennes high society. Between August 1919, when he moved with Édith into the ground floor of Flat 6, quai Richemont, below his in-laws, and late 1925, when his marriage was crumbling and he was working in Geneva for the League of Nations, he lived a settled, comfortable life that was in marked contrast to his peripatetic existence of the preceding years. But he found marriage stifling and sought to escape it via numerous affairs and unexplained trips away. He even participated in orgies with friends from that period; according to Germaine Constans, who was to become a lifelong friend of Céline's, a certain amount of 'partner swapping' went on behind Édith's back.[49] This did not prevent Céline from being insanely jealous of any man who went near Édith. The summer holidays of 1921 were spent by Édith and Colette at l'Aber Wrac'h in the Finistère, near Lannilis, where her mother's family was from. Céline turned up unexpectedly, after one of his many long absences, to discover that Édith had been taking boat rides with a certain eighteen-year-old family friend called Hilarion. Céline whisked Édith back to the hotel and told Hilarion in no uncertain terms that he would be taking no more boat rides.[50] He and Édith did share moments of happiness together – motorcycle rides in the Breton countryside (he had an American motorcycle with a sidecar), trips to the cinema in Rennes and occasional visits to the theatre, cabarets and concerts in Paris, where they stayed with his

Céline, Edith and friends in Rennes, *c.* 1920.

parents – but they were fleeting, and Céline quickly got bored and was always on the move.[51]

The young man from Courbevoie and the passage Choiseul was struggling with the regimented hypocrisy of bourgeois life. Only a few months after his marriage, in early 1920, he wrote scathingly of the bourgeois egocentricity he associated with his in-laws:

> The heart of the bourgeois is something that is unimaginably dull and insensitive to the suffering of others. This does not apply to Édith, even if altruism is not her strong point (where would she have learnt it from?) but to this band of hideous egotists whose fat and closed faces I randomly encounter in the street.[52]

While he did not dislike them as individuals, he resented the class they represented. He got on well with his father-in-law, who shared his irreverent sense of humour and love of literature and was equally unfaithful, having dalliances with, among others, the German governess.[53] Both Céline and his father-in-law liked to shock their respective spouses by citing Rabelais at the dinner table.[54] As a fellow philanderer, Céline chuckled at Athanase's infidelities. Moreover, there was considerable mutual intellectual respect between him and his mother-in-law, Marie-Louise Follet, whom he joked he should have married instead of her daughter.[55] She would regularly give him gifts, and he praised her prodigious memory in his *Interviews with Professor Y*, fondly comparing her to novelist George Sand in a letter to Édith on 10 April 1958, following her death.[56]

But Céline's irresponsible behaviour as husband and father should not detract from his extreme focus when it came to his studies. He read both literature and scientific texts voraciously. He largely kept his distance from the younger students at the University of Rennes, though he already stood out by wearing a cowboy hat. Perhaps most significantly, he seriously considered pursuing a career as a biologist.[57] Once he had passed his medical exams, with the encouragement of his zoology professor, Léon Bordas, his father-in-law and perhaps Professor Edmond Perrier, he was able to spend the summer of 1920 in the zoological institute at Roscoff.[58] There he experimented with the artificial hibernation of small algae, which resulted in the publication of an article for the Académie des sciences, 'Observations physiologiques sur *Convoluta roscoffensis*'. His subsequent experiments at the University of Rennes in techniques for prolonging life (which were consistent with his obsession with death) resulted in a paper: 'Prolongation de la vie chez les *Galleria mellonella*'. Céline's scientific ambitions and interest in the prolongation of life were further pursued thanks to his acquaintance with famous Nantes scientist Professeur Stéphane Leduc.[59]

Thus science, not literature, was very much Céline's central preoccupation at this point. Nevertheless, Édith and Céline did collaborate to produce a little-known work that reflects his nascent literary talents. In early 1923, when Colette was three and a half, her parents produced a short oriental fairy tale called *Histoire du petit Mouck* (The Story of Little Mouck). Although the text remained unfinished, it contained 44 illustrations by Édith (who was to become a respected children's illustrator in her own right) and some of Céline's emerging literary concerns. Petit Mouck is a 'little vagabond who is lost in the desert. He arrives at a palace, where he is generously taken in by a king and queen, before becoming unhappy and longing to escape. A genie grants his wish to 'travel far away, across the sea'. He then meets three sirens, who take him away to show him the treasures of the deep. The unmistakable hallmarks of Céline's fiction are present: travel and adventure, the constant urge to escape and the nagging feeling of dissatisfaction, all of which prefigure *Journey to the End of the Night*.[60]

As for his doctoral thesis, entitled *La Vie et l'œuvre de Philippe Ignace Semmelweis (1818–1865)* (The Life and Work of Philippe Ignace Semmelweis), this is a unique and important text because it encapsulates recurring motifs of Céline's life: literature, medicine, non-conformism and the ideas of persecution and marginalization. The thesis was about a Hungarian hygienist, Ignace Philippe Semmelweis, whose major contribution to medicine remained unacknowledged during his own lifetime: his discovery that when medical professionals – doctors and midwives – washed their hands prior to delivering a baby, this drastically reduced the number of deaths from puerperal fever, a disease which, at the time (the nineteenth century), was alarmingly high in many maternity wards. However, Semmelweis's colleagues, irritated by his lack of diplomacy and brusque manners, refused to heed his warning.[61] Céline would try to get his thesis published by Gallimard in 1928, but it was refused.

However, passing his doctorate in May 1924 suddenly opened up an exciting new career opportunity for him. In June, Selskar Gunn, the American professor and mentor who had recruited him in 1918 for the anti-tuberculosis campaign, recommended him for a post to Doctor

Ludwig Rajchman, director of the Health Section of the League of Nations in Geneva. Céline, who, by now, was fed up with life in Rennes and had only half-heartedly tried to open his own medical practice there, jumped at the chance and was recruited on a temporary contract.[62] He so impressed Rajchman with his intellect and ambition, that he was quickly made more permanent. Rajchman and Céline struck up a father–son relationship based on great mutual respect and affection, despite Rajchman being a Polish Jew.[63] Rajchman was a methodical, bright man of 43, with an impressive CV: a medical degree from Krakow, a stint studying at the Pasteur Institute in Paris and experience of running the National School of Hygiene and the Institute of Epidemiology in Poland. He, in turn, was impressed not only by Céline's intellect, but by his irreverent charm, which was a welcome change from the League's usual British formality. Céline became a regular at the Rajchman's, where Ludwig's wife was enthralled by his conversations about literature.[64] Céline's move to Geneva did little to reassure Édith about the state of their marriage, but he was not to be deterred. He saw this as a fresh start and was brimming with optimism at what this new job had in store for him, as his letter to Albert Milon makes abundantly clear:

> You see, this is where your old Louis is. Here, in the international beehive. I am headstrong, as you know. Here I am. This time, I am tackling problems of hygiene on a wide scale, and by God, I like it. Gunn, naturally, was my father. It will be said that the Rockefeller will take over my life. But you see, nothing is better than youth. Everything else is empty and the beautiful days are filled with hope.[65]

After a probationary period spent learning the administrative ropes, he was finally entrusted with his first foreign mission with the Health Section to the USA in February 1925. He was to head a delegation of eight Latin American doctors on a fact-finding mission on public health in North America, from Louisiana to Canada, for which he had to send back detailed reports to Geneva. One report, in particular, would leave a lasting impression on his fiction and social outlook: the one he wrote about his visit to the Ford Factory in May 1925. Here, he writes in his capacity as a bourgeois observer of the factory, who interviews his fellow medical professionals, rather than the workers. His visit coincided with the height of Ford's success and the production of the Model T.

At the time, Henry Ford defended his production methods according to his Midwest Protestant work ethic of self-reliance. His factories, he was quick to point out, employed people such as the disabled, who would be unable to find work elsewhere. Everyone could be socially and economically useful. Of course, Ford's critics also correctly pointed out that there was an underlying profit-driven motive to this 'inclusiveness': the wage of U.S.$6 a day may have been relatively generous, but it was also deliberately calculated so as to allow the employees to be able to afford to buy the Model T themselves. This would guarantee that the producer would also become a consumer.[66]

If Céline's primary brief was medical – to evaluate the health and sanitation of the workers – he also gives a penetrating overview of some of the contradictions in Ford's approach:

> This current state of affairs is, overall, hardly disastrous from a sanitary or even human standpoint, it offers many people a livelihood who would otherwise be quite incapable of obtaining one outside Ford. But Ford can subsidize this large surplus of useless people only to the extent that it has more advanced standardized machinery than the others. Irrespective of the ludicrous quality of its employees this machinery allows it to manufacture more competitively than anybody else.[67]

Ford machinery, in other words, takes precedence over its employees. Human labour has significantly less value than the equipment used. Now this idea is transposed to the novel in a way that is far more direct, visceral and satirical. As a worker, rather than a mere observer in the factory, Bardamu becomes so caught up in the noise of the machinery that it takes over his entire body to the extent that the two become indistinguishable from each other: 'We ourselves became machines, our flesh trembled in the furious din, it gripped us around our heads and in our bowels and rose up to the eyes in quick continuous jolts.'[68] In a second transposition from the report to the novel, we witness the factory doctor's dismissive and condescending description of the workers:

> The doctor in charge of admissions told us in fact that 'what they needed was chimpanzees, that this sufficed for the work they had been assigned,' he went on to claim that these animals were already used in the southern plantations. [. . .] I was somewhat surprised that

> he should make such disparaging remarks in public, always in a loud voice, assuring me that not only were the candidates physical invalids but mentally 'completely devoid of imagination, with no critical faculties, cretins, that is what we need, for us, the dream worker is the chimpanzee . . .'[69]

The novel remobilizes the *very same* chimpanzee metaphor and devaluing of the imagination, but with far greater satirical force. The reader is left in no doubt as to the individual's dehumanization by the production line, especially when Bardamu's attempts to assert his educated status as a thinking individual with a medical degree are swiftly dismissed as irrelevant:

> 'For the kind of work you'll be doing here,' the doctor assured me, 'your health is of no importance!'
>
> 'Glad to hear it,' I said. 'But you know, Doctor, I'm an educated man, I even studied medicine at one time . . .'
>
> At that he gave me a dirty look; I saw that I'd put my foot in it again, to my detriment.
>
> 'Your studies won't do you a bit of good around here, son! You're not here to think, you're here to make the movements you're told to. We don't need imaginative types in our factory. What we need is chimpanzees . . . Let me give you a piece of advice. Never mention your intelligence again! We'll think for you, my boy! A word to the wise.'[70]

The report's veiled critique thus becomes far more explicit in the novel. One reason for this was the greater freedom of expression he was afforded by the medium of fiction. He did not have to adhere to the conventions and protocols of the League. Another was that Céline's work for the Health Section brought him into direct conflict with America's self-serving economic and political agendas. By the time he wrote *Journey*, the League had gone down substantially in his estimations. Where he had once pinned his hopes on its capacity for change, he now saw it as structurally flawed and corrupt. The reasons for this lie in the origins of the League itself. At the first League of Nations conference in the autumn of 1920 it had been proposed to make the Health Section an integral part of the League, based on Article 23 of the League of Nations Pact, Paragraph F, which stipulated that the member states would 'make every effort to take measures on an international scale to prevent and fight diseases'.[71] Owing to the major health crisis caused by the war, the Health Section of the League was, in effect, set up before the rest of the organization and took on the bulk of its role. The Health Committee, made up of twelve members (later twenty) who were nominated by the Council, ratified the programmes and their implementation within the framework of the section.[72] But the Health Section's ability to operate independently was compromised from the outset by competing U.S. interests. The USA, having not signed up to the Treaty of Versailles, was not an official member of the League of Nations. Its government had no direct links to the League and made only negligible financial contributions towards it. But this did not prevent Rupert Blue and Hugh S. Cumming, who ran the U.S. Department of Public Health, from exerting considerable influence over the League via the 'back door' of the Health Section. First, they encouraged large subsidies to this section from the Rockefeller Foundation (about U.S.$941,000 for the period 1922–31); second, they facilitated the participation in its activities of U.S. scientists and researchers from different laboratories and universities. This meant that the Health Section became the 'unofficial' bridge between the USA and the other 54 members of the League. Despite partial funding from the League, it was heavily reliant on the Rockefeller Foundation. What further complicated matters for Céline was that his direct superiors, Rajchman and Gunn, were responsible for allocating the Rockefeller budget from New York. Since the United States, as a non-member, could not officially nominate one of their own for a post in the League, this had to be done via the Rockefeller Foundation on temporary contracts. On 23 March 1925, a shift in policy in the Health Section increased the U.S. government's influence on the League. Rajchman and the director general of the Rockefeller Foundation, General Frederick F. Russell, appointed Frank Boudreau, an epidemiologist from Ohio and head of the Bureau of Communicable Diseases, as deputy medical director of the section. Russell was himself pressured into this appointment by Colonel Huntingdon Gilchrist, who was director of the Medical Division in the Chemical Warfare Department.[73]

The conflict of interest was obvious, and it did not take long for someone of Céline's intellect and natural suspicion of authority to smell a rat. Matters came to a head during his fact-finding mission to North America, whose aim was to set up an international bureau of epidemiological information in Havana, Cuba. His early reports sent to

Rajchman from Havana already anticipate problems further down the line: 'Cuba, it is true, is flowing with gold. Even the Americans have designs upon this Eden.'[74] He continues: 'The country, as you know, is a kind of American protectorate, and its Constitution stipulates that the latter reserve the right to intervene in the case of "medical emergency".'[75] Céline was only too conscious of the U.S. influence over Cuba, as well as of Cuba's desire to wriggle free from it: 'The Cubans are scared of American intervention, which is always a realistic possibility in the case of an epidemic. They would really like us to provide them with sanitary protection in this regard.'[76] On 9 April, he warns that the Americans are trying to muscle in on the project he is heading with the Health Section: 'A frenzied pan-Americanism is circulating around Washington. American industry desperately needs outlets. Our delegates are being very carefully wooed. I'm keeping my cards close to my chest.'[77] Céline warned U.S. journalists that no article should appear without mentioning the League, but they completely ignored him. He was faced with an insuperable obstacle: his efforts, with the backing of Geneva, to set up an epidemiological bureau in South America, were being undermined by American attempts to set up *an almost identical project*. The inevitable confrontation with Surgeon General H. S. Cumming and Dr Leo S. Rowe, director general of the Pan-American Union, came when the League delegation was invited to a function in Washington, DC, with no less a figure than President Calvin Coolidge himself.[78] In an angry letter to Rachjman on 10 April 1925, Céline expresses his frustration that neither the League's existence nor its mission were even acknowledged: 'I understood that it was necessary to pass off this event as strictly pan-American. It was a deliberate ploy.'[79]

Since Céline was introduced to the president without even the merest mention of his name, nationality or official titles, it was simply assumed that he was South American. When the president asked Cumming what the purpose of the delegation's visit to the USA was, he merely said that they were doctors from Latin America 'whom we invite every year to study our public health organization'.[80] The president then addressed the delegation with 'very courteous and very Pan-American words'.[81]

Never one to forget a slight from those in power, Céline, on this occasion, uncharacteristically held his tongue. Though he was tempted to shout, 'Long live the League of Nations!' ('Vive la SDN'), he thought the better of it to avoid a scandal. But he did not mince his words about the Americans in his letter to Rajchman: 'These people are simply so proud that they do not even appear to have time for rudeness. Their political conduct reminds me of the Germans before the war.'[82] Nor did he refrain from systematically opposing communiqués from his American hosts, which caused a sufficient stir to make it into the *Washington Herald*.[83]

Another letter to Rajchman on 12 April further bemoans the delicate relations with Washington and the pan-American rivalry with the League's epidemiology committee. The newspapers continue to ignore him and all mention of the League, and by now, the Americans have got wind of the Cuban project from the League's Latin American doctors.[84]

On 16 May 1925, Rajchman is eventually forced to write a grovelling letter of apology to Cumming after the 'Washington incident'. He welcomes 'the opportunity of discussing with you in more detail all your impressions of the Latin-American Interchange and your observations concerning Dr. Destouches' and says he is 'very sorry indeed that there should have been some unpleasantness'.[85] Théodore Deltchev Dimitrov speculates that 'the complaint lodged by H. S. Cumming, U.S. Surgeon General, with the Rockefeller Foundation ruined the career of Docteur L. Destouches from the outset.'[86] This is an exaggeration, but the rot had set in.

The delegation's far more successful visit to Quebec in Canada temporarily cushioned the blow. The Canadians, including the press, warmly welcomed the League of Nations and its mission. Dr Destouches, in return, was quoted in the newspaper *Le Soleil Québec* of 22 May 1925, praising Quebec for its public hygiene system and the general prosperity of Canada as a country that had emerged largely unscathed from the war. A number of other Quebecois newspapers enthusiastically recounted the visit of the delegation, its mission and the favourable impression the Quebecois system made on them. This was a welcome change from the U.S. visit, where press coverage of the delegation had been non-existent.[87]

Once back in Geneva, however, Céline was summoned, like a naughty schoolboy, to Professor Gunn's office for a dressing down. As he sarcastically reported to Rajchman on 16 June 1925, 'Saw Gunn. He told me about Cumming's complaint about me to Rockefeller. I feel greatly honoured by his cowardice.'[88]

His growing disillusionment with the League mirrored his personal life. His reunion with Édith in London was hardly a happy one. Having disembarked at Liverpool at the end of May 1925 and feeling thoroughly deflated by his trip, he joined her in the capital, where she was convalescing in hospital for mumps, after visiting a close female friend who had

League of Nations delegation to study public health methods comprising Dr Destouches (second from right) and Latin American doctors, Toronto, May 1925.

settled there. Her poor health was, no doubt, a symptom that the marriage was in trouble, while he poured out his frustrations to her in hospital.[89]

Despite the U.S. incident, Céline was given some reprieve by the positive feedback he received about his Canada mission, which secured him a salary increase of 250 francs.[90] But the relentless pace of the delegation resumed in June and July: the Netherlands, Belgium, Switzerland and France (where Paris had just hosted the 1925 International Exhibition), culminating in an exhausting trip to Italy at the height of summer at the end of July and early August. Despite the warmth and hospitality of the Italian hosts, Céline tried, in vain, to lighten the load of his exhausted delegates. But it was difficult to duck out of a high-profile visit with Benito Mussolini himself, who was only too keen to promote Italy's antimalarial campaign, spearheaded by the draining of the Pontine Marshes.[91] By then, the Americans had put a further spanner in the works, with the appointment of Frank Boudreau as Rajchman's interim replacement as medical director. Céline took exception to his attempts to meddle with the individual itineraries of some of the doctors in his delegation on 25 and 27 July and told him so quite firmly in a letter on 28 July.[92]

The autumn and early winter of 1925–6 were spent kicking his heels in Geneva while waiting to take charge of a second delegation to Africa in 1926, with only the occasional visits to Paris, Brussels and The Hague to occupy him. During this time, he shifted his quarters from La Résidence Hotel to his own three-bed apartment in the residential suburb of Champel.[93] A visit by his daughter Colette, who was accompanied by Germaine Constans instead of Édith, was a sign that Édith had abandoned the marriage as a lost cause. She pushed for divorce. While Gibault claims this was at her father's instigation, she later told Vitoux that it was her idea, encouraged by her friends, and her father subsequently backed her.[94] Despite his own extramarital affairs, Follet's bourgeois Catholic provincial background meant that divorce still had a whiff of scandal, hence his initial reluctance. As for Céline himself, a combination of his 'old bourgeois reflex' ('vieux réflexe bourgeois'), his likely fear of disappointing his parents and a hypocritical desire to remain the dutiful husband and father, provided he did not have to live the conjugal life, also made him reluctant to end the marriage.[95] But he did not oppose Édith's divorce petition at the Rennes Palais de Justice on 9 March 1926, largely because he was unable to attend the attempt at reconciliation fixed for 19 March, having already embarked for Africa on 14 March. No doubt the final nail in the coffin of his marriage was his harsh letter to Édith, which her lawyer submitted as proof of his culpability, when the divorce was finalized on 21 June:

> You need to find something to give you independence in Paris. As for me, it is impossible for me to live with someone – I don't want to drag you behind me snivelling and miserable, you bore me, and that's it – don't try to hang on to me. I would rather kill myself than to live with you continuously – I want you to know that – and don't ever bother me again with clinginess, tenderness – but rather arrange your life as you see fit. I want to be alone, alone, not dominated, not in tutelage, not loved, free. I hate marriage, I abhor it, I spit upon it; it reminds me of a prison where I am dying.[96]

This cruel attack on Édith, marriage and love anticipates Robinson's similarly vicious diatribe against his lover Madelon and the stifling nature of love and sentimentality at the end of *Journey*. Madelon has repeatedly been goading him, declaring her love for him and imploring him to say that he loves her in return. After initially staying silent, he eventually explodes with anger and frustration, before she retaliates by shooting him in the back of the taxi:

> Only, if you want the whole truth . . . everything – absolutely everything! – disgusts me and turns my stomach! Not just you! . . . Everything! . . . And love most of all! . . . Yours as much as everyone else's! . . . The sentimental tripe you dish out . . . Want me to tell you what I think of it? I think it's like making love in the crapper! Do you get me now? . . . All the sentiment you trot out to make me stick with you hits me like an insult, if you want to know.[97]

Although they maintained civil relations for the sake of Colette, for whom he obtained custody one month a year, and they became closer again in 1958, when Édith's mother died, Céline bore a grudge towards Édith for initiating the divorce, as well as towards her father for finding letters to prove Céline's adultery in court.[98]

The one ray of light in his personal and professional gloom was his chance encounter with an attractive young American woman, who would become his muse and lover for the next six years: Elizabeth Craig. He accosted the 24-year-old outside a Geneva bookshop one day in early 1926, by asking her whether she liked a particular book.[99] The striking redhead responded favourably, explaining that she was from Los Angeles and spending a year with her family in Europe to recover from a bout of tuberculosis and also seeking opportunities as a dancer. Aside from her good looks and regal demeanour (she was nicknamed *l'Impératrice* (the Empress) by her friends), Céline was completely enchanted by her dancing background.[100] While she had started dancing too late to perform in ballets, she had performed in music halls and trained in Paris with the eminent Russian Alexandre Volinine. The only five surviving letters he wrote to her are in English, showing the limits of their communication: she knew very little French, and he spoke good, but by no means perfect, English. That this may have helped, rather than hindered, their relationship is certainly plausible, given Céline's profound aversion to outpourings of affection and neediness, as he had so cruelly made clear in his letter to Édith.[101]

His burgeoning relationship with Elizabeth was temporarily interrupted by his three-month trip to Africa. The absence of reports from there written by Céline implies that he had, by then, lost all interest and faith in the League.[102] Surviving letters and reports written by other members of the League suggest that the trip was as frustrating as the one in North America; only this time, it was not American interests that blocked the setting up of an epidemiological bureau, but those of the two traditional colonial powers in Africa: the British and the French. Céline was caught in the middle of numerous petty squabbles and competing agendas, including transport delays involving rival French and British shipping companies.[103]

Céline had had enough. His need to vent his frustrations about the League and colonialism resulted in his satirical play *L'Église* (The Church), which also afforded him the opportunity to create the role of a dancer for Elizabeth Craig. That he omitted all reference to the League in *Journey* may be because he got it out of his system in *L'Église* and also so as to avoid ruffling too many feathers in his debut novel.[104] But there is perhaps another reason: the League was simply too respectable an institution to be believable as a working environment for the anti-bourgeois Bardamu. *L'Église* lacks the sophistication and character development of *Journey*, flaws that are heightened by its inclusion of the crass antisemitic stereotype of the 'scheming Jew' who pulls the levers of power. Céline rather naively meant Rajchman to see the funny side, but he was, understandably, not amused.[105] The reality, as we have seen, was quite the opposite: Rajchman was the puppet on a string pulled by the Americans, since he was directly answerable to the Rockefeller Foundation. And it was Rajchman who, more than anyone else, had gone out of his way to help and promote Céline during his time at the League.

More generally, *L'Église* also reflects Céline's desire to cast off the shackles of bourgeois conformism, in order to rediscover his lower-middle-class roots. He was fed up with the dignitaries, the multinational corporations and his bourgeois wife and in-laws, and wanted to reconnect with hoi polloi. He requested a GP practice in the downtrodden suburb of Clichy, agreeing to undertake only occasional European-based missions for the League of Nations. This was the phase of his life he conducted, as Philippe Roussin aptly calls it, as the *médecin des pauvres*, the 'doctor of the poor'.

When Bardamu opens a new medical practice in the downtrodden suburb of La-Garenne-Rancy, a thinly disguised version of Clichy, we as readers are invited to acknowledge his valiant attempts to swim against the powerful tide of misery, cruelty and petty self-interest that characterizes this *banlieue*'s inhabitants. Rancy is a pun on the word 'rancid' (*rance* in French), a notion reinforced by the grey facades, 'soup-like' factory smoke and disenchanted workers, who urinate in the polluted river Seine. It belongs to that no man's land or 'zone' on the edges of Paris which, as James Cannon has eloquently shown, is neither quite the city nor the countryside, and full of disgruntled lower-middle-class commuters struggling to make ends meet.[106] Day after day, they pile into the trams and underground trains like sardines, to carry out unfulfilling work for their exploitative bosses in Paris.

Céline's psychological realism goes much further than the socio-economic analysis of naturalist writer Émile Zola, a fellow 'champion of the underdog', to whom he is sometimes compared. Where Zola's novels focus on the *outwardly visible* causes of urban misery – poverty and poor health – Céline digs beneath the surface to expose the hypocritical ways in which the victims of this misery seek to hide it from the outside world, just so that they can 'save face'. An example of this is the 'respectable' mother whose promiscuous daughter Bardamu tries in vain to treat for a botched abortion: the latest in a long line of unwanted pregnancies that result from affairs with married men who won't leave their wives. The mother sees the risk to her daughter's health as secondary to the scandal of malicious gossip. Better for her to suffer in silence at home than be treated properly in hospital, where her situation is more likely to become public knowledge: 'It'll kill me, Doctor! I'll die of shame!'[107] This reflects Céline's disgust at the obsession of his own petit bourgeois class with 'keeping up appearances', no matter how great the personal cost. As if this episode were not distressing enough, the 'glug-glug' (*glouglou*) of the blood Bardamu is trying to stem from her daughter's womb recalls in his mind that of the blood he witnessed pouring out of the decapitated colonel's neck: 'A glug-glug between her legs like in the decapitated colonel's neck during the war. All I could do was put back the big wad of cotton and pull up the blanket.'[108] This one incident summarizes Bardamu's struggles with his medical practice on three fronts: the medical crises themselves, his patients' social hypocrisy and the omnipresent shadow of his own post-traumatic stress disorder that is triggered by his exposure to suffering on a daily basis. War psychologically contaminates civilian life, even once it has ended. The hypocritical gap between public respectability and private scandal reaches its absolute nadir when Bardamu overhears his neighbours – apparently 'a normal family' – sadistically abusing their daughter inside their flat as a prelude to their lovemaking.[109] He is paralysed by guilt at his failure to intervene: 'I was no good for anything. I was helpless. I just stayed there listening, same as everywhere and always.'[110]

These episodes all suggest Céline's lack of faith in the medical profession. But nothing could be further from the truth. The very period he was writing the novel – 1928 to 1932 – coincided with his doctor's practice in Clichy, when he was also still undertaking European-based missions on behalf of the League. Take, for instance, his request of 8 February 1929, for a bursary from the Health Section to investigate medical conditions in deprived areas of London that are comparable to Clichy:

> I am anxious of [*sic*] making a study trip to England and chiefly to London, in order to study, at first hand, the functioning of the

> municipal dispensaries of general medicine and their relations to urban public health in a popular district and their administration. At the same time I should like to study the administrative system of blennoragia in London.
>
> My duties as physician in our municipal dispensary bring me, as well as my colleagues [...] into contact with a great number of very diverse and distinct problems of social and public hygiene and a study such as I desire to undertake in the crowded districts of London (similar I think to our own quarters) would be of great service to me and my colleagues.[111]

Throughout 1929 and 1930, he requests missions to the poorer quarters of various European cities (Antwerp, Oslo, Stockholm, Copenhagen, Dresden, Prague and Vienna), with the specific purpose of studying ways in which medical treatment of the urban poor can be improved. Above all, he strives to promote in his Clichy practice a collective 'therapeutic' medicine that focuses on curing patients, rather than the 'diagnostic' medicine practised in hospitals.[112] This medicine was to be both 'efficient' and 'standardized', with recourse to specialists, only when all other treatment options had failed.[113] In a particularly revealing paragraph relating to a mission in London that anticipates his depiction of the thick industrial smoke in La-Garenne-Rancy, he expresses his desire for a medicine that would be 'adapted to the needs of a population that is working class, poor, badly housed, in a rainy, inclement climate, and which is, moreover, near the factories, whose smoke has an additional noxious impact'.[114]

Philippe Roussin draws an important distinction between Céline's socially utopian medical writings as a public hygienist working for the League in the 1920s and his far more pessimistic tone as 'author-as-doctor' in his novel.[115] The latter essentially undermines his more optimistic outlook as public hygienist for the League, which envisaged the possibility of universal healthcare and access to medicine based on 'principles adopted in the domain of the scientific organization of work'. In other words, 'standardized medicine' would replace charity, philanthropy and social welfare, as well as private practices ('bourgeois medicine is dead, good and dead'). In an increasingly industrialized society, it made sense that 'health and sickness should be defined by the factory and through the factory – that is within the sphere of production rather than by the medical profession.'[116] However, by the time he adopts the narrative voice of the 'author-as-doctor' in *Journey*, Céline is commenting from the standpoint of the Great Depression and not the hygienist social utopianism of the 1920s. Therefore, his perspective and role change. He becomes 'the author of the time of crisis', whose new literary function is to 'register the explosion of the social ensemble and to report its defects'.[117]

Roussin's distinction between Destouches as the socially utopian public health professional of the 1920s and Céline the literary 'author-as-doctor' from 1929 onwards is well made, but insufficiently nuanced and chronologically too schematic. Whatever enthusiasm Céline may have felt about the methods of standardization he observed in the Ford factories was already tempered before the Depression by his serious reservations about the dehumanizing impact of the assembly line: specifically, that workers are treated like chimpanzees. Furthermore, by equating Céline's economic utopianism with the public health work he conducted for the League in the factories in the mid-1920s, Roussin ignores his profound disillusionment – which, again, started *well before* the Depression – with the League's internal politics and vested interests. This explains why he wished to return, even *before* the crash of 1929, to a grass-roots medicine centred around GP practices in deprived areas, rather than continue to focus on what happened in the factories. His extensive trips from 1928 onwards to downtrodden medical practices in European cities as a basis for comparison with his own branch in Clichy bear testament to that.

There is no more poignant example of Céline's heartfelt compassion for the poor than Bardamu's desperate attempts to save the child Bébert from a rare form of typhoid. Bébert is the scruffy, but cheerful nephew of the concierge, whom Bardamu befriends after frequently seeing him sweep the pavement. Amid all the squalor and misery he encounters on a daily basis in La-Garenne-Rancy, Bardamu's gloom is always lifted when he is greeted by the joyful sight of Bébert's face: 'I've never been able to forget the infinite little smile of pure affection that danced across his livid face. Enough gaiety to fill the universe.'[118]

To build up the boy's strength, he offers to take Bébert for walks in the cemetery, since there is no other green space available. When Bébert falls seriously ill with fever, the entire neighbourhood rallies around and counts on Bardamu to save him, despite his poor reputation as a doctor. After every treatment he can think of has failed ('baths, serum, dry diet, vaccines'), he consults other medics, but to no avail.[119] As a last resort, he visits the supposedly reputable Joseph Bioduret Institute in La Villette (a satire of the prestigious Pasteur Institute in Paris). The sight of unkempt, lethargic and badly paid 'men of science', who carry out 'niche' obscure experiments on rabbits and guinea pigs, does not fill him with confidence, and neither does Parapine, his former medical colleague who works there.[120] Bardamu soon discovers that 'In twenty years, he [Parapine] had learnt so many, so diverse, and so often contradictory things about typhoid that by that time he was just about unable to formulate any clear and definite opinion concerning that most commonplace ailment and its treatment.'[121] Thus the so-called experts are no more capable of curing Bébert than Bardamu, the humble GP, is. Was Céline having another subtle dig here at the medical hierarchy? Did he have in mind his own frustrating experiences with the many consultants and surgeons who treated his injuries in 1914–15, or with the petty internal politics of the Health Section of the League in the 1920s? Whatever the case, Bébert tragically dies, leaving his aunt, the community and Bardamu utterly devastated.

If science has failed to save him, then literature also offers scant consolation. Bardamu purchases an old copy of a book by philosopher and essayist Michel de Montaigne from a bookseller on the banks of the Seine. In it, he stumbles upon the letter Montaigne sent to his wife to console her for the death of their own infant son. The letter contains La Boétie's translation of a letter Plutarch sent to his wife to console her in similar circumstances.[122] Nothing in Montaigne's letter remotely resonates with Bardamu's overwhelming sense of grief and impotence:

> How happy his wife must have been to have a husband like her Michel, who never let anything get him down [. . .] But as far as Bébert was concerned, my day hadn't been so good. I had no luck with Bébert, dead or alive. It seemed to me that there was nothing for him on earth, not even in Montaigne.[123]

Céline's letter includes Montaigne as an 'intertext' to signal his desire to break free of a Classical literature that is no longer able to answer modern man's psychological and emotional needs. His despairing tone has more in common, as Henri Godard perceptively suggests, with Russian novelist Fyodor Dostoevsky than with Montaigne, whose pragmatic acceptance of death leaves Bardamu cold and perplexed. Godard cites the obvious parallel between the sadistic parents in the *Brothers Karamazov*, who torture their daughter, and Bardamu's own feeling of powerlessness, as mentioned above, when he hears his neighbours abusing their daughter.[124] But the Bébert episode is more hopeful: it shows that Céline's despair is, deep down, a sign of his compassion, rather than nihilism. And that his attitude is one of *defiance* in the face of injustice, instead of defeatism. This is confirmed by Bardamu's determination to cure Bébert, because as a child, he represents the possibility of a better future: 'You never mind very much when an adult passes on. If nothing else, you say to yourself, it's one less stinker on earth, but with a child you can never be so sure. There's always the future.'[125] The writer René Schwob, an early admirer of Céline's novel, perfectly understood that, beneath this cynical exterior, Céline was concealing a deep but frustrated love of humanity:

> After my initial impression that you hated all human beings, I realized that what made you suffer on the contrary – so great is your love of human beings – is that it is not actually greater; and that it remains powerless to save those whose every defect you nevertheless know. This impossibility of being useful to anyone, this is one of the biggest lessons of your book, and one which pushes our self-loathing to the point of delirium. I believe that you must really have suffered a great deal to be capable of urging us, without explicitly saying so, to love so much.[126]

This was the suffering Céline would pour out onto the pages of *Journey to the End of the Night*, the novel that would forever transform not only his own life, but the entire landscape of twentieth-century literature.

four

Novelist and Pamphleteer

Céline underwent three major transformative experiences in his life: fighting in the First World War, exile and imprisonment in Denmark, and his meteoric rise to fame following the huge success of *Journey to the End of the Night*. If two of these experiences were traumatic – most of his generation was sent to the trenches, and his fascist sympathies made him a wanted man from 1944 onwards – the third was mostly welcome, but totally unexpected.

Within months of its publication in October 1932, his novel's reputation as a masterpiece had spread like wildfire. Apart from a few detractors, the unknown Dr Destouches from the run-down suburb of Clichy found himself feted as the new writing sensation Louis-Ferdinand Céline. This was all the more remarkable, given the relative mediocrity of his previous literary efforts. Having initially dabbled in poetry, in 1917 he wrote a short story, 'Les Vagues' ('The Waves'), an ironic parody of petty colonial rivalries on a ship bound for Africa that foreshadows Bardamu's tense sea voyage with hostile colonialists on the *Admiral-Bragueton*. But whereas the style of *Journey* perfectly captures the psychology of its central character – Bardamu's sense of victimization is conveyed by short, punchy sentences that keep the reader on tenterhooks until they reach an explosive climax – 'Les Vagues' displays a glaring mismatch between language and content: specifically, through an over-elaborate and decadent prose that drains the narrative of all dramatic tension and satirical force. As for his plays – *L'Église* (The Church) and *Le Progrès* (Progress), written in 1926–7 but subsequently turned down by the *Nouvelle revue française* in 1928 – their reputation hangs largely on the coat-tails of the two much better novels that they foreshadowed: a one-dimensional version of

Bardamu appears in *The Church*, while *Progress* only loosely anticipates the complex family dramas of *Death on Credit*. Genre, as much as content, explains this gulf in quality: contrary to the novel, theatre does not readily lend itself to a first-person narrator speaking directly to the reader on an intimate, emotional level.

Céline had yet to establish a powerful voice that was recognizably his own. To make this voice stand out, he needed to find the right literary platform. *Progress* was a loosely stitched-together mishmash of genres that sought to blend realism and fable (*féerie*), but still lacked aesthetic cohesion: the first act is in the melodramatic style of boulevard theatre, the second is a dreamlike ballet, the third is a light comedy set in a bordello, and the fourth is in Heaven, with God and his angels.[1] Ironically, it is only in his medical thesis on Semmelweis, his one *non*-literary work from this period, that his creative originality begins to emerge, despite the third-person narrator. The central protagonist is sufficiently nuanced and psychologically complex to elicit empathy in the reader in ways that anticipate Bardamu in *Journey*. Although both men are flawed and feckless loners, their tragic plight as society's underdogs cannot fail to move us.

However, the floodgates to his literary talent only truly opened for Céline when he made a conscious decision to switch from theatre to the novel. At last, he had found a genre, a modern version of the picaresque tradition, that was far more personal. His use of a confessional, first-person narrator gave him the subjective freedom to mine and express his innermost thoughts and experiences with no generic constraints. This aesthetic masterstroke is also inseparable from his psychological motivation for writing the novel: it was a necessary form of catharsis. As we have already seen, Céline absolutely had to 'exorcize' the war and 'get it out of his system'. But there were also pragmatic considerations: in particular, the opportunity to make money. He was greatly encouraged by the huge success of Eugène Dabit's *L'Hôtel du Nord*, a populist novel that came out in November 1929.[2] Indeed, Elizabeth Craig later recalled how Céline equated literary success with financial freedom: 'Toward the end of the last year he began to believe that he had a chance to become a successful writer: *I'll make money and I'll be free*! Making money was more important to him than being famous, he didn't really care about fame.'[3] As to the actual writing of *Journey*, this was a Herculean task that set the tone for his remaining eight novels: it involved the painstaking reworking of multiple, handwritten drafts running into thousands of pages that he pored over down to the very last comma. Juggling this process with his medical practice and his relationship with Craig was both mentally and physically draining. As the only constant witness to Céline's writing of his masterpiece, her recollections shed valuable light on the huge sacrifice it entailed:

> He seemed to be divided between a need to be happy and a feeling that he would be deserting his duty if he let himself be. What prevented him from feeling happy was the book in which he was trying to say something he felt deeply [. . .] From time to time I used to open the door to bring him some cookies: *Aren't you getting hungry? Would you like to have coffee with me? I haven't seen you in hours.* He would look at me as if he hardly recognized me, then smiled graciously: *I'll be out a little later!* Hunched over his papers, he looked like an old man, his face looked old, everything about him looked old. It made me wonder; *Is that Louis?*[4]

His novel's bleak subject matter would plunge him into despair:

> He'd go in his study and come out an entirely different person, staring with a desperate look on his face that would make you want to cry. He'd look at me as if to say: 'Well, you don't understand anything, you just don't understand how tragic life is!'[5]

But at other times, he would use Elizabeth as a sounding board, despite her limited command of French and her inability to empathize with his characters' behaviour:[6]

> Sometimes he'd come out all excited: 'I'm going to read this to you, this is good! I'm going to read it in French.' I'd catch a few words here and there, but most of it escaped me. He'd translate the words, interpret the idiomatic expressions and explain the slang. He'd read it again in French, warned me that it won't be as good in English, translate it once more, then ask me:
>
> – What do you think?
>
> – I don't know enough about the characters you're developing, who they are, what caused them to feel and act that way. They seem to me rather brutal.
>
> – Well, they are brutal.

– Not everybody is brutal.
– Oh yes they are! Inside they all are![7]

Writing was an agony for Céline, certainly not something that came easily to him; and it would become even more so when his health further declined after his imprisonment in Denmark from 1945 to 1947. Inevitably, his complete absorption into his fictional universe eventually erected a barrier between him and Elizabeth that was too wide to bridge: 'I thought we'd stick it out. I always intended to be with him

Céline and Elizabeth Craig, 1931.

forever, never had any thoughts of leaving him. It was "Voyage" that really did it, he was becoming so involved in it, living its characters so intensely.'[8] Nevertheless, their move in August 1929 to 98, rue Lepic in Montmartre, the lively district that was to be his home until June 1944, provided welcome relief from the dreariness of Clichy.[9] In Montmartre, he became part of a close-knit, convivial community of bohemian and like-minded artists, especially the painters Henri Mahé and Eugène Paul, known as 'Gen' Paul. Mahé, in particular, whom he met in October via his friend from Rennes, Germaine Constans, would remain a lifelong friend. Twelve years Céline's junior, he was already established, at 22, as a successful artist who had first exhibited at the salon of 1926.[10] His main commissions, however, came from the world of popular culture: not only did he decorate the famous cinema Rex in the rue Poissonière, but he painted thirteen mythological erotic panels for 31 Cité d'Antin, a notorious *maison close* or bordello, for which Céline wrote a preface to an illustrated edition. Céline and Mahé were kindred spirits: both were handsome, charismatic men, who shared a love of women and louche milieus; both enjoyed swapping bawdy stories, and were proud of their northern origins, even though they were typical Parisians. Mahé's origins were Breton, and, like Céline, he loved the sea: they would share a number of happy holidays in Saint-Malo. Until 1933, Mahé lived with his wife Maguy on a barge called the *Malamoa* in Croissy-sur-Seine, where Céline and Elizabeth would spend many a happy Sunday singing, dressing up and revelling.[11]

Mahé sheds light on the writing of *Journey* in three important respects. First, he served as a confidant about the novel's genesis: upon his return from a League of Nations mission to Stockholm in December 1929, an excited Céline told Mahé about 'the death of his colonel'. The colonel was no doubt inspired by General Henry Blacque-Belair, who died in Paris on 9 January 1930, and had been the commander of Céline's cavalry regiment in 1914. At the end of February 1930, Céline wrote his famous war chapter, which is corroborated by a letter of 21 March to another friend and close confidant, war veteran Joseph Garcin.[12] Second, Mahé was a rich source of the novel's Parisian argot. According to their friend the film producer Gilbert Renault Decker, Céline would get Mahé drunk and angry, note down his expressions and use them in his novel. A mutual friend, film director Abel Gance, affectionately referred to the two of them as Verlaine and Rimbaud, owing to their colourful language and non-conformism.[13] Third, Mahé himself inspired a secondary

Publisher Robert Denoël, *c.* 1938.

character in the novel: the artist who lives with his wife on a houseboat near Toulouse, to which he invites Bardamu and Robinson.[14] So despite the monumental effort required to write his work, Céline was sufficiently energized by the buzz of Montmartre and the stimulus provided by the friends he acquired there to write the bulk of it between 1930 and 1932.

As for the actual discovery of the novel, this has become the stuff of legend. It all began when the ambitious young Belgian publisher Robert Denoël returned to his office one day to find an anonymous manuscript lying on his desk.[15] His assistant told him that a tall young man had quickly dropped it off without leaving his name or address. Intrigued, Denoël began reading the text there and then, only to realize that he could not tear his eyes away from it. He stayed up all night, handing page after page to his wife in bed, who soon became equally engrossed in this work. By the following morning, Denoël was so convinced that he had stumbled upon a masterpiece that he was determined to track down its mysterious author. The packaging had the name and address of a young woman, who had herself sent some of her own manuscripts to Denoël that week. Deploying his considerable charm and diplomacy, Denoël contacted the woman and feigned interest in her manuscripts as a ruse to get what he really wanted: the name and address of the author of the anonymous manuscript. She eventually admitted it was her neighbour, the Docteur Destouches, of 98, rue Lepic, and that she must have mistakenly left the packaging in his consultation rooms. Denoël immediately summoned Céline to his office, telling the initially sceptical doctor that he wished to publish him there and then. Céline, who was somewhat piqued that rival publisher Gaston Gallimard had already turned down the manuscript after keeping him waiting for several months, was incredulous, but grateful. Denoël may not have been his first choice, but his enthusiasm won him over. Thus was forged a close bond between the Belgian and the Parisian, which, like all of Céline's friendships, had its share of ups and downs, but was to prove to be arguably the most fruitful of his entire literary career. Like a loyal guard-dog, Denoël would fiercely protect Céline's reputation through thick and thin, until he was shot in mysterious circumstances in 1945 as a suspected collaborator.

The author and publisher had much in common. Both were autodidacts with an anarchist streak: intelligent, ambitious young men from relatively modest backgrounds, who considered themselves as outsiders to the intellectual Parisian elite and therefore had a point to prove. Contrary to Céline, Denoël felt marginalized by nationality rather than class, but he had similarly arrived at literature via a circuitous route. Like Céline, he had studied medicine, but unlike him, he quickly abandoned it when confronted with the sight of a dead child; he then switched to law, before realizing that literature was his true passion. He had a keen eye for young, undiscovered writers and was willing to take risks and publish them. One risk that paid off handsomely, was, coincidentally, his publication (by now he had entered into partnership with the American Bernard Steele) of Eugène Dabit's *L'Hôtel du Nord*. Denoël's championing of an author whom Céline admired and would subsequently befriend further drew him to the Belgian publisher.

Denoël wasted no time in marketing *Journey*. He shrewdly started out low-key and gradually stepped up the campaign. A limited number of copies were distributed to bookshops in early October, accompanied by a provocative insert designed to pique readers' curiosity: 'This book promises to be a resounding success. The author is making his debut in his prime, having lived an extremely full and varied life.'[16] A provocative statement underpinned its 'anti-establishment' credentials: 'Its target audience: doctors whom the author attacks with a particular violence, academics and men of letters.'[17] As was the custom, there then followed, for almost five months, the release of selective extracts (*bonnes feuilles*) to newspapers that were pitched to the political and intellectual tastes of its readership. This strategy was primarily aimed at the liberal and communist press (*Europe*, *Monde*) but encompassed the entire political spectrum from *Vu* to *Libertaire*. To give one example, the rebellious schoolteacher Princhard's subversive discourse appeared in the anarchist *Libertaire*! Up until 20 November, the novel was targeted primarily at a relatively niche group of open-minded critics. If not all of the reviews were entirely favourable (*L'Information*, *Comoedia*, *L'Ordre*, *La Volonté*, *La Presse*), the most reputable names sang its praises: Georges Altman, Jean Pallu, Noël Sabord, Pierre Descaves and Ramon Fernandez. A third, medium-term strategy adopted by Denoël was to publicize the novel in provincial journals and newspapers. This planted seeds throughout the country that bore fruit when the novel began to attract major acclaim from December 1932 onwards. In parallel with this campaign in the provinces, a massive publicity drive, unusual for its time, was launched in the Paris weeklies. This included, in the last week of October, the insertion in bold, large typeface that once again drew attention to the novel's controversial appeal: 'You will either love this book or hate it: it won't leave you indifferent. A cruel work, but so truthful, written in a tone that is at once so painful and truculent, that it will make an immediate impression, whatever backlash it may cause.'[18] In addition, Denoël's judicious use of leading columnists such as D'Artagnan and Cyrano for specialized weeklies, and the equivalent columns of the main newspapers – Les Treize (*L'Intransigeant*), Cacambo (*Candide*), Central 32-65 (*Les Nouvelles littéraires*), Pierre-Jean Launay (*Paris-Midi*) – created a kind of echo chamber of opinions which soon spilled into the public arena.

Book cover of Livre de Poche edition of *Voyage au bout de la nuit* (1961). The publicity blurb on the back cover translates as: 'One of the fiercest and most unbearable cries ever uttered by man.'

But Denoël had another card up his sleeve: he focused his campaign not just on the novel, but on the personality of Céline himself. He carefully fostered the public image of 'doctor first, author second'. In other words, he was promoted as a 'reluctant author', who wrote under the pseudonym of Céline (a name he took from his favourite, maternal grandmother Céline Guillou) because his main vocation was not that of a writer, but of a doctor, who tirelessly treated his patients in the downtrodden suburb of Clichy. This image of the publicity-shy 'doctor-as-author' was predicated on a clever form of reverse psychology: it created a mystique around Céline that increased, rather than decreased, the curiosity of journalists and public alike. The interviews that followed the publication of *Journey* reveal a Céline whose 'medical identity, far from disappearing into the world of literature, was, on the contrary, claimed and reaffirmed by him'.[19] Between December 1932 and April 1933, Céline regularly agreed to be interviewed and photographed at his dispensary in Clichy, in his hospital whites, surrounded by his medical colleagues. When courting Lucien Descaves, one of his key supporters and a member of the jury for the Goncourt prize, he did so on official headed letter paper from his clinic, stating, 'I am a doctor in this municipal practice, that is my job after twenty others.'[20] Newspaper headings such as 'Céline in a White Coat' ('Céline en blouse blanche') or 'Literary Diagnostics' ('Diagnostics littéraires') abounded with medical wordplay.[21]

The doctor figure invokes, as Philippe Roussin has shown, two types of cultural discourse. The first is that of late nineteenth-century realism and naturalism and is based on the idea that the doctor is an objectively reliable social investigator with a unique ability to uncover the 'truth'. This figure is epitomized by Zola's *Docteur Pascal*, who demonstrates a coherent capacity to 'present an ordered meaningful world' and to 'recognize and organize symptoms as signs of a reality that could be charted and described'.[22] The second cultural discourse is the hagiographical model of the *médecin des pauvres*, the doctor of the poor, which has much in common with the *vita*, or life, of a saint. Recalling the thesis advanced in the mid-1920s by writer and philosopher Bernard Groethuysen in *Origines de l'esprit bourgeois en France* (The Origins of the Bourgeois Spirit in France), Jean-Claude Bonnet has lamented France's tendency, since the Enlightenment, to celebrate her bourgeois men of letters as secular heroes. This secularizing discourse, however, merely reinforces the status of an intellectual urban elite that is completely disconnected from the ordinary working man. By promoting the image of the self-taught, jobbing medical doctor, who is discovered by chance in the *banlieue* and is not part of this Parisian secular elite, Céline, as Dr Destouches, thus revives a hagiographical discourse that is refreshingly associated with the innocent simplicity and humility of religious figures such as Francis of Assisi. In this regard, poverty, innocence and lack of formal education are valorized as marks of authenticity that recall Christ's special bond with the poor. And interestingly, both the scientific and hagiographical discourses converge in Docteur Pascal's monklike existence as a 'Benedictine'.[23]

For all Denoël's clever strategizing, however, *Journey* received its biggest publicity boost from a completely unexpected event: the so-called 'Goncourt scandal', or the controversial awarding of the prestigious annual Goncourt prize to Guy Mazeline, instead of to Céline. Aside from François Mauriac's *Le Nœud de vipères* (The Knot of Vipers), 1932 had been an unremarkable year for the French novel. It included such forgotten authors and titles as Édouard Peisson's *Parti de Liverpool*, Roger Vercel's *Au Large de L'Eden*, *La Femme maquillé* by André Billy and *Le Pari* by Ramon Fernandez. Two front runners stood out from the crowd: Guy Mazeline's *Les Loups* and Céline's *Journey*, in part owing to their above-average length. By the time the Goncourt Committee, headed by J.-H. Rosny (pseudonym of Joseph Henri Honoré Boex), met on 30 November, Céline was considered the winner in all but name: Guy Mazeline was, by now, considered the clear favourite for the rival Prix Femina, and Céline had received the strong backing of the influential literary elder statesmen Léon Daudet and Lucien Descaves, the latter returning to the Goncourt jury after an absence of fourteen years. An article in *L'Œil de Paris* on 3 December boldly predicting that the liberal-minded Goncourt jury would be put off by Mazeline's wealthy bourgeois background further raised expectations of Céline's victory. This is why all hell broke loose when Mazeline was announced the winner on 7 December by six votes to three for Céline's *Journey*, and one vote for Raymond de Rienzi's *Les Formiciens*. Descaves was so incensed that he stormed out of the committee. However, on 17 December, *Le Cri du jour* exposed a plausible conspiracy theory. Hachette, by far the most powerful publishing house and distribution chain in France, had exclusive rights to sell titles by the other publishers Gallimard, Fernczi and Tallandier. Aside from Larousse, Denoël was the only publisher who refused to collaborate with Hachette, whereas Mazeline's novel had been published by Gallimard. Had Céline won the Prix Goncourt, Hachette would have been forced to buy 20,000 copies of *Journey* at a cost of 300,000 francs. The hypothesis that members of the jury had been swayed by Hachette's clout (notably J.-H. Rosny, who switched his vote towards Mazeline's novel at the eleventh hour) was backed by Mazeline's own failure to win the Prix Femina by one vote on 5 December, an equally unexpected outcome that, some claimed, was made in cahoots with Hachette and the Goncourt jury. Fierce accusations, counter-accusations and strong denials filled newspapers and literary journals throughout 1933, Descaves himself hinting at the financial motives of Hachette and then swiftly retracting his statement so as to avoid being sued.

Despite the consolation of being awarded the Prix Renaudot, Céline was so utterly disenchanted by the Goncourt affair that he sought to escape from the limelight.[24] But Descaves twisted his arm to deliver a speech on Émile Zola at the annual celebration of the famous naturalist author at Meudon.[25] His talk provides a revealing snapshot of his fast-developing views on literature, politics and human nature, which owed a significant debt to Freud, whose theories he had probably discovered in the mid-1920s.[26] Today, Céline argues, Zola's naturalism is 'almost impossible' because he was able to give his readers access to a social reality that would now be denied to them: 'We would not be released from prison if we talked about life as we know it to be, starting with his own [...] Reality today would not be granted to anyone. So what we have, is symbols and dreams.'[27] In other words, symbols and dreams are the only forms of reality available to us that are beyond the reach of censorship or political dictatorship.

Céline's main objection to dictatorships, however, is not just their repressive nature, *but the fact that they lie*. And what they lie about is the *real* reason for man's violence: the universal death drive, *l'instinct de mort*, which triggers the same destructive behaviour in all human beings, whether or not we live under a dictatorship: 'We are well within our rights to ask ourselves whether the death drive in Man, in our societies, does not already override our desire to live. Germans, French, Chinese, Vlachs... Dictatorships or not! Nothing but pretexts to play the game of death!'[28] Freud's theory of the death drive is consistent not only with the ubiquitous theme of death in *Death on Credit*, published three years later, but with Céline's own staunch pacifism and well-founded conviction that political parties of all stripes want war: 'Liberals, Marxists, fascists agree only on one point: soldiers!'[29]

Military conflict aside, according to Céline, today's politicians further justify violence and repression as a necessary cure for society's grievances. The fascists invoke rampant nationalism and the Marxists class war as legitimate responses to the societal injustices of capitalism and poverty. But, Céline argues, neither extreme poverty ('misère profonde') nor heavy-handed policing ('l'accablement policier') can excuse political violence; nor can the thirst for war and violence more generally simply be blamed on the ruling class. Céline cites the example of Coupeau, the alcoholic protagonist of Zola's novel *L'Assommoir*, to personify what has changed between Zola's time and his own. The Coupeau of Zola's era was an alcoholic. This alcoholism was an unequivocal and stark reminder of man's destructive instincts. In Céline's era, by contrast, these instincts appear to have been curbed, since 'today's Coupeau drinks less', and the stigma of alcoholism has decreased. In fact, the instincts are still very much present, but far less visible. No longer do they openly display themselves in abnormal behaviours such as alcoholism, but they remain *hidden* behind the facade of social respectability that is provided by political power. So the fact that the new Coupeau 'has been educated' ('il a reçu de l'instruction') may make him more *outwardly* respectable than his alcoholic and illiterate predecessor, but he is no less prone to destructive instincts, because power goes to his head:

'his delirium is a standard desk with thirteen telephones. He barks orders at the whole world.'[30] The stigma of alcoholic delirium has been replaced by a socially legitimized political delirium. This is why Zola was able to analyse instinct from a purely scientific perspective as a discrete, externally visible phenomenon; whereas the challenge for writers in Céline's era is to expose how the political system tries to deny the very existence of that instinct in the first place. Literature can no longer analyse social reality from the outside; it must now delve deeper into man's inner psychology and hidden motives: 'We now work via our sensibility and no longer via analysis, in short "from within".'[31]

The Zola lecture was an inevitable part of Céline's demanding new life as 'celebrity author'. But there were undeniable perks, too: in particular, the opportunity to rub shoulders with key players on the cultural scene, who broadened his intellectual horizons and network of contacts. There were the established novelists who welcomed him into the literary fold: André Malraux (one of the few writers Céline openly praised) and, more surprisingly, the Catholics Georges Bernanos and François Mauriac. In the ultraconservative *L'Écho de Paris*, Mauriac considered the novel worthy of comparison to his own, despite their obvious differences, including Céline's 'immoral' use of language. The writers met at two separate dinners in late March 1933. Then, there were those authors to whom posterity has been less kind, but whose friendship to Céline at this time proved to be very useful: Emmanuel Berl, Joseph Delteil and, above all, Raymond Fernandez. Other writers, such as Blaise Cendrars, were much more grudging in their praise and had no wish to meet Céline at all. What especially irked Cendrars was that no one remembered his own 1927 novel *Moravagine*, even though it addressed the very themes for which *Journey* was now receiving rave reviews: war, flight, America, fraternizing with indigenous 'savages', madness, eroticism, the *banlieue*, medicine and so forth.[32]

The one fellow novelist to whom Céline became genuinely close following their initial meeting in the spring of 1933 was Eugène Dabit. His novel *L'Hôtel du Nord*, also published by Denoël, had not only incentivized Céline to write *Journey*, but was later adapted into a hugely successful film by Marcel Carné, starring Jean Gabin. Céline's feeling of kinship with Dabit as both man and author is not hard to understand. The two writers were close in age (although already established, Dabit was only four years younger) and had very similar backgrounds: the only children of families from modest Parisian backgrounds, they were close to their maternal uncles, essentially self-taught (having left the *lycée* early to undertake apprenticeships) and both were ex-army, an experience that enabled them to discover the harsh discipline of the barracks and the horrors of the trenches, at a similarly young age. In addition, they shared the same publisher in Robert Denoël. Dabit's two most famous novels, *L'Hôtel du Nord* (1929) and *Petit-Louis* (1930), had three stylistic traits that set them apart from other contemporary novels: the first was his focus on the daily life, *le quotidien* of the so-called *petites gens*, the ordinary, downtrodden people hitherto neglected by the novel. The second trait was that his first-person account of this daily grind was inextricably linked to his personal experience of war: just as Céline did with Bardamu, Dabit drew only on hardships he had lived through himself. Finally, there was Dabit's desire to strip away literary artifice by expressing his experiences in popular language. All of these attributes paved the way for Céline's *Journey*. Yet Dabit's explorations did not go quite far enough. The first time he publicly acknowledged Dabit's influence on *Journey*, Céline damned him with faint praise. Compared to his novel, not only did Dabit's suffer from a paucity of experience (Céline 'had more to say'), but he had 'not dared to go all the way, not to the point of revolt, and had remained "plaintive"'. What is more, he had allowed fame to go to his head and had donned the mantle of a 'writer' (écrivain).[33] His reservations about Dabit's writing aside, Céline still held him in sufficiently high regard to confide in him about his literary projects – a privilege he granted to no other author. He took on board, for instance, Dabit's advice not to write his second novel *Death on Credit* as a legend, an idea that Céline had seriously contemplated.[34]

But from 1933 to 1935, Céline's most influential intellectual mentor was the sixty-year-old eminent art historian Élie Faure. Another in a long line of Céline's surrogate father figures, Faure helped shape his aesthetic and political outlook. The older man's admiration for the author of *Journey* was reciprocated by the latter's regard for his erudition, especially his work *Histoire de l'art* (History of Art).[35] Not normally one to praise even his closest friends, Céline wrote gushingly: 'You know how much I admire, get enthused about and worship everything you know.'[36] The two would frequently meet and exchange ideas at the former's flat at 147, boulevard Saint-Germain, or in the Brasserie Lipp. It was probably Faure who put Céline in touch with the film-maker Abel Gance, whom he had already encountered in 1917 when working for Paul Laffitte's journal.[37]

Faure's eloquent social idealism brought out Céline's more visceral political scepticism:

> I absolutely and completely refuse to nail my colours to any one mast. I am an anarchist through and through. I have always been one and will remain so to the exclusion of everything else [. . .] Every political system is a hypocritical enterprise which consists in deflecting the personal ignominy of its members onto a system or onto 'other people.' I see all too clearly, I admit, I shout it from the rooftops, passionately and at the top of my voice, the full extent of our shared disgusting nature, whether on the Left or the Right, as human beings.[38]

His scepticism about politics because of his scepticism about man was something for which neither the Left nor the Right would forgive him: 'I have always been an anarchist, I have never voted, I shall never vote for anything, nor anyone. I do not believe in man.'[39] This statement provides more ammunition for those who see Céline as nothing more than a nihilistic misanthrope. But it was not so much man per se he despised, as his propensity for hypocrisy and idealistic abstraction. The main culprits are contemporary politicians and writers, whose falsely optimistic views of mankind are based exclusively on speculative ideas and platitudes, rather than on concrete examples of human feeling – and in particular suffering – they have experienced *themselves*. Faure, as a bourgeois and *lycée*-educated writer, is guilty of this type of abstraction, as he has been shielded from the reality of personal hardship:

> You are not of the people, you are not vulgar, you are an aristocrat, you say so yourself. You do not know what I know. You have been to the lycée. You have not earned your crust before going to school. You have no right to judge me. You don't know. You don't know everything I do – You do not know what I want. You do not know what I do. You do not know the excruciating effort I have to make every day, especially every night, just to remain standing, to hold a quill – When you are in agony, and only then, will you fully understand me. I speak the language of the intimacy of things – I have had to learn it, to spell it out, first. I've weighed everything up. Nothing I say is gratuitous.[40]

If Céline highlights the class division between himself and Faure, this is to make a literary, rather than a political, point. Faure writes only about things he has acquired at second hand from his bourgeois education. His writing is not rooted in any personal experience of life's difficulties – therefore, it is not authentic. Céline, on the other hand, who has not been to the *lycée*, writes only about experiences he has acquired at first hand from the 'school of life'. And this school comprises both the harsh reality of having to work for a living from an early age and the physical agony of the writing process itself (an agony, in Céline's case, that is exacerbated by his numerous physical ailments). So contrary to Faure, Céline's writing is never gratuitous because it is always authenticated by a reality he has actually lived himself. This desire for authenticity is what distinguishes Céline from the old Romantic cliché of the accursed artist having to suffer for his art. What he emphasizes instead is that this suffering is *at the service of the truth* – what he calls 'the intimacy of things'. It is this truth, as his Zola talk reminds us, that is continually suppressed by society: either by dictators, or by political ideologies who distort it (what he refers to as 'political delirium'). Especially guilty of this tendency, he says, are the Marxists, who claim to have a monopoly on 'the Truth':

> My only concern: to strike a chord with the maximum number of readers and when all is said and done I prefer those on the Right. Those on the Left are so certain about their Marxist truth that no one can teach them anything. They are much more entrenched than on the Right. No paper has damaged me more than the 'Populaire' in the name of human value and dignity!![41]

The intellectual stimulation of mentors such as Faure provided welcome relief from the emotional turmoil of his private life. He was dealt a bitter blow by his father's sudden death in March 1932, especially because Fernand did not live to see his son's success. Then Elizabeth Craig left for America to care for her own sick father, following her mother's death, which effectively marked the end of their relationship. Her brief return to Paris in 1933 merely delayed the inevitable. As was his wont, Céline sought solace in relationships with three attractive young women, all in their twenties: Erika Irrgang, Cillie Ambor (also known as Cillie Pam) and Evelyne Pollet. Irrgang, an elegant brunette student from Breslau, literally fell into Céline's arms after fainting on a café terrace in Montmartre's place du Tertre in May 1932. After taking her for a hearty meal on the Grand

Boulevards to recover, he offered her hospitality in his flat in rue Lepic, which quickly led to an affair.[42] He became a father–protector figure, dispensing advice in his letters about how to capitalize on her intellectual and cultural potential through her physical attractiveness, good health and practising 'safe sex' ('no love without protection').[43] As for Cillie Pam, she was a 26-year-old widowed gymnastics teacher from Vienna, who was both Jewish and open-minded. He met her in Café de la Paix in September 1932, and entertained her in Paris for two weeks, including an orgy in his flat.[44] The third of his lovers, Evelyne Pollet, was a married mother of two from Antwerp in Belgium. She had written him a fan letter to express her admiration for *Journey*, which subsequently led to a clandestine affair when he visited her in Antwerp in May 1933. He would continue to see her, on and off, until 1941, and she later published a novel, in 1956, that was significantly inspired by their relationship.

Despite exhibiting the hallmarks of an early midlife crisis, these relationships did pay literary dividends: specifically, via Céline's discovery of painting and psychoanalysis. He first discovered the Flemish masters – notably Pieter Bruegel (and later his predecessor Hieronymus Bosch) – while with Cillie in Vienna in December 1932, where he saw Bruegel's *The Fight between Carnival and Lent* (1559), the depiction of a popular feast day that juxtaposes carnivalesque amusements with beggars and cripples.[45] This shocking blend of celebration and suffering unsurprisingly resonated with Céline's own grotesque, tragicomic vision of humanity: two obvious examples are Madelon's shooting of Robinson as they leave the funfair at the end of *Journey*, or Courtial's grossly deformed head after he shoots himself in *Death on Credit*. In a letter to Léon Daudet shortly after his trip to Vienna, he enthusiastically refers to Bruegel's *délire* ('delirium'), a term frequently employed by Céline to designate his own literary inspiration.[46] The following year, he discovered another Bruegel painting, *Dulle Griet*, when visiting Evelyne Pollet in Antwerp.[47] It was also thanks to Cillie that he deepened his knowledge of Freud and psychoanalysis. She introduced him socially to her psychoanalyst friend Anny Angel, who later recalled that he spoke too much of sex and perversion, but – perhaps surprisingly – was sensitive to the threats she felt as a Jew. She also put him in touch with Anny Reich, wife of psychoanalyst Wilhelm Reich in Prague, whom he claimed 'told me a thousand useful things and made me almost intelligent within a few days'.[48]

But not even Freud or great art could fill the void left by Elizabeth. Most of 1934 was spent pining for her, promoting *Journey* and failing to make much headway with his second novel. He had, however, secured an English translator, John Marks, with whom he enjoyed a friendly relationship. They met in London in December 1933 to discuss the finer details of the translation and, over the next two years, regularly swapped bawdy letters discussing their amorous conquests as much as the novel and its various publishing outlets in the English-speaking world.[49]

As fond as Céline was of Marks, his translation with Little, Brown and Company did him no favours with his English-speaking market. It is perfectly competent, but inferior to Ralph Manheim's later version. Moreover, Marks cut phrases and sentences that were deemed too shocking for the American public by his editor Herbert Jenkins.[50] This meant that reactions to his novel varied from enthusiastic to lukewarm, depending on whether or not it was discovered and read in the original French, or the inferior English. The novelist Henry Miller and the critic Samuel Putnam respectively exemplify these two types of response. According to the sculptor Georges Brassaï, his friend Henry Miller was living in Paris in 1932 and 'struggling with his manuscript of *Tropic of Cancer*, which had already been rejected by publishers'. Frank Dobo, a literary agent connected with Céline's publisher Denoël and his partner Steele who would help sell and promote the English translation of his first novel with Little, Brown and Company, sent Miller the French galley proofs of *Journey*. Miller was allegedly so impressed that he told Brassaï that 'no writer had ever given him such a shock' and proceeded to rewrite *Tropic of Cancer*.[51] Miller subsequently sent his novel to Céline and was to champion him throughout his career, signing the famous petition for his rehabilitation in 1946.[52] Miller's 'positive' shock contrasts markedly with the decidedly negative view of Samuel Putnam, a translator of Rabelais, who knew Miller as a fellow Paris expatriate and would employ him at his literary magazine, the *New Review*. In his April 1934 review of the Marks translation, he wrote, 'It is safe to wager that nine out of ten non-French teachers in America would be unable to make head or tail out of the original, while the French-born ones would be terribly shocked, linguistically, as well as morally.'[53] Alice Kaplan draws two conclusions from this: that those, such as Miller, who first read Céline in French inevitably embraced him far more than those who discovered him via the English translation, which also had sections expurgated; and that artistic responses to Céline in America tended to be more positive than academic ones, thereby sealing Céline's reputation as a 'writer's writer'. Kaplan rightly concludes that 'it is astonishing that we had to

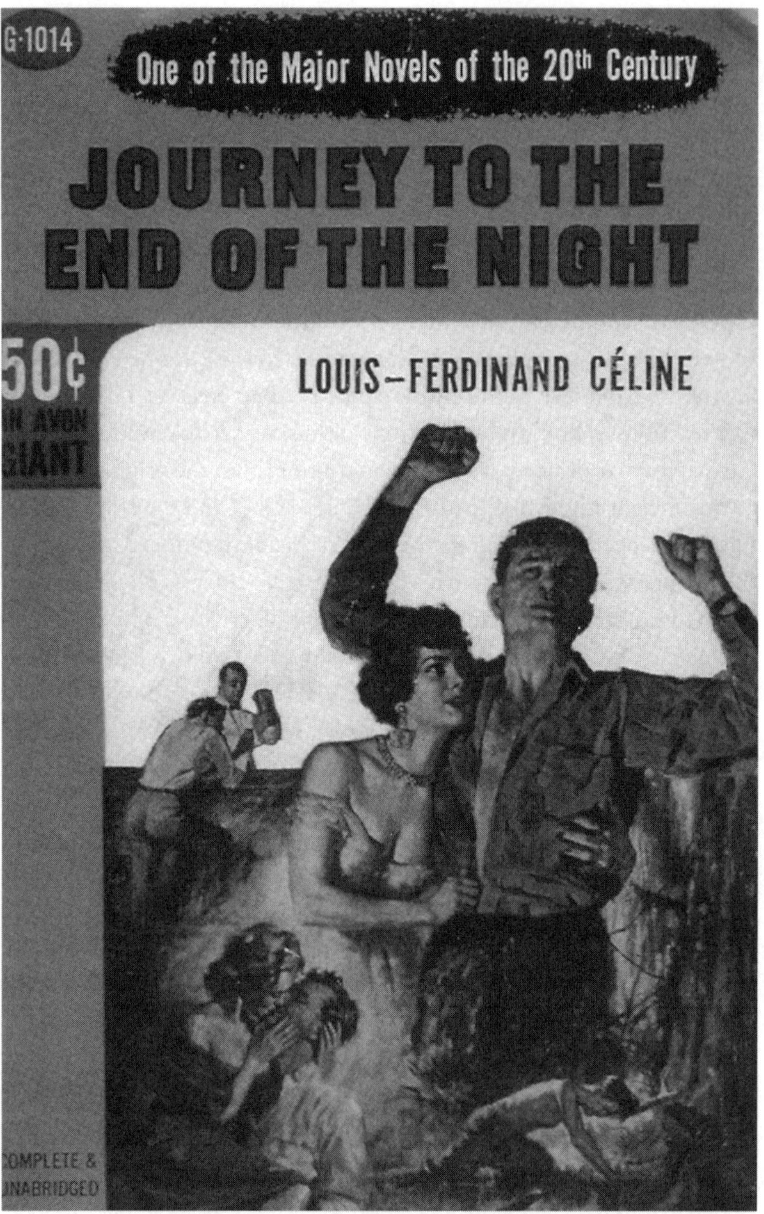

American cover of *Journey to the End of the Night* (Avon, 1951), reproduced in *Les Études céliniennes*, 4 (Autumn 2008. Collection O. Moncharmont).

wait until 1983 for Ralph Manheim's translation of *Journey*', by which time 'Céline's American reputation had waned considerably.'[54] Indeed, it is remarkable that *Journey* was still successful in the anglophone world, *despite* the Marks translation. That the very same Samuel Putnam wrote a separate, far more complimentary review of the *original* French version, as opposed to the Marks translation, lends further weight to Kaplan's theory. In this other review, Putman expresses deep regret that Céline has been 'edged out for the Goncourt prize by M. Guy Mazeline's *Les Loups*'. He considers Céline's novel 'a more fascinating one' than Mazeline's, praising it for its 'almost narcotic [. . .] hold over the reader', 'its human genuineness' and 'elusion of aesthetic criteria'.[55]

Little wonder, then, that Céline was concerned about the poor sales of his novel in the United States, despite its wide distribution in bookshops. He embarked on his publicity tour half-heartedly, although in his first interview there, with Sterling North, he could not resist displaying his customary irreverence. North writes that Céline 'was bitterly brilliant today in his indictment of man'. 'Punctuating his English with explosive French the young Parisian doctor told of the countless threats upon his life, the challenges to duels, the insults and vilifications that have been poured upon him since the appearance of his epochal novel last year.'[56] But Céline also tempers his complaints with some subtle self-promotion: in particular, his plan for Karen Marie Jensen (a Danish dancer friend of Elizabeth Craig, whose help would later prove invaluable to him during his exile in Denmark) to star in a film adaptation of *Journey*, as well as a new play.

Céline then proceeds – uncharacteristically for him – to debunk the myth that he had *deliberately* anonymously left a 50,000-page manuscript of *Journey* on Denoël's desk: 'Ooo la la – such an exaggeration,' he says. 'Yes,' his interviewer clarifies, 'He did write 50,000 pages, but that was including the many drafts of the book. As for leaving the manuscript without his name on it, that was an accident.'[57] And to the story that 'he is so indifferent to his success and to the accruing royalties that he never calls at the publisher's offices for a check', Céline responds, 'Then I will get all my money at once.' When asked his opinion about Americans, Céline is typically forthright. They are 'filled with beauty, with grace, but nevertheless are cultureless, radio-mad drunken bums'. He reserves his praise for American women: 'But, yes. They are queens of the universe. The tragedy of their lithe, sinuous, elusive beauty! [. . .] "Americans are the most erotic race on earth," says the cynical young Parisian. (High praise from a Frenchman!).'[58] No doubt he was thinking of Elizabeth Craig as he uttered these words.

The love–hate relationship with the United States Céline expresses in this interview – admiration of its alluring women on the one hand, dismissal of its culture on the other – is strikingly reminiscent of

Bardamu's ambivalent experience of New York in *Journey*. His reaction to the Big Apple similarly lurches between extreme fascination and profound revulsion. Having recently disembarked from Africa, destitute and malaria-ridden, he is quarantined along with the other immigrants, stumbling into a job as a 'flea-counter'. That this should be considered an important role at which he excels is a blatant satire of American bureaucracy's depersonalization of individuals – and especially immigrants – to the status of mere insects and statistics. His hard work is eventually rewarded with the permission to enter the promised land of Manhattan. But he soon finds himself sitting completely alone on a bench, 'slap-happy, drooling with erotico-mystical admiration and quinine' at the physical perfection of American women, 'Those blondes! Those brunettes! Those Titian redheads!', who provide a distraction and imaginative psychological escape from his desperate and uncertain predicament:

> I had come to the heart of my pilgrimage. And if my appetite hadn't kept calling itself to my attention, that would have struck me as one of those moments of supernatural aesthetic revelation. If I'd been a little more comfortable and confident, the incessant beauties I was discovering might have ravished me from my base human condition. In short, all I needed was a sandwich to make me believe in miracles.[59]

In those brilliantly concise pages that portray Bardamu stranded in Manhattan, Céline effectively deploys such religious vocabulary ('pilgrimage' and 'miracles') in order to satirize American capitalism and the banking district as its most revered incarnation: 'You can enter it only on foot, like a church. It's the banking heart and centre of the present-day world.'[60] In a powerfully imaginative satire of Christian liturgy, the dollar is personified as the secular substitute for the Communion Host, and interactions with bank tellers sitting behind their grills are the modern-day equivalent of confessing to a priest behind his screen:

> It's a district filled with gold, a miracle, and through the doors you can actually hear the miracle, the sound of dollars being crumpled, for the dollar is always too light, a genuine Holy Ghost, more precious than blood [. . .] When the faithful enter their bank, don't go thinking they can help themselves as they please. Far from it. In speaking to Dollar, they mumble words through a little grill; that's their confessional.[61]

Not even the American women whose erotic perfection provides Bardamu with temporary respite, can remain untainted by a capitalist machine that is intermeshed with the collective imaginary of the Hollywood dream factory. Deprived of food and sleep, Bardamu seeks solace in a cinema 'with posters of women in slips, and what legs! Boyohboy! Heavy! Ample! Shapely! And pretty faces on top, as though drawn for the contracts, no need of retouching, not a blemish not a flaw, perfect I tell you, delicate but firm and neat.'[62] Further extending the analogy between capitalism and religion, Bardamu compares the cinema to a church:

> It was warm and cosy in the movie house. An enormous organ, as mellow as in a cathedral, a heated cathedral I mean, organ pipes like thighs. They don't waste a moment. Before you know it, you're bathing in an all-forgiving warmth. Just let yourself go and you'll begin to think the world has been converted to a loving kindness. I almost was myself.
>
> Dreams rise in the darkness and catch fire from the mirage of moving light. What happens on the screen isn't quite real; it leaves open a vague cloudy space for the poor, for dreams and the dead. Hurry hurry, cram yourself full of dreams to carry you through the life that's waiting for you outside, when you leave here, to help you last a few days more in that nightmare of things and people.[63]

Hollywood serves a vital function in the American psyche: that of peddling the illusion to the poor and disadvantaged that their social deprivation is not as bad as it seems.

That American capitalism represents, to Bardamu, both the twin poles of luxury and social deprivation is brilliantly captured by his hotel, ironically called the 'Laugh Calvin' – a nod (through the allusion to Calvinism) towards the Protestant work ethic that underpins the pursuit of the American dream. Since he needs somewhere to stay, the majestic appeal of a hotel and the female occupants of its lobby lure him inside:

> Instant amazement . . . You had to divine, to imagine the majesty of the edifice, the generous proportions, because the lights were so veiled that it took you some time to know what you were looking at.
>
> Lots of young women in the half-light, plunged in deep armchairs as in jewel cases. Around them attentive men, moving silently, with

> timid curiosity, to and fro, just offshore from the row of crossed legs and magnificent silk-encased thighs.[64]

This hotel juxtaposes two contrasting worlds: the opulent lobby in which the rich guests are comfortably sprawled, and the distinctly less enticing quarters containing the cheapest rooms, that society's underdogs such as Bardamu can barely afford. The unbridgeable gulf that divides them is brilliantly symbolized by the vast distance he has to cover between the lobby and his shabby quarters, a 'big box with ebony walls', in which 'the only light was a faint ring surrounding the bashful greenish lamp on the table'.[65] The bell boy ushers him along an endless succession of dark, soulless corridors at breakneck speed. When he finally reaches his dark cubby hole, Bardamu sees the reverse side of the American dream: not the elegant, bejewelled women of the Manhattan streets or hotel lobby, but the suite of rooms across the court 'which was more like a well-shaft, and in which uncommunicative couples are preparing for bed'. Here, the women have 'very full, very pale thighs' and 'ate chocolates in bed, while waiting for their husbands to finish shaving'.[66] A grim social reality is concealed behind Manhattan's glamorous facade.

Bardamu is soon under no illusion that the United States is purely driven by a ruthless capitalism ('You can't get away from American business enterprise') that promotes the American dream in order to disguise poverty and suffering.[67] But he also realizes, when he visits his former girlfriend Lola, that this American dream is nothing more than an empty sham that fails to satisfy even those who achieve it. Although her 23rd-floor apartment 'was posh, pretty much as I'd imagined', and she employs a black manservant, her well-off female friends, 'painted, corpulent, middle-aged, muscular, bejewelled and very free and easy', seem to look down on her:[68] 'Judging by their rather arrogant manner towards her, I had the impression that in a certain society these women must have enjoyed greater prestige than Lola – a considerable authority, in fact.'[69] Far from bringing her happiness, Lola's wealth only serves to accentuate the feeling of emptiness in her own life; hence she becomes 'obsessed with adopting a child' and develops an attachment to a small boy to whom she gives dance lessons. And her affluence makes her largely oblivious to the social divide. Despite his later and unequivocal racism, Céline subtly shows that these social iniquities are exacerbated by racial ones. Lola refers to her black manservant as 'a maniac [. . .] but not dangerous' who 'belonged to a secret society for black emancipation'; but, she condescendingly continues: 'I keep him, he's an excellent servant. And all things considered, he's probably more honest than the ones who aren't revolutionaries.'[70]

Was this satire of Lola's apparent obliviousness to social inequality based on Céline's disapproval of Elizabeth Craig's own sheltered existence? We have already seen Craig's recollection that one of their rare arguments as a couple was caused by him taking her to Amsterdam's red-light district to see parents selling their own children into prostitution.

However, Bardamu's observations on America suggest Céline's cultural, as well as personal, influences: specifically, the contemporary trend in France for sociological and literary investigations of American life. *Journey* bears the unmistakable imprint of novelist Paul Morand and sociologist Georges Duhamel. Morand's publication between 1925 and 1930 of *Chronique du XXème siècle* (Chronicle of the Twentieth Century), four books devoted to each of the four continents, resonates with Céline's own desire to expand his horizons beyond the shores of Europe. And it is probably no coincidence that Morand published a novel called *Le Voyage* (1927), a title he attributed to the pent-up frustration of a generation scarred by war that desperately craved travel as a release. There are clear similarities between *Journey* and Morand's novel *New York* (1930), which is replete with images of imposing skyscrapers, self-service restaurants and descriptions of the Stock Exchange as a 'temple' and banknotes as 'hosts'.[71] Duhamel's 1930 *Scènes de la vie future* (Scenes from the Life of the Future) is an even more striking intertext. There is no doubt that some of his themes and images, based on his exhaustive visit to the USA in the autumn of 1928, find their way into Céline's novel, such as the labyrinthine hotel, the sculptural legs of American women, the haggard passengers in the subway and the communal toilets. But whatever images Céline borrowed, he carefully *reworked* and *recontextualized* them in his own vocabulary to express a completely different narrative point of view from Duhamel's. Where the latter adopted the patronizing ironic detachment of the bourgeois European observer, who is merely passing through the United States, full of preconceptions about his own cultural superiority, Bardamu, as we have seen, is forced to confront the reality of this alien environment head-on, and thus gives a far more impulsive and unfiltered response to it that constantly lurches between fascination and revulsion. The two writers' very different descriptions of the communal toilets encapsulate particularly well their contrasting perspectives. Duhamel's tone is one of incredulous disapproval: 'What do I see? Good

God! What do I see? Ten chaps, crouching in little cubicles, without doors.'[72] Céline's language, however, is far more coarse and hyperbolic, as if his imagination were dredging up instinctive reactions buried deep in his unconscious: 'In that state of undress, belching and worse, they settled down in the faecal grotto.'[73] Contrary to Duhamel, Céline's Bardamu does not have the luxury of keeping the more sordid aspects of American life at arm's length.

Nevertheless, this did not prevent Céline from being attracted to the glamorous side of American life. In June and July of 1934, he spent four weeks in Hollywood, staying with his friend, the author and director Jacques Deval (who would give him the briefest of cameo roles in his film *Tovaritch* the following year), hoping to sell the film rights for *Journey*.[74] Thanks to Deval's studio contacts, Céline secured a six-month option on the film rights with Lester Yard, the editor of *Variety*, but it seems, as he wrote to Henri Mahé on 4 July, that Hollywood puritanism prevented the project from ever getting off the ground: 'As far as the film is concerned, peanuts. Here they only tolerate chastity and gaiety. Can you believe it?'[75] In the United States, as in France – where he would regularly visit his friend the director Abel Gance on set at Joinville – Céline made no headway with his adaptations.[76] He found welcome respite from Hollywood's moral conservatism amid the decadent opulence of Deval's tycoon lifestyle, which involved consorting with an assortment of ambitious and compliant young starlets around his luxury swimming pool.[77] Céline became friends with Jacques Deval's mistress, French actress Junie Astor, whom he had got to know via Abel Gance, and to whom he later confided about his failed attempts to woo Karen-Marie Jensen.[78] But the sexual and other distractions of Hollywood were secondary to his main aim: to win back Elizabeth Craig, whom he knew to be staying in nearby Los Angeles.[79] But she would not be swayed. Years later, she admitted that – aside from the toll exerted by his writing of *Journey* – she feared their relationship was doomed because she was losing her youth and knew only too well that Louis liked physical perfection, especially that of dancers: 'I could see myself getting older and fatter and senile, and that was not what Lou loved and needed [. . .] I think it's because I loved him that I left him.'[80] For a while, she was torn between Céline and Ben Tankel, a property developer whom she met in 1934 and who was to become her husband. Despite her love for Louis, Tankel offered optimism and security instead of Céline's excitement and pessimism. Céline's summary of the situation, in a letter to Mahé, was that 'Elizabeth gave herself to gangsters.'[81] His double failure in Hollywood – both with Elizabeth and the film adaptation – effectively severed his ties with America once and for all, aside from his fruitful collaboration with Allerton Parker in 1937, who translated *Mea culpa* and *Semmelweis* into English.

If, in 1934, he was stuck in a rut, 1935 was far more productive. Literary inspiration was provided by a new lover and muse, the attractive and acclaimed 26-year-old pianist Lucienne Delforges, whom he first saw perform Frédéric Chopin's 'Le Révolutionnaire' in May. After the concert, he thanked her for the rendition, claiming that it had provided the violent tone he was looking for in the chapter in *Death on Credit* in which Ferdinand assaults his father. In return, she asked him to write a preface to her concert programme. At the end of the month, they spent a weekend together in London, followed by a whistle-stop tour of Europe in July: Denmark and then Austria, where, in Bad Gastein, Lucienne combined studying with a reputed pianist with climbing in the mountains, accompanied by Cillie Pam, who had joined the couple from Vienna.[82] Céline admired Lucienne's natural way of playing, drawing parallels with the emotional spontaneity he sought in his writing: 'She expresses herself with a natural lyricism. You can count on your fingers the number of virtuosos who don't kill music. Most of them don't know what they are doing: learnt, forced, music is not their language.'[83] She was also the inspiration for the piano-playing headmaster's wife, Nora Merrywin, in *Death on Credit*. But Céline abruptly ended their affair on 2 August, when he suddenly left Bad Gastein. He was immersed in his novel and didn't want the burden and responsibility of a long-term relationship. Perhaps, as Henri Godard speculates, the fact that she was a musician, rather than a dancer or gymnast, meant that their artistic temperaments were too similarly highly strung.[84] Indeed, it is no coincidence that in a letter he wrote to her four years later (they remained on friendly terms), he called her 'my dear little double' ('mon cher petit double').[85] In a long letter of 26 August 1935, he explains to her why their affair must end:

> But the routine of life, the reality of life, grinds me down. It is not you know that I want to act like the artist, the capricious hysteric, the exceptional-subject-who-needs-to-throw-his-tantrums.
>
> God only knows how I hate that type! But you know Lucienne I cannot, absolutely cannot be THERE. In order to be a serious lover one has to be THERE. I am far more present with people when I leave them.

> I have to admit to you that for me reality is a constant nightmare and God knows how life has dished out to me more than my fair share of experiences! How I have been served by reality! [. . .] What affects me is having to occupy myself with things that have not been transposed or are not transposable, unless a number of years, many years, have elapsed. I have no wish to die without having transposed everything I have had to endure from people and things. That is more or less the sum total of my ambitions.[86]

Here, he justifies the same self-sabotaging behaviour that characterized his previous serious relationships. He left his first two wives because to him, love equated to reality, which he found stifling and intolerable, having endured so much suffering already. As for Elizabeth Craig, she eventually left him because his novel took precedence over the reality of their relationship. In the end, Céline preferred to transpose reality into his fiction, than to live it directly. He regarded this transposition not as facile escapism, but as a necessary, painstaking form of catharsis that was driven by a sense of urgency: so overwhelming was the reality he carried deep inside him that he had to unburden himself of it in his writing before he died. And this transposition entailed an effort as monumental as that made by his mother when she worked her way through the daunting piles of lace, 'a mountain of work' ('une montagne de boulot') on the table in front of her: 'Like her I always have on my table a huge pile of suffering Horrors that I would like to patch up and then be done with it.'[87]

Following the huge effort needed to transpose this 'pile of suffering Horrors' into his second novel, in the late spring of 1936, he met the woman who was to become his third wife and by far the most important person in the remaining 25 years of his life: the 23-year-old dancer Lucie Almansor, who was known as Lucette Almanzor. Lucette, who would outlive Céline by an astonishing 58 years before eventually passing away aged 107 in November 2019, first caught his eye at the reputable dance studio of Blanche d'Alessandri-Valdine, in the Pigalle, which he would attend regularly to watch the dancers, in order to recover from the stress of writing *Death on Credit*. Céline was granted admission by the normally austere Alessandri, owing to his magnetic charm and dandyish elegance, which were also not lost on the impressionable Lucette:[88] 'He also had this Gatsby side to him, nonchalant, immaculately turned out, laid-back, he was extraordinarily handsome, with blue eyes that had

Lucette Almanzor, Céline, Dr Camus, Henri Mahé, Sergine Le Bannier, St Malo, summer 1938.

the merest hint of a black circle in the middle.'[89] She was also drawn to his sadness: 'I looked at him like an extraordinary being that one sees, who does not talk, but is there. He was sad and far away. Sadly far away. Naturally this made us curious to know what he wanted, he looked so unhappy.'[90] She could empathize with this sadness, since she herself was at a particularly low point in her life: 'I wanted to die, I found life so sad. I had no friends, I didn't talk, I was completely focused on myself and on dance.'[91] She had just spent the winter of 1935–6 dancing with a troupe in Miami and New York. But after the excitement and bright lights of Broadway, she found herself alone and penniless in Paris, without support from her family. Indeed, her entire childhood had been lonely and starved of love. Her father, Jules Almansor (the surname was of Arabic-Andalusian origin), was the manager of a struggling lace and embroidery store, who upped sticks and enlisted for the army in 1912, just after Lucette's birth; ironically, he would become, like his future son-in-law, *maréchal des logis*. By the time he came back in 1918, his marriage to Lucette's mother, Gabrielle Donas, was in trouble. Gabrielle Donas was an alcoholic with expensive tastes, who often neglected Lucette as a child, seeking solace in numerous affairs.[92] With a distant father and neglectful mother, the 42-year-old Céline no doubt filled the void of the older authority figure she had craved as a child. He, in turn, found her naivety endearing, while her self-sufficient and tolerant character was able to cope with both his pessimism and his own need for independence. That said, it took Lucette some time to get used to his mood swings, impatience and eccentricities. In the early days of their courtship, they would go to a restaurant, and he would order two steaks, wolf them down in five minutes and then demand that they leave before she had even started eating. The same thing happened when they went to the cinema: they would see the first few images and then he would drag her outside.[93] Overall, however, Lucette's stabilizing influence on Céline was such that, with very rare exceptions, he finally 'settled down' and almost completely refrained from sexual escapades with other women.[94] His fear of being tied down had been banished at long last.

Lucette's support proved especially valuable at this time, given the unexpectedly fierce backlash he faced when his second novel came out in early 1936. As Denoël acknowledged in an interview in 1939, 'Céline could never have imagined what the critics had in store for this book, which had cost him several years of painstaking effort when he was suffering terribly from ill health.'[95] Although around ten reviews were broadly favourable, the majority, on both sides of the political spectrum, were not.[96] 'Twenty-five francs of ignominy and abjection' ('Vingt-cinq francs d'ignominie et d'abjection'), cried *La Liberté* on 21 May; 'The biggest producer of garbage *in the world*, a sort of Ford for slush' ('Le plus grand producteur d'ordures *in the world*, une sorte de Ford de la gadoue'), said *Combat* the following month; 'Vocabulary from the sewer' ('Vocabulaire d'égout'), ranted *L'Ordre*.[97] The attacks on his use of argot did not just revolve around obscenity. Marcel Lapierre, in the left-wing *Le Peuple*, had no problem with Céline's inclusion of argot per se, but with its implausible use by a character who is a bourgeois doctor: 'it is a doctor speaking. He has no motive for speaking in this way.'[98] Moreover, he accused Céline of historical inaccuracy: the argot used is not that of 1912, when most of the novel is set, but from a later date.[99] This is one example of Céline's 'aesthetic extremism', which was clearly not to everyone's taste.

Indeed, even among those critics who had admired *Journey*, many were deeply unhappy with two aspects of Céline's style in *Death on Credit*. The first was the apparent disorder of his syntax, owing to his spoken use of slang. In *Journey*, the style – sentence structure and vocabulary – is still, as Céline's second translator into English Ralph Manheim aptly points out, 'relatively literary', but already contains 'a strong popular admixture' that 'lends a tone that had never before been heard in French prose'.[100] *Death on Credit* was merely an attempt to take this spoken style one step further. The second stylistic shift between the two novels – which infuriated many academics at the time – was his frequent use of the *trois points*, or three dots. These were an attempt to capture speech in a more authentic way: 'They mark the incompleteness, the abruptness, the sudden shifts of direction characteristic of everyday speech, and signify a declaration of war on the flowing prose period.'[101]

Céline was both incensed and crestfallen at the negative responses, especially because he and Denoël had already had heated discussions over certain obscene sections of the novel. The Belgian had refused to print the most explicit passages, and Céline could not be persuaded to rewrite them. They reached an uneasy compromise: the disputed words, phrases or paragraphs were left blank in the main edition, and a mere 117 copies appeared, outside the market, with the entire text. Céline felt particularly aggrieved at André Rousseaux's remark in *Le Figaro* that his 'prodigious verbal genius' ('prodigieux génie verbal') was in danger of becoming 'prisoner of its own artifices' ('prisonnier de ses propres artifices') through his excessive use of argot.[102] Céline countered in his published response that argot was necessary to inject 'spoken emotion' into the written word, that 'the only mode of expression possible for emotion' ('le seul mode d'expression possible pour l'émotion') is to 'render the spoken in writing' ('rendre le parlé en écrit').[103] His new style seeks to break with the traditional academic prose of the novel: 'I don't want to narrate, I want to evoke FEELING. It is impossible to do this with the usual academic language – the beautiful style.'[104] The problem with this *langage classique* (classical language) is that 'emotive rendering is not there' ('le rendu émotif n'y est pas'); it is, therefore, a 'dead' language, in the emotive sense, as illegible as Latin. Argot, by contrast, gives language, if only temporarily, a new lease of life, owing to its

> critical superiority over so-called pure language, very French, refined, ALWAYS DEAD, dead from the beginning, dead since Voltaire, a corpse, *dead as a door nail*. Everybody feels it, nobody says it, or dares to say it. A language is like everything else, IT IS ALWAYS DYING, IT IS DESTINED TO DIE.[105]

Céline further vented his spleen in a letter to Daudet, a few weeks after the novel's publication, hoping for his support.[106] He defends his 'spoken emotion' as the manifestation of his northern, rather than southern, background and temperament. Thus, if his style is not 'Latin, classic, southern', this is because 'I am not from the south. I am Parisian. Of Breton and Flemish descent. I write as I feel.'[107] If people accuse him of being 'foul-mouthed, talking slang' ('d'être ordurier, de parler vert'), then the same thing must surely apply to other canonical writers and artists such as Rabelais, Villon and Bruegel. Then, with some justification, he denounces the hypocritical 'sudden purists' who accuse him of 'systematic cruelty', yet say nothing against gangster films. This he puts down to cowardice: a 'solitary author' is a far easier target than the 'formidable interests' of cinema or a publisher like Hachette. He also speculates that critics are jealous of his life experience, and that despite never having attended the *lycée*, he still managed to obtain his *baccalauréat* and medical degree while earning a living: 'You learn a lot that way. This is perhaps what people will have most trouble forgiving me for.'[108] He believes this jealousy extends to his profession as a doctor: 'people hate doctors, as well as their experience' ('on haït les médecins, leur expérience aussi'). Finally, he counters accusations of implausibility by saying that he writes in the mode of 'waking dream' ('rêve éveillé'), which is a 'Nordic formula' ('formule nordique').

Despite their disagreement over the passages, Denoël also came to Céline's rescue. His 'Apologie de *Mort à crédit*', published two months after the novel's release, eloquently rebuffed the critics' short-sighted accusations of obscenity. He cites works now widely regarded as masterpieces, but which were lambasted at the time for immorality. Balzac was heavily criticized for *Le Père Goriot*, *Le Lys dans la vallée* and *Les Illusions perdues*; Flaubert received similar treatment for *Madame Bovary*, and Zola was even accused of 'an odour of bestiality' for his novels *La Terre* and *L'Assommoir*, today considered among his very best. Denoël concedes that if Céline is the 'only author slated in France in the last forty years' ('*seul auteur ereinté* en France depuis quarante ans'), then this is only because he refuses to 'play the game' of self-promotion by attending book launches and marketing campaigns or cultivating strategic political and literary affiliations, in salons or political parties.[109] Denoël upholds Céline's own defence of his 'jargon' and syntactical use of slang, in his response to André Rousseaux in *Le Figaro*: its injection of 'life' – even if only temporarily – back into language.[110] Finally, he quotes, at length, his fellow Belgian Charles Bernard in *La Nation belge*, who compares the capacious architectural scope and variety of Céline's novel to that of Gothic cathedrals. They, too, sought to encompass the entire spectrum of human moral behaviour, warts and all:

> the author wanted to put everything into his book. As one puts everything into a cathedral, the earth, the sky, hell, purgatory, virtues, sins, the spirit and the flesh. There are not just the pillars, the vaults, the walls, the entire architectural edifice. There are the statues, the thousands of statues, the incredible pullulation of statues. And if there are edifying statues among these, there are unseemly ones as well.[111]

Denoël was also remarkably prescient. In *Le Petit parisien*, he correctly anticipates that the novel will one day receive the recognition it is due: '[it] will occupy, of that I have absolutely no doubt, a place in the highest echelons of French letters.'[112] That this novel is today considered a masterpiece and has influenced, among other classics, Philip Roth's *Portnoy's Complaint* fully vindicates his prediction.

Indeed, in the Anglo-American world, reactions to the novel, despite another translation by Marks, were generally more favourable – and often more perceptive – than in France. John Walcott, for instance, writes that even though Céline 'is lacking in the French virtues of a clear intelligence wedded to a sympathetic understanding', the novel's workmanship 'is better, the life less picaresque than the *Voyage*, and there are signs of discipline in the novel that give it iron. It is a better book than the first.'[113] He praises Céline's 'admirable qualities of imagination, gusto, invective, a coarse and brutal humour'. Its comic qualities are similarly praised on 20 June 1936 by the *New Statesman*, which calls it 'one of the most savagely amusing books ever written', claiming that 'Swift is the only other writer whose hatred is as all-embracing as M. Céline's.' The review praises the seasickness passage and Courtial's death: 'the mess made by a man blowing out his brains'.[114]

Nobert Guterman of the *New Republic* rightly spots, before anyone else, Céline's increasing desire to focus on form and style rather than conventional narrative, which paradoxically aligns him with more 'elitist' writers such as Paul Valéry:

> The stress is no longer on the subject matter, but on the style. To discuss the 'social implications' of a work like this seems utterly irrelevant – except in so far as 'Death on the Instalment Plan' is part of the disappearing school of art for art's sake. For in spite of Céline's use of the most 'popular' language, his violence and abundance and 'impurity' are just as formalistic as Paul Valéry's restraint and purity.[115]

Justin O'Brien of *The Nation* attacks the prevailing critical tendency to compare Céline to other major writers, especially Rabelais and Joyce. He argues that while all three authors share 'lengthiness, a love of scatology, and a dissatisfaction with the current vocabulary', he finds that 'he [Céline] lacks their learning and careful composition'. Where Joyce and Rabelais 'enrich the language [. . .] make subtle graftings and invent onomatopoeic images [. . .], Céline simply scrambles common words as a strong man bends iron'. As for 'his special sense of the comic', praised by so many, this 'manifests itself most often in elephantine exaggeration, not unlike Rabelais at his worst'.[116] A more valid comparison is with Lautréamont, who 'wrote with the same unrelieved intensity, the same Gargantuan exaggeration, and the same hallucinatory manner'. In particular, O'Brien highlights the novel's various 'stampede' episodes, which 'sound as if they had come directly from "Maldoror" save that they lack Lautréamont's brilliant flashes and startling images'.

As for G. W. Stonier, if he unflatteringly compares the Courtial episode to another major nineteenth-century writer, Flaubert ('an overblown chapter of *Bouvard et Pecuchet*'), he also praises the novel's overall style: 'the quality of Céline's writing is so remarkable (and it loses comparatively little in Marks's brilliant translation) that any book written by him is an experience.'[117]

But in 1936–7, Céline was still licking his wounds from the poor reception of *Death on Credit* in his home country. To add insult to injury, two of the staunchest supporters of his previous novel, Lucien Descaves and Léon Daudet, had not gone out of their way to defend him. As he wrote furiously to Henri Mahé at the end of May, 'Daudet and Descaves have this time massively chickened out.'[118] The deep hurt and bitter disappointment felt by Céline were undoubtedly catalysts in his decision to publish his first antisemitic pamphlet the following year. It would be naive, however, to assume that he was transformed into a rabid antisemite overnight. The signs were already there, but latent. He had grown up with a father who supported the antisemitic newspaper *La Patrie*; his play *The Church* had contained a crass antisemitic stereotype of the 'all-powerful Jew'.[119] There was also his difficult relationship with the head of his medical practice in Clichy, the Jewish doctor Grégoire Ichok.[120] By 1937 his frequent absences to travel in Europe and rumours of orgies he organized in his flat (which Céline blamed on women he claimed to have helped escape from prostitution) made his position at Clichy untenable. Even his letter to Élie Faure, in which he attacks him for his bourgeois privilege, warns against the dangers of 'drooling like a Jew' ('baver comme un juif').[121] His letter to Karen-Marie Jensen on 7 February 1935 contains a lengthy anti-American diatribe that presages a 'Jewish takeover': 'a nation of drunken garage mechanics, who shout and will soon become completely Jewish'.[122] His belief that Jews ran America was only reinforced by his discovery that Elizabeth Craig's new husband Ben Tankel was descended from Russian-Jewish immigrants.[123] And just after the setback of *Death on Credit*, he suffered another double blow in the summer of 1936: he submitted to the Paris Opera a ballet he wrote, *La Naissance d'une fée* (The Birth of a Fairy), based on *Gisèle* and Shakespeare's *A Midsummer Night's Dream*, and also tried to secure Lucette a dancing role there. Both requests were rejected by the supposedly Jewish-dominated institution.[124] With the election of a Jewish prime minister, Léon Blum, on 4 June 1936, it did not take much to convince Céline that a 'Jewish conspiracy' was being waged against him professionally, personally and politically.

The first step towards his official 'outing' as an antisemite was his radical decision to switch from the novel to the pamphlet – specifically, his vehemently anti-communist pamphlet *Mea culpa*. The catalyst for this text was his three-week trip to the Stalinist Soviet Union in September 1936, which he saw as an opportunity to vent his spleen, after the negative reception of *Death on Credit*. Elsa Triolet, wife of communist author Louis Aragon, had translated *Journey* into Russian. Despite some cuts and editing enforced by the Stalinist censors and Maxim Gorki's attack on its 'nihilism of despair', it had sold very well indeed in Russia. Trotsky, already sent into exile by Stalin, had even praised the novel for its sympathy with the proletariat.[125] Financial considerations finally pushed Céline to visit a country he had long wanted to discover. The disappointing sales of *Death on Credit* meant he had cancelled a planned visit to the United States; moreover, royalties from his book translations in the USSR could only be spent there, as the rouble was not convertible. *Death on Credit*, however, was deemed unfit for translation by the Soviets, who found it nihilistic, anarchical, mediocre and cynical.

French writers had already paved the way for his visit. A propaganda drive was under way by Stalin, to show off his nation's achievements to Western authors: Georges Duhamel, Henri Barbusse, André Malraux and, most recently and infamously, André Gide had all been invited to Soviet Russia. (Accompanied by Eugène Dabit, who died suddenly in Sebastopol on 21 August, and Louis Guilloux, Gide's two-month trip from June to August 1936 had resulted in his less-than-flattering publication *Retour de l'USSR*.)[126] Arriving in Leningrad via Copenhagen and Helsinki only a few weeks after Gide's departure, Céline was met by an official delegation at the train station. A guided tour of the city to demonstrate the supposed pre-eminence of Soviet workers failed to convince him, and he declined the opportunity to meet other writers, preferring to visit the city alone, after checking into the luxurious Hôtel de l'Europe.[127] In fact, he was accompanied by a pretty young guide and translator, Natalia, who (so he later told Karen Jensen and Lucette) wanted to marry him as a way out of the Soviet Union, after he had seduced her.[128]

A recently discovered 2006 police report on his visit reveals that he used his medical background to insist on a tour of a hospital, the Peterhof Institute of venereal disease.[129] Céline was shocked at the awful conditions. Culturally and aesthetically speaking, however, he was enchanted by Leningrad: the Hermitage, the Winter Palace, the canals and, above all, given his love of dance, the Kirov Theatre, where he saw a number of ballets, including *Swan Lake*, and praised the ballerina Galina Oulanova.[130] This points to a further motive for his trip to the USSR: his attempt to have his ballets performed, after failing to do so in Paris and London. He obtained a meeting with the reading committee, including eminent retired dancer Agrippina Vaganova, to consider his ballet *The Birth of a Fairy*. They politely declined, saying that the subject was not 'social' enough and that he should return the following year with a subject more in line with Soviet policy.[131] This refusal added to his sense of disillusionment with Stalinist Russia, and the ballet was included, with a dig at the critics, in his pamphlet *Trifles for a Massacre* the following year.[132]

His frustration with his Soviet experience found an outlet in his fifteen-page pamphlet *Mea culpa*, which was published by the ever-loyal Denoël.[133] As in the Zola lecture, he lambasts society, especially dictatorships, for hypocritically hiding the truth from their citizens. Stalinism perpetuates the illusion of happiness, when, in reality, man is just as unhappy as he was before: 'The great pretension to happiness, that's the main big fraud; that's what complicates all living! That's what makes people so poisonous, so filthy, so hard to take!'[134] As for the class divisions supposedly eradicated by Stalinism, they are still present in the vast disparities in living standards between high-ranking communist officials on the one hand, and 'Prolo' (Céline's ironic name for the ordinary working man) on the other. Prolo 'can look up and watch the Commissar ride by in his second-hand Packard'; a 'fine engineer' earns 7,000 rubles a month, but 'the charwoman only 50'.[135] As a doctor, he is especially shocked that 'with the exception of the Kremlin and the In-tourist wards and rooms', the hospitals are 'openly sordid'.[136] Nor does he spare Stalin for terrorizing those citizens who dare to disagree with him: 'The proletarian? Into your house! Read my newspaper! Read my rumors . . . but no other. Dip into the wisdom of my speeches! But take care you don't go beyond them, swine! Or I shall cut off your head!'[137]

In the end, for all its valid criticisms of Stalinism, *Mea culpa* does not reach the stylistic heights of Céline's novels. If the pamphlet has been regarded as Céline's philosophical vision of a 'communism of suffering', the style is disjointed, repetitive, vituperative and over-declamatory and lacks the novelist's usual verbal inventiveness.[138] His metaphors are few and contrived and tend to revolve around dance, his main aesthetic obsession just after *Death on Credit*: 'If we compare this life under communism to a dance, its tune seems even more hobble-dehoy, more clodhopping, a sort of blindman's bluff of a dance, even more stupid than here at home; but everyone must join in, no limping cripple can drag behind.'[139] Perhaps the most probing observation of *Mea culpa* is that Soviet communism and American capitalism are paradoxically the same: 'Just look, in this USSR, how quickly money has been rehabilitated. How money has recaptured its tyranny right away!'[140] Soviet industry reminds Céline of the Ford factories. The Soviet Union promotes industrial technology – what he calls 'the Machine' – as 'The true Promised Land!' and promotes its factories, as Ford did with his car plants, as the socially inclusive guarantor of a stable wage: 'Machinery is now "good form." It means "mass production"; it means work, it means "basic" industry, it means three meals a day. So it makes a great hit with the masses. It makes them feel like technicians and specialists; it inspires loyalty.'[141] Céline makes the link with Ford explicit. His comparison of workers in the Detroit car plant to chimpanzees finds its dehumanized equivalent in the Soviet factories:

> But all during this time, one must not think!' [. . .] Machinery is infection itself. The supreme defeat! What a sorry joke! The best machine ever invented has never affected deliverance for anyone. It has brutalized Man more cruelly and that is all there is to it! I have been a doctor in the Ford factories and I know what I am talking

about. All Ford factories resemble each other, whether in the Soviets or anywhere else.[142]

Céline was desperate to counter the negative press generated by *Death on Credit*. He therefore decided to publish *Mea culpa* together with his medical thesis *Semmelweis*, since, as he wrote to his American editor at Little and Brown, James W. MacIntyre, he saw both works as united by a common humanity in the face of injustice that would 'make readers think twice before accusing *Death on Credit* of being dirty eroticism etc.'[143] It was little wonder that the Left in France reacted furiously to the pamphlet, and Céline forever burnt his bridges with the communists. Chief among these was Paul Nizan, who attacked Céline for the social conscience expected of him after *Journey*: 'In *Journey* there was an unforgettable denunciation of war, of the colonies. Today Céline denounces nothing but the poor and the vanquished.' Among the few critics who defended him were Georges Altman, who had praised *Journey* in 1932. In the freemasonic publication *La Lumière*, he observed that Céline 'poses the entire moral problem of mankind'.[144] But Céline did not just want to reach a French audience. He went to great lengths to persuade Robert Allerton Parker to translate both *Mea culpa* and *Semmelweis* into English, since he also wished to restore his critical reputation internationally.

In his last ever trip to the United States, Céline met and befriended Parker in New York in February 1937, probably through the academic Milton Hindus, who would later visit Céline in Denmark in 1948.[145] The reactions of the anglophone press ranged from moderate praise to downright hostility, with polite bafflement being the most typical response. Critics were generally more receptive to *Semmelweis* than to *Mea culpa*, but often unfavourably compared both works to his novels. Thus the *New English Weekly* of 6 January 1938 wrote, 'There is little in this present volume of the wild war humours of "Journey", or its after-phantasy of modern progressive civilization in USA and France. This book is bleak with anger but commands respect and interest due to all genuine protest in the name of truth.'

The *Times Literary Supplement* wrote, 'The first essay in this volume is one prolonged denunciation of Soviet Russia today, written with all the bitterness of the deceived admirer [. . .] The other essay [. . .] is one of the tragedies of science, told with the utmost vigour and dramatic effect.'[146] Unsurprisingly, as in France, Leftist publications, such as *The Statesman*, were particularly harsh on *Mea culpa*: 'A short essay in vituperation against Communism in particular and life in general. It is slangy, explosive, staccato, and fiercely independent of syntax, a tirade, a diatribe, a hysterical hymn of hate.'[147] It was more forgiving of *Semmelweis*'s humanism:

> This is Céline in a different mood and a different style, telling the story of the great doctor who discovered the origin of puerperal fever. The author has command of irony and understanding of the value of unadorned fact. Even in translation the economy and concentration of his style are evident.[148]

Similarly, *Weekly* comments that while *Semmelweis* is 'more lucid [than *Mea culpa*], though hardly a work of art', Céline 'seems to dislike not only Communism but human nature with a frenetic fervour'.[149]

But by now, Céline was undeterred. After the backlash against *Death on Credit*, such criticisms were like water off a duck's back. He considered his pamphlet a success and a psychologically liberating experience. So much so, in fact, that he felt sufficiently emboldened to embark down a sinister path, from which there would be no return: that of writing three antisemitic pamphlets. Once he published the first of these, *Trifles for a Massacre*, in December 1937 his life would never be the same again.

five

Antisemite and Fascist Sympathizer

Most Céline scholars today are reluctant to confront an inconvenient truth: that despite its antisemitic content, his second pamphlet, *Trifles for a Massacre*, was a critically praised bestseller. Published at the end of 1937, the first print run quickly sold 20,000 copies, prompting Robert Denoël to publish a second one a mere three months later.[1] By the time it was withdrawn from circulation, in May 1939, it had reached 76,000 copies.[2]

If Godard simply expresses consternation and surprise at the pamphlet's success, Nicholas Hewitt attributes it to a textual ambiguity that caused Céline's readers to dismiss his racism as mere satire.[3] Hewitt's argument hinges on a paradox: Céline was an unabashed racist, but deliberately wrote in an elusive, satirical style that allowed him to *disguise* this racism. On the one hand, Hewitt correctly distinguishes the biologically racist component of Céline's antisemitism from most French antisemites at that time, who were more concerned about Jewish economic and political power. Anticipating a recent book by Annick Duraffour and Pierre-André Taguieff, he highlights Céline's increasing intellectual debt, after *Trifles for a Massacre*, to racist ethnologist George Montandon, whom he met in 1938 via Henry-Robert Petit, the editor of the extreme Right-wing journal *Au Pilori*.[4] Montandon belonged to a Right-wing tradition of public health thinking that perceived alien ethnic groups as a major health risk to the French nation. He upheld a 'public-health model of society as an organism beset by an alien infection', and considered 'the racial purity of France' to be 'at risk from the increasing presence of the Jews who, in their turn, are attempting to undermine the health of the Aryan population'.[5] Céline's own earlier background in hygiene and public health with the League of Nations thus provided a springboard for his transition to biological racism in the late 1930s. His intellectual debt to Montandon, contrary to most French antisemites, 'brings him unfashionably closer to Nazi ideology'.[6] Moreover, his endorsement of racial purity stems from his opposition to racial hybridity, a theoretical position he derived from Joseph Arthur de Gobineau's work *Essai sur l'inégalité des races humaines* (Essay on the Inequality of the Human Races). This attempts to reconstruct human history according to the supposed existence (and irretrievable loss) of three distinct and original races – white, black and yellow – each of which has particular psychological and corporeal characteristics. These races have now allegedly become so intermingled and 'impure' that the future of humanity is doomed.[7]

On the other hand, if Hewitt correctly pinpoints Céline's racism, he also maintains that this racism was deliberately *camouflaged* in *Trifles for a Massacre* via a strategy that philosopher and critic Walter Benjamin called the 'cult of the joke'. This practice, typical of many fascist propagandists at the time, 'consists of saying the unacceptable in such a way that it can be taken as a joke while still insidiously making its point'. Céline thus allegedly cloaks his violent antisemitism 'in a fictional and ironic form' as a means of self-preservation that is intended to provide him with an 'escape route' from prosecution.[8] So his inclusion of three ballets, of the same playful literary narrator Ferdinand as in his novel *Death on Credit* and of the word 'bagatelles' in the original French title, which means a piece of 'light music' and, more archaically, the sales pitch given by performers at fairgrounds to attract customers, are examples of both the pamphlet's satire and its artistic leitmotifs.[9] This is thus as much an *art poétique* as it is a polemical work, allegedly prompting literary aesthetes such as Gide to interpret it as a purely satirical text.[10]

However, the seductive notion that Céline's racism hides behind an ironic aesthetic facade both overestimates the ambivalence of his text and underestimates the moral responsibility of his readers. Specifically, it completely ignores the institutionalized racism and culturally embedded attitudes of the time. These societal factors, as much as the intrinsic qualities of the text itself, explain the pamphlet's popularity. A sample of some sixty journal reviews from across the political spectrum shows that only fewer than half of these reviews openly condemned the pamphlet for its antisemitism, while well over half either endorsed it, or played down its importance.[11] How do we explain the fact that, by today's standards, the reaction was relatively benign, with the exception of a few articles published by Jewish groups and one full-length study, Hans Eric Kaminski's *Céline en chemise brune* (Céline in a Brown Shirt), which directly accused his pamphlet of inciting a pogrom against the Jews? Despite the relative failure of *Death on Credit*, Céline's stock in the literary world was still high following the huge critical and commercial success of *Journey*. Nor should we forget France's complacent, even tolerant, attitude towards antisemitism at that time, which was exacerbated by the wave of Jewish immigration into the country from 1933. Drawing attention to the xenophobia that typically scapegoats the newly arrived foreigner as a potential threat to the indigenous population, French philosopher Alain Badiou has argued that this influx of Jewish immigrants was the 1930s equivalent of the present-day disenfranchized, working-class French Arabs of the Parisian *banlieues*.[12] Common to both groups is their exclusion from, and stigmatization by, mainstream Republican society, and regular targeting by the police. Unprovoked police raids in 1934 and 1938 in Paris's Jewish quarters resulted in the random arrest, beating and insulting of Jews on the pretext of not having papers. Anticipating the populist appeal of present-day anti-immigration rhetoric, 1935 also saw high-profile strikes by non-Jewish French doctors and lawyers in protest at the influx of Jewish medical practitioners into both the public and private health systems. The swift passing of a law to make it more difficult for immigrant doctors to practise or dispense medicine is a clear indication that antisemitism was not only socially widespread, but institutionally entrenched in a way that it had not been since the Dreyfus affair in the 1890s.[13] Céline's pamphlet also owed its success to a prevailing cultural attitude at that time: the perception of literature as an autonomous practice that was completely separate from morality and politics. Sociologist Gisèle Sapiro calls this an 'art for art's sake' approach to literature that was primarily manifested in the two dominant interwar literary movements: the *Nouvelle Revue française* (N.R.F.), spearheaded by André Gide, and Surrealism, led by André Breton.[14] Both championed, albeit in different ways, the idea of the disinterested writer who is not held morally accountable to the state for what he or she writes.

This notion of literature as an intrinsic, depoliticized practice, thriving against a backdrop of antisemitism, provides relevant cultural context for Gide's favourable reaction to Céline's pamphlet in April 1938. Gide himself was no antisemite, nor did he belong to the far Right. But he dismisses Céline's antisemitic attacks – for instance, his blaming of the Jews for the poor sale of *Death on Credit* – as a deliberate joke on the reader. Instead, Gide claims, we should praise *Trifles for a Massacre* for its bold stylistic experimentation and creativity, the same qualities that are to be found in certain visceral descriptive passages from his novel:

> When Céline comes to us talking about a conspiracy of silence, a coalition to prevent the sale of his books, it is quite clear that he is joking. And when he holds the Jew responsible for the poor sales, it goes without saying that it is only a joke. And if it was not just a joke, then he, Céline, would be completely crazy . . . He does his utmost not to be taken seriously . . . He is a creator. He talks of Jews in *Trifles* in the same way that he talked, in *Death on Credit*, about the maggots that his powers of evocation had brought forth.[15]

It is worth contrasting Gide's primarily literary response with that of the far-Right journal *Gringoire* in March 1938. Where Gide praises Céline the novelist and stylistic innovator but minimizes the antisemitic pamphleteer, Jean-Pierre Maxence, on the contrary, flags up his antisemitism as evidence of his talents as pamphleteer rather than novelist:

> Above all, he is a pamphleteer. That was evident in the best pages of *Journey* [. . .], in the best pages of *Death on Credit* . . . We ask of him one talent, and one talent only: to find the underlying weakness of the person he attacks, to go beyond the ludicrous, trivialities; with the first blow to get to the very core, the heart, the hypocrisy of the problem . . . His 'attacks' are admirable.[16]

This praise of Céline's devastating attack on his target and of his denunciation of hypocrisy in the best traditions of the French pamphlet, points to a second generic preconception at that time: the pamphlet, as opposed to the novel, was a genre highly valued, by *both* the Left and the Right, as a type of polemical writing that exposed the hypocrisy of state authority. (Zola's *J'accuse* (I Accuse) of 1898 is the model pamphlet in this regard.) The pamphlet is typically written by a solitary individual who demonstrates intellectual courage by speaking out against a scandal, who posits a truth in order to expose an institutionalized lie. Contrary to established writers, whose language is authorized by institutions such as the Académie française, the pamphleteer's legitimacy lies in his autonomy and the risk he takes in combating the dominant ideology. His break with conventional discourse and language is the mark of his anti-conformism and assigns to his words a subversive potential.[17] It is precisely Céline's anti-conformism, the cathartic purity of the language of his pamphlet, that in January 1938 is contrasted favourably with the vulgarity of his literature by Jules Rivet, this time in the Left-leaning *Le Canard enchaîné*, France's most established satirical journal:

> I didn't like *Death on Credit* very much . . . Everything was rotten, muddy, greenish and nauseating . . . In *Trifles for a Massacre*, [there is] nothing dirty, nothing that is not, on the contrary, very healthy and breezy. Here we find clean and good old-fashioned hatred, proper violence with its sleeves rolled up . . . Here the non-conformist soldiers on manfully, the solitary individual stamps his authority, shows his teeth, settles scores . . . I would not wish to trivialize this liberating, torrential and irresistible book with the word masterpiece. It is far greater than that, and purer.[18]

To sum up, the popularity of *Trifles for a Massacre* owes at least as much to entrenched societal and cultural attitudes as it does to textual ambiguity. But it comes as no surprise, in a twenty-first-century post-Holocaust world, that most Céline scholars, especially in France, avoid broaching the question of complacency towards antisemitism at that time, for to do so would pose the embarrassing dilemma of having to explain why Céline's pamphlet was praised not just by the far Right, but by highly revered liberal readers such as Gide. But as I have already suggested, it is perfectly possible to acknowledge society's high *tolerance* of antisemitism, without accusing Gide of being an antisemite. Rather, he was an intellectual aesthete for whom inflammatory language against Jews was of secondary concern to questions of literary style. Equally, we must also avoid erring in the opposite direction by *overemphasizing* antisemitism as a normalized societal phenomenon in 1930s France. If we do so, then we risk *trivializing* what Céline actually wrote by conceding that since antisemitism was so deeply entrenched anyway, his opinions were not particularly unusual for that era, and hence not especially reprehensible. In 1939, as we shall see, a new law eventually intervened to condemn his second, and even more explicitly, antisemitic pamphlet *School for Corpses* (*L'École des cadavres*).

The most objective position to adopt is thus as follows: to condemn Céline for his pamphlet's racist content, but without completely exonerating those readers who responded positively to it, even if we allow for textual ambivalence. It must be recognized that either they explicitly or tacitly endorsed his opinions or, at the very least, did not consider them to be sufficiently inflammatory to be worth opposing.

As for Céline himself, to escape the publicity surrounding *Trifles* and also to identify a possible long-term refuge both from his critics and from a Europe he believed was about to be plunged into war, he set sail for Canada and the island of Saint-Pierre-et-Miquelon.[19] From there, on 5 and 6 May 1938, he went to Montreal, where he gave several interviews on his political opposition to war, rather than on his literature. For the first time, he expressed his sympathy for a French alliance with Hitler. He also attended a meeting of the far-Right-wing Christian Nationalist party led by Adrien Arcand, as well as a dinner hosted by Victor Barbeau, president of the Society of Writers in the French Language in Canada.[20] From Canada, he went to New York, no doubt to coincide with the American release of the English translation of *Death on Credit*. However, matters were delayed by the modifications requested by the American publisher, Little, Brown and Company, to the John Marks translation: they wished to 'Americanize' certain of Marks's British expressions. Moreover, Céline's friendship with Robert Allerton Parker, the American translator of *Semmelweis* and *Mea culpa*, whom he had met in New York the previous spring, had cooled. Owing to its antisemitism, Parker understandably had grave reservations, despite Céline's protestations, about translating *Trifles* into English, as did the publisher Little, Brown. This point is crucial because if, as Hewitt alleges, many in France were duped by the pamphlet's 'textual ambiguity', the Americans most definitely were not: they were under no illusions as to its antisemitic content and intentions. Céline even said so himself in a letter (written in English) to Parker on 27 January 1938: 'I have just published a very méchant pamphlet on the Jews called *Trifles for a Massacre*.'[21] When Little, Brown imposed what Céline saw as draconian editorial conditions, he angrily wrote to Parker on 17 March 1938 (this time in French), requesting his help in finding a different publisher: 'I nevertheless want to try and find an anti-Jewish publisher in America.'[22] Again, his antisemitic intentions are unmistakable. Nothing came of this request, and Céline's already negative feelings towards America, especially as an alleged capitalist ally of the Jews, became even more acute.

This anti-Americanism, the short-lived reappointment of the Jewish Léon Blum as French prime minister following the cabinet reshuffle of

March 1938 and the imminent prospect of war gave Céline plenty of ammunition to write another highly polemical pamphlet, *School for Corpses*. Published shortly after the Munich Agreement of September 1938, not even French readers of the time could have any doubts as to its anti-Jewish sentiments. To all but an extremist, this pamphlet is virtually unreadable from start to finish, so shockingly crude and unambiguous is its racism. Taken in isolation, its core intellectual premise – that only an alliance with Hitler can save France from military conflict – has some legitimacy as a desperate, last-ditch attempt to avert another disastrous war. But what is clearly indefensible is his use of pacifism as a peg on which to hang a whole host of unrelated grievances against the Jews. He embarks on a long, vituperative anti-Jewish diatribe, frequently expressed in a language so repulsive and inflammatory as to be scarcely believable. The Jew is a moving target who has simply shifted from the communist Russia and Hollywood denounced in *Trifles* to American capitalist society more generally, together with its Anglo-Saxon ally Great Britain. He satirically refers to this unholy trinity as 'Moscow–Torture, Washington–Oil, London–the Stuffed' ('Moscou–la Torture, Washington–Pétrole, Londres–la Gavée').[23]

Contrary to his positive depiction of London in his novel *Guignol's Band*, the British capital is presented here as a sinister hub of Jewish power, concentrated almost exclusively in the hands of the City's financiers and the freemasons in the intelligence services. The hapless prime minister Neville Chamberlain is merely at their beck and call. His recent Munich Agreement with Hitler is satirically presented as a sham theatrical performance, mere window dressing for the completely different agenda driven by his Jewish 'stage directors', whose sole preoccupation is to go to war with Hitler.[24] As for America, it is presented as an impregnable fortress of vast Jewish power, that it is barely dented by the persecution of the Jews in Nazi Germany: 'The danger is vague, it is being exaggerated! The USA, so absolutely Jewish, still possesses 70 percent of world industry!'[25] American anti-fascist propaganda, Céline disingenuously alleges in a torrent of violent meteorological metaphors, is far harsher in tone than the Nazi propaganda directed at Jews and freemasons. He claims that 'all the ranting and raving' ('tout ce que peuvent tempêter') of the German Hitlerites against the Jews and freemasons is 'no more than grumbling, common old moaning in comparison to the storm, whirlwind, tornado of insults, challenges, vituperation, curses, virulent madness towards Rome, Berlin, Franco, Japan, which the whole of America literally roars, unleashes, day and night [. . .] War against Hitler! And right now!'[26]

Nothing but a pact with Nazi Germany will negate the twin threat of Jewish, pro-militarist Anglo-Saxon democracies and Soviet communism. This pro-German stance is fundamentally what separates him from Charles Maurras, a fellow member of the far Right, who espouses an anti-German and pro-Latin brand of fascism. If both men hate Soviet communism, their attitude to Germany is diametrically opposed: 'Neither Berlin, nor Moscow, means nothing! Rather it should be "Washington–London–Moscow" against "Berlin–Rome–Burgos". Take it, or leave it! You have to choose! This minute! This instant! No horse-trading with the Latins.'[27] Contrary to Maurras, Céline's valorization of Aryan, rather than Latin, identity naturally leads him to criticize fascist Italy's antisemitism for not going far enough: 'I find Italian anti-Semitism too tepid for my taste, meek and insufficient. I find it dangerous. A distinction between good Jews and bad Jews? It makes no sense. Allowing Jews who are patriots and not allowing those who are anti-patriots? That's a farce.'[28]

Had Céline merely advocated a purely strategic alliance with Hitler on pacifist grounds, he could perhaps be given the benefit of the doubt. After all, Chamberlain had just signed the Munich Agreement, and the German and Russian foreign ministers Joachim von Ribbentrop and Vyacheslav Molotov signed a Nazi–Soviet non-aggression pact on 23 August 1939. That both agreements were broken (by Hitler) is beside the point. Desperate times called for desperate measures. But making a hard-nosed pragmatic alliance with the Führer is not the same as actively endorsing the man and his policies. Céline presents Hitler not just as a necessary ally in the quest for peace, but as the defender of the underdog and the supporter of an Aryan identity that embraces life:

> What is the people's real friend? Fascism. Who has done the most for the worker? The USSR or Hitler? It's Hitler. You only have to look without all that red shit in your eyes. Who has done the most for the small shopkeeper? It's not Thorez, it's Hitler! Who is preventing us from going to war? It's Hitler! All the communists (Jewish or Jewified) think about, is resending us to our deaths, for us to croak in a crusade. Hitler is good at raising a people, he is on the side of Life, he cares about the life of peoples, and even ours. He's an Aryan.[29]

Any misconceptions about Céline's endorsement of biological racism are quickly dispelled by his favourable comparison of Aryan racial purity – synonymous with 'life' – with France's decadence and declining birth rate. He blames these on a racial hybridity that has made France too weak to withstand another war: 'Our indigenous population, already so bastardized by the negro and Afro-Asiatic cross-fertilizations, the contribution of twisted Jews, masonic confusion, racial treason, degeneration erected into a sublimely humanitarian religion won't withstand two years of systematic killings.'[30]

Vitriolic excerpts such as these undermine Hewitt's assertion that Céline's readers, especially those on the far Right, did not know whether to take *School for Corpses* seriously or not. 'It is difficult to see', he says, how Céline's attacks on Right-wing leaders such as Doriot or La Rocque, the criticism of Maurras' 'Jewish' style, the deliberate spelling of racist theorist Drumont's name as 'Drummont' and the 'blurring of categories' between Jews and non-Jews 'can be taken totally seriously'.[31] He contends that because Céline 'shows as much contempt for his fellow antisemites as for the ostensible enemy', then 'it is this which accounts for the disorientation of Rebatet's Fascist colleagues', who did not praise this pamphlet as they had *Trifles*, preferring instead to maintain a diplomatic silence.

It is certainly true that, unlike *Trifles for a Massacre*, *School for Corpses* sold badly. At the outbreak of war, it had managed only 27,700 copies and was poorly received, even by the far Right.[32] But this had far less to do with textual ambiguity, than the sheer bad timing of its proposed alliance with Hitler. The main problem, as Rebatet himself acknowledged, was that Céline was calling for an economic, political and military alliance with Hitler at the precise moment when the Führer had just ordered the occupation of Prague, in direct contravention of the Munich Agreement.[33] The far Right – even those members who tacitly approved of Hitler – could not possibly endorse a pamphlet that supported an alliance with a man who was equally likely to invade France.

To make matters worse, Céline was sued for defamation by two plaintiffs, whom he inaccurately referred to as being Jewish. The first was Left-wing journalist Léon Treich, whom he wrongly accused of belonging to Colonel François de La Rocque's entourage; the second was de La Rocque himself, the former leader of the Right-wing league Croix de feu and now of the proto-Gaullist Parti social français. Treich withdrew his complaint when Céline wrote a letter of apology, but de La Rocque took him to court, successfully suing him and Denoël for defamation. In addition, the court condemned the pamphlet's inflammatory language, in light of the new Marchandeau decree of April 1939, which sought to clamp down on the defamation and incitement of hatred towards a specific race or religion.[34] This merely fuelled Céline's paranoia that a Jewish conspiracy was specifically being targeted at his two antisemitic pamphlets. Consequently, he and Denoël thought it prudent to withdraw both antisemitic pamphlets from print in France prior to the judgment being passed on 21 June.

This led to a heated dispute with fascist author Robert Brasillach, with whom Céline always had a testy relationship, despite their shared antisemitism. Brasillach published an anonymous and ironic article in the pro-fascist journal he edited, *Je suis partout*, ending with the provocative phrase 'Ferdinand, you are chickening out' ('Ferdinand, tu te dégonfles'). To someone as touchy as Céline, this accusation of cowardice was like a red rag to a bull. He sent a vituperative response to *Je suis partout*, of which only four lines, in telegrammatic style, were deemed suitable for publication: 'Ferdinand never chickened out. *School*, *Trifles* withdrawn. Court ruling Police. Your journal nothing to fear.'[35] The matter did not end there. A new controversy was triggered by the release of the German translation of *Trifles*. Céline was accused by the anti-fascist journals *Le Canard enchaîné* and *L'Humanité* of securing this translation by colluding with future German ambassador in occupied France Otto Abetz and Louis Darquier de Pellepoix, the future commissioner-general for Jewish affairs under the Vichy government.[36] Céline correctly responded in his usual provocative tone that he had never met Abetz (this would come later, during the Occupation).

But this does not detract from the unequivocal racism of both *Trifles* and *School for Corpses*. The 1939 court ruling is evidence that, *despite* French complacency towards antisemitism in the 1930s, Céline's views were eventually deemed sufficiently extreme to warrant legal intervention. The question remains, however, as to whether Céline's antisemitism was confined to his pamphlets, or if it *also* extended to his novels. Duraffour and Taguieff are adamant that it does. Since he was an unapologetic antisemite, they claim, then this antisemitism, especially from 1937 onwards, must be considered as much a part of his literary works as his political ones. We should avoid deluding ourselves that the novels and pamphlets are separate entities, and instead regard them as the shared expression of the *same* racist ideology.[37] They stress Céline's biological pro-Aryan racism and his familiarity with, and endorsement of, a variety of doctrines and thinkers aligned with Nazi racial ideology. However, at times their justifiable outrage at his antisemitism clouds their judgement about the literary merit of his novels. In other words, they use his racism as a stick with which to beat his fictional works, especially all those that he published after *Death on Credit*.[38]

The pamphlets and novels should, instead, be regarded as *distinctive* works, despite occasional areas of overlap when it comes to Céline's aesthetic ideas. To make this distinction in no way excuses or minimizes his antisemitism, nor does it reflect a culturally elitist bias towards the novel as a genre that is considered superior to the pamphlet. Rather, we first need to acknowledge the clear distinction in terms of genre between novels and pamphlets, in terms of the very different *functions* they serve. The pamphlet is a political, polemical text that asserts a truth that directly challenges the dominant ideology of the present. By contrast, while the novel can also be subversive, it is a work that is primarily focused, especially in Céline's case, on past events rather than current affairs. Whatever basis these events may have in autobiographical or historical fact, they are ultimately transposed to the written page via the medium of the author's imagination.

What is more, the ethnic and racial stereotypes that are so clearly offensive in the pamphlet are usually subverted in his novels. In *Guignol's Band*, the first novel Céline published after the pamphlets, two Jewish characters, Titus Van Claben and the doctor Clodovitz, are presented in sympathetic terms. Clodovitz displays a 'friendly smile' ('aimable sourire') and is 'never brusque, never impatient' ('jamais brusque, jamais impatient') towards his patients. As for Van Claben, he may invoke the stereotype of the thrifty Jewish usurer (like Balzac's character Gobseck), but he is also a virtuoso pianist, whose talent is greatly admired by Ferdinand and his friends.[39]

Nor should we forget that *before* his racist turn in 1937, Céline had already set out in several key letters to private individuals the fundamentals of his aesthetic theory according to intrinsically *literary*, rather than racist, criteria. We have already seen his 1936 letter to Léon Daudet, in which he defends *Death on Credit* with his theory of *le rendu émotif*, or 'emotive rendering', as the cornerstone of his literary enterprise. His decision to adopt an antisemitic stance from 1937 onwards does not automatically mean he abandoned his original literary objectives in favour of a completely new racist aesthetic. Instead of replacing these objectives, his *poétique raciste* (racist poetics) merely *alternated* with them in accordance with his target audience. Race did not dislodge literature from the aesthetic pedestal onto which he had carefully placed it; it simply became a junior partner that played an important but secondary role. This is perfectly demonstrated in two contrasting letters he wrote to Robert Brasillach in 1943 and 1944:

> It seemed to me before *Journey*, when I observed (by way of comparison) road traffic, which is so chaotic – these cars, these people, who hit and jostle each other out of the way, who fight one another in order to make headway , all this zigzagging, the incoherence of these nonsensical and stupidly wasteful manoeuvres, that there should be, *like the metro*, a clearer, more intimate path that allows us to reach a given point without all this idiotic wastefulness, this tiresome chaos – in the same way, also, that I *tell* my stories. So I will spell out the difficulty to you in a nutshell: to be able to enter into the intimacy of language, the inner core of emotion and language, blindly so to speak, like the metro without paying heed to the annoying external incidents. Having set off in this manner, to arrive at the destination via each successive emotion – always taking the nearest, the shortest, the most accurate route, rhythmically and once a sort of intimate music has been chosen, *economically*, by avoiding anything that reverts back to objectivity – description – and always via *transposition*.[40]

The first letter speaks of literature as a purely aesthetic pursuit that strives for the most economical and direct means possible of transposing emotion to the written page. The metro metaphorically encapsulates this desired speed and incisiveness, as distinct from road traffic. With its exasperating congestion, delays and digressions, the latter is reminiscent of the long, cluttered and over-descriptive sentences that Céline regarded as antithetical to his own narrative style.

Céline's second letter to Brasillach, by contrast, refers to literature in terms of *race*, rather than aesthetic style, in order to distinguish his own 'biological' conception of literature from what he sees as Brasillach's excessively cerebral approach:

> I admire you, but I do have one minor criticism – all told, you focus too much on thought and not enough on emotion. Emotion in the physiological sense – 'emotive Rendering'. This, God damn it, is what our race and language needs most of all. So shrivelled, dry,

so calculating, so boorish, so clumsy, so unfeeling behind all those poetic and sensible exteriors.[41]

The second letter's racial references in no way contradict, override or invalidate the irreducibly literary intentions of the first. Rather, this racist dimension is superimposed onto a pre-existing aesthetic theory that was already carefully conceived as intrinsically literary in nature, prior to 1937. With its introduction of the metro metaphor, the 1943 letter is a logical development of the purely literary emphasis on emotion previously set out in the 1936 letter to Daudet. This disproves those claims, made by Céline's more sceptical critics, that his increasingly frequent use of the metro metaphor after 1945 was part of a cynical, disingenuous strategy to 'reinvent' himself as a literary *stylist*, rather than a political writer, in order to gain favour with a hostile, anti-fascist public. But his detailed explanation of this very same metaphor to a fellow racist and fascist sympathizer whom he had no need or desire to appease shows that style was *already* central to his aesthetic aims, *before* his exile from France.

If Céline's racism does not compromise his stylistic integrity, this does not mean to say he could not make tough, pragmatic decisions about his writing when the occasion demanded it. This is evident from his abandonment of his novel *Cannon Fodder*, on which he worked from the autumn of 1936 to the summer of 1937, before switching his attention to *Trifles for a Massacre*. This he saw as the more urgent text, given the looming threat of a new war. In 1934 this threat had yet to appear, and Céline was still basking in the afterglow of his anti-militarist black humour in *Journey*. He therefore originally envisaged *Cannon Fodder* in a similar vein, as a comical, semi-fictionalized satire of the oppressive military life he had known in the barracks of Rambouillet from 1912 to 1914. *Cannon Fodder* was to form part of a semi-autobiographical triptych – Childhood–War–London – that would channel his personal experiences into a revival of the highly popular French anti-militarist novel tradition of the 1880s.[42] This tradition had garnered great acclaim in satirizing the French military as an incompetent and elitist institution. If *Death on Credit* had covered his childhood, and *Journey* the First World War, the two missing pieces of the jigsaw were his life in the barracks and his stint in London. The London episode was to have featured in *Journey* itself, but in July 1931 he wrote to Joseph Garcin that he preferred to defer it to a later, standalone work, in which he could do it full justice.[43] Today all that survives of *Cannon Fodder* is the introduction, which gives us a flavour of its comical, irreverential tone, although a fuller draft of the work may have been lost when Céline's Montmartre flat was ransacked in 1944, following his hasty escape to Germany. By 1937, however, not only had a satire of the French barracks lost its historical relevance – the French military could no longer be blamed for the external threat of war from Nazi Germany – but it was completely out of touch with public sentiment. Céline realized that French readers were in no mood to joke about anything to do with the military, even if his novel were set in the past. What is more, he himself was never comfortable about writing novels that bore too much relation to contemporary events. As we have already seen, the present was the time frame reserved for his pamphlets, whereas the past was the province of his novels. As Godard aptly puts it,

> Deep down, the *célinien* novel is always the recapturing of an experience from the past that is transposed via an imaginative route. When it comes to people or places, the history of his works shows that in every case, Céline needs to be separated from them by circumstances in order for them to become transposable material.[44]

This explains Céline's urge to transpose London, and not the military barracks, to his fiction: the British capital was linked to an event from his past that was as far removed from the concerns of the present as possible. The result was his novel *Guignol's Band*, which he wrote between 1940 and 1944. Moreover, unlike with *Cannon Fodder*, he no longer had to worry about employing a comic tone. The subject was not the military, but its polar opposite: the euphoric city life that had helped him exorcize the demons of the front in 1915 and 1916. In 1940, the year he started writing *Guignol's Band*, the Occupation in France made London even more out of reach, so he felt sufficiently removed from it in terms of both time and place to begin to transpose his experiences to the written page.

Before he could do so, however, Céline had more pressing material matters to attend to. At the outbreak of the so-called 'Phoney War' in September 1939, the nine months prior to Germany's invasion of France in May 1940, he was 45 years old, a war invalid and hence deemed unsuitable for any military role. His double disillusionment with the court case and the outbreak of a war he had always feared was exacerbated by his languishing medical practice: by now, he was increasingly reliant on temporary, sporadic and poorly paid replacement posts, following his ignominious discharge from the Clichy practice in 1936. He therefore took the radical decision, in September 1939, to up sticks from his mother's house in the rue Marsollier (where he and Lucette were now living, in order to save money) to set up a new practice in the quiet and more bourgeois Saint-Germain-en-Laye. Hoping to capitalize on the patriotic mood of the times, he got Lucette and his mother to distribute business cards that emphasized both his medical and military credentials. But to no avail. After one month and not a single patient, Céline decided, with his customary impatience, to abandon the project and move back to rue Marsollier in October.[45]

Fortunately for him, another job opportunity quickly arose, thanks to his artist friend Gen Paul, who had contacts in Paquet, a shipping company based in Marseille. A ship's doctor was needed, Céline's name was put forward, and he duly found himself on board the *Chella*, a transport ship tasked with ferrying troops between Morocco and France. His childhood love of the sea, his taste for adventure and freedom – especially following his recent personal and professional setbacks – as well as the prospect of making money, all lifted his spirits. His letters indicate his pride, euphoria and sheer relief at feeling useful and valued on the open sea, far away from the prying eyes of the public: 'My discipline and adherence to the rules has been noted.'[46] Given his staunch pacifism and anti-militarism, it is ironic that he was soon promoted to the rank of temporary navy officer, third class, because the *Chella* was requisitioned by the navy. Thus, he could later lay claim to having 'signed up' for both world wars. But his main priority was to occupy his time productively, in an atmosphere of freedom and anonymity, away from the spotlight. He duly persuaded the ship's captain to conceal his identity as the novelist Céline, and simply introduce him to the crew as the medical Dr Destouches. This relaxed atmosphere got his creative juices flowing once again, and he secretly worked on a literary manuscript 'La Légende du roi Krogold' ('The Legend of King Krogold'), a medieval legend he had begun in 1933 and abandoned in favour of *Death on Credit*, although he included fragments of it in the novel.

However, this maritime and literary idyll was brutally interrupted by the accidental sinking of his ship by the British vessel *Kingston Cornelian* in the Straits of Gibraltar on 4 January 1940.[47] The seventeen-man crew was rescued by lifeboat, resulting in Céline's eventual repatriation back to Marseille on 23 January, after having tended to some of the wounded. The traumas of military combat of 1914 had been reawakened. Nevertheless,

Céline and ambulance, Sartrouville Exodus, June 1940.

Céline had still enjoyed this assignment, even if he did not seek to renew his contract, which expired on 30 January. Instead, between February and June 1940, he commuted three days a week from his mother's residence in rue Marsollier to a replacement doctor's position he had found in the satellite town of Sartrouville.

But on 22 June 1940, everything changed: France signed an armistice with Germany after the Wehrmacht's rapid and successful invasion. It was a complete and utter rout. As the Germans were about to enter Paris on 10 June, Céline, accompanied by Lucette, who was dressed as a nurse, was ordered by the mayor of Sartrouville to escort by ambulance, as part of a convoy destined for Pressigny-les-Pins in the Loiret, an elderly lady and two newborn children. Their final destination was to be Saint-Jean-d'Angely, near La Rochelle.[48] But the ambulance soon became separated from the convoy, and Céline and Lucette desperately sought sanctuary by crossing the Loire.

However, upon arriving in Orléans on 15 June, they found that both the town and the bridge were being showered by German bombs. The sheer horror, chaos and panic of this episode was to mark, as we shall see, a major turning point in his writing.[49] Henceforth, a new, terrifying type of technological warfare was wreaking havoc on mankind and would continue to do so for the next five years. Both the German blitzkreig and, later, the Allied bombings of Paris were so overwhelming that they presented him with a fresh literary challenge. Just as he had sought to recapture the horror of the trenches in *Journey*, so too he now saw it as his duty to find a new style of narration that would do justice to the emotional turmoil and total saturation of the senses that these bombing raids elicited in those who experienced them. Once again, he made a literary virtue out of a military and political necessity.

Céline eventually completed his mission by dropping off, first, the babies to the Red Cross in the Indre, and second, on 19 June, the elderly lady to safety in La Rochelle. Once he and Lucette reached the refugee camp in Saint-Jean-d'Angely on 21 June, he tended to the sick and wounded for ten days, before leaving for Paris again at the end of the month. Upon his return in mid-July, however, an administrative mix-up meant that his medical post in Sartrouville was discontinued. But he had no regrets. He was pleased to have participated in 'an adventure, which must only repeat itself, I imagine, every three or four centuries'.[50]

Nevertheless, he had to secure new employment. After lobbying, among other officials, Frédéric Empayatz, fellow First World War veteran and the new collaborationist mayor of Bezons, a small town near Sartrouville, he was appointed as the town's new doctor in November, with an annual salary of 36,000 francs. He replaced Dr Hogarth, a Haitian, who was fired according to the new racial laws. But the suggestion that Céline deliberately got him sacked has since been disproven, and he enjoyed a good working relationship with Hogarth's French wife, who was also a doctor.[51] Céline's lobbying of collaborationist officials for professional reasons did not prevent him from being openly critical of collaborationist policy, especially that of the new Vichy government recently installed in the Unoccupied Zone in July 1940.

His profound dissatisfaction prompted him to write his fourth and final polemical pamphlet *A Fine Mess* (*Les Beaux draps*). He castigated Vichy for its new statutes on Jews of 3 October 1940, implemented before the Nazi forces of the Occupied Zone had even demanded any anti-Jewish measures (deportation would come later, in 1942). Jews were disbarred from the army, the judiciary and the arts.[52] But Céline felt that these laws did not go far enough. They would satisfy supporters of Charles Maurras, but not him. He wanted total exclusion of Jews from all professions, including medicine, journalism, universities and literature.[53] Moreover, he mocked Vichy's *révolution nationale*, or desire for a new moral order based on the values of *Travail, Famille, Patrie* ('Work, Family, Homeland'). This new moral order threatened polemical writers such as him, by imposing strict censorship laws on any perceived attack on French moral values. Indeed, it was these very laws that got him into serious trouble for his most pointed criticism: that of the French army. He took exception to Vichy blaming French citizens for the defeat – for Céline, the army alone was at fault, and he made no bones about it.

The pamphlet was published in February 1941 in both the Occupied and Unoccupied Zones, but the Vichy authorities were furious over sentences such as 'It was expensive, the French army, 400 billion to save its own skin, 8 months of playing cards and a one-month rout.'[54] Admiral François Darlan, Vichy's minister of defence, was incandescent. In a letter to Henri Moysset, the minister of information, Darlan ordered the seizure of all works, including *A Fine Mess*, in which the author 'expresses regrettable personal opinions or unjustified criticisms in relation to the army and its commanders'.[55] The details of the implementation of this law and the extent to which the pamphlets were confiscated remain hazy. Céline alleged in a letter to journalist Jean Lestandi in early January 1942 that seventeen copies of his pamphlet were seized in a Toulouse bookshop; philologist Frank-Rutger Hausmann quotes a testimony from Céline, in which he obtained an audience with the Vichy War Ministry, who merely offered him 'some vague explanations' ('quelques explications vasouilleuses') and refused to lift the ban on his pamphlet.[56] As for the Nazis themselves, they appear to have had mixed reactions. Some, such as Céline's loyal supporter, the head of the German Institute, Karl Epting, thought the Vichy ban too draconian. But others, such as linguist Bernhard Payr, who was responsible for French cultural affairs and the suppression of anti-Nazi ideology in the so-called Amt Schrifttum, the Berlin Office headed by Alfred Rosenberg, criticized *A Fine Mess* as a 'hysterical' work, written in an 'unacceptably popular and filthy French . . . abominable gutter French'.[57]

This was not the first time Céline would criticize and anger Vichy and its supporters: he would do so again – albeit after the war – in his novel *Castle to Castle*, in which he brutally satirized Philippe Pétain and Pierre Laval, Vichy's head of government from 18 April 1942 to 20 August 1944. Be that as it may, the pamphlet does contain some valuable aesthetic insights. To counter the 'moral renewal' advocated by Vichy, he proposes a far more liberating 'artistic renewal' that should begin in childhood. In line with his prioritization of emotion in his novels, he advocates a far less rigid and academic school system that fosters and encourages, rather than stifles, the spontaneous creative emotion that he believes is innate to children:

> Childhood is our only salvation [. . .] Without continuous, artistic creation, and by everyone, no lasting society is possible, especially in the present times, when everything around us is mechanical, aggressive, awful [. . .] There needs to be a long and huge effort made by those in charge of the Syllabus to kill the artist in the child. This does not happen alone. Schools operate with this goal in mind, they are the torture chambers of perfect innocence, spontaneous joy, the joy of birds, they manufacture mourning which already seeps out of every wall, primitive social hoodoo, the coating which penetrates everywhere, suffocates, crushes once and for all zest for life.[58]

Instead of having their natural spontaneity and zest for life crushed by 'dry' subjects such as grammar, geometry and physics, children should have it nurtured through participation in the creative arts:

> We need to challenge received ideas, prioritize music, singing in the choir, painting, composition especially, the discovery of personal dances, specific rigadoons, everything that gives flavour to life, perks us up, allows the spirit to blossom, embellishes our sad hours, ensures we have some Happiness, enthusiasm, warmth that is uplifting, in short, that allows us to glide through existence as if on a cloud.[59]

His emphasis on dance as the most emotionally uplifting of the arts is reflected in his desire that children should emerge from school 'all imbued with music and lovely rhythms, uplifting examples, all bewitched by grandeur'.[60] As we shall see, the call in *A Fine Mess* for a liberating artistic renewal that is rooted in spontaneous childhood emotion is reflected in certain episodes of his novel *Guignol's Band*, on which he was working at the same time. The difference, however, is that *A Fine Mess* is *also* racist, while *Guignol's Band* is not.

If Céline's racist views are undeniable, a second moral question needs to be addressed: to what extent did he *collaborate* with the occupying German forces? The complex legal and literary ramifications of the term 'collaboration' and Céline's protracted trial will be examined later. For now, suffice to say that Céline was not considered a 'collabo' in any official capacity, even if he frequently mingled with French collaborators and some prominent Nazis. Two main factors need to be considered. The first pertains to the intellectual climate in general, and the second to Céline specifically. Historian Frederic Spotts has called the French cultural climate under the Occupation the 'shameful peace': an oxymoronic term coined by writer and playwright Jean Cocteau.[61] It designates the insufficiently recognized moral grey area that lies between Résistance and Collaboration, which forces us to re-evaluate the polarizing mentality that was prevalent during the anti-fascist purges (*épuration*) from 1944 onwards. At the height of the purges, people were schematically divided into two categories: the 'good' Résistance 'heroes', who bravely opposed the Nazi oppressor, or the cowardly and 'evil' collabos, who supported or accommodated them. This *résistantialiste* narrative has since been shown to be over-simplistic and historically revisionist. In reality, many French intellectuals were neither members of the Résistance, nor collaborators, but merely pragmatic opportunists who were just trying to survive in uncertain and difficult times. During the early, ambivalent stages of the Occupation, writers such as Gide, Malraux, Roger Martin du Gard and Paul Éluard fled to the Unoccupied Zone, fearing that life under the Germans would be intolerable. Others did so for political or racial reasons, fearing for their safety: Louis Aragon and Elsa Triolet as communists, Julien Benda and Tristan Tzara as Jews. Some held out in Paris until they found life there unbearable and escaped abroad: the sculptor Alberto Giacometti to Switzerland, the playwright Samuel Beckett to Provence and conceptual artist Marcel Duchamp to New York.[62] However, 'the attraction of Paris was too great to resist and most cultural figures returned, however warily, to the capital.'[63] Artists and intellectuals quickly realized that culture was a major element of Nazi occupation policy, and an elaborate infrastructure was set up to implement it. As Spotts aptly summarizes it,

> This was not out of any humanitarian concern for the French. Hitler did not want problems on his western flank and, while France was to be exploited materially and made to behave politically, the population was to be anesthetized by means of a rich cultural life. No newspapers, books, plays, art exhibitions or films that were anti-German or by Jews, Freemasons and (later) communists were allowed. Otherwise – a big otherwise, to be sure – French artists were to enjoy a preferred status, be cultivated, even feted, but largely left to themselves.[64]

The infrastructure in question was primarily the German Institute spearheaded by Karl Epting, who was an inveterate admirer and connoisseur of French culture. Established in the former Polish embassy in the Hotel Sagan by German ambassador Otto Abetz in the autumn of 1940, the institute was under the umbrella of the German Foreign Office. It competed with its fierce rival, the Wehrmacht's Propaganda-Abteilung that was guided by Joseph Goebbels' Propaganda Ministry, to establish a series of cultural events, conferences and functions. These proved highly popular both with French intellectuals and the wider public. Given the absence of a language barrier, music proved to be the most popular means of cultural assimilation: no fewer than 71 classical concerts, usually featuring German composers and orchestras such as the Berlin Philharmonic, were organized and often fully booked between May 1942 and July 1943.[65] Also highly successful were German-language courses and numerous conferences with a pro-Germanic political theme on historical figures such as philosopher Johann Gottfried Herder and eminent pro-Nazi speakers on the vision of the 'new Germany', such as the economist Ferdinand Fried (pseudonym of Ferdinand Zimmermann), author Anton Zischka and the lawyer Carl Schmitt.[66] Even non-fascist French intellectuals could not resist the lure of social functions organized by the institute, although the Left Bank crowd that congregated in the Café Flore, and comprised such figures as Simone de Beauvoir, Jean-Paul Sartre and Albert Camus, kept their distance.[67]

Against this morally ambivalent cultural backdrop, we also need to consider Céline's own highly contrarian, maverick personality – his individualist and anarchist streak – that made him naturally resistant to, and suspicious of, any kind of ideological authority, group identity or conformism. He was his own man, who far preferred to cultivate relations on an individual basis, rather than along party lines. Indeed, he steadfastly refused to join any extreme Right-wing political party or league such as Action française, George Valois' Le Faisceau, Pierre Taittinger's Jeunesses patriotes, François Coty's Solidarité française, Colonel de La Rocque's Croix de feu, nor even the Parti populaire français (P.P.F.), headed by Jacques Doriot.[68] Doriot was keen to recruit him, but Céline turned him down. Despite meeting the man two or three times, Céline writes scathingly of his party's internal politics: 'The man was interesting, but I hated the clique of small-minded political spongers who surrounded him, and the P.P.F. felt the same way about me.'[69] Similarly – and this was to prove crucial in his legal defence after the war – Céline was never paid by the Nazis or any French collaborators for pro-fascist writings or activities. To pro-fascist journals, he submitted around 25 private letters, three interviews, three oral interventions and two answers to surveys during the Occupation: seven in *Au pilori*, six in *Je suis partout*, four each in *La Gerbe* and *L'Appel*, and three in *L'Émancipation nationale*. Their content was invariably antisemitic and racist (though sometimes he criticized the Nazis as well), and Céline would complain that his letters appeared in edited or distorted form. But for none of these was he ever paid.[70] Nor is there any evidence that he supported the extermination of the Jews, either in his pamphlets, or elsewhere. To a survey about the extermination of Jews conducted in *La Gerbe* on 23 October, he responded in very general terms and referred back to his previous pamphlets.[71]

But Céline's maverick personality was a two-way street: if his pragmatic desire for self-preservation and natural aversion to authority led him deliberately to refuse all officially sanctioned forms of collaboration – whether political or economic – he was, in any case, considered far too much of a loose cannon by most of the Nazis themselves. Even those, such as Gerhard Heller, who appreciated 'the power and novelty of Céline's style' ('la puissance et la nouveauté du style de Céline'), and saw him as the equal of Rabelais and Hugo, were wary of using him for propaganda purposes.[72] Assigned to the Schrifttum (literature) section of the Propagandastaffel (propaganda squadron), under the aegis of Joseph Goebbels' Ministry of Propaganda, Heller was primarily responsible for censorship and enlisting the support of French writers for the Nazi vision of a 'New Europe'.[73] In 1981 he fondly recalled two encounters with Céline: one was with actor Robert Le Vigan in a Montmartre café, where Céline gave him some sunglasses (which he later put to good use during a bombing raid on Berlin in February 1945); the other was in Sigmaringen, in February 1945, where a compassionate Céline gave Heller medical advice about his arm injury. But Heller was also 'repulsed' by Céline's hysterical antisemitism and did not invite him on a trip to Germany in October 1941 for fascist French writers. Heller was in close contact with Bernhard Payr in Berlin. Payr, as we have already seen, wrote not only a scathing report on *A Fine Mess* in January 1942, but, at the end of that year, *Phönix oder Asche?* (Phoenix or Ashes?), a work on French literature, in which he questioned both Céline's 'nihilo-pacifism' and his suitability to be involved in the struggle against Judaism and freemasonry.[74] The fact that Céline's staunch defender and friend Karl Epting had, meanwhile, published an article explicitly defending *A Fine*

Mess and regretting its confiscation by Vichy was one of the reasons why he was called back to Berlin between June 1942 and February 1943 and kept 'under observation', before being sent back to Paris.[75]

As to social gatherings organized by the German occupiers – whether at the German embassy, the institute or elsewhere – Céline attended these only occasionally and even then, he was considered not just 'an intellectual catch' but a 'terrible embarrassment'.[76] His slovenly appearance was invariably exacerbated, as Epting's wife Alice recalled, by his tendency to cause a scene. At one German Institute dinner, he shouted across the table, 'Don't you agree, Madame Epting, when I say that if things go on this way, one fine day it will be the Jews who will be dancing on our graves?'[77] According to Lucien Rebatet, at the inauguration of the Institut d'études des questions juives (Institute for the Study of Jewish Questions) on 15 May 1941, Céline interrupted the chairman's interminable speech by saying 'Say, and what about Aryan stupidity? You've got nothing to say about that?' ('Et la connerie aryenne, dis, t'en cause pas?'). Fifty pairs of scandalized eyes turned to the author, who remained in his seat.[78] But the most embarrassing episode of all occurred in February 1944, when Céline was invited to dinner by Ambassador Otto Abetz at the German embassy on Rue de Lille, along with two other fascist intellectuals: writer Pierre Drieu La Rochelle and historian Jacque Benoist-Méchin, who recounted the scene. Abetz, according to author Ernst Jünger, was as enamoured with Céline's literary and intellectual authority as Epting. Working in close collaboration with the Sicherheitsdienst (security service, SD) from late 1940, he had seriously considered Céline as a potential member of the Office central juif, but had been advised against it by Kurt Ihlefeld, a former member of the Propagandastaffel.[79] Abetz's attempts to reassure his French guests that Germany's 'secret weapons' would soon turn the tide of the war back in Germany's favour were forcefully rebuffed by Céline, who banged his fists on the table before launching into an apocalyptic rant about Germany's imminent and catastrophic defeat. If that were not enough, he claimed that Hitler was dead and had been replaced by a doppelgänger. To demonstrate just how easy it was to replace Hitler, he asked his friend Gen Paul, whom he had brought with him, to imitate the Führer, by using tobacco as a fake moustache, combing his hair forward and placing one hand behind his back and the other inside his waistcoat. Céline, much to the relief of the stunned guests, eventually got up, and Abetz, fearing he was mentally deranged, insisted that the security forces escort him home.[80]

Little wonder, then, that most Nazis regarded Céline as a potential liability, rather than an asset, in their propaganda campaign. Even the most reluctant Nazis, such as Ernst Jünger, viewed him with considerable suspicion. A hero of the First World War and later a renowned lepidopterist, Jünger was stationed as an army captain in occupied Paris, where he was given nominal responsibilities for censorship. As a cultured aesthete and bibliophile, much of his time was actually spent frequenting Right Bank bookshops, and calling in on film director Sacha Guitry, the painters Pablo Picasso and Georges Braque, and the playwright Jean Cocteau. His intense dislike of Hitler, to whom he referred as Kniébolo in his wartime diaries, was evident from his 1939 fable *The Marble Cliffs* and his later tacit support of the assassination attempt on the Führer in July 1944.[81] Upon first meeting Céline at the institute in December 1941, the refined Jünger was appalled by his crude and subversive behaviour. Referring with horror to 'the monstrous power of [his] nihilism', he recalled Céline's astonishment that 'we soldiers were not out, hanging, exterminating the Jews. It is astounding that anyone having a bayonet on him does not make full use of it.'[82] Duraffour and Taguieff cite this account as evidence of Céline's support of the Holocaust; but it is more plausible, given his long-standing anti-establishment views, that he was merely trying to provoke and shock the aristocratic Jünger.[83] This was as much a clash of personalities as it was of ideologies. Jünger alleged that Céline told him, when their paths crossed again on 22 April 1943 at the home of Paul Morand, the author and Vichy ambassador to Switzerland and Romania, that he had visited the mass grave of the Polish soldiers killed by the Soviets at Katyn. However, it is well documented that Céline never once went to Katyn. It is thus plausible that Jünger responded to Céline's provocativeness with some subtle character assassination of his own.[84]

However, there were two more active members of the Nazi party who were genuinely fond of Céline and always made time to see him. The first was Hermann Bickler, the head in Paris of the SD, who set up a police antiterrorist unit (Selbstschutzpolizei) made up of French collaborators, and also trained SS and Gestapo agents. Bickler was 'specifically responsible for infiltrating resistance organizations and protecting important collaborators'. Interrogated after the war, he recalled how he would walk with the author in the Bois de Boulogne or have a chat in his office and always 'met him with pleasure and interest', despite Céline's unreserved criticism of Nazi policy in France and of fellow Germans such as Abetz.[85] Céline even invited Bickler to his flat in Montmartre.[86]

The second of Céline's Nazi supporters was Karl Epting. As a fervent admirer of the author's literary style and, unusually for a member of the Nazi party, of his non-conformist personality, he went to great lengths to help him. He praised his novels both in his 1943 work *Frankreich in Widerspruch* (France in Contradiction) and in an article, 'Céline est proche de nous' ('Céline is close to us'), published in early 1942.[87] He would later write a nostalgic and insightful article, 'Il ne nous aimait pas', ('He didn't like us'), published two years after the novelist's death. He perspicaciously summed up Céline's literary contribution thus: 'Céline's cultural critique represents one of the great counterpoints to the development of rationalist, technical and industrial civilization of the 1930s and '40s, providing a more profound and human testimony than the hundreds of sociological analyses to which we have since become accustomed.'[88] Thus it was Epting who granted Céline's requests for paper to help with his writing, when it was in desperately short supply, and Epting who organized a 'medical visit' to Berlin for Céline, his wife and Gen Paul in 1942, as an official cover to allow the author to hand over his gold to Karen Jensen for her to deposit in Denmark on his behalf.[89] Epting even risked his own reputation to defend Céline's *A Fine Mess* in early 1942, much to the displeasure of Bernhard Payr. And Céline's escape to Baden Baden in June 1944, and from there to Kränzlin, would have been impossible had it not been for the intervention of Epting and his contacts. The friendship with Karl and Alice Epting was to last beyond the war: they came to visit Céline and Lucette in Meudon in early 1961, just a few months before Céline's death in July of that year.[90]

Despite his friendship with Epting, Céline's main support group and source of solace was predominantly French: specifically, his Montmartre circle of artistic friends who were sympathetic towards the fascist cause. With them, he felt safe and relaxed. The regulars at his Montmartre flat in rue Girardon, especially on Sunday mornings, included Gen Paul, author Marcel Aymé, the actors Robert Le Vigan (who was to become a central character in Céline's German trilogy) and Jean Bonvilliers, the artist and engraver Jean-Gabriel Daragnès, the painter Louis Chervin, the playwright René Fauchois, the violinist Jean Noceti, singer Max Revol and Antonio Zuloaga, cultural attaché at the Spanish embassy in Paris.[91] The most politically active of this group was the caricaturist Ralph Soupault, who often contributed to far-Right journals and was a member of Doriot's party, the P.P.F. Owing to his journalistic connections, Céline used him as an informant, but stuck to his policy of not writing anything pro-fascist for money by refusing to write a preface for one of Soupault's illustrated works. Other visitors to his flat included theatre actress Marie Bell and her friend, wealthy American author, socialite and organizer of literary salons, Florence Gould. When not receiving guests in his own flat, Céline would visit not only the Morands, but Josée Laval, a huge admirer of his work, and daughter of Pierre Laval. It was at Josée's that, in 1941, Céline first met another literary admirer, with whom he was to form a lifelong friendship: the actress Arletty, who, like him, hailed from Courbevoie.[92]

The only other French cultural figure during the Occupation who was comparable to Céline for his 'maverick' status was the writer and playwright Jean Cocteau. Both men were *provocateurs*, irreverential and highly individualistic cultural creators, but in completely different ways. Cocteau was openly gay, flamboyant, and loved the high life and hedonism of both the German Institute and the anti-fascist Left Bank café culture of Café Flore. He was something of a social butterfly, who moved seamlessly between opposing camps, without ever explicitly endorsing either. The staunchly heterosexual Céline, on the other hand, was more of a misfit: unkempt, generally antisocial, apart from a close-knit group of friends, and, as we have seen, someone who shunned most official gatherings organized by the Germans, even if his sympathies were clearly fascist. Cocteau was just as friendly with Jünger and Heller – whom he admired for their knowledge of French culture – as he was with Picasso, with whom he shared Left Bank friends.[93] He adopted the detached stance of the dandyish aesthete who rises above politics, in the sole pursuit of art. This, unsurprisingly, angered both anti-fascists and fascists, who regarded his frivolity as morally irresponsible in the context of war and occupation. Surrealist poet and anti-fascist Paul Éluard wrote a furious letter to Cocteau, criticizing his support of an exhibition by Nazi sculptor Arnold Breker (who was also friendly with Céline and made a bust of him) in May 1942.[94] By the same token, in the fascist journal *Je suis partout*, theatre critic Alain Laubreaux, who had already lambasted Cocteau's play *Les Parents terribles* for being too 'Jewish' in 1938, launched an even more virulent attack on his play *La Machine à écrire* (The Typewriter) in 1941.[95] So vicious was the attack that the play was closed by the police. Céline, who had met Cocteau shortly before at a reception given by the Groupe Collaboration, and no doubt recalling his own hurt at being criticized for *Death on Credit*, felt sufficiently moved to defend a fellow artist, and offered to mediate by meeting Laubreaux. He took, as Vitoux puts it, the 'side of the creator against the critic' ('côté du créateur contre la critique').[96] But not for long. Upon discovering that, before the war, Cocteau had expressed support for the head of the International League against Anti-Semitism, he sent him a harsh letter withdrawing his offer to help: 'To me, Race as a Rationale supersedes the Rationale of Art or the Rationale of Friendship. Are you, my dear Cocteau, anti-Semitic? That is the crux of the matter. If you are, then for God's sake shout it from the rooftops and everyone will know.'[97]

This is one of those instances in which Céline prioritized race over art, specifically in order to clarify his moral position. What he could not abide was Cocteau's *amoral* attitude: the playwright wanted to have his cake and eat it. His non-committal, frivolous aestheticism made his stance on racial politics unclear. To Céline, this was a cardinal sin, because he prided himself on being completely unambiguous about where he stood. His views may have been abhorrent, but he was not afraid to express them, even when they contradicted official Nazi policy implemented by friends such as Karl Epting.

An example of this, in a letter to his friend Henri Poulain in June 1943, is his vocal denunciation of German cultural policy, which he saw as too bourgeois and decadent. Surely, now that the Nazis were beginning to lose the war, what was needed between France and Germany was *military* and not cultural rapprochement, in order to make up for the 'shortage of fighting soldiers' ('pénurie de soldats combattants'). In any case, culture was a lost cause because it was the exclusive domain of a dying and indolent bourgeoisie, and excluded the common man. The French bourgeoisie has been courted by the Germans: 'German diplomacy has given it a veneer of importance' ('La diplomatie allemande lui a donné un semblant d'importance'), even though it has become as 'politically insignificant' ('politiquement insignifiante') as the nobility. Thus he mocks 'the Franco-German rapprochement via the salons and the Deux magots' ('Le rapprochement franco-allemand par les salons et les Deux magots!') and 'under the guise of Parisian Life' ('sous le signe de la Vie Parisienne'). No doubt, he had Cocteau's own extravagant bourgeois dilettantism in mind when he wrote these lines. Cultured aesthetes such as Cocteau were certainly not about to strengthen the ranks of the military by providing officers:

> A privileged class has no utility, meaning, or life when it is no longer capable of supplying officers to the army. That's the one and only

> criterion. [. . .] The moment it is no longer able to fulfil this role, where it no longer produces children or officers – it is only parasitical and hence disastrous.[98]

In the end, Céline's position was deeply paradoxical, in accordance with his wilfully anarchic streak. He supported Aryan racial theory, but frequently criticized Nazi policy; he was friendly with a handful of Nazi officials, but he alienated many others. Even more astonishing – and casting further doubt on the *résistantialiste* narrative – is that he maintained a cordial, even friendly, bond with his neighbour and member of the Résistance, Robert de Champfleury. Champfleury and his wife Simone lived in the fourth-floor flat, directly below Céline and Lucette. Céline and Champfleury were at opposite ends of the political spectrum and, by all accounts, should have been sworn enemies. And yet in an article of March 1962, the year after Céline's death, Champfleury rushed to his defence, in light of an earlier 1958 article attacking Céline, published by fellow member of the Résistance, the writer Roger Vailland:

> I can well recall that one evening you said to me in all sincerity, 'Don't worry, Champfleury, I pretty much know what you're up to, you and your wife, but you have nothing to fear from me . . . I give you my word . . . and, he even added, if I can help you at all!'
>
> There was such a ring of truth to your statement that I was completely reassured.
>
> Even better, one day, I came to knock on your door, accompanied by a member of the Résistance who had been tortured by the Gestapo. You let me in, you examined my companion's injured hand, and without asking a single question, you bandaged it up in suitable fashion, having guessed entirely correctly how this wound had come about.[99]

This, in a nutshell, encapsulates to an extreme degree Céline's frequent privileging of personal relationships over ideological allegiance: he was friends with Hermann Bickler, who had close links with the very organization – the Gestapo – that was responsible for torturing the man he had just treated.

A return to fiction was a welcome release from this moral minefield. It came in the form of *Guignol's Band*. Originally planned as a three-volume work (it ended up as two), the first volume was published in March 1944. Deeply preoccupied with war and the Occupation, the French public was largely unreceptive. What is more, Céline's exile in June 1944, an increasingly hostile political climate and Denoël's unexpected assassination in December 1945 meant that publication of the second volume was deferred until 1964, three years after Céline's death. But he carried on working on that, as well as on an early draft of the incomplete third volume, right up to his imprisonment in Denmark in December 1945. The novel's frantic pace and occasionally bloated quality no doubt reflect the less-than-ideal writing conditions for a man on the run, whose creative bursts could now only come in fits and starts.

But, these trying conditions aside, we should not underestimate the deliberate change of tone on Céline's part. *Death on Credit* had been a novel about hardship, lack and deprivation: it reflected Céline's parsimonious and strict upbringing in a lower-middle-class Paris that did not share in the spoils of the Belle Époque. Conversely, *Guignol's Band* was a novel of enjoyment, excess and abundance: it shows its narrator Ferdinand's fascination with the wealth and global influence of London as the epicentre of the British Empire, still at the height of its stupendous power and prosperity. Ferdinand watches in awe as a vast profusion of exotic goods from far-off lands is unloaded from the docked ships:

> I'm now talking about jam, really colossal sweetness, forums of jars of Mirabelle plums, surging oceans of oranges, rising up on all sides, overflowing the roofs, fleet-loads from Afghanistan, sweet golden Turkish delights from Istanbul, pure sugar, all in acacia leaves . . . Myrtles from Smyrna and Karachi . . . sloes from Finland . . . Chaos, vales of precious fruits stored behind triple doors, incredible choice of flavours, exquisite sugared Arabian Nights' magic in amphora jars, eternal joys for childhood promised from the depths of the Scriptures, so dense, so eager, that sometimes they crack the wall, they're squeezed in so thick, burst the sheet metal, roll into the street, cascade right into the gutter![100]

In this regard, London symbolizes for Céline the *anti*-Paris – not the oppressive, stingy Paris of his childhood, but the euphoric, plentiful London of his adulthood in 1915 and 1916, when he spent a recuperative year in the capital to escape the horrors of the Great War in 1914.[101] Something of his footloose and fancy-free life of post-war hedonism comes across in the supercharged celebratory atmosphere in which Ferdinand is immersed. His life is like a non-stop merry-go-round that takes in the music halls, vaudeville and brothels of Soho, and the pubs of the Wapping docks. The revelry, singing and dancing of the imperial city have replaced the horrors of the front and the misery of his Paris childhood. The likely autobiographical influences were touched on earlier: the character Sosthène is probably inspired by the mystic inventor Édouard Bénédictus and theatrical performer Sung Ling Soo; Colonel O'Conogham may have been based on the protector of Céline's first wife Suzanne Nebout; and the novel's pimp, Cascade, on Joseph Garcin and another acquaintance, Jean Cive, both of whom had alleged dealings with the louche seedy underworld of London's brothels. Yet the novel's main source material is neither autobiographical, nor historical (even if he did glean some details about London's brothels, music halls and topography from Garcin, Cive and his English translator John Marks): most of it comes from Céline's own, fertile comic imagination. Of all Céline's nine novels, *Guignol's Band* is the one in which he gives the greatest licence to his imagination. As for comedy, this is often celebrated for its own sake and not just used as a weapon of social satire, as in *Death on Credit*. As we saw earlier in the description of the passport office, much of the novel's humour is slapstick – evoking both the worlds of vaudeville and the silent movies of that era. Moreover, the word 'Guignol' recalls the intersecting worlds of comedy and popular culture. It is the name of the puppet who is the French equivalent of Britain's Punch and Judy, and the expression *faire le guignol*, meaning to 'act the goat', summarizes the often farcical scrapes Ferdinand gets himself into (for instance, his and Sosthène's ridiculous attempts to build a gas mask or the lengths to which he goes to evade the clutches of Police Inspector Matthews, who suspects him of the murder of the moneylender Titus Van Claben). 'Grand Guignol' was also both the name of a famous theatre opened in Pigalle in 1897 and a horror genre which can be traced back to plays from the Shakespearean and Jacobean eras, such as *Titus Andronicus*. Finally, the very title *Guignol's Band* has a knowing tongue-in-cheek quality (it shares the same initials as Great Britain, where the novel is set), and the word 'band' bears a resemblance to the French word *bande*, meaning 'gang' or 'group', thereby suggesting the festive spirit of communal solidarity that characterizes the story. Indeed, the first-person narrator Ferdinand is not as central to the action as he is in *Journey* and *Death on Credit*; more often than not, he is a bit player in an ensemble cast of characters, all of whom carry equal weight. This communal atmosphere speaks to the novel's homage to the shared experience of popular culture. Readers are frequently made to feel that they have a privileged ringside seat at a 'live' performance.

Both the prologue and opening chapter knowingly prepare the reader for entry into this dreamlike fictional universe, which, as we shall see, owes a great deal to Shakespeare. They serve a transitional function of transporting the reader from the harsh, political reality and material conditions of the present – expressed in the polemical, highly personal pamphleteering style to which Céline's readers had, by now, become accustomed – to the imaginative and blissfully depoliticized universe of Ferdinand, the first-person narrator. If 1936–41 had marked Céline's shift from the novel to the pamphlet, the prologue signalled his return to the novel.

The prologue immediately adopts a pre-emptive, defensive tone, in which Céline laments the hardship of war, including the difficulties of printing the book in its complete form. He thus urges the reader not to judge him too soon:

> Readers, friends, less than friends, enemies, Critics! Here I am at it again with Book 1 of Guignol! Don't judge me too soon! [. . .] It had to be printed fast because with things as they are you don't know who's living or dead! Denoël? You? Me? . . . I was off for 1,200 pages! Just imagine![102]

He includes an ironic dialogue with his publisher Robert Denoël, whose scepticism about the violent content of Céline's book he dismisses by highlighting the frequent presence of violence in Shakespeare: '"All I see in your book is brawling! It's not even a book! We're heading straight for disaster! Neither head nor tail!" I could bring him *King Lear* so he could see massacres.'[103]

Céline further legitimizes his new novel both by stressing that his literary talents are inherited from his grandfather and by comparing his own bold literary innovations to similarly radical stylistic evolutions in music and painting. He compares his much-maligned style – especially his use of the 'three dots' and his 'telegraphic' sentences – to the spontaneous art forms of jazz and impressionist painting that broke free of the strictures of their more conservative predecessors:

> Jazz knocked out the waltz, impressionism killed 'fauxjour', you'll write in 'telegraphic' or you won't write at all

Excitement's everything in life!
Got to know how to use it!
Excitement's everything in life!
When you're dead it's over![104]

The prologue highlights a combination of high-brow literary tradition – Shakespeare – and more popular modern art forms – jazz – as major influences on his novel. It also foreshadows the status of his novel as a nostalgic, self-contained, aesthetic world located in the past (London in 1915–16) that offers an escape from the horrors of the present (the occupied France of 1940–44). But before entering this different world, the reader must first be reminded of the horrors from which he or she is about to escape.

The opening chapter begins with a violently powerful description of the bombing of the bridge of Orléans in June 1940. This, of course, was based on his actual witnessing of the bombing of Orléans while driving the ambulance from Sartrouville. Strict historical objectivity takes a back seat to his highly subjective, and almost-hallucinatory, account of an aerial bombardment whose apocalyptic proportions act as a symbolic warning of the lengthy war that is to follow. The bombing of the bridge of Orléans was Céline's first literary transposition of warfare since depicting the horror of the trenches in *Journey*. Certain images and stylistic tropes remain the same in the two novels, such as the comparison of humans to insects to designate their insignificance when confronted with violence: 'We're going to die mashed up! . . . Like bedbugs!' is reminiscent of the bedbugs in the trenches.[105] Then there is once again the notion of death as the great equalizer, which is no respecter of hierarchies: 'Other airmen trying to finish us up! . . . They don't give a damn, men, cattle or things!'[106] There is the implicit satire of military heroism and patriotic rhetoric that was so prevalent in the description of the shelling of the colonel in *Journey*: 'You can see a colonel, of Zouaves I think, floundering in the cataract . . . He succumbs beneath the weight of the corpses! . . . Topples down to the bottom! . . . "Vive la France!" he finally cries . . . vanquished beneath the pile of bodies! . . .'[107]

But the stylistic differences between the two novels outnumber the similarities, specifically in his greater use of hyperbole, onomatopoeia, ellipses (his famous three dots) and metonymy, not to mention metaphors taken from the lexical fields of dance and religion. Hyperbole – his favoured rhetorical trope in a novel that is about excess – emphasizes man's powerlessness in the face of military technology, a theme that picks up on Céline's growing dismay at the dehumanization of man by machine, which was epitomized by the downfall of Courtial de Pereires in *Death on Credit*: 'The two hundred eighteen thousand trucks, tanks and handcarts massed and melted in the horror, straddling one another to get by first, arse over heels, the bridge crumbling, are tangled up, ripping each other, squashing wildly . . .'[108]

If hyperbole captures the destructiveness of aerial bombardment, then the personification of weapons and armoury as creatures that are at once half-human and half-animal suggests a blurring of boundaries between the biological and technological realms. The increasing encroachment of the mechanized world upon the human sphere that he lamented in *A Fine Mess* is given extreme prominence in the description of one of the airmen as 'the rubber man' ('l'homme caouthouc').[109]

Onomatopoeia, which was used sparingly in *Journey* (for instance, to describe the 'glugging' of the colonel's neck wound or the abortion on Bardamu's patient) is now given much greater prominence, to emphasize how the rapidity and intensity of this military arsenal short-circuits all rational understanding, being filtered only through the senses: 'Rraap! . . . Whah! . . . Rraango! . . . Whah! . . . Rrong! . . That's about the real noise made by a real molten torpedo . . . the most enormous!'[110]

Technology's tyrannical hold over man is shockingly depicted in the death of a young child, as his hapless father watches on: 'A baby all naked surges up on the hood of a flaming truck. He's roasted, done to a turn . . . "Good God! . . . Good God! . . . Shit! It's not right" . . . It's the father in a sweat . . . Those are his very words . . .'[111] Synecdoche further emphasizes this dehumanization, especially in its depiction of dismembered body parts: 'Arms everywhere all mixed up . . . smashed, melted into jitters!'; or 'His leg hanging out in shreds'.[112] The lexical fields of religion and dance further enrich the passage. The description of the pilots as 'Death's acrobats' is indicative of the novel's overall apocalyptic tone: not only has its author correctly predicted the war, but the worst is yet to come.

However, this intolerable and hellish experience in the present paves the way for the reader's complete and sudden immersion into a nostalgic and poetic past. The narrator desperately steers his ambulance and dog away from the bombardment towards the shelter of poplars and warehouses. This does not just evoke a geographical landmark, but a symbolic one: the warehouses of the Thames docks and the area of 'Poplar' that constitutes the urban landscape in which Ferdinand circulates in London:

> Me, the little terrier and the cart bore towards the left . . . in another volley of grenades . . . towards the poplars . . . the Warehouse . . . at a good height and full of drive . . . I saw higher than the clouds . . . and bleeding drop by drop . . . a pale white hand and all about clouds of birds . . . all red . . . flitting about sprung from the wounds . . . the fingers all studded with stars . . . strewn on the margins of space . . . in long gentle veils . . . light and graceful . . . lulling the Worlds . . . and grazing you . . . and your pretty eyes . . . caressingly . . .[113]

The narrator's panicky and frenzied account of this military and technological apocalypse gradually recedes into the background, giving way to a more soothing, ethereal, almost-dreamlike realm of calm introspection and contemplation. And this surreal atmosphere – this *féerie* – immediately transports us into a literary, aesthetic world that owes a significant debt to Shakespeare.

Two of Shakespeare's plays dominate *Guignol's Band*: *Macbeth* and *The Tempest*. The first serves as an ironic counterpoint to the murder of Van Claben. In the fantasy world of Delphine, the mad schoolteacher, who recites *Macbeth* in the concluding Zeppelin attack of the novel, she is Lady Macbeth, Van Claben is the murdered king Duncan, the narrator Ferdinand becomes Macbeth, and Borokrom becomes the ghost Banquo, who represents his guilt.[114] As for *The Tempest*, Céline's favourite literary work, its influence hovers over his novel even more strongly. Prospero Jim, the landlord of the Dingby Cruise and The Moor and Cheese pubs, recalls Prospero, the Duke of Milan, who has been exiled on a magic island through the treachery of his brother Antonio. Just as Prospero is an exile who discovers magic to dominate the spirits of the island (notably the beast Caliban), the landlord is an Italian exile living in London, who dominates his clientele through his well-kept secret of 'sailor's vitriol'.[115] More generally, the enchanted setting of *The Tempest* is reproduced in the dreamlike atmosphere of the novel, in which the 'leprechauns' of the streets of London 'play the same role as the elves and spirits of Shakespearean comedy'.[116] Finally, Prospero's demonstration of his magical powers, shown through two magically contrived storms at both the beginning and end of his exile, is echoed by the initial bombing of the bridge of Orléans and the Zeppelin raid at the end of the novel.[117]

But in *London Bridge* (*Guignol's Band II*), there is another Shakespearean character whom critics have overlooked: the mischievous figure of Ten-Paw ('Mille-Pattes'), who recalls Puck, or Robin

Goodfellow, the spirit of mischief, in *A Midsummer Night's Dream*, described in Act II as 'that shrewd and knavish sprite . . . That frights the maidens of the villagery . . . Mislead[s] night wanderers, laughing at their harm' (II.i.33, 35, 39).[118] Puck's endless capacity for mischief is summarized by the fact that things please him best 'that befall preposterously'. Like Ten-Paw, Puck is most active at night. In his penultimate chant he says,

> Now it is the time of night
> That graves all gaping wide
> Everyone lets forth his sprite
> In the church-way paths to glide.
> And we fairies, that do run
> By the triple Hecat's team
> From the presence of the sun
> Following darkness like a dream
> Now are frolic.

As critic Harold Bloom noted,

> Everything problematic about Puck is summed up there; a domestic, workaday spirit, yet always uncannily *between*, between men and women, faeries and humans, nobles and mechanicals, nature and art, space and time. Puck is a spirit cheerfully amoral, free because never in love and always more amused even than amusing. The triple Hecat – heavenly moon maiden, earthly Artemis, and ruler of Hades – is more especially Puck's deity than she is the goddess worshipped by the other faeries.[119]

This description could equally apply to Ten-Paw: he causes mischief and discord between Ferdinand and Virginie; he is always laughing, teasing and playing to the crowd; and he eventually disappears into a cemetery (the realm of Hades) at night, accompanied by a gravedigger.

Critics have generally highlighted Ten-Paw's role as a projection of Ferdinand's guilt for his involvement in the death of Van Claben.[120] He unexpectedly returns from the dead after Ferdinand has pushed him onto a Tube line, suspecting him of spying on behalf of Cascade. But he also possesses life-affirming and aesthetic qualities. Despite his shape-shifting, elusive and 'trickster' behaviour, his constant teasing of

Ferdinand, who becomes jealous when he dazzles his fourteen-year-old love interest Virginie with his performances, it is Ten-Paw who ushers the young couple from the expensive restaurant into the jazz club, the Tweet-Tweet. Artistic modernity and tradition push each other to ever greater heights when Ten-Paw seeks to compete with the black jazz musicians. The rhythm and music generated by the jazz musicians compete for the audience's attention with Ten-Paw's spritelike, dazzling movements as he floats around the room above them:

> From the big bass drum, a blast that sends the whole mob, the joyful swarm flying up into the air . . . with each whack they leap three feet off the floor . . . the whole scene a riot of black and bright . . . satin, dresses, sequins . . . and the way everybody's hopping, hooting . . . it's seething down here, people dancing in threesomes, tensomes, twenty-somes! [. . .] And Tweet-tweet everybody sings in chorus, hollering out the words! Ten Paw can really let it rip! Nobody's bothering him! [. . .] he's putting on his act, amazing his audience! He wants to outshine the Negro! [. . .] they're wowed by Ten-Paw, all hot watching him . . . true, he's out of this world, fluttering everywhere at once . . . lighter than air, totally weightless . . . floating, a bundle of rags above the audience . . . a genuine freak, a literal flake hovering in the air, drifting, swaying however he likes . . .[121]

Traditional Shakespearean theatre – symbolized by the ethereal Ten-Paw – vies for artistic supremacy with the new art form – the hypnotic rhythm of jazz – to create a supercharged atmosphere of emotionally spontaneous artistic freedom. If this scene ultimately degenerates into an orgy, in which Virginie is raped by various musicians and revellers and then impregnated by Ferdinand, this perhaps reflects Céline's conflicted state of mind at this time: the short-lived euphoria of aesthetic escapism is able to keep the harshness of reality at bay only for so long. By the same token, however, this episode also shows Céline's desire to push back aesthetic boundaries. His symbolic juxtaposition of Shakespeare and jazz overturns the entrenched hierarchies that exist between tradition and modernity, 'high-' and 'low-brow' culture, underscoring his preference for popular over elitist art forms. Above all, he pays homage to Shakespeare as the 'people's playwright', a reminder that his plays cater not just to a cultured elite, but to the common man. Moreover, Céline's depiction of aesthetic escapism fulfils the bold experimental mandate of his prologue – where jazz is presented as radically innovative, just as impressionism had been in the previous century. The 'Tweet-Tweet' Club thus exemplifies the spontaneous creativity he had valorized in *A Fine Mess*: his desire to shatter the rigid, academic mould he attributes to the French school system – a system that is exacerbated by Vichy's moral conservatism and stifles the natural artistic creativity of children. As for Virginie's delirious enjoyment of Ten-Paw's performances ('"*Isn't he wonderful*" she asks, fascinated as well . . .'), as well as those of the jazz musicians, this also recalls the pamphlet's mutual valorization of childhood and artistic creativity.[122]

As the tide began to turn against Germany, aesthetic escapism – whether acquired through his own writing or the performances of others – became ever more important to Céline. Music, singing and dancing offered both a refuge and a liberation from an increasingly intolerable reality. On 15 April 1943, for instance, he wrote to congratulate his friend, the theatre actress Marie Bell, for her performance in a Cocteau play: 'There should be more music [. . .] Everything should join together – voice and music never forget that man *sang* before he spoke. Singing is natural, speech is *learnt*. The sources of poetry are in song, not chatting.'[123]

But art also provided respite from disappointments of a more personal nature, such as his daughter Colette's decision to marry Yves Turpin on 10 June 1942, upon discovering that she was pregnant. Céline, who had continued to see Colette on a regular basis, was so distraught that he refused to attend the wedding, or the birth of his grandchild in August. He would not see Colette again until his return from exile in 1951. His hopes of a glorious medical career for his beloved daughter were now dashed. Even his own marriage to Lucette on 23 February 1943 was prompted mainly by his fears about the future and his desire to give her a minimum of legal and financial security. She was not bothered about getting married, but he insisted on it. The only two witnesses were Gen Paul and an employee of the Mairie of the 18th arrondissement.[124] Artistic distractions aside, a welcome bonus was the acquisition by Céline and Lucette of their beloved cat Bébert, at the end of 1942. Originally owned by their actor friend Robert Le Vigan and his recently estranged wife, they were only too happy to take the cat in. He was to become both their loyal and cherished companion and a central protagonist in the German trilogy.

By the spring of 1944, the net was closing in around Céline. On the one hand, *Guignol's Band* came out in late March to relatively few, but largely favourable, reviews, from the Right-wing press. Aside from René Gerin, who accused Céline of being an epileptic afflicted by delirium tremens, who was dismissive of his readers, the critic Roger de Lafforest lavished praise on his creation of a 'new language which is exactly in tune with the soul' ('langue nouvelle qui est l'expression exacte du pouls de l'âme'). Céline was ecstatic. The academic Claude Janet produced the first comprehensive and positive study of Céline's opus in his book *Préliminaires à l'esthétique de L.-F. Céline*.[125]

On the other hand, as the Nazis were now facing defeat, Céline genuinely began to fear for his safety as a fascist sympathizer. Since 1942, he had already been denounced by BBC radio and begun to receive ever more frequent and threatening letters. As he later recalled in an early draft of *Fable for Another Time*, he even had three small coffins delivered to his flat.[126] In the months preceding his exile, he began to be followed in the streets of Montmartre, and strangers would loiter in front of his home. The last time his mother came to visit him, he was too scared to accompany her back to the metro, preferring to let Lucette do so instead.[127] But what he found most upsetting was the sudden distancing of even close friends, who increasingly feared being compromised because they frequented him, especially the painter Gen Paul. This led to a furious confrontation in the avenue Junot in Montmartre, witnessed by passers-by, in which Céline hurled insults at the painter.[128] Gen Paul attempted to make amends by rushing to Céline's flat on the day of his departure from Paris, but it was too little, too late. They would never meet again. Even so, more loyal friends and acquaintances offered Céline and Lucette potential getaways, even his neighbour from the Résistance Robert Champfleury. Champfleury offered Brittany, his painter friend Ignacio Zuloaga the Basque region in Spain. In the end, however, Céline opted for Denmark, since he had deposited savings there in the form of gold, and was offered refuge by his loyal friend, the dancer Karen Marie Jensen. The political and military situation dictated that Denmark could only be reached via Germany, with the approval of the Nazi authorities. The catalyst for his departure, together with Lucette and Bébert, was the Allied Normandy landings of June 1944. The end was nigh. On 8 June, with Epting's help (who asked Doctor Knapp, the medical attaché at the German embassy), he obtained German passports.[129] Lucette's dancing colleague Serge Perrault had a brother in the Préfecture de police, who had helped them secure false French identity papers back in February.[130] Céline posed as Louis-François Deletang, a French-Canadian commercial

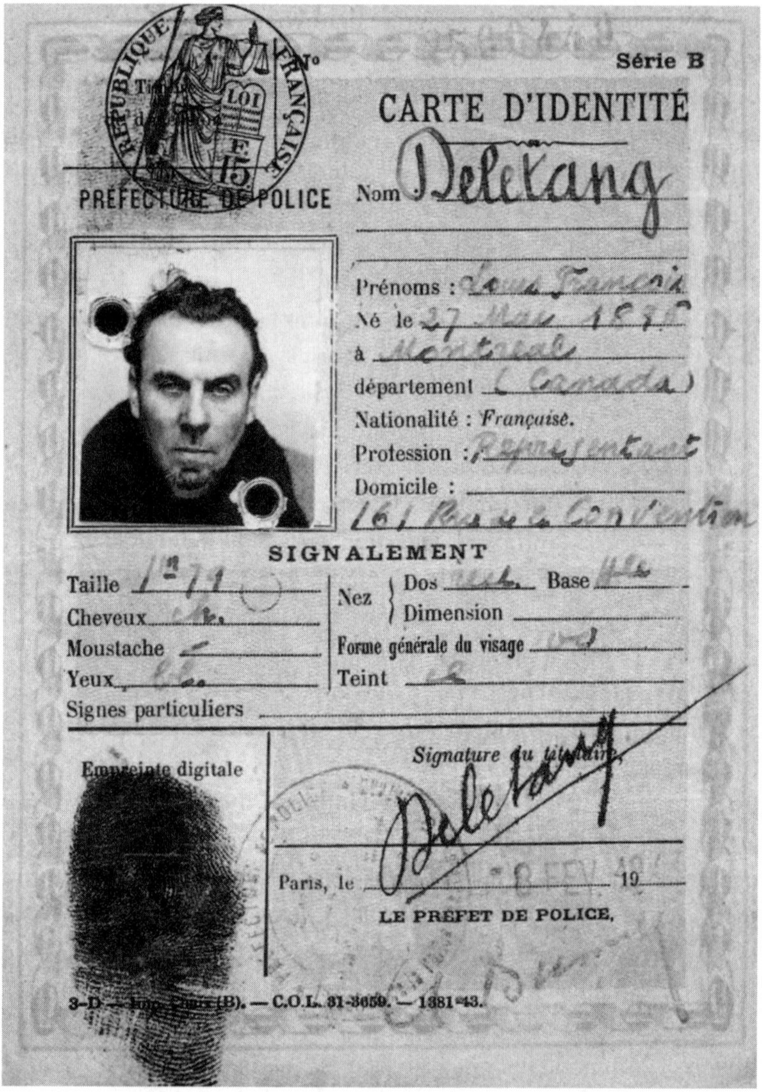

Photo for Céline's fake identity card, with which he fled France in June 1944.

traveller, born in Montreal on 27 May 1896; Lucette was Lucile Alcante, a physical education instructor (*professeur de culture physique*), born in Pondicherry on 20 June 1914.[131]

The fateful day of departure was 17 June. For security reasons, only Céline's mother and Karen Marie Jensen were informed.[132] Even Lucette's mother was kept in the dark. Céline withdrew all his remaining assets in France – principally, gold pieces he had kept in a safety deposit box at the Crédit Lyonnais, which Lucette had sewn into her garments. No doubt hoping that they would be able to return in a few months, baggage was kept to a minimum. Lucette insisted on bringing her silver teapot – which helped perpetuate the illusion of normality as they crossed a war-torn Germany. As for Céline's manuscripts, some he left in Paris – the unfinished manuscripts of *Cannon Fodder* and *The Legend of King Krogold* (*La Légende du roi Krogold*) – and others he brought with him, including one of the two versions he had of the second volume of *Guignol's Band* (the other he entrusted to his ever-loyal secretary Marie Canavaggia).[133]

Following their traumatic and stressful journey, their destination, the elegant spa town of Baden-Baden, just across the Rhine from Strasbourg, was akin to an oasis. In a letter to Karl Epting, Céline says that it is almost too good to be true, despite the occasional reminder of war from aeroplanes up above:

> It has taken us a few days to accept the reality of this enchanting place! To get used to this incredible peace – Selfishly we are enjoying, alas, so many creature comforts, fortunately for the anxiousness of our souls, death and thunder occasionally fly above us! Everything is too beautiful everything is too good.[134]

They were joined in this sanctuary by other French collaborators or fascist sympathizers: their actor friend, Robert Le Vigan; Céline's former lover, the pianist Lucienne Delforges; writer Alphonse de Châteaubriant; Jean Luchaire, president of the Parisian Press Association during the Occupation; and Otto Abetz.[135] In *North*, the second instalment of his three novels known as the 'German trilogy', Céline gave a typically hyperbolic and satirical edge to his letter's guilty and anxious depiction of the Simplon Hotel at Baden-Baden as a self-enclosed island of fascist decadence that remains completely oblivious to the conflict and suffering that rages around it. He depicts a hedonistic world of Vichy collaborators and anti-Hitlerite German aristocrats, who pin their naive hopes of staving off catastrophic German defeat on the plot to assassinate Hitler in July 1944. Céline's starkly contrasting portrayal of the haves and the have-nots of society – a leitmotif that runs through all his novels – is here brilliantly overlaid by political and sexual intrigue. The hotel's luxurious display of opulence masks a veritable nest of vipers made up on the one hand, of the crème de la crème of German society – bankers, industrialists and generals – who are all aware of the plot to get rid of Hitler, and on the other hand, the spying waiters, whose task it is to lift their spirits and loosen their tongues by providing them with an endless supply of fine wines and gourmet cuisine:

> Believe me, those folks wanted for nothing . . . choice food not to mention the plots, conspiracies and timetables . . . you'll say I'm making it up . . . not at all . . . faithful chronicler! . . . of course you had to be there, not everybody's luck . . . the end of the meals, flushed with roasts, heavy secrets, burgundy . . . irresistible menus! . . . delicacies from start to finish, from the hors d'oeuvres to the strawberries and whipped cream . . . melba? . . . syrup? . . . more? . . . less? . . . lemon peel? . . . and all those waiters, so attentive, listening and taking note, hesitations, ja, and sighs . . . the finest flower of the espionage networks.[136]

But political and economic power, as so often with Céline, is merely a respectable front for the simmering human passions and impulses that lie just below the surface. Following the failed assassination attempt, political tensions begin to run so high that the Freudian death – and sex – drives spill out into the public arena and puncture the genteel facade of upper-class propriety.

Upon discovering that the plot has failed, the conspirators' original desire to kill gives way to a primal fear for their own lives and a complete regression to their baser instincts. They all but lose control of their libidos when they see an attractive young French woman, Mademoiselle de Chamarande, wearing a succession of ever more provocative bathing suits at the swimming pool:

> For the last three weeks . . . ever since she arrived . . . our young lady had done her best to drive the swimming pool males up the wall . . . every day a new bathing suit, more and more provocative . . . oh, a magnificent ass, I admit [. . .] enough to turn the pool upside down . . . the customers, I mean . . . barbers, croupiers, bath attendants . . . and the lounge lizards from our hotel . . . convalescent officers . . . yes of course, their nerves shot to hell . . . that attempt on Hitler's life had raised the temperature . . .[137]

Mademoiselle Chamarande, however, has ended up here because she fell in love with a member of the Milice, the French police force that collaborated with the Germans. She has escaped to Baden-Baden as a *tondu* or 'scalp', the term designating women who had German or collaborationist lovers and were sheared, painted with swastikas and chased down the street after the Liberation.[138] Writing with the benefit of hindsight, Céline wanted to show his readers that collaborators could be victims, too.

But at the time, neither he nor Lucette could have known that Baden-Baden was but the deceptively luxurious prelude to what would be the worst period of his life since the trenches of 1914. When they were obliged to leave the quiet town at the end of July 1944, it was probably a blessing in disguise that they had no idea what the next seven years had in store for them.

six

Prison and Exile

At 7.30 p.m. on 17 December 1945, Céline, Lucette and their beloved cat Bébert were startled by an ominous knock at the front door of 20, Ved Stranden, the small Copenhagen flat owned by their dancer friend Karen Marie Jensen. She had let them use it in her absence, shortly after their arrival from Sigmaringen in Germany, on 27 March. Standing behind that door were two Danish policemen. Until that fateful evening, Céline had managed to keep one step ahead of the French and Danish authorities. On 19 April, unbeknownst to him, Judge André Alexis Zousman back in France had issued him with an arrest warrant for treason. He, meanwhile, was already taking precautions: he grew a beard as a disguise, received letters from his faithful secretary Marie Canavaggia under the pseudonym Henri Courtial, and mostly stayed indoors to work on a new ballet, *Foudres et flèches* (Lightning Bolts and Arrows). The couple eked out a living from dance lessons Lucette gave through their choreographer friend Birger Bartholin. Hella Johansen, a friend of Karen's, would also give them money she managed to convert on the black market from the gold they had entrusted to Karen in 1942.[1] At the end of September, an anonymous tip-off alerted the French Foreign Ministry to the author's presence in Copenhagen, but no action was taken. French newspapers furiously speculated as to his whereabouts: Oslo, said *L'Aurore* on 9 October; Sweden via Denmark, countered *Le Figaro* on the 25th.[2]

The net truly began to close when the French wife of a Danish citizen recognized Céline in the street on 10 December. On the 14th, he refused to grant an interview to the correspondent for Agence France-Presse in Copenhagen, who wrote under the name of Samuelson. It was almost certainly Samuelson who alerted the French press to Céline's presence in the capital, since it was revealed in the newspaper *Samedi-soir* the following evening. Lucette and Céline's friend Jytte Seidenfaden, daughter-in-law of Copenhagen's chief of police, Aage Seidenfaden, warned them by telephone to flee to Sweden immediately. But, without passports and believing themselves to be protected, they decided to stay put. On 16 December, a translation of the *Samedi-soir* article made the front page of the Danish daily *Politiken*, citing a 'confidential source'. It said that 'A French Nazi is hiding in Copenhagen. It is the writer Céline who fled with the Vichy government.'[3] That same evening, the Danish police were probably given Céline's address by his local newsagent. Recognizing the novelist as a major scalp, the ambitious forty-year-old French ambassador to Denmark, Girard de Charbonnières, who would become a thorn in Céline's side, wasted no time in ringing Gustav Rasmussen, the Danish foreign minister, on the afternoon of 17 December. Rasmussen then urged his minister of justice, Aage Elmquist, to arrest the writer without delay.[4] Céline's world was about to collapse.

Lucette later recalled how, after peering through the keyhole, she and Céline initially refused to let the plain-clothed policemen in, believing them to be assassins. The two men knocked again, this time more loudly. Panic-stricken, the couple considered fleeing via the skylight through which Bébert had already escaped. But the older and less agile Céline could not squeeze through. Lucette then rang Birger Bartholin for advice. They eventually agreed to let the men in. According to the Danish police report, the couple were profoundly shaken and terrified by their arrest, and a Mauser gun with two bullets was found on Céline's bedside table. Lucette admitted that, although they never would have used the gun against the police, they briefly contemplated turning it on themselves in a moment of panic. They were searched on the spot, and Céline's papers and money (3,765 Danish crowns) were confiscated. They were then whisked away for interrogation in a prison van, after which Céline was locked in a men's prison cell, and Lucette in the women's section. She was released after eleven days and went to live with a friend of Karen Jensen; he was to spend the next fourteen months in Vestre Faengsel prison.

In his novel *Castle to Castle*, this terrifying sequence of events is slightly exaggerated, for dramatic effect, as a desperate bid for freedom across the rooftops: 'from roof to roof! hunted beasts ['bêtes traquées'] do wonders to escape the butchers!'[5] The visceral force of the verb *traquer* in the original French ('hunted') is similarly exploited in many of Céline's letters from 1945 onwards to convey the dehumanization he feels at being pursued relentlessly like a wounded animal. When he is taken away in a heavily guarded prison van, people look on apprehensively: 'Guarded by a dozen tommy guns . . . what a show! . . . the passers-by weave and waver, cling to the shopfronts . . . for fear this might happen to them . . . their consciences quake! scared shitless!'[6] The vertical Ls of the original French version below visually recall the bars of the prison van (my emphasis), thereby reinforcing his feeling of entrapment. Since they also belong to the word *trouille*, a colloquialism for 'fear', these same vertical consonants emphasize just how scared he, as well as the onlookers, feels: 'Sous garde de douze *mitraillettes*! . . . jugez! l'effet! Les passants flanchent, *oscillent*, se racrochent aux devantures . . . que ca pourrait leur arriver! . . . leurs consciences *flageolent*! *Trouille*! *mille fois trouille*!'[7] If Céline's arrest both traumatized him and completely caught him off guard, he was already well aware of the *épuration*: the purge of fascist collaborators. He therefore decided to appoint a lawyer, Thorvald Mikkelsen, in May 1945, through their mutual photographer friend Anne-Marie Lindequist. The sixty-year-old Mikkelsen was a tall, charismatic and fluent French-speaker, whose late wife was from France. Despite his connections to the Danish Resistance, the cultured Francophile was both drawn to the idea of defending a persecuted writer and shocked at how far the *épuration* had gone.[8] In his first known letter to Mikkelsen in May 1945, Céline consciously pandered to his lawyer's literary sensibilities by placing himself in a distinguished line of persecuted and exiled French writers:

> How numerous are those French writers who at one time or another have had to flee their Homeland! . . . *Almost all of them were exiled* . . . From *Villon* to *Verlaine*, *Daudet*, not forgetting *Zola*, *Chateaubriand*, *Lamartine*, *Chénier*, guillotined alas . . . Of course, it is no secret that persecution is almost the norm in the History of our literature and exile . . .[9]

Critics and biographers agree that Mikkelsen's vigorous legal interventions during Céline's first nine months in Denmark probably saved his life, as did, ironically, his fourteen-month spell in prison, which prevented him from being extradited back to France.[10] The will for a thorough *épuration* evaporated rapidly in France after a few months of rage. He was thus spared the fate of many collabos who were executed, such as author Robert Brasillach (6 February 1945), Vichy minister Joseph Darnand (10 October), Jean Hérold-Pacquis (11 October) and Pierre Laval (15 October). In a letter to Marie Canavaggia, Céline's first so-called 'Mémoire en défense', he builds an impassioned case that he would repeatedly use in his letters to lawyers and judges: his steadfast refusal to collaborate, which was proof of his sincerity and independence. He also adopts the pose of the persecuted writer and scapegoat that typifies many of his post-1945 letters and fiction:

> Naturally I was the most targeted person in Sigmaringen, if I had been found there. I would have once again been the scapegoat. But neither in Germany nor in France did I ever have a job, a role or the semblance of a role that was political. I was free, neither the employee nor supporter of anything or anyone – That is what that completely salaried <sell-out> arsehole never wanted to admit nor anyone else – hence their outrage [. . .] I shouted it from the rooftops – the Franco-German history from 1940 onwards seemed to me to be carried out and implemented in the most ridiculous way [. . .] and could only end in disaster [. . .] Had I been more of a coward, I would have fled to Spain from [19]40 onwards since I was free of all engagements or making money [. . .][11]

He emphasizes the hostility of a Nazi regime that viewed him with considerable suspicion: 'Abetz hated me. All my books are banned in Germany since Hitler. I was considered there to be an intolerable anarchist. Had Germany won the war, the Gestapo would have got rid of me.'[12] And he pulls no punches when it comes to Hérold-Pacquis, who 'always hated me and was extremely jealous', and is 'still talking nonsense even though he's dead'.[13] He refutes his accusations of defeatism, by emphasizing his heroic role as doctor in Sigmaringen, while Hérold-Pacquis himself was hypocritically living elsewhere and leading a decadent lifestyle:

> In Sigmaringen, I practised medicine in conditions that I consider to be quite heroic – there are a thousand witnesses [. . .] In any case, he wasn't there, he was on Lake Constance getting drunk and playing cards. It's the gossip of a microphone obsessive, who is furious to have lost after twenty attempts to save his skin.[14]

If he shed no tears over Hérold-Pacquis' death, he was very shaken by that of his former publisher Robert Denoël on 2 December 1945.[15] Even though Denoël was assassinated rather than executed (most likely by the Résistance), their friendship and his intimate connection to Céline's writings meant that this news hit him hard.

Still, he was relieved to be granted a residence permit in Denmark, thanks to a letter Mikkelsen sent to the Danish chief of police on 1 June 1945, which was followed by an interview on 20 June. The letter emphasized Céline's towering literary stature as the author of *Journey*, his lack of collaboration or political involvement and the fact that he was not considered a war criminal. He was unpopular in France only because of his pamphlets, which were banned both there and in Germany. Their antisemitism was mitigated by their pacifist intentions. Finally, his client's fragile health and Denmark's strong liberal traditions made it the government's duty to let him stay in the country.[16]

Even allowing for his tendency towards self-pity, Céline's situation unquestionably deteriorated once he was in prison. To begin with, there was a noticeable drop in Mikkelsen's efforts on his behalf. This stemmed, in part, from the lawyer's three-month trip to New York in late 1945 and early 1946. A terribly distraught Céline only gently admonished Mikkelsen, knowing full well that he could not afford to alienate his most important ally: 'Our only hope was your return! But I am completely to blame. I must have been hovering around you like a ghost during your whole journey! You who were hoping to have a nice relaxing time free from worries!'[17] In fairness to Mikkelsen, he had put his own reputation on the line by defending Céline, incurring the wrath of the Danish Left. But he continued to fight on his behalf. What is more, although it was largely self-inflicted because of his antisemitic pamphlets and fascist sympathies, Céline's incarceration was the worst period of his life. The trenches in 1914 had been truly horrific, but he was at least considered a war hero and had youth on his side. Now, though, he was a 51-year-old social pariah, whose political and literary reputations both lay in ruins. He was also racked with guilt about Lucette, and thus tried to shield her from his pain by confiding instead in Mikkelsen. Her visits were limited to Monday afternoons, and dialogue was kept to a minimum, since the prison guards demanded that they speak in English. Until he was given his own cell in February 1946, Céline had to share with a Yugoslav called Tito and a Pole named Vitali, who did not get along. To prevent them from coming to blows, he told them the story of the *Three Musketeers* and the *Count of Monte Cristo* by Alexandre Dumas.[18] Worst of all, he experienced severe health problems, which aged him by some twenty years, according to his former friend and patient from Clichy, Éliane Bonabel, one of the rare visitors who was admitted to see him, on 27 January 1946.[19] He suffered from depression, enteritis, constipation, pellagra, eczema, rheumatism, vertigo, headaches and insomnia.[20] His dramatic weight loss required frequent visits to the prison infirmary and hospital, and his symptoms were exacerbated by pre-existing conditions: the dysentery he had contracted in Cameroon in 1917 and his Ménière's disease. He reached a particularly low point on 25 March 1946, when he told Mikkelsen about the humiliating state of his bowels:

> I am quite unable to pass stool of my own accord. I need paraffin, pills, enemas etc. . . . If I was not alone in my cell, I would not know how to hold it in, it is not uncommon for emergencies to force me to go to the 'Toilet' ten or twenty times a day, *which is impossible in prison*. I use the only potty in my cell (despite the regulations).[21]

But just as he had exorcized his depression in his *Cahiers du cuirassier Destouches* in the Rambouillet barracks in 1913, so too he found some salvation through his writing. This spawned his prison diaries, the *Cahiers de prison*, which comprised ten booklets written in pencil, in fragmentary form, between February and October 1946.[22] These diaries provided not only an essential form of catharsis, but a written record of his exile up to that point, which laid the groundwork for a new novel: they allowed him to jot down his tumultuous experiences in writing, before he forgot them. These had begun with the Allied bombings of Paris on 21 and 22 April 1944 – the moment he realized he would have to go into exile – and ended with his incarceration up until late 1946. The literary account of his exile was to centre, albeit not in strict chronological order, on the nine-month odyssey that began in Montmartre on 17 June 1944, taking him, Lucette and Bébert through an apocalyptic war-torn Germany that was staring defeat in the face. It would encompass their stay in Baden-Baden in July and August, a relative idyll that left them ill-prepared for the hardships to come, followed by a brief stopover in Berlin, before proceeding, at the request of their German contact, Dr Hauboldt, the president of the Chamber of Doctors in Berlin, to Kränzlin in Brandenburg in September. By now accompanied by their actor friend Robert Le Vigan, they endured hunger, poor lodgings and a decidedly frosty reception from their hosts. Matters slightly improved in late October, with their transfer to Sigmaringen, the seat of the Vichy government in southern Germany, where Céline spent almost five months treating Vichy collaborators. The German authorities finally allowed him and Lucette to travel to Denmark on 24 March 1945, leaving Le Vigan behind after a falling-out (he was arrested and tried for collaboration in 1946, eventually emigrating to Argentina). The final leg of their journey included the bombing of Céline and Lucette's train by the Allies and the injuries they sustained. Originally planned as just one novel that would be entitled *Féerie* (Fable), it eventually became five: the two volumes of *Féerie pour une autre fois* (Fable for Another Time) (1952 and 1954), which were a critical and commercial failure, followed by the far more successful 'German trilogy' of *D'un château l'autre* (Castle to Castle) (1957), *Nord* (North) (1960) and the posthumously published *Rigodon* (Rigadoon) (1969).

The diaries provided not only catharsis and a plot outline, but the seeds of a new literary style. By scribbling down experiences and events as they came to him, Céline discovered a more spontaneous way of writing – what Godard calls writing 'in its brute state' ('à l'état brut') – that allowed a stream of powerful memories to rise up from deep within his unconscious.[23] Putting pencil to paper in the harsh prison environment brought out irrepressible feelings of pain, longing and nostalgia that he transposed to both volumes of *Fable for Another Time*, thereby infusing his prose with a searing honesty and emotional immediacy. These two novels merit closer attention, as a prelude to an analysis of the trilogy.

The gamble of *Fable for Another Time* was to prioritize style over story. Neither volume had a coherent plot that logically unfolded across readily identifiable time frames or locations. Instead, each one revolved around one key moment and place: Denmark and his 1946 imprisonment in *Fable for Another Time*, and Montmartre and the 1944 Allied bombing of Paris in the second volume, which would subsequently be translated into English as *Normance*.[24] Since prison was not just the subject of his novel, but the place where he started writing it, the *Cahiers de prison* are regarded as the very first, rough draft of *Féerie*. Imprisonment and the bombings generate a productive tension: they are both painful emotional memories – moments of intense suffering that he wants his sceptical reader to acknowledge – and the catalysts for his stylistic creativity. Céline channels this productive tension into two nineteenth-century cultural tropes. The first is the Romantic notion of the literary martyr: the writer is a persecuted, misunderstood genius – one of the many authors he listed in his letter to Mikkelsen – who suffers for his art, despite a society that rejects him. Céline had already applied this trope to a scientist, in his medical thesis on Ignace Philippe Semmelweis, the Hungarian doctor who discovered the cause of puerperal fever. Vilified by both his peers and society at the time, Semmelweis died in abject circumstances, only posthumously to be vindicated. The second cultural trope is that of the writer as alchemist. This draws on the medieval belief that base metal can be turned into gold, a notion revived by nineteenth-century poet Charles Baudelaire as the perfect metaphor for the poetic process itself. His poem 'Une Charogne' famously exemplifies his creative ability to transform even the most grotesque and artistically unpromising material – in this case, the rotting animal carcass – into a work of lasting beauty. Style is thus the key to Céline's artistic redemption: it provides a creative outlet for his suffering that is legitimized by his literary martyrdom and linguistic alchemy.

But style is of little use if it does not meet with the approval of his reader. How did a writer whose popularity had plummeted owing to his fascist past regain a readership in a deeply anti-fascist climate? He had two choices: either to be contrite and apologetic, in keeping with the mood of the times, or to be defiant and polemical. Since it was not in his nature to show remorse or suppress his opinions, he chose the latter option. Counter-intuitively, he employed an ironic and confrontational first-person narrator, a move that would have been especially shocking to his readers, given the historical sensitivity surrounding the Holocaust:

> Céline knew that nothing would shock the reader more than distancing himself from the general feeling about the Nazi camps whose existence was just being revealed, and from the tone everyone was using in speaking about them [. . .] he was certain that by touching this most sensitive spot, he would provoke a reaction, even if it was one of rejection.[25]

However, Céline's polemical tone was not reckless, but calculated, because what Godard refers to as 'the violence done to the reader [that is] inflicted playfully' at least guaranteed a *reaction* from the reader, rather than mere indifference. For Céline, 'the important thing is that there should be between him and the reader an emotional link' and therefore 'hostility will do just as well as complicity'.[26]

There is no shortage of hostility in the twenty opening pages of the novel, which are directed at the narrator's former friend, Clémence Arlon, who comes to visit Céline in his Montmartre flat with her teenaged son in 1944. Clémence and her son represent the sadistic 'voyeurism' of friends and acquaintances – and, by extension, the public more generally – who hope to profit from his downfall before his reputation is completely destroyed. Céline takes verbal revenge on his tormentors:

> She's all puffed-up, wrinkled, ashen . . . I'm gonna tell her so: Sweetie-pie, you deadly bitch, you're nothing but a big fat dirty whore! Fuck off! You and your brat. Out o' here! Out! They deserve rough treatment. They came to see a soon-to-be-dead man, a tomorrow-he'll-be-hung, she, who's almost dead already herself![27]

This vituperative, polemical tone initially suggests a regression to the aggressive verbal assault of his pamphlets: his language is physically degrading, offensive and scatological. But this tone is frequently tempered and enriched by a prose style that is at once more autobiographical and more 'spoken'. The seeds of these two stylistic developments – autobiography and orality – had already been planted with the semi-autobiographical narrator, Ferdinand Bardamu, in *Journey*. In the subsequent novels, he simply became Ferdinand, thereby suggesting a possible identification with the author, whose pseudonym is, of course, Louis-Ferdinand Céline. From *Fable* onwards, the shoots blossomed into the more explicitly autobiographical voice who says 'I': this voice alternates between Ferdinand, Céline, Dr Destouches (his real and professional name) and 'Louis' (the name used by those who are close to him). Céline's gradual move towards autobiography made sense, given that he was writing about events from his life that were already well known to the public.[28] At the same time, he wanted to create characters who are so obviously caricatured and exaggerated, and in a tone that is 'so cavalierly indifferent to verisimilitude', that 'the reader always senses the role of invention and the imaginary'. The result was 'a new novelistic formula destined for a great future in France and elsewhere: a novel in which invention is grafted onto a presumed autobiography'.[29]

As for *Fable*'s 'spoken' style, this too was the culmination of a process that had initially begun in *Journey* and would reach fruition in his German trilogy. In *Journey*, Céline had introduced slang and popular language, but had done so within the parameters of traditional syntactical structures. In *Death on Credit*, however, his use of Parisian argot was enhanced by ellipses, or the famous 'three dots' (*trois points*). These convey the hesitations and interruptions that are inherent to human speech. By 'simulating' speech in this way, Céline's sentences give the impression of being in the present, even if the time when he wrote the novel and most of the events to which he refers belong to the past. The spoken word, by its very nature, is always inextricably linked to our experience of the present:

> *Fable for Another Time* is also the novel in which Céline becomes fully conscious of the possibilities of a discourse that is supposed to be oral. In particular, he realized that the more a fragment carries the weight of emotion, the more it will have the ring of the present.[30]

This discovery is crucial. This 'ring of the present' conveyed by the narrator's spoken emotion blurs the boundaries between past, present and future that are normally visible in a conventional, rationally ordered narrative. This impression of the 'immediate present', Céline explains, is part of the reason why he calls his novel a 'fable' (*féerie*), a timeless genre that transcends temporal boundaries:

> I'm writing you from everywhere, by the way, from my place in Montmartre! From the depths of my Baltavian prison! And at the same time from the seaside, from our hut. Time and place all mixed up! Shit! It's Fable isn't it? . . . That's what a Fable is: the Future! The Past! The False! The True! All the same, I'm thinking something – I'm thinking that the mangiest stray dog who's wandering around there in the gutter, who's sticking his nose everywhere, let's say he's called Piram, *he's* got less to fear than yours truly here. Hounded as no dog is![31]

Céline shows us that neither the exact dates and locations that he wrote his novel – Montmartre (1944), the prison in Copenhagen (1946), Klarskovgaard (1947–50), his residence on Denmark's North Sea coast after his release – nor those of the events that constitute its plot, are anywhere near as important as the *emotional immediacy* he feels when he describes them through his oral style of writing. This style conveys such strength of feeling – in this case, that of being more hounded than a stray dog – that we forget to distinguish between the different time frames to which he refers.

No more is this true than in his portrayal of prison, which makes us feel, when we read it, as if we are right there by his side, even though the date of his incarceration was 1945–7. His emotions express both his intense suffering – especially from the intolerable prison noise – and his desperation to overcome and transform that suffering into something positive: specifically, through nostalgic memories that spur him into creativity. Prison noise is a constant presence in *Fable*: the screaming prisoners, the howling wind outside, the prison guards who march up and down the corridors blowing their whistles, unlocking cells and jangling their keys, allowing their dogs to bark loudly. Céline employs harsh sound patterning here – onomatopoeia – to highlight the unbearable torment this causes him:

> If the guards weren't so drunk, if they didn't blow their whistles for every goddamn piddling thing, if they'd stop fiddling with the twenty thousand latches . . . and if they poisoned the seven dog packs! . . . Ah, the seven dog packs! Seven packs of them outside barking! . . . then I could talk to you more intimately . . . not bothered by anyone! . . . because it's humiliation itself, brutal, the last straw, that you're fuckin' nuts and a thousand times worse, with the noise from the iron bars! *crrrrttt! crrrttt!* that never stops! The way the guards get their kicks, here, let me scrape the bars for you! And scrape them again for you! . . . the harp of the iron bars! They run their keys through them! *crrrrttt! crrrrttt!*[32]

His feeling of constant exposure to spiky and grating sounds is further accentuated by the frustrating lack of visual stimulus. His dwindling physical state no longer allows him to hoist himself up to look through the small barred window. And even if he were still able to do so, he could only glimpse a world of comfort and freedom that is tantalizingly out of reach:

> Heaven is houses three kilometres away, with lots of people in them, with seven floors! all the comforts! Windows! Wispy curtains! Elevator! Seen like that by us, peeking through a cell window . . . Anyway, I couldn't hoist myself up anymore . . . My scabs are sticking too much! . . .[33]

This powerful mix of sensory overload – noise – and sensory deprivation – sight – plays havoc with his feelings to the point that they explode into his writing with a powerful cathartic immediacy.

Writing thus allows him to articulate his ordeal. But it also offers him *sanctuary* from this anguish in the form of nostalgic escape. This nostalgia may be tinged with regret for what is no more, but it also allows him to access a happier, more innocent past that helps him block out – if only momentarily – the torment of the present. This was the nostalgia he discovered through writing his prison diaries. As he jots down a particular memory, this memory triggers a whole host of other memories that had previously not occurred to him. He initially recalls, in his telegrammatic style, that crucial moment, at the beginning of his exile, when he and Lucette were about to leave Montmartre in June 1944. He remembers the agonizing dilemma they faced of whether or not to take the cat Bébert with them:

> Will we leave Bébert? No we'll take him [. . .] Just a little jaunt to Denmark – faced with the enormity of this misfortune, courage is lacking . . . A long time lingering at the window there – we both cry . . . All those lines there, those roads, those rooftops, the long meandering Seine – Opéra – my district – Temple where I went with grandmother – République.[34]

This initial recollection of his cat reawakens, in turn, an indelible visual memory: the sight of the Paris skyline. As soon as he and Lucette stared out of their Montmartre window, they started crying, because it suddenly dawned on them that they may never return to their beloved city. But, like a Russian doll, this visual memory of Montmartre in 1944 contains within it an even earlier memory that is also emotionally intertwined with the sight of Paris: specifically, those districts he can see from the window that he had frequented with his grandmother as a young child. These memories – of leaving Montmartre in 1944 and of cherished childhood moments with his grandmother – converge in his mind with equal force to elicit the same emotional response: that of shedding tears at what has been lost, or what he is about to lose. His tears at having to leave Montmartre in 1944 become mingled with those he sheds when recalling his treasured childhood recollections of his grandmother.

Céline's diaries thus acted as a safety valve from the pressure cooker of prison. They provided an emotional release from reality by triggering an outpouring of memories that were located deep inside him. In *Fable*, he strives for the same result through his writing. Since he cannot physically escape his cell, the only solace he can find is *from within*. He turns to his memories as a comfort blanket that shields him from the intolerable world outside. He therefore internalizes the jarring prison noises and transforms them, through his sense perceptions, into little islands of nostalgia that allow him to blot them out:

> Just my walls! . . . that's all there is! . . . Confidence in my walls! . . . Oh, I confine myself! [. . .] ears ever at the listen! . . . and eyes waiting to see! . . . I pick up everything! . . . aside from my internal noises, the goods trains . . . in twos and threes! . . . anything that moves in Batignolles . . . both under the Flanders Bridge and under three adjacent tunnels . . . and I never mix up the whistles! . . . the prison ones, the railroad ones, the ones in my ear . . . the imaginary ones, the real ones . . . Never the tiniest inkling of a doubt! . . . The exquisiteness of my hearing . . . I'm like a bloody conductor! . . .[35]

Prison makes his hearing so acute that he is able to distinguish between real and imaginary noises, even though they appear to be indiscriminately interwoven into his narrative. Initially, the real noises are themselves subdivided into the internal tinnitus he hears as a result of his Ménière's disease ('my internal noises'), and the external noise of goods trains and the whistles of the prison guards. But these actual sounds of whistles and trains quickly rekindle within him memories of similar trains and whistles from his past life that he used to hear when living in Montmartre (close to Batignolles) and even earlier, when fighting in Flanders in 1914.

His mind is thus caught between, on one hand, his need for psychological release from the intolerable prison din, and, on the other, his desire for that noise to sustain and replenish the creative power of his memory. Once he has artistically exhausted one source of sound, he seeks a new one, in order to kick-start the cycle all over again. Thus the cries of the abortionist in cell 28 above him ('she goes at it like twenty-five newborns! . . . the cries out of her!') reawaken memories of the shrieking mothers giving birth when he delivered babies as a doctor: 'Push, now, my good woman! Push! . . . I've heard many a cry . . . I'm a hearer but the duo of childbirth, mama and the little guy, now there's a chord you won't soon forget . . .'[36] The cycle of one sound replacing another is symbolized by the cry of the newborn baby: 'as soon as the mother stops shouting the little guy pipes up . . .'[37] This segues into his recollections of the pigmy celebrations in Cameroon in 1916: 'the noises in Cameroon, now, you can have as many as you want of them! . . . talk about forestial orchestrations! . . .

[...] "Ding... a! bouay!" [...] sixteen drumsticks going at a hollow tree-trunk...'; his charging cavalry regiment in the First World War ('Giddyap! Giddyap! Something to hear again ... [...] I create the grand manoeuver charges'); and the sound of the death rattle of dying patients.[38] He even links this sound to ones that have become obsolete because they belong to practices from a bygone era: 'like the watermills of a thousand years ago and the din raised by anvils ... Museum noises!'[39]

By dint of his creative alchemy, he transforms the very source of his ordeal – harsh noise – into an intricate tapestry of 'sound memories', what he calls his 'petite musique'. In so doing, he takes ownership of his suffering and removes it from the clutches of his persecutors. These include journalists, who exploit his torment for their own nefarious ends. He imagines one such journalist coming to visit him in prison in order to get a scoop. In Céline's savagely ironic parody, the journalist invokes the very same trope as he does – literary martyrdom – but for purely sensationalist, rather than aesthetic, purposes. After praising him as 'The Greatest Writer of the Century!', as opposed to dead writers such as Robert Brasillach, the reporter tells Céline that the best way to recapture the public and critics is to play the role of the angry, humiliated fallen victim.[40] Thus, he asks him to crouch down on all fours, expose his anus to the world and lash out at those who persecute him:

> France can't sleep, you've been outraged so! Spoliated! Slandered! Spat upon! Brasillach, nobody gives a shit about him, he's dead! What people want is pictures! Records! Words! They want meat and photos! Show me your ass where it's bleeding! Move over here, Maestro! Maestro! Your drawers! Get on your knees! ... [...] repeat after me: 'I hate them!' ... with feeling, dear maestro, with feeling! ... and now weep! weep![41]

His literary martyrdom becomes a vulgar parody of ruthless journalists who will stop at nothing to satisfy a sensationalist readership, and also a self-parody of the terrible intestinal problems from which he suffered in prison. But this self-debasement is not so much an act of self-loathing, as it is a provocative dig at his readers. By taking this parody to a scatological extreme, he shocks them into questioning their own voyeuristic tendencies. By giving the readers *too much* of what they want – the spectacle of the humiliated fallen hero – they actually end up asking themselves whether they really want it at all.

But style also fulfils the wider artistic function of providing the public with a more inclusive and honest depiction of reality. In other words, style is also a mark of Céline's artistic *integrity*. It recalls, once again, Baudelaire's notion of 'creative alchemy', only this time in an ethical, as well as an aesthetic, sense. Céline, like the poet, wanted to incorporate the unpleasant or grotesque aspects of reality into his literature, not only in order to demonstrate his own literary talents, but to avoid cheating his readers. Excluding or disguising those aspects of real life that are unacceptable to conventional bourgeois taste would be an act of deliberate hypocrisy and dishonesty.

This is precisely why he measures his own creativity against that of his former close friend and Montmartre neighbour Gen Paul, referred to as Jules in both *Fable for Another Time* and the second volume, *Normance*. The true gauge of his artistic honesty is to be willing to depict reality in a way that other artists are not. To Céline, Jules represents two things: his nostalgia for a bygone era and an artistic and sexual rivalry. The nostalgia is not just for a lost friendship – as we saw in Chapter Five, the two men had a major falling out when Gen Paul distanced himself from Céline in 1944 – but for Montmartre itself and its vibrant, bohemian community of artists, writers and musicians: it is no coincidence that Gen Paul was born and raised there. Over a twelve-year period, he and Céline were close friends and neighbours. The artist even illustrated two editions of Céline's novels. Despite a brief thawing of relations and an exchange of letters in 1947, Céline's sense of hurt and betrayal was heightened by the painter's point-blank refusal to visit him in Denmark in 1947. In his place, he sent his estranged second wife.[42]

Céline projects his love–hate relationship with Gen Paul via his narrator. He mocks Jules' sexual frustration as an invalid artist (Gen Paul had his leg amputated when he was injured in the First World War), who lusts after his attractive female models; but he also self-mockingly portrays himself as a cuckold. Jules invites Lucette to pose as his model, makes a pass at her and also dismisses Céline's artistic tastes. Céline's sexual jealousy of Jules is intermingled with his grudging admiration for his artistic talents. These are on full parodic display when he climbs to the top of Montmartre's famous windmill, the Moulin de la Galette, gesturing furiously to the bombers up above with his walking stick, as if he were an orchestra conductor:

> there's something supernatural about Jules, the way he balances, straightens up, floats, and rolls round and round! Woaah horsey! pivots! pirouettes! . . . what they admired him for in his studio: abracadabra and voila – masterpieces . . . I mean, if you ask me . . . all that was nothing compared to this, now! Compared to what he's displaying over Paris! The way he held the storm in his grasp, smearing the sky with blue, green, yellow! Making the geysers erupt! . . . where he liked! as he liked! with his cane! with his signals! . . . spurring on the rafaplanes! The explosives criss-crossing each other in the sky! . . . and the way he had them blow up with the factories! . . . the churches flipped over in the clouds! . . . bell towers upside-down! I'd seen him varnish his paintings . . . me the perfect rube not knowing a thing about art, I said to myself: he's got it all worked out! He's bluffing those bourgeois clients of his he paints them buses on an icy sea . . . and even the Alps in mauve, orange, with crimson snow, and cows grazing on daggers! . . .[43]

His apparent praise of Jules' magician-like capacity to 'conduct' the new artistic display of the bombs contains a veiled criticism: his studio paintings, by comparison, are artificial conceits that dupe his bourgeois clients with unrealistic images ('crimson snow' and 'cows grazing on daggers!'). The visual spectacle of the bombs, on the other hand – with its bold painterly colours splashed across the sky – is generated by something real and thus has far greater artistic potential. The unmooring and overturning of buildings may *look* more implausible and incongruous than the crimson snow and cows eating daggers in Jules' paintings, but as a direct consequence of the bombs, this real phenomenon constitutes a far more artistically authentic image. Thus, the comical tone masks a serious statement of literary intent: artistic integrity means depicting those aspects of reality that are considered too controversial or unpalatable to fall within the traditional cultural domain. As we shall discover, aerial bombardment was exactly the type of painful reality to which no artist or writer had hitherto ever given adequate expression. Like Baudelaire before him, Céline shows his willingness to tread where no writer has dared to tread before. Failure to do so would be to cheat his readers by shielding then from the truth.

Céline's allusion, in his parodic description of Jules, to two major works from the literary canon offers further evidence that both *Fable* and *Normance* are a serious meditation on his own aesthetic style: Miguel de

Cervantes's *Don Quixote* and Victor Hugo's *Notre-Dame de Paris*. As is well known, Don Quixote tilts at windmills, a metaphor for being out of touch with reality, and Quasimodo is a solitary hunchback who rings the bells of Notre-Dame. Since Jules is described both as a 'slimy hunchback of an artist' and stands defiantly at the top of a windmill, the symbolism is far from coincidental.[44]

If, in the end, both volumes of *Fable for Another Time* were a gamble that backfired with the critics, they have now come to be regarded as one of Céline's very finest literary achievements. At the time, however, his pariah status, and his stylistic difficulty, proved to be a bridge too far for both the public and critics. When it was published in 1954, *Normance* was even more harshly criticized than the first volume. To console Céline after the poor reception of *Fable* (*Féerie I*) in 1952, Gaston Gallimard, Céline's new publisher, pertinently observed,

> The new book *Féerie*, you wrote out of necessity, to satisfy your taste for style, and you were right. It is a fine work, accomplished, that I am proud to have published. But it is not a commercial work that sells quickly. It is not written for a wider public. I am not complaining about it, but neither should you.[45]

Céline's relationship with Gallimard was to become as instrumental to the second half of his career as his relationship with Robert Denoël had been to the first. He was desperate to secure a prestigious and influential publisher, especially after Denoël's brutal death and his inability to publish during his exile. As for Gallimard, he was being offered a second bite at the cherry, having made the mistake of turning down *Journey* in 1932. Just after Céline's return to France in July 1951, a contract was mutually agreed via Céline's friend Pierre Monnier, who had laid the initial groundwork. The terms were generous: Gallimard not only agreed to republish Céline's previous novels, but to pay him 18 per cent royalties, plus an advance to the value of 25,000 copies, upon receipt of the manuscript of *Fable for Another Time*.[46] When Céline and Gallimard finally met in Neuilly in August, at the house of Céline's admirer, the wealthy industrialist Paul Marteau, the two men got along well.

But as so often with Céline, especially when it came to publishers, whom he saw as ruthless capitalists, their relationship quickly became testy, albeit never to the point of a total breakdown in communication: Céline knew what side his bread was buttered, which is why his letters to Gallimard are akin to those of a naughty child who pushes his parents to the limit and then behaves just in time to avoid getting into trouble. Being thirteen years older than Céline, Gallimard soon fell into the role of the firm but patient parent who indulges his wayward offspring's precocious tantrums, but who lays down the rules when needed. Their lengthy correspondence is a highly amusing game of tit-for-tat, which betrays, beneath their many disagreements, a degree of underlying affection on both their parts. Céline's frequent complaints – which are usually unreasonable – are that he feels exploited, paid too little or too late, and routinely neglected by an aloof publisher who is impossible to get hold of. Gallimard does not take him seriously and gives him sound advice:

> Your humour is nothing but rhetoric. You fail to make me believe in your violence. You mix everything up – on purpose [. . .] You want to sell, so then provide a product that's easy to sell! And then play to the gallery like a good salesman: radio – photos, interviews etc. . . . That way, you draw attention to your books. Your diatribes against your publisher achieve nothing.[47]

Céline eventually swallowed his pride and published, with the older man's full cooperation, a comical pseudo-interview with an academic known as 'Professor Y', who, according to critic and translator Stanford Luce, acts as a 'foil for his jibes at traditional literature'.[48] He realized, especially after the failure of *Fable*, that this 1955 pseudo-interview, entitled *Entretiens avec professeur Y* (Conversations with Professor Y) was a light-hearted and less confrontational way of trying to regain public support. It was also far more accessible to his readers than the difficult prose that had alienated them in *Fable*. Instead of showing how his style worked, he would explain, in simple dialogue form, *why* it was important. The initial part of the text depicts Céline racing through Paris to meet the reluctant interviewer on a park bench, in the district of Arts et Métiers. The text indulges in considerable parody and self-irony: he openly acknowledges that he is conducting an interview in order to placate his publisher, even though he despises the publicity machine and literature's assimilation to the consumerist rat race, in which it is sold just like any other commercial product:

> 'You're not playing the game!' . . . is how he ended up . . . no reproach . . . but just the same! . . . a patron of the arts, Gaston, of course . . . but a business man, too . . . I didn't want to give him any trouble [. . .]

> I understood toot sweet, presto, two shakes! that playing the game meant getting on the radio . . . setting all else aside! . . . stammering out something or other, but spelling out your name loud and clear at least a hundred times! a thousand times! . . . whether you're pushing the new Big Bubbly soap product . . . or the Nickless no-blade razor . . . or the eager genius! . . . the same broth! same cloth![49]

Just as he does in his letters, he is quite prepared to bite the hand that feeds him – Gaston Gallimard – by depicting his publisher as a rich profiteer who, contrary to the impoverished writer ('you'll see any number of writers end their days as rag-pickers'), wields considerable power over numerous authors and academics, including Professor Y himself, who are desperate to be published by him: 'Professor Y, of course, he had his little pensum too, which had been waiting for years in the Gallimard catacombs, for Gaston to request it, thumb through . . .'[50] In order to get his readers back on side, Céline is prepared to poke fun both at his own fallen reputation, and at the publisher on whom he depends. But having learnt his lesson the hard way, he no longer uses the violent tone of the pamphlets, nor the extreme scatological humour of his imagined interview with the journalist in *Fable*.

Conversations with Professor Y sparked mild curiosity among the public, which gave him the confidence to attempt another literary comeback. He had explained why style was important, but he still needed that style to be legitimized by a story that would hold his readers' interest. A happy coincidence came to his rescue: after eleven years of embarrassed silence, enough time had passed to trigger a renewal of public interest in Sigmaringen, an episode of French extreme Collaborationism that he was one of the few to have witnessed. He admitted as much in an interview with Albert Zbinden in July 1957, when the first novel of his so-called trilogy, *Castle to Castle*, came out:

> I have been subject to a kind of prohibition for a number of years, and, by releasing a work that, all things considered, is quite public, since it is based on well-known facts, and which are of interest, after all, to the French, – since it is a small part [. . .] of France's history, I talk about Pétain, I talk about Laval, I talk about Sigmaringen.[51]

Given his pariah status, Céline knew full well that an intimate account of his exile alone was not enough to win back the public. This is why he decided to link his personal story to the *collective history* of France, and specifically to an episode that was suddenly in the public eye. This gave him a distinct advantage over Louis Noguères, the author of a book on Sigmaringen that had been published a short time before and sparked public interest – he was a *witness* to Sigmaringen, whereas Noguères was not: 'I get to think about Noguares [*sic*] . . . Where does he come off, writing about Siegmaringen? He could have gone there at least. The lousy pompous bastard! He'd sooner have shat in bed!'[52]

To legitimize his claims to historical authenticity by providing a witness account, Céline frequently uses the word *chronique*, or chronicle. Exactly how apt this word is to describe *Castle to Castle* is open to debate. Vichy historian Henri Rousso, for instance, remarked in 1996 that the word is a misnomer when it comes to Céline, since his account of Sigmaringen contains many factual and chronological inaccuracies. While this is technically correct, it is also true, as Rousso himself concedes, that Céline's work did more than any other to put Sigmaringen back on the historical map.[53] Literary critic Philip Watts is even harder on Céline, by labelling him a historical revisionist. He dismisses his righteous stance as a reliable chronicler as a clever ruse that allowed him to reverse the dominant anti-fascist narrative propagated by the Allied 'victors' by subtly 'smuggling' a counter-narrative into his novels that instead portrays fascists as history's *victims*. Thus, for example, in *Castle to Castle*, Céline takes the French public to task for refusing to acknowledge the Allied bombing of Montmartre in April 1944: 'What the readers want is a laugh . . . in the first place Paris was never bombed . . . not a single commemorative tablet, isn't that proof enough? . . . I'm the only one who remembers, two, three families buried under the ruins . . .'[54] What both these commentators fail to recognize, however, is exactly what Céline means by 'chronicle'. His goal was never historical objectivity in the conventional sense, but rather to convey a deeply subjective *emotional memory* of the period in question. He understood all too well that the distinct advantage emotional memory has over a purely fact-based account is that it gives a far more authentic and powerful sense of how people *felt* at the time. No more is this apparent than in his novel *Rigadoon*, of which cultural historian Alain Corbin writes, 'Is there any history of the bombings that gives the reader a better sense of their emotional spectrum than their description in *Rigadoon*?'[55]

This is the same emotional memory as in *Fable for Another Time*, when Céline recalled his imprisonment and the bombs. The only difference is that he now applies it to a topic that is of *public*, rather than personal, relevance: an episode taken from France's collective history, rather than from his own very individual experience of literary martyrdom. The fact that Céline called the three works in his German trilogy *romans*, or 'novels', is making a clear statement: he is not completely abandoning his fictional roots, nor is he relinquishing the role of the imagination. The German trilogy is thus a unique genre: a blend of autobiography, history and fiction.

This hybrid genre needs to be set against the political context of Sigmaringen, and in particular of its two main factions. The first faction, known as the *actifs*, comprised those French collaborators from Vichy who purported to maintain a legitimate French government in Sigmaringen that worked closely with the Germans. Known as the Délégation gouvernementale française pour la défense des intérêts nationaux (French government delegation for the defence of national interests), this group had been set up in September 1944 by Hitler's Foreign Secretary, Joachim von Ribbentrop, and the German ambassador in Paris, Otto Abetz. The French delegation included Fernand de Brinon, the delegate general of the French government in the Occupied Zone; the founder of the Milice, Joseph Darnand; and the two fascist parties of diehard Collaborationists: Marcel Déat's Rassemblement national populaire and Jacques Doriot's P.P.F. Brinon was appointed as the Délégation's interim head, with a view to Doriot eventually taking over. Doriot, however, was killed by an Allied air attack while travelling in his car to Sigmaringen in February 1945, just when he was poised to supplant Brinon. The Délégation, which remained in place until the bitter end, had Déat as Secretary of State for Labour and Foreign Affairs, Darnand as Secretary of State for the Interior, General Bridoux as minister of war and Jean Luchaire as 'commissioner for information'. Luchaire was, by far, the most active delegate, even if the others also had offices in the village of Sigmaringen.

In the opposing camp were the so-called *passifs*, who refused to have anything to do with the *actifs*. It comprised members of the Vichy government who were brought to Sigmaringen against their will, refused to cooperate with the Germans and considered themselves their prisoners. Its two most prominent figureheads were Maréchal Philippe Pétain, who was appointed Chief of State of the Vichy government in July 1940, and his successor, Pierre Laval, who took over in April 1942, until Germany invaded the Unoccupied Zone in November of that year, following the Allied invasion of North Africa. Both Pétain and Laval remained in their own quarters, in the castle of Hohenzollern, consulting only a few close ministers. Other notable *passifs* included Jean Bichelonne, the brilliant minister for industry and commerce in several Vichy cabinets; famous writer and former minister of education and culture Abel Bonnard; Maurice Gabolde, the minister for education in the 1940 Vichy government; Pierre Mathé, the minister of justice; Jacques Guérard, secretary general of the government; and Charles Rochat, secretary general of foreign affairs.

Neither camp would have anything to do with the other, despite the efforts of Otto Abetz, the German ambassador to the exiled French government, who had collaborated with Laval and was given three months by von Ribbentrop to persuade Pétain and Laval to renounce their passivity. Having failed to achieve this, he was replaced as ambassador by Otto Reinebeck in mid-December.[56]

This was the political situation Céline faced. Some of these ministers were his patients, but not all of them. But as a doctor who moved seamlessly between the upper and lower echelons of society in Sigmaringen, he had plenty of ammunition to denounce the political system as both deeply flawed and in complete denial of a glaring reality: the imminence of Germany's defeat. His vicious satire of the far Right does not, however, prevent him from refusing to incriminate some collaborators whom he knew to be still alive in 1957, including personal friends and acquaintances. This is why he makes no mention in the novel of the Swiss ambassador Paul Bonny and his wife, who had befriended Céline and Lucette at Baden-Baden. Nor does he name his friend the author Lucien Rebatet, writer of the infamous and recently republished fascist pamphlet *Les Décombres*. Another friend, Abel Bonnard, is mentioned only in passing. Bonnard accompanied Céline and Lucette to Sigmaringen station as they left for Denmark on 22 March 1945 and was hiding in Spain when the novel was published. Céline does, however, paint a flattering portrait of Bonnard's cultured mother, to whom he grew close while treating her, and was greatly upset when she died. Then there are those whom Céline knew less well or not at all, but whom he included in the novel to provide relevant political context. He slightly modified their names so that they remained recognizable to the reader without being named outright: Gabold for Gabolde, Bridou for Bridoux, Mathey for Mathé, Rochas for Rochat.[57]

Céline decided to switch emphasis from the literary style of *Fable for Another Time* to his second vocation: medicine. He underlines his role as a conscientious doctor who selflessly serves his community, despite his advancing years and a hostile clientele. His tone, although still polemical, is now softened by the resignation of old age. He laments his status as an ageing man of 63, living in the quiet suburb of Belleville, near the Courbevoie where he grew up. His declining health and physique count against him, especially among the gossiping women in his neighbourhood, who reject him for younger and more attractive doctors ('wait and see what they have to say about you: "Crabby, toothless, ignorant, hunchbacked, always hawking and spitting . . ."').[58]

He plays down his literary career, referring to himself as a 'jobbing novelist', rather than the innovative creator of *Fable*. Writing is no longer about creative alchemy or style, but good, old-fashioned hard graft. It is undertaken reluctantly for an exploitative and disinterested publisher, Achille Brottin (his fictional name for Gaston Gallimard), whose only concern is profit. Brottin does not share his previous publisher Robert Denoël's passion for literature:

> Let me tell you about Denoël . . . Denoël who was assassinated . . . oh, he had his nasty ways . . . [. . .] but he had one saving grace . . . his passion for literature . . . he really recognised good work, he had respect for writers . . . Brottin is a horse of a different colour . . . Achille Brottin is your sordid grocer, an implacable idiot . . . the only thing he can think about is his dough![59]

In a passage of bold, imaginative brilliance, the doctor–narrator leaves his home to administer morphine to one of his ageing patients, Madame Niçois, who lives a few minutes away. As he wistfully contemplates the barges on the Seine from the window of her house, he spots a *bateau-mouche*, with a sign saying 'La Publique' and a number, 114. Intrigued, he leaves the sleeping Madame Niçois and approaches the river. This boat nostalgically reminds him of the authentic barges he would board as a child, to enjoy an invigorating cruise down the river with his parents on Sunday afternoons ('every Sunday when I was little, for my complexion, we took one to Port Royal, the nearest landing . . . twenty-five centimes round trip to Suresnes . . .').[60] The barge he observes resembles the ones from his childhood, as opposed to the hideous, modern-day *bateaux-mouches* that are crammed with tourists: 'none of the phony bateaux-mouches you see today . . . showcases for tourists . . . all glass! . . .').[61]

As he approaches the barge, he is suddenly greeted by a sight that appears to be half-memory, half-vision: his actor friend Robert Le Vigan disembarks, dressed in a gaucho costume: 'we hadn't seen each other in a long time . . . since Siegmaringen . . .'[62] Céline punningly introduces an 'e' into Sigmaringen to satirize the German word for victory (*Sieg*) that was used in the Nazi greeting 'Sieg Heil!', and the gaucho costume alludes to Le Vigan's new life in Argentina. The actor explains that the barge belongs to Charon and that all the people on it, including his new wife Anita and Émile – a former garage-owner who belonged to the L.V.F. (the volunteer corps of Frenchmen fighting for the Germans on the eastern front) and was lynched by the Résistance – are actually dead: '"Then these are all dead people?" [. . .] "What else would they be?"'[63] This demands of his reader some familiarity with Classical literature: Charon is the ferryman of Hades, who carries the souls of the newly deceased across the rivers Styx and Acheron, which divided the world of the living from the world of the dead. A coin to pay Charon for safe passage, usually an obol or *danake*, was sometimes placed in or on the mouth of a dead person. And in accordance with the myth, Le Vigan asks Céline for money to embark on the barge.

He goes on to describe Charon as a gruesome monster ('at least three . . . four times my size! . . . built like a barrel . . . with a face . . . that face! . . . like an ape . . . part tiger . . . part ape . . .') who beats all the passengers with his oar.[64] The narrator cannot distinguish dream from reality: the dead passengers smell bad, and his dog Agar refuses to bark: 'Agar sniffed . . . sniffed at all these beings . . . one by one . . . but not a murmur out of him!'[65] Feeling increasingly uneasy, the narrator says that he has to tend to his patient, Madame Niçois, promising Le Vigan that he won't tell anyone what he has seen. But the passengers get angry that he won't join them on the barge, hurling insults as he leaves: 'Stinker! Eel! No-good! . . . Go?' on! Traitor! Traitor!'[66] Given that the number 114 on the barge is a likely symbolic nod to the 1,142 French collaborators who ended up in Sigmaringen, this Charon episode is open to allegorical interpretation.[67] It suggests a certain anxiety about revealing what he saw at Sigmaringen: will he be accused of betraying the collaborators? In addition, his refusal to join the others on the barge separates him from the herd: contrary to Le Vigan and the other collaborators in Sigmaringen, he wants his readers to know that he did not participate in the propaganda activities that took place there. Finally, this is perhaps a form of psychological wish-fulfilment: a wistful fantasy of what might have been had he chosen not to join the others in Sigmaringen. His dream-vision acts as a corrective to his real-life decision to join the 'living dead'.

The doctor–narrator and the Charon episode are thus intended to present Céline in a favourable light to the reader: as a non-collaborator and an empathetic, eminently relatable man who tends to the sick. As such, the reader is psychologically prepared for his evocation of the similar medical role he carried out in Sigmaringen twelve years earlier. Céline stresses his tireless work in harsh and dangerous conditions, which set him apart from the more pampered and ineffectual political figures, many of whom are also his patients. What is more, the reputation of the doctor as a 'rational observer' lends credence to his role as reliable 'chronicler' of history. Even if, as we have seen, Céline's notion of the *chronique* was predicated on a unique blend of his emotional memory and his imagination, he still wanted his account of Sigmaringen to be perceived as authentic and trustworthy by his readers. The reliability of the doctor as narrator is further strengthened by his similarity with the detective in crime fiction: as Fredric Jameson has noted, both are privileged observers of the inner workings of society, with the ability to move seamlessly between different social classes and geographical spaces.[68] This was certainly true of Céline. Even though he and Lucette had to live, and even treat, patients in their own room in the Löwen, one of Sigmaringen's overcrowded hotels, they had virtually unlimited access to the castle up above, the opulent and luxurious residence of senior members of the Vichy government and of the Nazi hierarchy. Moreover, he had access to the hospital–convent, the Fidelis and the headquarters of the district administration, the *Landrat*. Ever the defender of the underdog, Céline was thus exposed to vast disparities in wealth and privilege, which he did not fail to denounce in his novel.

This can be seen in his satire of Pétain himself. Contrary to Laval, Pétain refused to be treated by Céline, whose pamphlet, *A Fine Mess*, had launched a coruscating attack not only on his Vichy government, but on the French army. It is hardly surprising that the Maréchal took a very dim view of a novelist who mocked the very military establishment on which his reputation rested. When the Nazis sacked Pétain's personal doctor Ménétrel, considering him an obstacle to their attempts to get the Maréchal on side, Céline purportedly wanted to replace him, but this was immediately blocked. Cleverly reinforcing the link between his roles as doctor in 1957 with that of 1944–5, Céline compares Pétain's hostility towards him to that of his patients in Meudon: 'I attended Laval now and then ... I never came near Pétain ... Brinon had suggested me, Ménétrel had just been arrested ... "I'd rather die right away!" ... that was the impression I made on Pétain, same as the people around here in Lower Meudon ...'[69] Pétain is a satirical goldmine for Céline, since he was known for his legendary appetite: cultural historian Christine Sautermeister has even retraced some of his lavish menus from Sigmaringen.[70] His gluttony is used to accentuate the inequities between the Vichy hierarchy and the hungry 1,142 refugees who were clamouring for bread beneath the castle drawbridge: 'Pétain up there, housed like a dream! ... a whole floor to himself! ... heated! ... with four meals a day! ... sixteen cards plus presents from the Führer, coffee, cologne, silk shirts ... a regiment of cops at his beck and call ... a staff general ... four cars ...'[71] Céline reinforces the self-image of the humble, devoted doctor by contrasting this gastronomic excess with his own measly rations and stressful life treating patients, despite acute shortages of medicine: 'I didn't have sixteen food cards ... or eight ... just one ... [...] I was admitted to the Castle, yes, ... but not to eat ... to keep tabs ... how many cases of flu? How many pregnant women? New cases of scabies? ... and how much morphine had I left? ...'[72] These shortages were genuine, leading to constant battles with the pharmacist. But Céline reserves his most biting satire for the Maréchal's daily walk. In reality, Pétain was driven every day to the forest outside Sigmaringen for a quiet stroll. Céline, however, claims to be an eyewitness to the grandiose procession of an ageing king ('Pétain was our last King of France, "Philip the Last! ..."'), who is accompanied by a stately and pompous retinue of ministers ('the whole procession at least two miles long').[73] They all descend from the castle drawbridge like feudal lords, who brush disdainfully past their starving but loyal subjects: 'Oh, Monsieur le Maréchal, how you incarnate France!'[74] The daily walk of the ageing Pétain and his entourage is like a slow death march along the river Danube, in which they are completely oblivious to RAF bombers up above trying to attack the bridge:

> The RAF was looking for the bridge ... at that precise moment ... no razzledazzle! ... dropping their strings of bombs over the bridge ... straight down ... every which way three four planes at a time ... how did they manage to miss it? ... their bombs sent up geysers! The Danube was boiling! And the muck splashing all over ... and in the fields ... two, three miles away ... We were squeezed under the arch, pressed against the enormous granite abutment ... a good

> chance to piss, the ministers and the party chiefs and the Marshal . . . I knew all their prostates . . . some had big business . . . for that the bushes were more convenient . . .[75]

Like his favourite Renaissance writer, François Rabelais, who savaged authority figures with his scatological humour, Céline completely debunks Pétain's stature in France by recounting how he and his ministers relieve themselves in the bushes, owing to their ailing prostates. Their complete removal from the reality of military defeat is demonstrated by their greater concern with their bodily functions than with the threat of the Allied bombers up above.

The reality of defeat is denied just as emphatically by those collaborators who are indoctrinated by cultural propaganda. Céline recalls being accosted by an extremely dapper actor by the name of Raoul Orphize (a fictional character), whom he had treated for sinus problems in the Fidelis hospital. Orphize enthusiastically tells Céline that he plans to direct and produce a film for which he wants him to write the script. Orphize is accompanied by an equally glamorous and well-dressed actress by the name of Odette Clarisse, who reminds Céline of two well-known actresses of the time, his friend Arletty and Marlene Dietrich. The first indication that this project is a ridiculous pipe dream is the fact that not only does the Vichy government support it ('I've just come from Brinon's . . . he's given his okay [. . .] I've just seen Laval, he's all for it!), but so too do the Russians: 'ah Céline, that authorization from the Russians, you can't imagine! But I've finally got it!'[76] Since the Russians were both communists and part of the Allied forces under Stalin, this already strikes the reader as fanciful.

Céline himself wonders how these two immaculately dressed individuals have been able to make their way from the cultural centre of Dresden to Sigmaringen, when Dresden has just been heavily bombed by the RAF: 'the Mecca of the arts, meanwhile burned down . . . 200,000 dead'.[77] How did they emerge unscathed from a city that had suffered one of the worst bombings of the Second World War?

> I don't surprise easily, but there . . . I've got to admit . . . Orphize, Odette . . . the veil, the alligator handbag, the triple soles! . . . and coming from Leipzig! . . . from Dresden! . . . especially as I know a thing or two about Dresden . . . I'd seen the Consul from Dresden a week before [. . .] he'd told me all about it . . . the tactic of totally

> squashing and frying in phosphorus . . . American invention! . . . really perfected! The last 'new look' before the A-bomb . . . first the suburbs, the periphery . . . with liquid sulphur and avalanches of torpedoes . . . then general roasting . . . the whole center! Act II! . . . churches, parks, museums . . . no survivors wanted! . . .[78]

Should this be read as historical revisionism on Céline's part: portraying the fascists as the innocent victims of vengeful Allies? His indignation at the complete absence of moral condemnation of these bombings would suggest so, especially when less serious mining accidents and the Russian invasion of Budapest in 1956 (the time he was writing the novel) are perceived as scandalous:

> they never say a word . . . and they're wrong! . . . about how their brethren were roasted alive in Germany beneath the spreading wings of democracy . . . one doesn't speak of such things, it's embarrassing! . . . the victims? . . . they shouldn't have been there, that's all! . . .[79]

But this needs to be put into context. Céline is not denouncing attacks against Nazis, but on *ordinary German civilians*. His sympathy with the common man – irrespective of ideological allegiance – is later confirmed by his empathy with the Berliners rebuilding their bombed homes at the beginning of *North*. By drawing attention to the horrors of Dresden, he emphasizes, by way of counterpoint, the fantasy world in which Orphize and Clarisse live: they appear to be 'sleepwalking' – rather like the half-dead refugees on Charon's raft – into Germany's imminent defeat, despite having been in Dresden themselves.

Jean Bichelonne's funeral is a wake-up call for the 'sleepwalkers' of Sigmaringen: they are confronted with the reality of military defeat. Bichelonne was a brilliant graduate from the prestigious École polytechnique, whose analytical mind was deployed in the Department of Labour and also the organization of the railways under Vichy. Céline depicts him as an eccentric, neurotic genius, who interrupts his meeting with Laval because he is distressed that he has broken his foot on a tile. Bichelonne was also employed in more sinister activities in the implementation of anti-Jewish laws in 1942–3, although Maurice Gabolde defended him as an ivory-tower dreamer, who had no real consciousness of politics. Bichelonne died in Hohenlychen on 21 December 1944, after a failed operation on his knee, supervised by a Nazi surgeon, Karl Gebhardt.[80]

A delegation was sent from Sigmaringen comprising Gabolde; his friend and executor of his will, Paul Marion; Guérard, former Secretary of State for the Foreign Office and collaborator with Laval; an embassy official; and Darnand, head of the Milice. According to Gabolde, the journey was comfortable and unproblematic, and took 21 hours. Fog provided cover from Allied air attacks. The funeral was also attended by the sculptor Arno Breker and his wife, high-ranking German officials and Gebhardt. It was a funeral befitting a high-ranking French official, with three speeches, followed by a banquet, light music and a film projection of the operation. The Marseillaise was played, as the officials were accompanied back to catch their train to Ulm, where they were collected by their chauffeur.

Céline considerably embellishes the episode for satirical purposes. The train journey does not take a day, but a week; is not in the fog, but a blizzard; is not smooth and comfortable, but constantly interrupted and in freezing conditions. Instead of being dignified and long, the funeral is farcical and brief. The delegates struggle on slippery ice to make their way to the hospital where Bichelonne's body is kept. They are briefly greeted by Gebhardt, do not utter a word and then struggle through the windswept snow to carry back a French flag they had promised for Pétain. On the train back, they are so cold that Horace Restif, one of Céline's semi-fictional characters, has to rip some of the fabric in the compartments to give to the others to keep them warm. Céline's decision to substitute Restif for the real head of the Milice, Darnand, is, according to Sautermeister, satirical. Restif was based on the real Jean Filliol, a trained Milice assassin, who, under the supervision of German security service (SD), trained 'counter-terrorist' commandos to conduct operations to kill members of the Résistance. Restif thus personifies survival skills and calmness under pressure. But by transposing him to this farcical scenario, Céline satirizes the inanity of these clandestine counter-terrorist activities, which, in reality, proved to be unsuccessful. The real Filliol managed to flee to Spain after the war, worked for cosmetics company L'Oréal and was largely forgotten, despite being given three death sentences in 1948. It is entirely plausible that Céline was scared to depict such a sinister figure, other than in disguised form.

But Céline's satire works on another level: it punctures the bubble of self-delusion of the Sigmaringen delegates by confronting them with the looming spectre of military defeat. The harsh elements – the snow, the cold, the creaking train, the ice, the ludicrous funeral, the flag that blows uncontrollably in the wind – are all metaphors for exposure to the naked truth. When he ironically wonders whether the train has taken them all the way to Russia, this too is a symbolic reminder of the advancing Allied forces: specifically, of the eastern front and the Russian army that will enter Berlin in a matter of months. The final nail in the coffin, the ultimate intrusion of reality into their fantasy, is when their train is suddenly invaded by a swarm of forty or fifty Red Cross refugees, comprising children and pregnant women. These starving children, who have been cooped up in a train for five days, devour the Red Cross supplies like a bunch of savages, jostling and stamping uncontrollably all over the delegates, while their supervisor struggles in vain to discipline them. The starving refugees are in stark opposition to the gastronomic delights the delegates are used to consuming in the sanctuary of Sigmaringen. And this shattering of their illusion by the harsh reality of war reaches its humiliating climax when the children tear off their uniforms, leaving them semi-naked and practically in rags. They are literally stripped of their dignity and symbolically divested of whatever little political power they still possess.

In this world of catastrophic self-delusion, the only minister to emerge with any credibility in Céline's eyes is Pierre Laval. Prior to Sigmaringen, Céline had been less than charitable to the Vichy minister, commenting to Marcel Déat in 1942 that his swarthy appearance made him look like a *Juif* (Jew) and a *nègre* (negro). But when he treated him in Sigmaringen, he changed his mind. In the novel, it is Laval who restores peace at the train station when starving, angry refugees have killed a German officer; and it is also Laval who promises Céline a diplomatic post at the French overseas *département* of Saint-Pierre-et-Miquelonne, in exchange for a cyanide capsule that Céline, as a doctor, can procure him. This alludes to two aspects of Laval's life: his pacifism, which he shared with Céline, and the fact that he attempted suicide by cyanide poisoning just before his execution. Céline's relatively positive portrayal of Laval in the novel was anticipated by a comment he gave in an interview to journalist Jacques Robert on 28 November 1947: 'My relationship with Laval was indeed very bad when he was in power, but in Sigmaringen he never gave me any trouble. On the contrary I always found him very dignified in adversity, very patriotic, very pacifist, all qualities that appeal to me.'[81]

Castle to Castle was generally very well received, even if – inevitably – it angered many members of the far Right, as well as the Left.

But its overall success was welcome news to Céline after the setback of *Fable for Another Time* and *Normance.* He wasted no time in working on the second instalment of his trilogy: *North*. If the two volumes of *Fable* had prioritized style over story and *Castle to Castle* history over autobiography, *North* marked a return to plot and characterization. This is because this novel, after briefly portraying his stay in Baden-Baden in the summer of 1944 and his visit to Berlin in early September, primarily focuses on a period and location in his exile – the two months he spent in the village of Kränzlin, some 60 kilometres (37 mi.) northwest of Berlin, between late August and late October 1944 – that were of negligible historical significance. Céline was thus relieved of the burden of 'historical responsibility' that he felt when writing *Castle to Castle*.

The prospect of greater artistic freedom offered by Kränzlin, after the rigid historical scrutiny of Sigmaringen, no doubt explains why he chose to focus on that part of his exile that came *before* rather than after his stay in southern Germany. Thus the final leg of his journey from Sigmaringen to Denmark was deferred to *Rigadoon*, the third novel of his trilogy. With the straitjacket of public opinion partially removed, he produced what many critics considered to be his best novel since *Journey*. To begin with, he had greater scope for intricate character development. *Castle to Castle* had principally been a succession of disjointed tableaux of real or adapted historical figures, whose lives were not directly intertwined. However, Kränzlin's more intimate and self-contained small community setting gave Céline the opportunity to delve deeply into each character's psychology and to explore his or her relationships with the other characters. There is thus more of an 'ensemble cast' feel to the novel that recalls *Guignol's Band*. Moreover, political controversy aside, the success of *Castle to Castle* made Céline less prone to dwell on his literary persecution and personal gripes and more focused on plot. His sense of injustice is still present, but less intrusive. Finally, following Gustave Flaubert's famous statement about *Madame Bovary* that he wanted to write a 'novel about nothing' ('roman sur rien'), Kränzlin's great virtue is its monotonous, unsophisticated rural setting: removed from the intrigue of political and military action, it is a space inhabited by ordinary people, whose stories of day-to-day universal human suffering come to the fore. Contrary to Berlin, Sigmaringen or even Baden-Baden, there are no external distractions: no bombs, no fighting, no high-level political intrigue or key historical players. Yet Zornhof, as he called Kränzlin in the novel, also provides a microcosm of society as a whole: as an overcrowded wartime farm that is owned by Prussian aristocrats, it comprises low-level Nazi officials, ordinary Germans and French, Polish and Russian forced labourers of all political persuasions, plus a gypsy community nearby. Céline thus has the perfect opportunity to revisit two of his favourite literary themes: war and social class; or more precisely, the exacerbation by the former of the innate injustices of the latter. If *Castle to Castle* had gradually stripped away the fanciful ideological and military illusions of a political elite who inhabit a fantasy world, *North* exposes the more visceral and impulsive behaviour of simple folk who are just trying to survive.

This contrast between the ordinary citizen and the political elite is brought into sharp relief by the narrator–protagonist's arresting portrayal of the bombed-out houses of Berlin. Céline had indeed visited Berlin twice during his exile: the first time, briefly, from Baden-Baden to meet officials to obtain papers; the second time, in early September 1944, when he met Karl Epting's contact Dr Helmut Haubold, who ratified his medical papers and secured his transfer to Kränzlin. In *North*, Haubold becomes the gregarious, but rather slippery, Dr Harras, who similarly escorts the trio to Zornhof. As Céline enters Berlin with Lili, Bébert and Robert Le Vigan, he portrays it as an eerie ghost town, which is reminiscent of Italian neo-realist director Roberto Rossellini's film *Germany Year Zero* (1945):

> ... [T]he city was all stage sets ... whole streets of facades, the insides had caved in, sunk into holes ... not all, but pretty near ... much cleaner I hear, in Hiroshima, neat, clipped ... decoration by bombing is a science, it hadn't been perfected yet ... here the two sides of the streets still created an illusion[.][82]

Céline's focus is not on France's German enemy, but on the universal plight of the dispossessed. As we shall see, if his novel occasionally invokes certain German stereotypes, these are far less present than in *Castle to Castle*. His primary concern is human hardship and the gap between rich and poor. Those who are rebuilding are aged, even disabled, Berliners, whose city has a long history of suffering:

> ... [A]nd there in that dismal Berlin I saw men and women about my age and even older, maybe seventy or eighty ... some of them blind ... hard at work ... bringing everything back to the sidewalk,

> piling it up in front of every house front, putting on numbers . . . bricks here! yellow tiles there! . . . broken glass in a hole! everything! . . . no goofing off! . . . rain, sun or snow, Berlin was never funny . . .[83]

These are normal German civilians, rather than Nazis, vulnerable underdogs and not ideological fanatics.

These stoic, unexceptional citizens are quite different from the character the trio subsequently encounter during their stay in the half-gutted rooms at the Zenith Hotel in Berlin. Directly opposite, they spot a flat that stands out in splendid isolation from the rest, a furnished mezzanine that is tastefully bedecked with flowers. Assuming that it belongs to a florist, they wander over, hoping to purchase a bouquet to spruce up their sparse, half-destroyed rooms. Its occupant turns out to be an eminent lawyer called Dr Pretorius, who explains to them, in perfect French, how he has legally come into possession of the flat: 'I am entitled by law. . . . as long as I rebuild, occupy the premises residentially and pay my taxes, the place is mine . . . law of 1700, never abrogated.'[84] Their charming host not only offers them a bouquet of flowers, but the use of his flat. They readily take up his offer to escort them on a guided tour of Berlin, starting with the nearby Chancellery.

At this point, however, Céline starts to feel uneasy. He is immediately struck by the Chancellery's sinister appearance, retrospectively making a symbolic connection with Hitler's subsequent suicide on 30 April 1945: 'Good grief, is that their Chancellery? . . . a big stone rectangle, something like granite . . . but much more dismal than granite, more funereal . . . no wonder what happened there!'[85] He is then taken aback by Pretorius's sudden claim to be able to hear music, when the Chancellery square is eerily empty and quiet:

> 'Sh! Sh!' he goes . . . 'There they are! hear the band?' I don't hear a thing . . . there's nobody but us on the little square . . . the three of us, the four, Lili, me, Le Vig, and him, nobody else . . . we stand there and wait . . . this Chancellery Square is really empty . . . not a sentry, not a soldier, not a *schupo* [short for Schutzpolizei, uniformed police in Nazi Germany] . . . It's beginning to look fishy to me . . . why'd he bring us here? . . .[86]

Alarm bells are raised when Pretorius claims to see Hitler entering the Chancellery, when there is nobody there: 'The square is deserted . . .

all the shops are closed . . . and he sees Hitler! "See him? He's going in? . . . the gates are opening! . . . magnificent! Magnificent! *heil!*'"[87] Pretorius is the German equivalent of the French collaborator and director Raoul Orphize in *Castle to Castle*: both men belong to a cultured, urban political elite, whose seductive outward charm hides their delusional grasp of reality. Orphize wanted to make a film glorifying Vichy; Pretorius still believes in the glory of the Führer. Both are mirages, the psychological projection of their ideological brainwashing. Their self-deception shields them from an inescapable fact that they refuse to accept: imminent and catastrophic German defeat. The flowers covering the empty shell of Pretorius's bombed-out flat thus also have a metaphorical function: their enticing appearance hides an unpalatable truth. In this respect, both men's falsification or denial of reality is the political equivalent of what the painter and sculptor Jules (Gen Paul) was doing in art: he too was deceiving his public with seductive 'surreal' images that refrained from showing the world as it really was.

And sugar-coating reality is precisely what Céline refused to do in his novel. *North* very deliberately shifts our focus from the self-deluded political elite, who take refuge in abstract fantasies, to ordinary citizens who struggle to survive at a very basic human level. What lends authenticity to his depiction is Céline's *own* experience of hunger. His friend Lucien Rebatet recalled how both the author and Robert Le Vigan vociferously complained about 'a sinister backwater, crazy Krauts, who hated the *Franzosen* (French people), a famine in the middle of a gaggle of geese and ducks'.[88] Lucette confirmed this in an interview in 1962:

> I can't say we have very fond memories of it. It was a family of country squires, who were not remotely friendly. Very hard people. The Nazis had requisitioned their house to place people like us, who were not involved with politics. We starved there. If in the end we went to Sigmaringen, it's because we couldn't take it anymore.[89]

If the conditions in Sigmaringen were tough, at least Céline's profession as a doctor afforded him and Lucette certain privileges and a minimum standard of living. While they did not partake of Pétain's gourmet lunches, neither did they starve. In the 'backwater' of Kränzlin, however, as unwelcome refugees who have the status of second-class citizens, they felt the full brunt of war deprivation. As soon as Céline, Lucette and Le Vigan arrive, they are alerted to the hypocrisy and meanness of their

German hosts by two French farm workers, Joseph and Leonard. Even if they are prisoners of war, their warnings that the hosts are well fed and eat secretly in their rooms, while virtually starving the French residents with a sparse evening meal, prove to be accurate:

> Their pockets . . . bursting! . . . enormous! . . . like this! look around! The barns are full! But they let us starve! . . . they're loaded . . . and they won't give us a carrot! You'll get a load of their System! . . . they'll roll you in clover! . . . that's what you came for, isn't it? . . . you're not the first! . . . take it from me, they're not fat when they leave . . . skin and bones! . . . you'll never see them eat! . . . they stoke in their rooms! At the table, nothing![90]

This was based on reality: Le Vigan's bedroom was located near a kitchen where the staff secretly prepared meals, and he was tormented by the cooking smells.[91] If Berliners had bombs to contend with, Kränzlin's inhabitants had hunger. Its rural setting, away from the fighting, shifts our gaze away from war as military conflict to war as a basic human struggle for survival. Hunger is the narrator's abiding obsession, even infiltrating his unconscious memories. But these memories do not alleviate suffering as they did in *Fable for Another Time*: they only serve to exacerbate it. Thus, when the narrator enters the grocer's shop, the sight of stacked shelves rekindles memories of his own trading post in Cameroon in 1917. This was a period of his life when, contrary to his stay in Zornhof, he had plentiful supplies:

> Speaking of trading posts, I had one like that myself, a straw hut, strings of shelves all around . . . that was in '17, with the Mafeas in Bikomimbo . . . quite an edifice, three stories, built entirely by myself and the village carpenters . . . cannibals, it seems . . . I never saw them eating dinner . . . but bandits, I'm sure of that . . . looters as bad as my Fifis on rue Girardon [. . .] I had everything, not like Zornhof! *cassoulet*, rice, cod fillets, loincloths . . .[92]

His memory of Cameroon thus starts off promisingly, with a nostalgic evocation of food; but it soon degenerates into his recollection of loss and deprivation. The trading post was built with the help of village carpenters, who were suspected cannibals and probable bandits. They, in turn, remind him of the looters who took his possessions in Montmartre in 1944. Cannibalism's connotations of human cruelty and savagery are thus applied to those who raided his flat. His memory transforms hunger from an uncontrollable primal urge into the direct manifestation of man's innate cruelty. And even though he had food in Cameroon, his ability to consume it was severely compromised both by the dirty water and tornadoes:

> that bog water is fatal . . . applesauce bowels for the rest of your life . . . At the first tornado everything flies away . . . shelves, merchandise, liana rigging, rice, kegs of tobacco! . . . [. . .] nothing left but scorpions, snakes and chiggers . . . everything else had taken off, absolutely . . . like my pad on rue Girardon . . .[93]

The tornado literally blows away his food and merchandise in Cameroon and metaphorically takes away his Montmartre flat in one fell swoop. This extreme weather, like hunger itself, becomes assimilated to ruthless human avarice: those who looted his flat. In Zornhof, he faces not only hunger, but the hostility of the German housewives in the grocer's shop, who leave as soon as they see French refugees entering: '*komm! Komm*! They gather up their baskets and kids'. But he speculates that the French equivalent of these housewives in Montmartre would have behaved no better towards him: 'the same women [. . .] would have rushed us, cut us up small and fought over our kidneys . . . a bit of liver . . . carried us away in their shopping bags . . . oh, that could happen here, too! . . .'[94]

By depicting the housewives as cannibals, he turns the earlier reference to the cannibals in Cameroon into a metaphor to designate both the ruthless nature of the *épuration* and of human beings more generally when they are faced with the harsh realities of war, irrespective of their nationality.

Céline's universalist view of human behaviour means that he avoids a purely negative stereotyping of Germans. If anything, he is more exasperated by Leonard and Joseph, the two French prisoners, who interrupt his medical treatment of the ageing 'Rittmeister' (commissioned cavalry officer), the 84-year-old debauched aristocratic head of the family ('old von Leiden who enjoyed getting himself whipped by his little imps').[95] That he is called von Leiden punningly alludes to the German verb *leiden*, which means 'to suffer'. Leonard and Joseph demand that the narrator smuggle in alcohol from a secret stash he has been told about by Dr Harras. They expect him to be more loyal to them as fellow Frenchmen than to the German patient he is trying to treat: 'let 'em croak! . . . what about us! Don't we exist?'[96] By the same token, he has every reason to be angry at the anti-French housekeeper, Frau Kretzer, for deliberately withholding his ration cards because her two sons have been killed on the front by the Allies. Yet he understands that her obstructive behaviour emanates from an irreducibly human emotion: grief. Her grief even drives her to madness, since she starts dancing hysterically and shouting accusations: '"*sie! sie franzosen*!" we'd murdered her sons! . . .'[97] What angers him is not so much her accusations, as the fact that his compatriots took his furniture from Montmartre, and members of his own family accused him of killing his mother (she died in March 1945, when he was already in exile), while at the same time raiding her flat in his absence, thinking he would never return from exile:

> It was only natural . . . this lunatic accusing me of everything . . . what with her grief over her two sons . . . but now . . . twenty-five years later and in my own family, it's a little funnier . . . and no chicken feed the crimes they accuse me of! Murdering my mother! [. . .] they stole everything from my mother's place . . . very sure of themselves! 'he'll never come back!'[98]

His ability to empathize with Frau Kretzer on the level of family and common humanity overrides any nationalist hostility he feels at the suffering she causes him. The Germans who deprive him of food while eating it themselves, are no worse than the French parents of Bezons, whom he witnessed stealing their own children's rations when he practised there as a doctor:

> Everywhere, in every country at war, it's the same vice . . . you never see what they eat and drink . . . the kids' rations, especially the milk, are raided for daddy's coffee . . . in Bezons, for instance, I prescribed extra milk for children under four, they never saw a drop of it . . .[99]

In the cauldron of war, primal human urges – hunger and sex – inevitably come to the fore in ways that overturn conventional morality and norms of behaviour. War is often messy, embarrassing and unheroic, and this is just as true of the First World War as it is of the Second. He recalls how in October 1914,

> [When] our regiment of dismounted cavalry was waiting for dawn under the constant fire of the batteries across the river, a crowd of women and young girls, middle and working class, came out under cover of darkness to feel us up and hoist their skirts, no talk, not a word wasted, from one dismounted cavalryman to the next . . .[100]

In *North*, Céline thus repeatedly shows this 'hidden face' of war to justify his pacifist, anti-war stance. He sheds light not on the military and political battles of the elite, but on the unglamorous, visceral human struggle for survival that affects ordinary people when they are under extreme duress. And these struggles are the same, whether it is the First or the Second World War. But another element common to all wars, and which also recalls the pacifist stance of *Journey*, is the exacerbation of social inequalities. He satirizes the condescending attitude of a local German aristocrat towards people like him, who manifestly do not belong to the social elite:

> The real iron curtain is between the rich and the down-and-outers . . . between people of equal fortune ideas don't count . . . when you take a good look, your opulent Nazi, an inhabitant of the Kremlin, directors of Gnome et Rhone . . . asshole buddies . . . they exchange wives, gargle the same Scotch, traipse around the same golf courses, buy and sell the same helicopters, and open the hunt together [. . .] Filthy sweat tramps, butt-picking bellyachers, back where you belong! That's what they think of us for sure![101]

The vast gulf between rich and poor is exposed when Rittmeister von Leiden is found in a field, having been viciously beaten by prostitutes from the nearby village of Moorsburg. Alongside him, and almost as badly bruised, is the Revizor (auditor). Céline is part of a search party organized by Herr Kracht, the estate's officious pharmacist and local member of the SS, who regularly joins Céline, Lucette and Le Vigan for their measly dinners, alongside various secretaries from the *Dienstelle* (office) and Herr and Frau Kretzer, the cook and housekeeper. The narrator reveals what caused it: the prostitutes were driven by hunger, poor sanitation, rationing and curfews to make a bid for a better life in the west ('sick of the sewers and garbage cans! . . . sick of the sidewalks! . . . sick of obeying! . . .').[102] En route, they encountered the Revizor and Rittmeister: the latter, in a fit of senility, was heading east in his full military attire thinking he could defeat the advancing Russian army. The prostitutes, worried that the two men would denounce them, beat them up and stripped them of their clothes and possessions in order to resell them. And as a sign of their desperation – which echoes the cannibalism evoked in the grocer's shop – they kill the Rittmeister's horse, chop it up and cook it:

> How the mare had died . . . how they'd roasted her . . . beginning with how they'd killed her . . . they'd taken their pickaxes to her head and belly! . . . and then they cut her up . . . dismembered her . . . and roasted the meat . . . that we could see! . . . they'd eaten some already . . . quite a lot! . . .[103]

Society's ultimate underdogs – prostitutes – are driven to kill an animal for food. Céline is too nuanced a writer to present this as a blatant revenge fantasy of the poor against the rich. Instead, he wants to remind the reader, by way of counterpoint, that there is not just one war going on, but two: not only the military conflict taking place in Berlin some 60 kilometres (37 mi.) away, but the less well publicized, visceral human struggle for survival that is happening in this rural setting: 'Boom! Booom! . . . it was rumbling and thundering as bad at the bottom of that gully as in our tower or Le Vig's cell at the manor . . . the whole plain was shaking . . . north, south and west . . . to give you an idea of what was going on in Berlin!'[104] He gives a powerful voice to the socially excluded: their war is very different from that of the political and military elites of Sigmaringen, Berlin and Baden-Baden.

Céline's pacifist social conscience, however, did not curtail his taste for literary innovation or comedy. *North* concludes strongly with a comical parody of a well-known genre: detective fiction, or the 'whodunnit'. A series of unexplained deaths occurs that have nothing to do with the war: that of Rittmeister von Leiden, whom Céline has treated for his wounds, and of his epileptic son, who is found strangled at the bottom of a murky pond. Céline finds himself thrust into the role of detective, as well as doctor, when he tries to piece together what has happened. He ponders a number of suspects and motives: Isis (known as Inge in the English translation), the sexually frustrated wife of the epileptic, who is of illegitimate birth and covets the estate's inheritance; Nicholas, the faithful Russian servant, who has been badly treated by the younger von Leiden; and Leonard and Joseph, the two French workers, who provide Céline with an alibi by insisting that he, Lucette and Le Vigan attend a performance given by the local gypsies while the murders take place. The attractive Isis has already used her sexual charms to try to entice the narrator, in his capacity as doctor, to buy poison at the pharmacy, which he refuses to do. She and Frau Kretzer are also caught trying to set fire to the estate.

Some levity is added to this serious catalogue of events by Robert Le Vigan, to whom Céline affectionately refers as 'Le Vigue'. He exploits his potential as 'temperamental actor', whose behaviour in real life was often unpredictable, to defuse the tension of a scene in which all the murder suspects are gathered around, while Nazi officials sent from Berlin conduct their investigation. Le Vigan suddenly blurts out that he is the murderer: '*Leute! Leute!... ich bin der mörder!... ich! Ich*!'[105] Céline tells him to shut up – that he was not the murderer, since everyone saw him attending the gypsy performance – and even Kracht, the local SS officer, explains that he is a temperamental actor: '*schauspieler! nervös!* actor! hysterical!' Céline adds that Le Vigue's fragile ego could not bear to see someone else perform instead of him: 'seeing a stage and not being on it! ... the long and short of it! A fit of jealousy!'[106] By the time he wrote the novel, Céline had forgiven Le Vigan for their bust-up in Sigmaringen. Céline had accused him of fraternizing too much with the collaborators; but when he later learnt that the actor had refused to testify against him at his trial, all was forgiven.[107]

Céline had produced a novel that was taut, suspenseful, moving and with his abundant gifts for tragicomedy and sharp social observation on full display. When the book came out on 20 May 1960, the critics were ecstatic. Even André Rousseaux, the critic from *Le Figaro littéraire*, who had so lambasted *Death on Credit*, was jubilant.[108] But the novel's reception was not without its problems. Céline's unflattering portrayal of two of its main characters, Isis von Leiden and Dr Harras, was based on two individuals, Frau Asta S. and Doctor H., who were still alive and recognized themselves in the book. They therefore sued Gallimard for defamation in 1962 and 1964 respectively, shortly after Céline's death in 1961. Not only was Frau S. awarded damages, but her lawyers managed to suspend the publication of the novel for three years until October 1964, by which time Gallimard had agreed to publish a new version in which all the original proper names would be replaced. Since then, Godard's Classiques Garnier edition, to which I refer in this book, has restored some, but not all, of the original names of the 1960 edition.[109] But back in 1960, Céline's main concern was to finish recounting his odyssey.

Rigadoon, his last ever novel, and the final instalment of the German trilogy, was all but complete when he suddenly passed away from a brain aneurysm on 1 July 1961.[110] The lack of final proofreading for a writer as meticulous as Céline and his ailing health no doubt explain why, despite its moments of brilliance and characteristic inventive flourishes, this is the weakest novel of the German trilogy. It was not published until 1969, after Lucette, assisted by her lawyer and Céline's biographer François Gibault, had agreed, after much agonizing, on a final manuscript version.

The novel's main plot required a degree of chronological subterfuge and modification to account for the fact that *Castle to Castle* had focused on Sigmaringen, and *North* on Kränzlin, the two episodes he had chosen to portray in reverse order. Céline's solution is to gloss over Sigmaringen altogether. He turns a succession of discreet episodes into one long continuous train journey that lasts eighteen days. This journey takes Céline and Lucette from Zornhof (Kränzlin) to Warnemünde via Rostock, on the Baltic Sea coast, from Warnemünde to Sigmaringen (via Berlin-Anhalt, where they have to change trains) and from Sigmaringen to Copenhagen (in other words, from the North Sea to the North Sea via southern Germany). The couple are told upon arrival in Sigmaringen to leave immediately and continue on to Denmark, while Robert Le Vigan is instructed to make his way to Italy. This obviously overlooks the four months that were spent in Sigmaringen, the fact that Le Vigan ended up in Argentina, not Italy, and that the train journey from Sigmaringen to Denmark took only four days.

This non-stop movement adds symbolic weight to the two main axes of the novel: trains and death. The train is a symbol of escape: Céline's desire to escape to Denmark, but also, just like the countless refugees he encounters along the way, from death. The zigzagging motion associated with the term *rigodon*, which is the name of a seventeenth- and eighteenth-century dance, personifies the train's constant attempts to dodge death from the bombs above. The second meaning of *rigodon* is the ringing sound made when a bullet hits its target on a shooting range. Thus, the military context of the novel is also evoked.[111] Of all the novels in the trilogy, this is the one that depicts human mortality in the most direct and gruesome terms. Céline's final novel implicitly evokes Émile Zola's 1890 novel *The Beast in Man* (*La Bête humaine*). This is the story of a murdering train driver, Lantier, whose atavistic urge to kill is also personified in the mechanical ferocity of his train locomotive *La Lison*. The novel ends with Lantier and his locomotive carrying troops, full steam ahead, towards the Franco-Prussian War, spelling France's imminent defeat. *Rigadoon* both repeats and reverses this link between the train, death and war: the train is not only an agent of death, as in Zola's novel, but the means of escaping it; it spells the imminent defeat not of France, but of Germany; and the final outcome is not disaster, but freedom.

The link between trains and death is first made when Céline and Lucette arrive in Rostock from Kränzlin on a scouting mission, to see how feasible it is to catch a ferry to Denmark from the nearby port of Warnemünde. They had indeed undertaken such a mission, under the guise of looking for a medical post there. In Rostock, they encounter a 'Nietzschean doctor', Oberarzt Haupt, who is responsible for 'treating' injured citizens who have been evacuated by train from Berlin. Another doctor, a disillusioned Greek communist by the name of Pröseidon, explains that Haupt applies Nietszche's theory of 'survival of the fittest'. Those injured Berliners who are strong enough to get up and walk can be treated; the others are just left to die in the snow: 'they clear the cars, they put the bodies out in the field . . . [. . .] the ones that are able to get up are invigorated'.[112] Céline is shocked by this method, denouncing its inhumanity: 'how could he operate in such a place? . . . the Greek had told me: he eliminates a lot of them!'[113]

Another link between trains and death is symbolized by the sight of a train turned upside down by a bomb, lying on a mountain-top:

> This locomotive way up there . . . upside down . . . I'm like St. Thomas, I only believe what I see! . . . 'behold, Thomas! Touch! . . .' as long as our train with all its flatcars and caboodle had stopped, I might as well go take a look . . . at this phenomenon, I mean this mountain of scrap and the locomotive on the summit . . .[114]

The allusion to the biblical figure of 'doubting Thomas' echoes Céline's description of the bombs that fell on Montmartre in *Normance*, when Jules was standing on the windmill: both episodes encapsulate aspects of war that seem so implausible, that they have to be seen to be believed.

This is also the case with the bombed cities that they encounter in between their train journeys. Céline compares Hamburg's plight to that of the ancient Roman city of Pompeii after the eruption of Vesuvius: 'Hamburg had been destroyed with liquid phosphorus . . . the Pompeii deal . . . the whole place had caught fire, houses, streets, asphalt, and the people running in all directions . . .'[115] As he plots his way through the ruins in search of food, he encounters charred bodies, just like the ones preserved by Vesuvius' volcanic ash thousands of years ago:

> It's not a foot this time, it's whole bodies in the sludge . . . melted asphalt, a sticky sludge all over them . . . greasy and black . . . hey! . . . a man, a woman, a child! . . . the child in the middle . . . they're still holding each other by the hand . . . and a little dog right next to them . . . a lesson . . . people trying to get away, the phosphorus set fire to the asphalt . . . I heard about it later, thousands and thousands . . . we weren't there for the fun of it, our aim in life was milk and a loaf of bread . . .[116]

Céline's own survival instincts are reinforced by the sight of those who did not make it. In *Castle to Castle*, he describes the bombing of Dresden according to a second-hand account, and in *North* he directly describes the bombed-out ruins of Berlin; but here he goes one step further: he portrays in visceral, gruesome terms the sight of the human carnage left behind by the bombs. In a scene that recalls his portrayal of Courtial's dismembered corpse in *Death on Credit* – which, as we have seen, draws on the grotesque portrayals of the painter Pieter Bruegel – he comes across a horrifically disfigured dead shopkeeper:

> The corpse . . . dead five six days, I'd say . . . cold in here, it hasn't fermented very much, but it stinks all the same . . . I go over . . . it's a storekeeper . . . sitting . . . at his cash desk . . . slumped forward . . . pharmacist? . . . grocer? . . . cash desk, I said . . . that's definite, the drawer's open, all full of paper marks . . . and a box full of food coupons . . . the box is open too . . . you see, I'm giving you all the details . . . but what interests me . . . is the cause of death . . . now I see! a fragment! His guts were hanging out . . . cut him open from hip to navel . . . disembowelled, in short . . . his intestines and epiploon on his knees . . . a fragment? from where? . . . Felipe catches on quicker than I do . . . he shows me . . . at the top of the roof . . . a breach . . . what I was calling the crater . . . boom! Dottore! An aerial bomb, direct hit! . . .[117]

The ellipses reinforce his slow, careful scrutiny, like a forensic investigator, of the shocking sight that he beholds. They show his painstaking attempt to understand and convey as accurately as possible, with the help of his Italian companion, exactly what happened. This level of detail adds authenticity to his role as 'chronicler'.

The extreme precision of his recollection is commensurate with the experience itself: that of having to be careful and hyper-vigilant as he picks his way through the still-burning ruins. But more often than not, Céline's *chronique* draws on his emotional memory, a memory which, in *Rigadoon*, is more authentic in describing the bombings than a standard historical account. This is especially the case when Céline suddenly is hit by a brick from a nearby exploding bomb, from which he suffers pain and concussion. This physical injury causes a psychological confusion that makes it impossible for him to remember this event rationally and analytically:

> I'm not the fainting kind, but there I was, kind of stunned . . . pain, but not bad, and blood . . . on my neck . . . I'm bleeding, yes, blood from my cerebrum . . . no! my medulla . . . I think . . . anyway, that area . . . I know I tried to stay lucid . . . I thought about Lili . . . and Bébert . . . but as if they'd gone away somewhere . . . far away . . . and me too, still further . . . in a different direction! that's all I can honestly remember . . . that bomb . . . where'd it come from?[118]

These hesitations, contradictions and words of self-doubt convey far more authentically the confusion that arises from his injury than any rational and analytical account, which would inevitably attempt to 'fill in the gaps' and thus come across as forced and artificial.

Realizing that his rational intellect is ill-suited to the task of portraying this event, Céline instead conjures up his sensory memory. He remembers hearing a particular sound – a melody – at that precise time, but he struggles to remember, as he transposes his recollection of the bombings to the page many years later, exactly what that sound was:

> But a melody! A melody! . . . and as I've said, magnificent! As magnificent as the panorama . . . a symphonic melody, so to speak, just right for this ocean of ruins . . . wild ruins . . . this fiery surf . . . pink . . . green . . . [. . .] *wheesh!* Listen! . . . I need another ear, the one I have left is no use at all . . . maybe at the piano, groping . . .[119]

When he was in his prison cell in Copenhagen, this event was still recent enough, and he also had the time, to recreate the sound of the bombs:

'Later in Copenhagen up there, two years in the clink, I had time . . . I composed grandiose melodies for myself, still in memory of Hanover.'[120]

But now, many years later, as he writes in 1961, and feels frustration at being unable to remember the exact sound, he requires some fresh memory trigger. As he hears the music wafting down from the dance studio up above, where Lucette is giving lessons, he decides to rush up later that night to try and identify the melody he is trying to recall, by playing the piano: 'A miracle! Twenty years you've been racking your brains, and damned if you haven't got it! . . . [. . .] I go back down, I've got my four notes . . . G sharp! G A sharp! . . . Got to remember them!'[121]

In *Fable for Another Time*, transposing his emotional memories to the page was easier: they were originally recorded as they came to him in his prison diaries, and they were constantly replenished by the sensory stimulus provided by the prison environment. In *Rigadoon*, however, he faces two additional challenges: that of trying to write about an experience fifteen years later, and one that was itself *already confusing at the time.* But the very fact that he acknowledges his difficulty in remembering is itself a testament to the authenticity of Céline's account.

And just as in *North*, this artistic integrity also means writing about the *untold* stories of the war, not the well-documented accounts of the political elites or of key historical players. This is especially apparent when one of the many trains that he, Lucette and Le Vigan have to catch is trapped in a tunnel because of an RAF bombing raid. Chaos ensues as a swarm of refugees of different nationalities, including mothers, children and heavily pregnant women, take shelter on the railway tracks and refuse to get back on the train, for fear of being killed. Céline implores a French-speaking German, Captain Hoffmann, to escort a woman, whose baby is desperate for milk, to the nearest town of Furth. The captain eventually agrees, but he asks a favour in return: Céline is to deliver a message to a friend of Hoffman's, Captain Lemmelrich, who will be attending the military funeral of Field Marshal Rommel in Ulm. Lemmelrich is a member of Marshal von Rundstedt's staff. Rommel was one of Hitler's most brilliant generals, but he was forced to commit suicide following his involvement in the July 1944 bomb plot against the Führer. But in the novel, Céline is completely ignorant as to who Rommel is: 'Rommel? . . . never heard of him.'[122] And the message he is to deliver on Hoffmann's behalf has nothing to do with military conflict, only family: 'just one sentence . . . "your daughter in Berlin is better"'.[123]

This episode echoes the perspective of *North*: Céline wants to tell the untold story of war from an ordinary, human perspective that has nothing to do with military strategy or political ideology. Even army captains like Hoffmann and Lemmelrich have families and friends and the same concerns and worries as everyone else. Céline's downplaying of Rommel's celebrity and the fact that he, Lucette and Le Vigan never make it to his funeral because they are waylaid in Ulm by a fireman and a group of French refugees, reinforces his emphasis on the common humanity that unites all sides during a war. And Hoffmann's genuine concern for his colleague and willingness to escort the mother and her starving baby to safety presents him in a far better light than the fanatical ideologue Haupt, the Nietzschean doctor who left injured citizens to die in the snow.

Céline did not ignore historical facts completely. Rommel's funeral did indeed take place at Ulm on 18 October 1944, with Marshall von Rundstedt in attendance, as well as officers from the French Milice, who were stationed there. Céline would have learned about the funeral when he arrived in Sigmaringen a couple of weeks later. If there is no record of his having met the fireman and his wife, Céline and Lucette did pass through Ulm twice, on their way to Sigmaringen in late October 1944 and to Denmark in March 1945. They were shocked by the transformation that had taken place: a small picturesque town with a splendid cathedral, the Münster, whose tower was 161 metres (528 ft) high, had been reduced to a mountain of rubble.[124]

Little wonder, after all the bombings, injuries, corpses, hunger and hardships that he had experienced, that the closing pages of *Rigadoon* that conclude his apocalyptic trilogy of novels switch to a poetic tone to express his relief at arriving in the promised land of Denmark: 'Oh well, this is Denmark, we'll see . . . [. . .] the sea was tourist-blue . . . a healthy swell, though, just enough to put a pretty crest of foam on the waves . . . the gulls are circling around them . . . just the thing for a poster, irresistible . . .'[125] Thus ended Céline's account of his nine-month odyssey that had begun in Montmartre on 17 June 1944.

His journey may have been difficult, but at least it was eventful. However, the three and a half remaining years of Céline's exile between his release from prison in June 1947 and his return to France in early 1951 did not make it into his novels. Whether they would have done so had he lived longer is debatable, given how tedious and frankly uneventful his life was during this period. Dominated by legal questions, writing letters, working on both volumes of *Fable* and hosting occasional visitors, it could hardly compare in excitement to what had preceded it. It was still, however, preferable to being in prison. He continued to languish there – thereby at least avoiding extradition – owing to a legal deadlock between France and Denmark. Although an extradition treaty had been signed between the two nations in 1877, Article 75 of the French penal code, for treason or *intelligence avec l'ennemi*, was not included under the terms of the treaty, a fact that the sympathetic Danish chief of police Aage Seidenfaden exploited in late December 1945, to buy Céline valuable time.[126] Article 75, to which Céline frequently refers in the German trilogy, was the main accusation levelled against him. Moreover, there was a lack of fit between French law and the French public's overriding desire to see him prosecuted for his antisemitic writings. Aside from the brief period between April 1939 and October 1940 when the Marchandeau decree was valid (resulting in Céline's prosecution for his antisemitic opinions in *Trifles for a Massacre*), there was no law in France condemning the incitement of racial hatred, until 1972. Thus the antisemitic pamphlets legally fell under the category of freedom of expression.[127] The accusations under Article 75 that were initially sent by the French Ministry of Justice on 31 January 1946 were considered by the Danish government to be legally vague and without foundation. Allegations that he was an 'honourary member' of a group of pro-German doctors; that his novel *Guignol's Band* and his preface to *Bezons à travers les âges* (Bezons Through the Ages), a historical work published by his friend Albert Serrouille, were 'favourable to Germany'; and that he had 'facilitated German propaganda' were baseless and inaccurate.[128] In May, the Danish Ministry of Justice, therefore, requested a more detailed list of charges as well as an interrogation of Céline by its French counterpart. Both were declined. Realizing the difficulty of getting Céline extradited, the ultra-zealous French ambassador Guy de Girard de Charbonnières tried desperately to restart proceedings, but made little headway.[129]

As for Céline, he pounced on the legal weaknesses of the accusations by drafting, in November 1946, an impassioned thirteen-page riposte, which was essentially a fleshed-out version of the letter to Marie Canavaggia, analysed above, in response to the accusations of Hérold-Pacquis. It reiterated his refusal to publish or receive payment for any article in the Collaborationist press (although some thirty letters he sent were published by the editors), when many other writers who had done so had gone unpunished. His pamphlet *A Fine Mess* was reviled by many collaborators, even being banned by the Vichy government. As for the nine months he spent in Germany, these were merely a stepping stone to getting to Denmark. His time in Sigmaringen was exclusively spent as a doctor, treating his compatriots and avoiding all propaganda activities.

If Céline's assertions were largely true (though he conveniently forgot to mention his invitation to the German embassy by Otto Abetz, or his requests for paper from Karl Epting), he is disingenuous about the *real* reason he was wanted in France, even if it fell outside the remit of Article 75: his antisemitism. Even though his pamphlets had been published before the Holocaust, and therefore could not be shown to have any causal relationship to it, he makes no mention of the death camps other than in private conversations or letters, and his prison diaries, in which he states, 'The Jewish masseuse is sending us to Bouchenwald [*sic*] – we are overwhelmed by the dead of the concentration camps – we are suffocating.'[130] He more explicitly distances himself from the Holocaust when he justifies his anti-Jewish pamphlets purely on the grounds of his pacifism and patriotism, a mantra he was to repeat throughout his legal trial and which is typified by this 1948 letter to his friend Jean Paulhan:

> When I was attacking Jews, when I was writing *Trifles for a Massacre*, I did not mean or recommend that Jews should be massacred. Bollocks, quite the opposite! I was pleading with the Jews that they shouldn't hysterically drag us into another massacre more disastrous than the one of [19]14–18! It is quite different. The meaning of my pamphlets has been distorted in the most underhand way. There is a persistent attempt to label me as someone who massacres Jews. I am a staunchly patriotic preserver of French people and Aryans – and also, as it happens, of Jews! I did not want Auschwitz, Buchenwald.[131]

In his novels, the nearest he comes to evoking the gas chambers is in *Castle to Castle*, via his fictionalized head of the Gestapo in Sigmaringen, von Raumnitz. This character was based on Karl Boemelburg, who was the real head of the Gestapo in Paris until November 1943, when he was transferred to Vichy, owing to his age. It was Boemelburg, a Nazi with a sinister reputation, who arranged Pétain's transfer from Vichy to Sigmaringen. Céline had met him in August 1942 via Fernand de Brinon, Vichy ambassador in Paris, and it was he who authorized his visa to Denmark in March 1945. Céline's fictionalization of Boemelburg, who was from the Rhineland, as the noble Prussian von Raumnitz, is intended, according to Sautermeister, to appeal to his French readers' familiarity with the negative stereotype of militarist Germans that had emerged during the Franco-Prussian war of 1870. Von Raumnitz's Lebanese wife, Aïcha (her ethnicity is itself an ironic satire of Nazi racial policy), is even more threatening than he is: not only is she accompanied by sinister mastiffs (a satire of Nazi oppression), but she also escorts various detainees in Sigmaringen to the mysterious 'room 36' from which they are never seen again:

> It seems they shipped people out at night . . . a truck came by on certain nights . . . [. . .] the legend, the rumor was that nobody was ever supposed to see that truck . . . that they chained them and piled them in . . . all these so-called fugitives . . . and hauled them away to the East . . . further than Posen . . . supposedly to some camp . . .[132]

Given that collaborators, rather than Jews, are the people who disappear from 'room 36', it is difficult to draw definitive conclusions from this passage. It is a satire of Nazi oppression that avoids discussing the camps directly. Céline was certainly an antisemite, but there is no evidence, in any of his writings or statements, that he ever supported the Holocaust.

Had he done so, it is unlikely that he would have received the support of prominent Americans from the legal and cultural world, some of whom were Jewish. In late 1946, Julian Cornwell, a New York attorney, translated his *Mémoire en défense* into English. With the help of a young Jewish professor of English at Brandeis University, Milton Hindus – who visited Céline in Denmark in 1948, resulting in his memorable interview of the writer – he also organized a petition in Céline's favour. Among the signatories were the author Henry Miller, the composer Edgar Varèse and the publisher James Laughlin. The petition demanded Céline's release from prison on the grounds that he should not be prosecuted for freedom of expression; it also emphasized his military record in both world wars and the climate of vengeance that was reigning in France at the time.[133] The ironic outcome of the petition was not lost on Céline: it relaunched his publishing career more quickly in America than in his home country. In June 1947, he signed a contract for a new edition of *Death on Credit*, for which Milton Hindus wrote a generous preface, and another one for *Guignol's Band*, with James Laughlin, that would eventually be translated and published in English in 1954.

Seeking to capitalize on this international support to break the deadlock between France and Denmark, Mikkelsen wrote a furious letter, including a copy of the American petition, to the Danish Ministry of Justice on 27 January. He highlighted Céline's rapidly declining health and his fundamental human right to know where he stood; round-the-clock surveillance in such harsh conditions was completely unnecessary, since he was not a wanted criminal. His client was duly transferred, much to the annoyance of Danish communists, to the more pleasant surroundings of Copenhagen's Rigshospitalet on 26 February, where he began a period of 'semi-liberation' until his official release on 24 June 1947.[134] Lucette, in the meantime, had been living, since August 1946, in a Copenhagen flat at 8, Kronprincessegade that belonged to one of the prison wardens and his wife, in exchange for their use of her mother and stepfather's flat in Menton in the south of France. This had followed a huge bust-up with Karen Jensen, who had returned from Spain to reclaim her flat. After a brief period of cohabitation with Lucette, Karen had complained to Céline while visiting him in hospital that Lucette was squandering the gold entrusted to Karen on items such as a fur coat. This caused a huge row with Lucette, but he eventually took her side after Karen admitted to having spent some of the money herself. Mikkelsen henceforth took charge of the money, which he gave to Céline and Lucette in regular payments, and thus was ended the friendship with Karen.

But they could no longer afford to rent a flat in Copenhagen. Once the prison warden and his wife returned from Menton in 1948, Céline, who by now had joined Lucette in their flat following his release from prison, found himself homeless. Mikkelsen offered them a house he owned in Klarskovgaard, 8 kilometres (5 mi.) from Korsor on the North Sea coast. This was far away from the city lights of Copenhagen, only basically furnished and freezing cold in the winter. To Céline, this was an 'exile within an exile'. Although Mikkelsen came to visit them every week, and they befriended the local family who looked after it, Céline was bored, frustrated and bereft of cultural stimulation. He laboured away at *Fable* and his letters, while Lucette danced and swam in the sea. They built up a menagerie of cats and dogs to keep them entertained, Céline by now having lost all faith in humanity.

Added to his financial and legal woes was an existential one: that of being cut off from the French language. Language and literature were his lifeblood. Of course, he spoke French to Lucette, but she was no great conversationalist: her talents lay in dance. Two fellow French expats came to his rescue in the autumn of 1947. The first was Pastor François Löchen, head of the French Reformed Church in Copenhagen, whom Céline approached one day after his sermon. Although Céline was an atheist, he appreciated this erudite man's conversation, letters and support. Löchen tried in vain to intercede on Céline's behalf with the hostile French ambassador, and even offered him financial assistance. Céline was greatly touched, but too proud to accept.[135] His second contact was bookshop owner Denise Thomassen and her Danish husband. They had been forced into exile from France in 1943 for selling books that were considered Collaborationist. Denise contacted Céline after his release from prison, and he became a regular in their bookshop in Copenhagen, where they gave him books and French pastries. Although their tastes were too conservative to appreciate his literature, they discussed more traditional authors such as Balzac, and he regaled them with exaggerated stories about his childhood. Denise's daughter recalled how he would embellish the truth, saying that he had grown up without a father and

The house where Céline and Lucette lived in 1948, Klarskovgaard, Denmark.

Céline and Lucette with their dog Bessy, Klarskovgaard, 1950. (*Cahiers de L'Herne*).

that his mother was a cleaner. The Thomassens continued to send parcels of meat to Céline (as a vegetarian, he would feed the meat to his dogs) once he had moved to Klarskovgaard in July 1948, and he thanked them by sending them copies of *Journey*. Although they were offended when he left Denmark without saying goodbye, they at least provided a small slice of the France that he so missed and the opportunity to speak the French language he so loved.[136]

These few expats aside, Céline's intellectual sustenance came from writing letters. More than half his entire correspondence was written during his exile. His most important correspondent from late May 1946 onwards was Albert Paraz, a minor author whom Céline had recommended to Denoël in 1934, and who had frequented anarchist and surrealist circles in the 1920s. His value to Céline was as a non-conformist who had led a varied and interesting life (which included sustaining lung damage from a gas explosion while working at the Ben-Ounif research centre in the Sahara in 1939), and whose dedication to helping him as a humble admirer, was total. Céline sent Paraz no fewer than 353 letters until his death in 1957; with their shared love of colourful language and popular slang, they frequently exchanged thoughts on style. Paraz kept Céline abreast of any press reports about him, put him back in touch with his friend Arletty, lobbied hard to lift an embargo on publishers who were blacklisted for publishing Collaborationist writers and forged new contacts for Céline in the changed literary landscape of post-war France.

It was Paraz, together with a fellow Céline fanatic, the painter Jean Dubuffet, who put him in touch with Jean Paulhan, the editor of *Cahiers de la Pléiade*, the journal he set up to replace the *Nouvelle Revue française* (N.R.F.). Co-founded by André Gide in 1908, the original journal had spawned the Éditions de la Nouvelle Revue française in 1911, headed by Gaston Gallimard, which eventually became Éditions Gallimard. But from 1944, the N.R.F. was suspended for its Collaborationist activities under the editorship of Pierre Drieu La Rochelle, between 1940 and 1943. However, Paulhan's close ties with Gallimard helped smooth the passage for Céline's generous contract with the publisher in 1951. In the meantime, Paulhan was willing to publish a text by Céline in his new journal, but not his ballet *Foudres et flèches* (Lightning and Arrows), or the vicious text he wrote attacking Sartre, *À l'Agité du bocal* (To the Nutcase). This was deemed by Paulhan to be too controversial and incendiary. Céline's lawyers wholeheartedly agreed. By now, Albert Naud, a French lawyer, had been added to Céline's legal team, via their mutual friend, Antonio Zuluaga. Naud had the advantage of being a former member of the Résistance, who had defended Pierre Laval, albeit in vain.[137] Eventually, Maria Canavaggia, Céline's faithful secretary, suggested a compromise: Paulhan could publish the unfinished manuscript of *Cannon Fodder*. Paraz agreed to include the text on Sartre among his personal memoirs, *Le Gala des vâches* (The Cow Gala), published in 1948.

The third Frenchman to help Céline was a young admirer in his thirties and a Right-wing illustrator for the journal *Aux Écoutes*, Pierre Monnier. He went to visit the author in Klarskovgaard in the late summer of 1948.[138] After liaising with Paraz, Monnier published the first 'official' interview of Céline in the Belgian journal *Europe-Amérique* in August 1949.[139] This was essentially conceived as a public relations exercise to remind French readers of Céline's unjust treatment, poor health, literary genius and war record. The five photographs include a decrepit-looking Céline and Lucette in front of their simple house on the Baltic, and one with him and the famous actress Arletty at Vence in 1941. There was also a reproduction of the 1915 illustration from *L'Illustré national*, which shows Céline heroically brandishing a sword on horseback, during the First World War. Monnier describes Céline as 'overwhelmed, reduced to poverty, stranded in one of the most godforsaken corners of the Danish countryside, but not defeated'.[140] His literary credentials are emphasized by a décor that is 'fit for *King Lear*' and his comparison to another French writer who was exiled by the sea (Guernsey), Victor Hugo. His shoulders slump under the weight of the illness he contracted in prison, and he is quoted as saying, 'There is only one thing on my mind . . . to see my homeland again.'[141] He complains that what most hurts him 'is not hatred, since that is directed at a man that I never was, but lies'.[142] Monnier cleverly tugs at the readers' heartstrings and minimizes the seriousness of Céline's antisemitism, by quoting an (apocryphal) story: that of a man who saw Céline only once during his exile, but who still went to lay flowers on his mother's tomb in Paris. She had died in March 1945, without saying goodbye to her exiled son: 'That man was a rabbi.' And Monnier cites two Jews who are 'fervent admirers' of the author: Milton Hindus and Paul Lévy, the editor of *Aux Écoutes* in Paris.[143]

Monnier's article was conceived as a necessary corrective to the bad press Céline was receiving in his homeland, over which he had no control. Although extracts from the article were reproduced in a less than complimentary fashion in *Paris Match*, any favourable publicity, however small, could assist with his legal trial. In October 1948, on the advice of an industrialist friend and admirer, Paul Marteau, Céline switched lawyers from Albert Naud to Jean-Louis Tixier-Vignancourt. Although Tixier had far-Right leanings, he was well connected in the French courts and more energetic than the Left-wing Naud.[144] It so happened that Tixier also had good relations with the new magistrate who was assigned to Céline's case in May 1949, Jean Seltensperger, whose own wife was a fan of the writer.[145] After receiving numerous letters from Céline, written with his customary verve, and a visit from Mikkelsen in person to plead his case, Seltensperger concluded that, of the accusations levelled against

Céline with his lawyer Jean-Louis Tixier-Vignancour, 12 October 1951.

him, only certain passages from *A Fine Mess* (1941) and his consent for Denoël to republish *Trifles for a Massacre* in 1943 were problematic. That said, Céline had not modified anything from *Trifles* from its original 1937 version, which was published *before* the Occupation. Nor was there any evidence of collaboration with the Nazis, or that Céline gave consent to publish his letters in Right-wing journals during the Occupation. Nevertheless, all hell broke loose when this news was leaked, possibly by Tixier, to the Left-wing journal *L'Aurore* on 26 October. This scandal led to Seltensperger's replacement as magistrate by René Charrasse, who was less well disposed towards Céline, but at least repealed Article 75 against him (for treason). He retained only Article 83, for acts of 'national indignity', which carried only heavy fines and short prison terms.[146]

The 'Cas Céline' was also making front-page news in France. A survey conducted among writers and artists in January 1950, by liberal journalist Maurice Lemaître for *Le Libertaire*, deeply divided opinion. Painter Jean

Dubuffet and writer Marcel Aymé were among those who defended him; the surrealist and communist writers Benjamin Péret and André Breton vehemently condemned his antisemitism, fascism and literature. Writer Albert Camus was more balanced: he said that 'political justice disgusts me', and that Céline's case should be dropped, but expressed his equal disgust at antisemitism and especially the antisemitism of the 1940s. A judicial verdict was to be pronounced on 21 February. Numerous witness testimonies were gathered by Céline's friends and prominent supporters, including the actress Arletty, American author Henry Miller (even though Céline had dismissed his novel *Tropic of Cancer*) and even Raoul Nordling, the Swedish consul general to France, who had famously intervened to stop the Germans destroying Paris in 1944 and briefly visited Céline in Klarskovgaard in 1948.[147]

Under Article 83, Céline was found guilty of 'national indignity', given a one-year prison sentence in absentia and fined 50,000 francs, with confiscation of half his assets, including, much to his fury, his military pension. Commentators disagree about whether this verdict could be considered good or bad for Céline in the context of the times. Biographer Frédéric Vitoux argues that in the anti-fascist and pro-communist climate, he could not have hoped for a better outcome.[148] But the more sceptical historian Odile Roynette argues that after the hard line taken by the communist-led Résistance in 1946, the *épuration* began to soften from 1948. The Christian Democrats in the Mouvement républicain populaire (MRP) and the Rassemblement du peuple français (RPF) began to advocate a culture of clemency, national unity and reconciliation, even if this risked offending the memory of the Résistance. By 1950 Céline himself was more conscious of this more tolerant attitude.[149]

However, what finally broke the deadlock for Céline was Tixier's shrewd opportunism. Instead of appealing to a normal French court, he presented Céline's case to a military tribunal, invoking the law of partial amnesty (*loi d'amnistie partielle*) of 16 August 1949, whereby former combatants and war-wounded in both wars, even criminals (*délinquants*), could be granted amnesty. This was based on a law of 23 October 1919, according to which former war-wounded, *délinquants* and their widows and relatives were granted amnesty. Tixier kept his strategy top secret and, as a precaution, presented his client under the name Louis Destouches, hoping that the judge would not make the connection with the notorious author Louis-Ferdinand Céline. This is indeed what happened, and the amnesty was granted on 20 April 1951. It is quite possible that one of the officials present at the hearing, André Camadeau, knew exactly what was going on but said nothing, partly because he knew Tixier as a fellow native of Pau and partly because he bore a grudge towards the Gaullists who were condemning former fascists.[150]

Either way, Céline was a free man, and the French courts could not overrule the military tribunal. Tixier informed the French press on 26 April. On 30 June, Céline; Lucette; their three cats Bébert, Thomine and Flûte; and their dog Bessy left Klarskovgaard for Copenhagen, where they spent two nights at Mikkelsen's home. On 1 July, they took a flight to Nice, followed by the short ride to Menton, where Lucette's mother lived with her stepfather, Ercole Pirazzoli. They stayed with them until 23 July, Céline finding it difficult to tolerate the heat and his mother-in-law. They then took another flight, this time to Céline's beloved native city: Paris. After seven long and painful years, he was finally back on familiar turf.

seven

Death, Legacy and the Céline Culture Wars

The end of Céline's seven-year exile lifted an enormous weight off his shoulders. But his long-awaited freedom came at a price: he had burnt too many bridges, not least with the close-knit bohemian community of Montmartre that had once embraced him as one of their own. Having previously fraternized with the locals and held court to an admiring coterie of artists and writers in its bustling cafes, he was now considered the pantomime villain. He and Lucette had no option but to make a fresh start somewhere else. Their prayers were answered when they acquired a large house at 25, rue des Gardes, in the quiet Paris suburb of Meudon, with money Lucette had inherited from her recently deceased grandmother. Meudon was not just some name plucked out of a hat: Céline fondly remembered visiting it as a child, when he would accompany his mother there to sell lace.

Meudon was reminiscent of Montmartre in one important respect: it provided breathtaking views of Paris. This time, however, the capital could be contemplated not from up above, but down below: specifically, from a sprawling riverside garden, from which it loomed majestically on the opposite banks of the Seine. It is ironic that the same author whose novel *Journey* had so satirized the exploitative conditions of the Ford factories in Detroit should choose to live in a house whose previous owner was none other than the car manufacturer Louis Renault. Despite its proximity to his factory in Billancourt, Renault abandoned the house during the Occupation, before it was almost destroyed by a stray bomb that landed in the garden. Céline had thus unwittingly joined the ranks of the industrial bourgeoisie he so despised. But by now, his longing for discretion and space superseded all other considerations. The former was provided by a tall, imposing gate that allowed visitors to be screened, and the latter by two upper floors that were converted into a studio where Lucette could give dance lessons to a prestigious clientele, and a ground floor that served as Céline's study. The summer heat would drive him to the cooler cellar down below, which was equipped with a bed, on which he would lie down when his increasingly frequent migraines became unbearable. Nor was the house a total betrayal of his humble roots and populist sympathies: he was back in a Paris riverside *banlieue* that recalled the Courbevoie where he was born. Moreover, the house was in a part of Meudon that, like Céline himself, was neither quite working class nor bourgeois: it was situated halfway between the most affluent part of the suburb, near the observatory, and the working-class district around the Renault factories of Billancourt.[1] Having once lost everything, he was now leaving nothing to chance: he put the house in Lucette's name to give her security, should anything happen to him. This decision was as much psychological as it was financial: the suffering of his exile – even if it was largely self-inflicted – had made him extremely edgy, suspicious and paranoid.

His paranoia, though at times excessive, was not entirely unfounded. Once the locals discovered who he was, there was uproar. The communists circulated a petition quoting extracts from his controversial writings and the names of some of his far-Right acquaintances during the Occupation. This backlash was swiftly stopped in its tracks by the mayor of Meudon, Henry Albert, who announced that Céline had paid his debt to society, been granted amnesty and deserved to be left in peace; otherwise, the police would have to intervene.[2]

Thereafter, Céline was largely left alone, and spent the last ten years of his life as a virtual recluse, writing his novels or tending to the odd medical patient.[3] His tiny clientele made the doctor's plaque on his gate largely symbolic: it was only really thanks to eminent literary critic Henri Mondor, whose own background as a surgeon made him sympathetic to Céline's plight, that he was granted permission to practice again in 1953, until his retirement in May 1959, when he was eligible for his doctor's pension (his military pension having been confiscated).[4] He seldom ventured into Paris and avoided socializing or going to the cinema; although he had always wanted to visit the Maritime Museum (Le Musée de la Marine), he could never quite bring himself to do so. He would rise early at six and write until nine, when Lucette would bring him a breakfast of croissants and tea; the rest of the morning would be devoted to writing, reading the newspaper – *Le Figaro* or *Le Monde* – and answering his correspondence. He took a perverse pleasure in reading the obituaries of those who had wanted him dead. He would sometimes venture down to lower Meudon to do some shopping or visit the occasional patient. He usually fixed his own lunch, while Lucette gave dance lessons upstairs. In the afternoon, he would return to his manuscripts, or see the handful of patients who dared to visit him at home. His supper with Lucette was frugal, owing to his delicate stomach, and was followed by an early bedtime of no later than nine o'clock. The couple possessed neither radio nor television, both of which he hated.[5]

Despite this rather spartan existence (with the exception of the cleaner they employed), he felt guilty about the sacrifices Lucette had made during his exile. Knowing that she had been deprived of culture for so long, he encouraged her to attend Gaston Gallimard's cocktail parties (or 'coquetèles', as he called them), which were frequented by the fashionable literary elite of Paris and where she was chaperoned by Gaston's son, Claude. But Céline's paranoia was never far from the surface: not only did he worry about Lucette's spending (she was prone to impulse buying), but if she was gone for too long, he would ring the police in a panic to check that she had not been run over. He would come to greet her with their dogs at Bellevue train station, the nearest to their house, where she would surprise him with jars of his favourite breakfast jam, purchased in Paris. His fear of crowds and public exposure meant that Lucette provided his only vicarious contact with the common man: he would urge her to tell him stories of her encounters with Paris taxi drivers. Despite his increasing dependency on, and overprotective attitude towards Lucette, he did not interfere with her domain: the dance studio. She quickly put a stop to his slightly voyeuristic habit of greeting her younger dance pupils from his chair as they arrived and asking them to curtsy.[6]

Family visits, from both his side and hers, were kept to a minimum. Jules Almansor, Lucette's father (who passed away in 1952), was allowed to visit once a week, but alone: Céline disliked Jules's second wife, Fanny de Azpeitia, almost as much as he did his mother-in-law, Lucette's mother Gabrielle Pirazzoli, who was not among the invited guests. It is not exactly known how often Céline saw his daughter Colette, although he was in touch with her mother, his first wife, Édith Follet, in 1958, when her mother died. They were on sufficiently friendly terms for him to ask Édith (she had, by then, remarried and was a renowned illustrator) to illustrate his latest ballet, but she politely declined.[7] However, he made little effort to get to know his grandchildren. Lucette arranged for his fifteen-year-old grandson, Yves Turpin, to visit them in Meudon. Although he was initially polite, Céline suddenly cut the visit short and asked the boy to come back once he had completed his *baccalauréat*. He never came back.[8]

Before 1944, Céline had been a pessimist, but a sociable one. After his exile, he became a misanthrope who preferred the company of animals to that of humans. Consequently, the house became a virtual menagerie, much to the chagrin of the neighbours, with whom he got into heated disputes about the barking dogs. He greatly mourned the death of his favourite cat Bébert in 1952, but found solace in his many other pets, including his beloved dog Bessy and parrot Toto, who was not averse to repeating Céline's expletives.[9] Those few who were admitted to Meudon were mainly loyal friends from the Montmartre years. These included Albert Paraz, Fréderic Monnier, Clément Camus and Maria Le Bannier, the ex-mistress of Athanase Follet, his former father-in-law, who came to visit with her daughter Sergine. Céline and Lucette had spent several happy summers in their flat in Saint-Malo in the late 1930s. There was also the illustrator Éliane Bonabel, whose uncle he knew from his Clichy medical practice and whom he had treated as a child.

Two other regulars were the author Marcel Aymé and the iconic actress Arletty, his fellow *payse*, or native of Courbevoie, whom he had first befriended in 1941.[10] Arletty's own fascist associations during the war had damaged her career and reputation, although far less than Céline's. In March 1941, she had embarked on an ill-advised, passionate love affair with a dashing officer in the Luftwaffe, Hans Jürgen Soerhing.[11] She was 42 and he a decade younger. Despite not being a Nazi fanatic, he still worked closely with Reichsmarschall Hermann Goering, the head of the Luftwaffe and one of Hitler's most senior and trusted advisors, whom Arletty herself met at a function. By 1944, she was tarred with the brush of 'horizontal collaboration', the term used to designate French women who had affairs with the Nazi enemy, though she avoided the fate of the *tondues*, who had their heads forcibly shaved in public as a punishment.[12] She also refused Soehring's pleas to flee with him from France in July 1944. Her attempts to hide at the home of a countess in Choisy-le-Roi and then the Hotel Lancaster near the Champs-Elysées were thwarted by her arrest on 20 October. She then spent eleven nights in the Concièrgerie prison, several weeks in the internment camp at

Drancy and then around two years under house arrest in Château de la Houssaye in Seine-et-Marne. Even though she had refused to work for the Nazi-approved film production company La Continental, she was still banned from making films. Eventually, on 6 November 1946, she received the relatively light sentence of *blamé* (blamed) from the Comité d'épuration. Not that this prevented her from continuing her affair with Soehring in secret. By 1947, she was back filming *La Fleur de l'âge* with Marcel Carné.[13]

If Arletty had managed to bounce back relatively unscathed, Céline, by contrast, was a shadow of his former self. He was 'a different man' ('un autre homme'), recalled Marcel Aymé in 1952, observing his steep physical decline.[14] It is a testament to his long-standing affection for Arletty that he was coaxed out of Meudon by a young literary admirer, Paul Chambrillon, to record a reading of his first two novels with her, alongside her fellow actor Michel Simon. Following a technical hitch in a studio in avenue de Versailles in Paris, a grumpy Céline agreed to undertake two further recordings at the end of the year in Arletty's

Céline with his dogs, Meudon, *c.* 1955.

and Simon's respective flats.[15] He also went to Arletty's flat to record two songs he had written, entitled 'À Nœud coulant' and 'Règlement'.[16] Such nostalgic moments of happiness were rare. The successive failures of his novels *Fable for Another Time* in 1952 and *Normance* in 1954 knocked his confidence. A new literary generation was emerging: the novelists of the *nouveau roman*, who would soon be followed by Françoise Sagan, author of *Bonjour Tristesse*, whom Céline did not rate as a writer.[17]

He had also managed to alienate previous literary supporters, most notably his former admirer Jean-Paul Sartre, the leading intellectual figure of the day and a staunch anti-fascist. When it first came out, both he and his lifelong partner, Simone de Beauvoir, had nothing but praise for Céline's *Journey*. If they disapproved of *Death on Credit*'s 'hateful scorn for little people, which is a prefascist attitude', *Journey* was still very much at the forefront of Sartre's mind on a summer trip to Greece in 1937.[18] As he contemplated from a distance the majestic city of Salonica, he compared it to the novel's evocative description of New York as the 'ville debout' ('standing city').[19]

By the mid-1940s, however, Sartre could no longer stay silent about Céline's pro-fascist, antisemitic views. In 'Portrait of an Anti-Semite', an essay he published in the journal *Temps modernes* in December 1945, and which he included in 'Réflexions sur la question juive' ('Anti-Semite and Jew') the following year, he wrote, 'If Céline felt able to support the

Céline in Meudon, *c.* 1955.

The French actress Arletty with Céline, Meudon, 14 April 1958.

socialist theses of the Nazis, then it is because he was paid.'[20] Céline was incensed. Despite still being exiled in Denmark, he responded, in 1948, with a vituperative mini-pamphlet, *À l'Agité du bocal* (To the Nutcase), that went straight for the jugular.[21] In an all-out character assassination of the Left Bank philosopher, he furiously denied the allegation (it is true that he was not paid by the Nazis). He mockingly refers to him as Jean-Baptiste Sartre and minimizes his intellectual and literary originality, by stating, 'Still at secondary school, this J.-B. S! still doing pastiches, in "Themannerof" . . . In the manner of Céline too . . . and quite a few others . . .'[22] Céline snidely alludes here to the epigraph Sartre placed at the beginning of his novel *Nausea*, which was taken from Céline's play *The Church*. He also denounces, with the most shockingly scatological insult he can muster, Sartre's sneaky cowardice for kicking a man when he is down: 'This is what this little dung beetle wrote while I was in prison in real danger of being hanged. Damned piece of trash full of shit, you come out of my buttocks to soil me on the outside.'[23] He then derides Sartre's unattractive appearance and small stature, comparing him to a tapeworm: 'Tapeworm, of course, tapeworm of a man, located you know where . . . and a philosopher! . . .'[24] These distasteful personal insults aside, Céline also questions – not entirely without justification – Sartre's exaggerated role in the Résistance ('He apparently freed Paris, while riding his bicycle').[25] Sartre's ego, he suggests, has become grossly inflated by his recent fame: 'But times change, and look how he is growing, massively expanding, J.-B. S.!'[26] Céline's trademark satirical wordplay hits its mark when he renames Sartre's famous play *Les Mouches* (The Flies), staged during the Occupation in 1943, as *Les Mouchards*, which means 'The Snitches'. He stops just short of accusing Sartre of 'sending your detested colleagues, known as "Collaborators" to prison, to the stake, into exile . . .'[27]

Sartre's diplomatic silence suggests that he saw Céline's pamphlet for what it was: a paranoid rant, with a touch of jealousy and resentment thrown in. While his own star was in the ascendancy, Céline's was very much on the wane. Céline's fragile ego had been dealt a double blow: not only had a former, reputable admirer turned against him, but he had replaced him in the public's affections.

Still, there was one writer who would prove instrumental in salvaging Céline's reputation: the charismatic and dashing Roger Nimier. A monarchist and early admirer of the Catholic novelist Georges Bernanos, Nimier, as a 24-year-old in February 1949, had sent Céline (who was then still exiled in Denmark) a copy of his first novel *Les Épées* (The Swords), accompanied by a self-deprecating fan letter in which he offered to help the author in any way he could. Greatly touched, Céline graciously replied with some literary tips. Nimier's next novel, *Le Hussard bleu* (The Blue Hussar), published in 1950, established his credentials as a promising writer, who spearheaded a new literary group, the Hussards, that was opposed both to Sartrean existentialism and the *nouveau roman*. He would later collaborate with director Louis Malle on the screenplay for his 1958 film *Ascenseur pour l'échafaud* (Elevator to the Gallows). But it was as a probing critic with influential press contacts that Nimier would truly prove useful to Céline. In August 1952, he wrote a balanced review of *Fable for Another Time*. While he lamented the 'monotony' of the prison descriptions, which 'often weighed' on the novel, he was quick to praise Céline's genius for placing emotion at the heart of his writing. If Nimier leapt to Céline's defence to refute the criminal charges that had been levelled against him, he did not let him off the hook when it came to his pamphlets. Céline's failure to recognize that 'the anti-Semitic rage of the petit-bourgeois French became monstrous in German hands – and sometimes French hands' he put down to his pride ('fierté'), rather than 'thoughtlessness' ('inconscience').[28] Céline duly thanked Nimier for his review in a letter, deftly sidestepping the topic of antisemitism. So thrilled was he with Nimier's favourable review in April 1955 of *Conversations with Professor Y*, that he invited him and his pregnant wife to Meudon. The charismatic Nimier quickly became a firm favourite of the couple and a regular visitor, who would frequently lavish them with generous gifts. He and Céline soon established a father–son bond, in which the former would give his young protégé advice and listen patiently as the latter showed off his latest sports car (Nimier would die, aged only 36, when he crashed his Aston Martin in 1962). In October 1956, Nimier even wrote an article praising Céline, entitled 'Donnez à Céline le prix Nobel' ('Give Céline the Nobel Prize').[29]

Nimier's close personal ties with Céline were cemented by their professional relationship, which came about somewhat serendipitously, as the result of one of Céline's many notorious fallings-out. Since 1951, Céline's main contact and editor at Gallimard had been Jean Paulhan. As a former *résistant*, Paulhan had to endure threats and abuse from those who regarded his association with Céline as treachery. Yet for all that Paulhan stood by him, Céline had no qualms in sending him the same offensive letters (he nicknamed him the 'Languid Anenome', or 'l'Anenome Languide'), as he did to Gallimard, when things did not go his way. Paulhan, however, was far less willing than Gallimard to shrug off Céline's outbursts as those of a petulant child. In January 1955, he finally snapped, when Céline lambasted him for daring to suggest that he make cuts to *Conversations with Professor Y*. This was the final straw. Paulhan ended their association once and for all by letter, in which he accused Céline (not without justification) of ingratitude, with a final parting shot: 'This is all rather distressing, and when all is said and done, I was rather fond of you. But why the devil must you be so bad-tempered?'[30]

This is where Nimier came to the rescue. At the end of 1956, he was appointed as literary advisor to Gallimard, thereby emerging as the obvious candidate to replace Paulhan as Céline's editor. And for all Paulhan's commendable loyalty, it was Nimier who had the more influential media contacts. He used them to great effect to revive Céline's flagging literary career, when he organized an infamous interview with journalist Madeleine Chapsal in the Left-wing newspaper *L'Express*, to publicize the publication of *Castle to Castle* in 1957. Nimier effectively became what the critic Marc Dambre has called Céline's 'propagandist'.[31] As we shall see, the Chapsal interview triggered a sudden upsurge in newspaper, TV and radio interviews in the last four years of Céline's life. If many still refused to have anything to do with Céline, he was in much higher demand from 1957 to 1961 than between 1951 and 1957, and certainly more so than at any time since the publication of *Death on Credit* in 1936. Céline himself was ambivalent about his rediscovered celebrity status. On the one hand, he was undoubtedly relieved to feel relevant and respected again; on the other, he regarded the media attention and growing band of literary admirers who came to Meudon in the hope of meeting him as an irritating intrusion into his reclusive existence. The opening pages of his final novel *Rigadoon* comically satirize the constant bombardment of phone calls he receives from journalists, while trying to write.

Céline made an exception for the two young Beat writers and huge admirers of his work, Allen Ginsberg and William Burroughs. A meeting was arranged in July 1958 via the editor and novelist Michel Mohrt. An amused Burroughs later recalled that the eccentric who came to greet them at the gates of his house with five large, intimidating dogs 'looked exactly like an old reactionary concierge, with shawls all around himself'.[32] Among the topics the three men discussed were Céline's favourite writers (he was dismissive of Sartre), his struggling medical practice (he lamented, as he did in *Castle to Castle*, that his female clientele preferred younger male doctors to him) and perhaps most intriguingly, his experience of prison, which he shared with Burroughs. 'You don't know a country', Céline surmised, 'unless you've seen the jails.'[33] Feeling that their meeting had gone rather well, the two young Americans gave him copies of *On the Road* (by their fellow Beat writer Jack Kerouac) and Burroughs's own novel *Junk*; however, Burroughs ruefully recalled, 'I could tell by the way he touched them and put them aside that he was never going to look at them again.'[34]

Encounters such as these were no doubt a welcome boost to Céline's ego, and a reminder that he was still, at least outside France, a much-admired writer. This made him all the more determined to restore his literary reputation in his homeland. A particular bee in his bonnet was that his novels had yet to be included in Gallimard's prestigious Pléiade collection. The Pléiade, as Céline knew only too well, has long been the ultimate benchmark of cultural consecration and official admission into the French literary canon. It was an exclusive club, and Céline wanted to belong to it. This was partly for financial reasons (the Pléiade edition is more expensive), but also because, for all his non-conformism, anti-elitism and 'outsider' status, he still craved recognition from the literary elite he claimed to despise. Between 1956 and 2 June 1959 (when his contract for the Pléiade edition was finally signed), he constantly harangued Gaston Gallimard in his letters, accusing him of stalling, while granting lesser writers, such as Montherlant, admission into the exclusive club.[35] Gaston's weary but patient responses reiterated the same commercial imperatives: Céline's book sales needed to be high enough, and the Gallimard publishing house was dependent on the support of its main distributor, Hachette. To Gaston's credit, he was at least able to satisfy one of Céline's other demands: he obtained permission from Hachette, in November 1956, to publish *Death on Credit* in the paperback (*livre de poche*) edition (though it did not appear until March 1958).[36] Such was Céline's 'Pléiade obsession' that he would use Roger Nimier as an intermediary: an amused Nimier would report back to Céline about Gaston's response to his latest insulting letter.[37]

But for all these humorous epistolary exchanges, Céline's mounting exasperation was also symptomatic of an impending sense of his own mortality. By 1960, his health was declining. In February of that year, aged almost 66, he wrote to Gaston's son Claude that he was running out of time (he exaggerated his age) and that the Pléiade edition had yet to be published, even though the contract had been signed: 'I should be very grateful if you would shake things up with the Pléiade, and publish me this year, since at 67 years of age [*sic*], I do not have the luxury of waiting around for God knows what coup d'État . . .'[38] The positive reception of *North*, when it came out a few months later, only galvanized Céline to husband what little resources he had left to finish the last instalment of his trilogy: his final novel, *Rigadoon*. Originally entitled *Colin-maillard* (Blind Man's Bluff), Céline eventually decided on the name *Rigadoon*, because of its allusion to his favourite art form.

But by early 1961 Lucette was seriously worried about her husband's health. He was able to work for barely one or two hours a day, owing to recurrent bouts of the fever he had first contracted in Africa and the excruciating pain in his right arm (his writing arm) that stemmed from the war injury to his radial nerve. Worst of all were his migraines: they were so crippling that he had to take regular rests on the camp bed that had been decked out for him in the cellar. He pressed on regardless. If he was increasingly short with visitors, especially journalists, this was mainly because he knew he was running out of time. Entertaining guests was now an ordeal for him.[39] One rare exception was Karl Epting and his wife, who came to see him and Lucette unexpectedly, only a few months before he died.[40] His condition worsened when a heatwave hit Paris at the end of June. Arletty was one of the last visitors to see him alive, when she came to say goodbye before departing for her summer holidays at Belle-Île. On 30 June he announced to Lucette that he had finished his novel, even though a few corrections were still needed. On 1 July Lucette's friend, the dancer Serge Perrault, came to Meudon for tea. Céline was too ill to greet him. Lucette would go downstairs every five minutes to press a cold compress on his forehead. By 6 p.m., he was no more. A devastated Lucette immediately rang the family doctor, André Willemin, who officially pronounced him dead. The autopsy revealed that the cause of death was a ruptured aneurysm.[41]

According to his wishes, news of his death was strictly kept to a small, loyal circle of friends and acquaintances: his daughter Colette and ex-wife Édith, his secretary Marie Canavaggia, Gaston and Claude Gallimard, Roger Nimier, Arletty, Serge Perrault, Maria and Sergine Le Bannier, Marcel Aymé and even his estranged artist friend Gen Paul, who was notified by Aymé.[42] Given his controversial reputation, Céline had been especially keen to avoid unwanted attention from his enemies. But rumours quickly began to spread among the press. To buy time until his funeral, Lucette issued a holding statement that his 'condition had suddenly worsened', owing to a heart condition from which he had been suffering for several months.[43] Under a light drizzle – appropriate for a writer who was not renowned for his sunny disposition – a quick burial ceremony took place in Meudon cemetery at 8 o'clock on the morning of 4 July. Around twenty people were present, including Lucien Rebatet and the actor and theatre director Max Revol. Arletty had been detained at Belle-Île, but she attended his cremation in October. The press was not notified, apart from two journalists and a photographer,

Céline's tombstone, Longs-Réages, Meudon. The photograph dates from 2012, prior to the death of Lucette, who had engraved her name and '1912–19 . . .' in preparation. She died in 2019, aged 107.

who had been vetted by Roger Nimier: André Helphen from *Paris-Presse-L'Intransigeant*, and Roger Grenier and Claude Lechevallier from *France-Soir*. A photograph published in the latter showed Lucette and Colette Turpin, standing side by side, blessing the coffin.[44] By an ironic twist of fate, the date of Céline's death coincided with that of another giant of twentieth-century literature, Ernest Hemingway. But whereas the American novelist won the Nobel Prize, Céline's literary greatness was to remain tainted by his political reputation.

The continued controversy surrounding Céline has tended to disprove the axiom that time is the greatest healer. Sixty years after his death, passions still run high, especially in France, about his exact place in the literary pantheon. Already, in the year 2000, Céline critic Philippe Muray sought to identify the roots of this problem in a new preface to the revised edition of his 1981 study of the author. Contrary to the early years of the Mitterrand presidency, he argued, the new millennium is characterized by a rigid climate of political correctness that makes it increasingly difficult to acknowledge any form of moral ambivalence. Society feels ever more compelled to make uncompromising value judgments about human beings and their actions, and so immediately divides them into one of two antithetical categories: good or evil. The idea that both good *and* evil could *coexist* in the same person, as was, in fact, the case with Céline, is now considered unacceptable, so he is expediently stigmatized as evil.[45] In 1981, a morally nuanced appraisal of this author was still possible; by 2000, it was not.

The Céline Culture Wars

In the twenty years since Muray wrote these words, this moral polarization has become even more prevalent. That which we might aptly label the 'Céline culture wars' – the fiercely contested, antithetical clash over his legacy that his admirers and detractors have been waging for at least seventy years – has only intensified, rather than abated, not least in light of the recent 'cancel culture' that often dominates public discourse. These wars continue to rage, often needlessly and with no tangible benefits, across a variety of cultural spheres: academia, literature, the media, politics, cinema, publishing and auction houses.

If ever confirmation were needed of the increasing incompatibility of Céline's moral contradictions with mainstream, normative opinion, then this was provided by the 2011 'Céline affair'.[46] In January 2011, under pressure from prominent Jewish leader and Nazi hunter Serge Klarsfeld, the French minister of culture Frédéric Mitterrand withdrew Céline from a list of famous French authors specifically selected for a national celebration of culture. This bold decision polarized opinion: while many welcomed Mitterrand's intervention, a number of prominent French writers, some of them Jewish, opposed it on the grounds that Céline's abhorrent political beliefs – expressed in the three antisemitic pamphlets he published in the late 1930s and early 1940s and his flirtation with Nazism – should in no way detract from his literary genius.

The backlash was furious. Novelist and *Tel Quel* critic Philippe Sollers, one of Céline's most vocal supporters, accused Frédéric Mitterrand of censorship and hypocrisy, given that his own uncle François Mitterrand was a friend of René Bosquet, who collaborated in the deportation of Jews: 'As for the Minister of Culture, he has become the Minister of Censorship,' he quipped.[47] Mitterrand, Sollers continued, was also guilty of double standards for excluding Céline, yet choosing to include other notoriously antisemitic writers such as Voltaire, as well as Genet, who allegedly slept with German soldiers, and Aragon, despite his support for the Stalinist gulags: 'Unfortunately, Monsieur Mitterrand preferred to capitulate (in record time!) in the face of a minority opinion, however worthy it may be.'[48] Another legitimate gripe was the lack of distinction made between commemoration and celebration, especially in the context of a national French Republican ideology keen to preserve its proud revolutionary heritage. Had the anniversary in question been a *commemoration* rather than celebration, argued historian Jean-Noël Jeanneney, then Céline's name could have been left on the list. For instance, we can celebrate the French Revolution, but only commemorate Robespierre and the Terror: 'This volume is not appropriately named [. . .] If we talked about "commemoration" instead of "celebration", there would be no ambiguity.'[49]

But the government's stance on Céline was morally inconsistent in relation not only to other writers, but to its earlier stance on the author *himself*. It was quite happy to exclude him from the celebration, yet it retained him on the secondary-school syllabus and the prestigious *agrégation*, an exam for which he has been studied since 1994. He is institutionally enshrined in the Republican education system, but he is considered unworthy of cultural consecration. More embarrassing still, during his tenure, the president himself, Nicolas Sarkozy, had no qualms whatsoever about heralding Céline as his favourite novelist. In November 2010, only two months before the Céline controversy, he even invited famous actor Fabrice Luchini to lunch at the Elysée Palace to discuss their mutual love of the author. The staunchly anti-Céline critic Antoine Peillon sought to discredit both Sarkozy and Luchini, by association. Their lunch, he claims, was arranged via Alain Carignon, the former minister of communications, who had been imprisoned for five years in the 1990s for corruption and witness intimidation.[50] Even respected scholars Annick Duraffour and Pierre-André Taguieff, in their important recent book denouncing Céline's racial politics, cannot resist personally targeting Philippe Sollers for his unstinting support of Céline's literature. They describe Sollers as a 'writer with nothing left to say', who, at the age of 79, 'wants to keep playing the rebellious and provocative adolescent'.[51] To condemn the odious far-Right groups who celebrate Céline's antisemitism is one thing, but to set out to ridicule anyone who merely professes their public admiration for his literature is quite another. The year 2011, then, seemed to make the Céline culture wars more personal. Not only was the moral reputation of the author now under the spotlight, but so too was that of anyone who supported him, whether politically or not.

This situation is a far cry from 1937, the year Céline published *Trifles for a Massacre*. As we saw earlier, that era was not only marked by a higher tolerance of antisemitism than there is today, but by an 'art for art's sake' approach to literature that considered words merely as disinterested opinion, rather than as ideologically pernicious. This is what allowed Gide, for instance, who was representative of liberal thought, to dismiss Céline's antisemitism as comically trivial, rather than politically serious. He focused on the aesthetic playfulness of Céline's pamphlets, refusing to attribute to them any malicious intent.

However, if we fast-forward twenty years to 1957 and the release of Céline's much-publicized 'comeback' novel *Castle to Castle*, we find that the literary and political landscape of the late 1930s has changed beyond all recognition. Nazism has been defeated. The Holocaust has made antisemitism, in whatever guise, strictly off limits. The 1944–6 purges of Collaborationist writers and intellectuals have prosecuted fascist authors, such as Robert Brasillach, for their words and not just their deeds. Words are no longer considered mere opinions, as in the Gidean era, but consequential.[52] This legal attribution of moral responsibility to the writer provides fertile ground for Sartre's existentialist doctrine of literature as a form of social and political engagement. This doctrine discredits as both obsolete and morally irresponsible the 'art for art's sake' pre-war notion of disinterested literary autonomy. So in the first half of the 1950s, Céline's stylistically experimental novel *Fable for Another Time* was out of step with a cultural landscape that valorized Sartrean *engagement* over Gidean style.

The major catalyst for thrusting Céline back into the media spotlight was his infamous 1957 interview with Madeleine Chapsal for *L'Express*. Both the very audacity of this interview and its controversial content spawned furious reactions from both sides of the political spectrum. Chapsal subsequently admitted in 2008 that the editors of *L'Express* were so nervous about publishing this interview, given the prevailing anti-Collaborationist and anti-Céline sentiments of the time, that they insisted on reproducing a caricature of the author, an unflattering heading 'Voyage au bout de la haine' ('Journey to the end of hatred') and a cautionary introduction, as a kind of disclaimer.[53] The editors were rightly wary of the potentially explosive impact of Céline's controversial comments. True to form, for much of the interview, he goads the journalist with deliberately provocative answers. But he also occasionally crosses the line from tongue-in-cheek irreverence to outright offensiveness, when he unapologetically defends his past comments against Jews on the grounds of pacifism: 'I wrote things about [some] Jews. I said that they were plotting a war, that they wanted to get their own back against Hitler. Fine. It was not our concern (the editor won't print that either).'[54]

He also makes overtly racist comments about the Chinese as the new threat to the white race: 'You are disappearing, you the white race [...] the background is yellow. White is not a colour, it's a mere tinge. The real colour is yellow. The Yellow [person] has all the necessary qualities to become king of the earth.'[55]

So not only does he remain an unrepentant antisemite, but he shifts the target of his racism from Jews to the Chinese. Unsurprisingly, the liberal Left was furious. *L'Express* spent the next several weeks publishing letters, both from ordinary readers and from prominent literary figures, most of which condemned both the interview and Céline. One notable example is a letter signed by some twenty writers, including the surrealists André Breton and Benjamin Péret, condemning Céline in the most impassioned and damning terms: 'Not one line of Céline's works indicates anything other than a purely physical capacity for holding a pen and dipping it in mud.'[56] The letter also attacks *L'Express* for granting space to 'the infamy and intellectual dirt of the man in question'.[57]

A further consequence of the *Express* article was the government's banning of a TV interview of Céline, at the angry request of anti-racist groups and the association of former *résistants*. A measure of the fear at that time of broadcasting Céline on television is the fact that it was reported in *Télémagazine* that the announcer was suspended for even mentioning Céline's very name on TV. The same *Télémagazine* published a few days later a robust denial by the Ministère de l'information that it had caved in to pressure.[58]

By the mid-1960s, Céline's reputation was still fiercely being debated, only this time along generational as well as political lines. A survey of francophone writers conducted in 1965 by the liberal *Le Nouvel Observateur*, aptly entitled 'Que doit-on faire avec Céline?' (What Are We to Do with Céline?) reveals that writers' opinions of the author depend not only on whether they belong to the Left or Right, but whether or not they identify with the literary generation that was influenced by Sartre's notion of *engagement*.[59] We find that the older, established writers, many of them former *résistants* and communists who supported Sartre's anti-Collaborationist notion of politically committed writing, still refused to read or forgive Céline. However, the younger generation, including the *nouveau roman* author Michel Butor and structuralist critic Roland Barthes, were not on the Right, but nevertheless saw in Céline's stylistic innovations a type of literature that struck a chord with their own ventures into a more formally experimental and depoliticized type of writing. Defending the Sartrean line, Cuban novelist Alejo Carpentier condemns Céline not only for his antisemitism, but because he does not conform to the Leftist notion of political engagement:

> I still believe that *Journey* and *Death on Credit* are remarkable books. But Céline's last works are of no interest. You see, I am a man who is *engagé* [that is, engaged politically] so for me, the Céline of *Trifles for a Massacre* is an absolute no-no. Céline going to live in a German castle, Céline following German troops, absolutely no way. I don't like that one bit.[60]

At the other end of the literary spectrum, the younger Roland Barthes more subtly and provocatively defends Céline:

> Céline belongs to everyone. His only mistake was to look at reality through a literary lens. He transformed reality with his language. Many writers come from him. Sartre, for a start. Sartre's writing, or if you will, his 'verbalized vision', vibrates in much the same way as Céline's [. . .] Anyway, what does 'engagement' mean today? During the Algerian War, writers were able to be fully engaged politically while at the same time writing works that were completely disengaged.[61]

Here, Barthes highlights Sartre's increasingly outdated notion of politically committed writing: the recent Algerian War had shown that it was perfectly possible for writers to be both politically engaged and *also* produce successful literary works that were apolitical. In a further dig at Sartre, Barthes flags up the existentialist's own debt to Céline's literary style: it has often been noted that his novel *Nausea* is influenced by *Journey to the End of the Night*.

These three snapshots – 1937, 1957 and 1965 – demonstrate how much opinion on Céline has fluctuated over the years, and also that these fluctuations alert us to the historically determined and context-specific nature of his reception. Even his most discerning critics have based their judgments on preconceptions that invariably reflect the prevailing political and cultural values of their respective eras. But there is a second problem: not only do reactions to Céline directly reflect their specific era, but these eras and their corresponding reactions tend to repeat themselves. The mid-1960s polemic surrounding Céline remobilizes and rearticulates the earlier 1930s and 1940s rivalry between the 'art for art's sake' and *engagé* notions of literature. By the same token, the 2011 'scandal' is essentially a repetition of 1957: the government caves in to public opinion and pressure groups – it intervenes to cancel a TV interview of Céline, and to remove his name – and then denies having been forced to do so. These striking parallels point to a depressing sense of déjà vu in the Céline culture wars: history repeats itself, and the same old arguments are played out over and over again, albeit in a different context.

The problem we face, then, is twofold. There is the blinkered self-righteousness and lack of moral nuance that is characteristic of the new millennium – an era, as Muray has shown, that forces us to choose between a good Céline and an evil one, but denies us the possibility of both – and there is the depressing realization that the moral polarization of opinion on Céline has, in fact, always existed. It has simply lurched from one polarity to the other depending on the dominant values of a given period. In the 1930s and late 1960s, Céline's 'evil' side – his fascist politics and antisemitism – were minimized in favour of his 'good' side – his style and aesthetics; whereas from the late 1940s to the mid-1960s, the opposite was true. What, then, are we to do as critics? There is no easy answer, but we should try, as far as possible, to exercise greater moral latitude and self-reflection. Moral latitude allows us to do full justice to the *coexistence* of good and evil in Céline, rather than having to choose between them. And moral self-reflection would prevent the prevailing political and cultural values of a specific era – and especially our own – from unduly prejudicing our objective evaluation of Céline. At all times, we must ask ourselves whether we are truly judging what Céline said and wrote on its own terms, viewed in its proper context, or unwittingly projecting our own values onto his work, regardless?

Unsurprisingly, critics from both the pro- and anti-Céline camps rarely acknowledge the degree to which historical context can shape their own political or cultural prejudices towards the author. They naturally prefer instead to focus on how history shaped *him*. The main bone of contention between them is explaining his 'stylistic turn' in the mid-1940s. His defenders say that his drastic shift towards style was a deliberate gesture of withdrawal from history and politics. According to novelist and critic Philippe Sollers, this was a logical move because Céline's politics were so discredited. Moreover, style allowed him to play to his strengths. Other writers – especially Sartre – attacked Céline politically because deep down, they were jealous of his superior stylistic gifts. Style, therefore, was the terrain on which Céline felt able to gain the upper hand over the philosopher.[62] Céline's style signalled his renunciation of ideas, which he equated with the domain of morality and theology. And his ideas – the equivalent of theology and morality – were contained in the antisemitism of his pamphlets. But once he realized that these pamphlets had failed, Céline naturally concluded that style was preferable to, and separate from, ideas. Henceforth, he would leave the ideas of his pamphlets behind him, to dedicate himself exclusively to the style of his novels.[63]

Céline's detractors take the opposite view. For them, his style is not so much a withdrawal from history, as an active desire to rewrite it. It is not divorced from politics, but an integral part of the politics itself. This is especially true of the novelist's repeated claims, from his letters to Milton Hindus onwards, that his stylistic aim was to transpose spoken emotion to the written page. According to this reading, Céline used style as a political strategy. Following his Danish exile, imprisonment, trial and amnesty, he was shrewd enough to realize that he needed to restore his reputation, but he had no desire to renounce his antisemitism or Nazism. So he used style as a lure or mask to give the impression he had renounced politics, while deep down, he was seeking to promote a pro-Nazi ideology. He peppered his fiction with references to his literary martyrdom, the notion that he was one of many purged fascist writers who had suffered unjustly at the hands of the French state. This idea is encapsulated in his metaphor of the 'rendu émotif', or 'emotive rendering' that he ascribed to his literature. *Rendu*, Philip Watts suggests, also punningly suggests 'vomiting', thereby drawing attention to Céline's body as a site of physical purging that viscerally demonstrates the political suffering to which he has been subjected.[64] Worse still, Céline was also a historical revisionist: his later novels, beginning with *Fable for Another Time*, aim to reorientate his reader's perspective away from the suffering inflicted by the Nazis and *towards* the violence perpetrated by the Allies. Is it pure coincidence, Watts asks, that the allied bombings of Montmartre are the subject of his entire novel?

Those who subscribe to the 'historical-revisionism' argument also tend to emphasize Céline's 'poetic racism' (*poétique raciste*). In other words, he ascribed to his much-vaunted *petite musique* ('little music') and 'authentic emotion' racial, as well as aesthetic, qualities: specifically, qualities that distinguished the supposedly 'superior' Aryans from the 'inferior' Jews. As the 'born enemies of Aryan emotiveness' ('ennemis nés de l'émotivité aryenne'), Jews are lacking in this direct, spontaneous emotion.[65] This emphasis on the racialization of Céline's style refutes the notion, held by many of Céline's defenders, that his poetic vision has nothing to do with his politics. It underlines Céline's indebtedness to biological theories of race that were advanced by his friend Georges Montadon, as well as the oft-forgotten racial theorist Vacher de Lapouge. The latter combined eugenics with the nineteenth-century ideas on race of Gobineau to attack democracy for encouraging a mixing of the races (especially with Jews) that was allegedly conducive to the degeneration of humanity. These were the dominant ideas that found their way, directly or indirectly, into Céline's pamphlets.[66]

There is no denying that, from *Mea culpa* onwards, the style of Céline's pamphlets and certain letters he wrote to the fascist press bear the unmistakable imprint of his racial politics. This constitutes his evil, abhorrent side. At the same time, merely to *reduce* Céline's style to his politics, whether in the name of Aryanism, or historical revisionism, underestimates three of its other, depoliticized attributes. His style is a vehicle of anti-ideological, anarchical satire; it aims to authenticate the author's lived emotion through his suffering; and it seeks to reconnect man to a modernity from which, as we have already seen in previous chapters, he has become profoundly alienated.

Let us take his employment of style as satire. What is often forgotten today is that in 1957, the far Right was just as furious with Céline as the Left, but for different reasons: primarily, because his novel *Castle to Castle* gave a caustically satirical depiction of the Vichy regime that took refuge in Sigmaringen in 1944–5. This is why Pierre Cousteau in the far-Right journal *Rivarol* portrays Céline as a traitor and turncoat, contrasting the pro-Hitler and pro-Nazi statements he made in his pamphlets with later disingenuous statements that contradicted them.[67] He lambasts Céline for portraying Pétain and Laval as *guignols* (puppets).[68] Cousteau received support from fellow members of the far Right. Jean Loustau accused Céline of hypocrisy, given that in Sigmaringen he had enjoyed 'exceptional favours from which no one else benefitted'; nor did he want Céline to become a 'martyr to a cause that is buried in History and drenched in the blood of its victims'.[69] Jean-André Faucher denounced the 'Célinien logic of denial' ('logique célinienne du reniement') and lambasted the 'promise of fidelity towards all that is foul in Céline's opus, starting with the very first line of *Journey*'.[70] Other members of the far Right were more forgiving. Paul Chambrillon defended Céline's right to freedom of expression: 'Céline is not settling scores, does not attack anyone, does no special pleading. He brings us his poetic, subjective, symbolic vision of an astonishing period that overwhelmed him.'[71] And his loyal friend Lucien Rebatet, who had also been at Sigmaringen, stressed Céline's *non*-ideological stance: he was an 'anarchist visionary' and it was 'rather excessive to speak of denial in relation to a man who has never adhered either to principles or a flag.'[72]

I emphasize this dissent and discord on the far Right in order to highlight the thorny ideological challenge France has consistently faced since the 1930s when it comes to evaluating Céline's legacy: if his antisemitism is, quite rightly, no longer minimized as it was at that time, neither is it possible or entirely accurate to pigeonhole Céline politically as belonging either to the far Left or the far Right, despite attempts by both sides to slot him into a reductive model of political binarism. It should be recalled that in the early 1930s, Marxists, including Trotsky, had initially welcomed his empathy with the urban industrial working class in *Journey*, and the communist writer Louis Aragon's wife even translated Céline's novel into Russian. But Céline's 1936 pamphlet *Mea culpa*, which heavily criticized Soviet Stalinism, was soon to place him squarely in the anti-communist camp. At the same time, since Céline always had an anarchical, individualistic streak – emphasized by critics such as Yves Pagès and Francesco Germinario – he was equally reluctant to subscribe to a far-Right orthodox position or assume any official role under the Nazi Occupation. Many Nazis, we should remember, considered Céline to be a loose cannon and potential political liability, and he was no friend of the Vichy regime, which he depicted as impotent, treacherous and debauched both in *Castle to Castle* and in his 1941 pamphlet *A Fine Mess*.[73] It is difficult to see how his depiction, in the German trilogy, of Pétain as decrepit and incontinent and Nazi generals as perverted sexual deviants, serves the cause of a pro-Nazi historical revisionism.

What is more, style seeks to reproduce spoken emotion as a hallmark of authenticity, as the following letter to Milton Hindus explains:

> I think I'm a stylist above all – and I repeat: what interests me most is rendering emotions through words. All those 'great' writers don't

get close enough to the nerve in my opinion ... In short, I hate prose ... I'm a poet and would-be musician.

What interests me is a direct message to the nervous system ... I can't stand idle chattering. Look at Aristide Bruant, Villon, Schackspeare [*sic*], du Bellay, Barbusse (in his Feu) – all horrified of explanations – Proust explains too much for my taste [...] I'm in as much of a hurry as the most frenetic American. Same business with Gide – his glory is to have made buggery permissible again in the best families (the neo-socratics). Fine by me. That's perfect too, but speed it up a little. All Shakespeare's works in 500 pages! The Misanthrope, scarcely 30! Economy!

[...] Of course the public has to be educated – and Sartre does that well enough. But he didn't earn his plays, didn't pay for them. He'd need a couple of years in prison – and three in the trenches – to teach him real existentialism and the meaning of the death penalty on his ass for ten years or more – or incapacitated a good old 75%. Then he wouldn't go round in circles, then he wouldn't create irresponsible monsters (a vice of American writers too – Passos, Steinbeck etc.)

They're even afraid of themselves – they cheat. They stink of cheating like Baudelaire, who plied himself with poison to be sure he was 'damned' ... Opium etc. People are still trying to find out why Rimbaud left for Africa so soon. I know why – he was fed up with cheating. Cervantes didn't cheat. He had really been in the galleys. The war really put Barbusse on the rack. All that's not enough, of course, but the poet is always haunted by a desire not to cheat any more. Proust's lungs were falling apart – and he ended up talking rather nicely about his grandmother. And that part comes off – it's the best in the whole work.[74]

Emotion, here, has a distinctly literary, rather than political, goal. It has the speed, directness and spontaneity that distinguish it from lengthy explanation and description. It goes straight to the heart of the nervous system, without being weighed down or diluted by the superfluous detail of 'idle chattering'. There are those writers who are able to capture it – Shakespeare, Barbusse and Molière – and those, such as Gide and Proust, who cannot, because their prose is bogged down by ornate descriptions and explanations. Emotion has to be lived *by the author himself*, not acquired at second hand. And it is all the more authentic when it emanates from suffering – such as Cervantes's real experience of being a galley slave. Sartre, by contrast, has not experienced real emotion because he has never known suffering. And under no circumstances must this emotion deliberately be cultivated with the specific purpose of writing a book. Otherwise, it constitutes a premeditated form of cheating, such as when Baudelaire seeks out a specific emotion through drugs. Rimbaud, on the other hand, was honest enough to abandon literature as soon as he realized that he could no longer write without resorting to cheating with his emotions. Even Proust, a writer whom Céline often criticized for his overly erudite style, he praises here for drawing on his own genuine suffering – his weak lungs – to convey genuine emotion.

Céline's emphasis on satire and emotion shows that style for him, even after 1945, was about far more than just politics – not only that, but style was also a means by which he could reappropriate modernity for aesthetic purposes. He looked to stylistic tropes – and especially metaphor – as a way of neutralizing the negative connotations of modernity by turning it into a positive, aesthetically transformative experience. This idea is first given prominence in a letter he wrote to Milton Hindus in 1947:

> I remember before launching into *Journey to the End of the Night* an idea struck me. I told myself there were two ways to cross Paris. First on the surface – by car, bicycle, or on foot – every impression, description, etc., from – say – Montmartre to Montparnasse. But then there's the other way – going by metro: going directly to your goal via the very intimacy [*intimité*] of things. But you can't do that without imposing a certain melodious, melodic turn on your thoughts – giving them a track to follow – being determined not to vary from the route, not to slip off the track at any cost! You have to plunge deep into the nervous system – into the emotions – and stay there until you reach your goal. Transposing the spoken word into writing isn't easy.[75]

Here Céline expands on his famous metro metaphor, which he had first introduced in his little-read letter to Brasillach in 1943, and would later flesh out in his *Conversations with Professor Y*. Critics have long speculated on its possible meanings: depth and the unconscious libido, or a modern-day analogy to Pascal's experience of the void (*le gouffre*).[76] More suggestively, the metro has been interpreted as a metaphor for the speed of his writing. He sought to capture in his prose a particular quality – speed – that made the rival medium of cinema so appealing, and was leaving literature languishing in its wake. Cinema's enviable speed was able to release the writer 'from the lengthy travail of description and information, thanks to its power to short-circuit traditional psychology and sentiment'.[77] Inspired by both cinema and the economy of expression found in Shakespeare, Barbusse and Molière, Céline's own writing strives for a speed that makes it 'akin to the metro'. The impact of this metro-like quality on the reader is a 'dissociation of sight from hearing' that 'switches the emphasis to the resonant element of language, to voice, to an immediate relation between the reader and the narrator, and to the oral dimension of writing.'[78] This speed is associated with a subtle strategy of coercion: the rapid oral rhythm of Céline's work possesses a forward propulsive energy that sweeps readers along, like a passenger forced onto the metro, thereby denying them the time to reflect rationally, and eliciting from them a purely spontaneous emotional reaction:[79] 'No "buts" about it! . . . all aboard! [*j'embarque tout*!] . . . I stash everything on my metro cars! . . . and I repeat! every emotion on my metro cars! with me! My emotive metro takes everything along, my books take everything along!'[80]

Not only does the metro connote the speed, orality and emotionally ensnaring power of Céline's sentences, but another dimension overlooked by critics: modernity itself. As the very embodiment of technological progress, the metro is not just a metaphor for literature (Céline's writing style), but man's love–hate relationship with the modern world. It is thus a dual-purpose metaphor, one that merges literature with modernity, thereby perfectly encapsulating one of Céline's post-war aesthetic objectives: to redefine man's relationship to modernity from one of alienation and resistance, to aesthetic assimilation and experience.

In his first two novels, as the early chapters have shown, modernity lurks as an ever-present threat: whether in the dehumanizing production line of the Detroit car factories in *Journey* or the mass industrialization of *Death on Credit* that rapidly encroaches on the late nineteenth-century world of individual artisans, such as Ferdinand's seamstress mother, who can no longer compete with the new clothes factories. And since Céline refers to lacework as a metaphor for writing, her extinction as a lacemaker can be read as an allegory of the precarious state of literature itself.

Modernity, too, as we have already seen, spells the demise of another late nineteenth-century figure who actively tries to resist it: the individualist autodidact and inventor Courtial de Pereires. His spontaneous intellectual energy, insatiable curiosity and fierce independence of spirit have no place in the new, rule-bound, homogenized world of mass production. In vain, he invents a self-assembly kit for the motor car to protect the individual from the depersonalized, mass-produced cars of the assembly line:

> *An Automobile made to order for 322 Francs 25* [. . .] His idea was to combat the rising peril of mass production . . . There wasn't a moment to be lost . . . Despite his resolute belief in progress, des Pereires had always detested standardization . . . From the very start he was bitterly opposed to it . . . He foresaw that the death of craftsmanship would inevitably shrink the human personality . . .[81]

His own financial ruin through gambling debts and scientific pipe dreams further epitomizes the extinction of the individual creator in the hard-nosed world of mass commerce. The pamphlets, too, give a withering assessment of modernity.

The ballet from *Trifles for a Massacre*, 'Paul et Virginie', allegorizes the clash between mechanized technology and authentic art. A wicked witch offers a phial of potion to the innocent Virginie's cousin, Mirella. This makes her lose all her inhibitions, unleashing an erotic energy that drives her into the arms of Paul, Virginie's beloved.[82] A jealous and mortified Virginie thus drinks the phial herself, which allows her to carry out a sexually charged dance with Paul in front of a captivated audience. But suddenly, out of nowhere, there emerges onto the stage a giant locomotive known as the 'Fulmicoach'. This is described as a 'machine infernale', one that makes an almighty noise – 'roaring, blowing, humming' – ('rugissant, soufflant, vrombrissant') that is exacerbated by a man playing a trumpet and cyclists firing pistols.[83] The locomotive is bedecked with the American flag and whips the crowd into an emotional frenzy: 'the emotion of the crowd has reached its zenith' ('l'émotion dans la foule est à son comble').[84] But this is not authentic emotion: it is loud, crass, superficial and synonymous with a form of collective brainwashing that 'bewitches' the crowd, rather than engaging with the individual: 'he follows the betwitched crowd' ('il suit la foule endiablée').[85] Mechanized modernity becomes a garish, commercialized spectacle that has the power to lure an impressionable crowd away from the traditional art form of dance. Even Paul eventually succumbs to this mass hysteria by following the locomotive, leaving the lifeless Virginie behind on the empty stage. Given that the locomotive is American, it could also symbolize the growing threat of Hollywood: 'the larger fear that America will take over the European imagination'.[86] Céline adds his anti-American voice to those of Blaise Cendrars and Joseph Kessel in critiquing the false superficiality of the Hollywood dream factory.

Whether it is interpreted as the threatening commercial ogre of Hollywood or mass industrialization, the locomotive unequivocally represents modernity as the enemy of true art, an obstacle to the authentic aesthetic emotion Céline sought to reproduce in his fiction. But in the mid-1940s, things begin to change: relations with modernity gradually thaw as he starts to explore ways not to repel it, but embrace it by assimilating it to new aesthetic experiences. This becomes apparent at the end of *London Bridge* when the First World War German Zeppelin attacks provide Ferdinand and his merry band of friends with a novel form of entertainment to which they joyfully react in unison, as if they were in the Soho music halls they habitually frequent: 'The first to spot the Zeppelin takes the pot! The searchlights were searching the sky . . . Whenever they turned up empty the crowd ahhed and awhed . . . miffed . . . a barrage of catcalls . . . Go ahead, boo the fireworks!'[87]

In *Normance* (1954), Céline's reappropriation of modernity into a new aesthetic style reaches maturity. This is the novel of which Taguieff, who questions the literary value of all Céline's novels after *Death on Credit*, is most dismissive. He regards it as a 'long exercice de style' ('exercise in style'), invoking Malraux's view of Céline's later novels: 'We are given the impression of a Rabelais who has nothing to say, but always has at his disposal, should he need them, an endless torrent of extraordinary adjectives.'[88]

But such comments underestimate Céline's recuperative aesthetic strategy. Despite the ogre of technological modernity – the destructive Allied bombs that rain down on their Montmartre flat – Ferdinand and Lilith's legitimate fear for their lives is assuaged by the visual and aural feast that surrounds them:

> [A] magnificent eruption out that way! . . . ten, twenty times the size of the Renault crater! And the bombs are still falling in clusters! spurting up green! Blue! geysers through the clouds! . . . ah, this is so terrible, it's become sublime! There are such outrageously magical colours out there that even I, who's not the least bit artistic, I'm

thinking, goodness gracious! There's no show in the world you can buy a ticket to that's as dazzling as this! Such onslaughts of beauty make the universe wobble![89]

Here, Céline's sentences not only depict the sinister destructiveness of modernity, but they assimilate and revalorize it. They initially absorb its impact and then gradually transform it into an aesthetic spectacle of unprecedented beauty. Even though wave after wave of bombs descends upon Montmartre, having already destroyed the Renault car factory and left a huge crater, the frightened narrator and, by extension, the reader, are slowly made to marvel at the unique and memorable scene they are experiencing. Bombs are poetically transmogrified from agents of death into a splendid array of colours that are fit for the artist's canvas. Modernity at its most barbaric becomes the unexpected catalyst of a new, emotionally transformative aesthetic experience. What was once 'terrible' has now become 'sublime'. This is a far cry from the narrator of *Trifles for a Massacre* who bemoans the equally noisy and intimidating locomotive as a threat to authentic art. Despite the carnage it inflicts via relentless bombing, this narrator does not flee modernity but embraces it, does not see it as art's enemy, but its *friend*. What is more, contrary to the locomotive of 'Paul et Virginie', which represents the threat of Hollywood or American mechanization, this aesthetic spectacle is free and entirely untainted by commercialization. There is nowhere else that anyone could pay to see such a spectacle. This is not like the 'contrived' reality that is depicted by the painter Jules (based on Gen Paul). As we saw earlier, the narrator of *Normance* accuses Jules of being a 'sell-out' who panders to his client's bourgeois taste for artificial beauty, instead of depicting reality, however harsh it may be.

This stylistic alchemy is brought about by a rapid succession of splendid visual metaphors: artificial light becomes daffodils, rooftops turn into jewels, and exploding bombs dissolve into carnations. These traditional poetic motifs of beauty are given a new lease of life by the unpromising context of mechanized mass murder:

> Out there . . . it's brighter than just daylight! . . . daffodil daylight, and bright! So bright! . . . all the air! The whole sky! . . . the roofs . . . all of Paris! it'd blind you even just the roofs! the slate, all sparkling! . . . jewels . . . diamonds! . . . the bombs bursting into flowers! Red ones! into carnations![90]

Céline practises what he preaches in his letters: as a writer, he draws on his own suffering (the relentless bombing of his flat) to reach a pitch of authentic emotional intensity with which he seeks to grab his reader's attention via a dizzying succession of metaphors. Having transformed the real bombs into a metaphorical bombardment of the senses, he immerses his reader into the rapid rhythm of his sentences that leave her no time to think, but instead sweep her along as if she were on the metro. Moreover, Céline's repeated reference to Pliny, the poet who died while rescuing his friend from an erupting Vesuvius, recalls his earlier admiration for writers whose emotion is authenticated and intensified by the suffering they themselves experience and transcribe to the page: 'If a catastrophe goes unobserved then your whole era's been wasted! All for nothing! . . . all of humanity suffering, and for what? For the maggots! . . . that's the blasphemy, the intolerable thing! Hail to Pliny!'[91] His reason for not wanting this catastrophe to go unobserved is not just so that he can record the terrible suffering of his era, but so that he is able to exploit the aesthetic opportunities that this suffering offers. The *real* catastrophe would be if all that is left of the bombings for posterity are the maggots from the corpses they leave behind. Like Baudelaire before him, what Céline strives for in his writing is a kind of poetic distillation of painful experiences that ennobles suffering through the creation of lasting aesthetic beauty. The bombs should not just be viewed as agents of destruction that obliterate people and reduce them to dust; they provide the artistic possibility of something more enduring: they generate an unprecedented multitude of sights and sounds that provide the novelist with the raw materials from which he can weave a dense tapestry of aural and visual metaphors. Céline thus both stays faithful to a brutal historical reality – the destruction of the bombings – while *also* immortalizing this terrible reality into a literary work of lasting beauty.

Yet any objective, balanced view of Céline must still overcome the two interrelated obstacles imposed by the Céline culture wars, especially in a French context. First, there are the morally polarizing, and continually recycled, cultural and political prejudices of specific eras, spanning the 1930s to the present. Second, there is the equally divisive debate over his style, which is either defended as an intrinsically aesthetic, ahistorical and depoliticized manifestation of Céline's literary genius, or condemned as a cynical vehicle employed to promote his racialized fascist politics. Upon closer examination, we have seen that this style more subtly favours aesthetic over ideological aims. These aims span the novels, correspondence, theoretical texts and even his controversial pamphlets, while also retaining a strong connection to socio-historical concerns: the anarchical satire of the Vichy regime; the recuperation of literary authenticity from the writer's lived experience of suffering; and the gradual revalorization of modernity as an aesthetically transformative source of this suffering, both for author and reader, even in the destructive context of war.

The fact remains, however, that a more nuanced appraisal of Céline requires breaking out of the circular impasse of the French culture wars. There are three potential ways of doing this: to examine Céline from a transnational – and especially American and American-Jewish – perspective; to consider his cultural value and contribution from the standpoint of literary auctions; and to republish his pamphlets. The last of these proposals, as I shall conclude at the end of this chapter, is especially controversial and fraught with difficulties, but nonetheless could help break the deadlock.

In her penetrating article 'The Céline Effect', American critic Alice Kaplan has shown how it is in the United States that Céline's rehabilitation has been most systematic, sustained and, in the main, objective and dispassionate.[92] American writers and intellectuals were the only ones to organize a petition in Céline's defence in 1946, when he was threatened with extradition from Denmark to France. If Céline's reputation in France in the early 1950s hit an all-time low, then conversely, it grew dramatically across the Atlantic. Why was this so? Céline was championed and introduced to American writers such as the Beats by Kenneth Rexroth at the publishing house New Directions, which reprinted translations of *Journey*, *Death on Credit* and *Guignol's Band* in the late 1940s and 1950s. To these writers, Céline represented an exciting new brand of literary rebellion that provided a timely aesthetic alternative to the stifling orthodox formalism of the so-called 'reactionary generation' of Ezra Pound and T. S. Eliot. By the mid-1960s, Céline's black humour and anti-war stance were also speaking to another generation of influential American writers – notably Philip Roth and Kurt Vonnegut – who were opposed to the Vietnam War. Both even taught courses on Céline at the Iowa Writer's Workshop.

In addition, Céline is not an American writer, and thus exempt from more local political passions, and in any case, the antisemitic pamphlets are not available in English translation and tend not to cloud his American reception, most American authors being familiar only with his fiction. But even among those few American-Jewish admirers of Céline to have read his pamphlets – Philip Roth being the most famous example – Kaplan argues that there is a particular American tradition which compels them, whatever their personal circumstances, to separate politics from aesthetic appreciation.

The transnational, specifically American, perspective on Céline has consistently offered a nuanced alternative and welcome counterweight to the repeatedly politicized and morally polarized French culture wars. Yet despite this, attempts have recently been made to re-appropriate – one might even say 'Gallicize' – this transnational, transatlantic view of Céline, by French film-maker Emmanuel Bourdieu in his recent movie *Louis Ferdinand Céline: Deux clowns pour une catastrophe* (2016). This film purports to be a faithful reconstruction of Milton Hindus's visit to Céline and his wife Lucette Almansor in the summer of 1948, while they were still exiled in Denmark. It addresses a by-now familiar dilemma: whether or not Céline's so-called stylistic genius is defensible in the face of his antisemitism. That this question is explored from the perspective of a real American Jew, the professor of English and American literature Milton Hindus, lends the film a welcome psychological complexity and a deeply subjective portrayal of personal conflict that is lacking in most academic books. The background to the encounter between Céline and Hindus is sketched out at the beginning of the film via voice-overs, as Hindus, a dapper, French-speaking, but slightly clumsy professor of American literature in Chicago, travels to Denmark with breathless anticipation to visit Céline. At this stage, Hindus has every reason to feel optimistic. He has established a warm epistolary relationship of some eighty-odd letters with the author he so admires – and takes justifiable pride in the central role he has played in organizing a petition of American writers and academics to overturn Céline's extradition. When he first meets Céline and his long-suffering but quietly shrewd wife, Lucette, Hindus is presented as akin to a tongue-tied, overgrown schoolboy, who is so star-struck by the 'literary genius' that he hangs on to his every word, eagerly jotting down his phrases, his notebook at the ready. When a slightly bemused but evidently flattered Céline asks him why he is writing down these phrases, Hindus notes that it is 'the way you say things' ('la façon dont vous dites les choses'). The atmosphere is one of light-hearted and slightly exaggerated politeness, in which Céline and Lucette bend over backwards to accommodate their guest, while he tags along in admiring diffidence, diligently cycling every day from his hotel to their house, scarcely believing his luck that he has exclusive access to such a literary giant. The attention-seeking Céline is clearly tickled by Hindus's undivided attention and initially responds enthusiastically to his questions. But the superficial atmosphere of bonhomie and the seemingly unproblematic dynamic of self-possessed master and eager pupil mask a multitude of conflicting and underlying tensions and agendas that slowly begin to bubble to the surface. To begin with, Hindus is economical with the truth about his intention to write a book on Céline based on their personal encounters. Upon discovering this essentially benign deceit, Céline, who is already paranoid and suffering from a persecution complex, explodes with rage at Hindus, launching into an antisemitic tirade that leaves the American professor floundering.

Bourdieu's film leaves us in no doubt that Céline's antisemitism is so virulent that any defence of his stylistic genius is morally untenable. It might almost be said that the first half of the movie reinforces the myth of the genius through Hindus's initially admiring gaze, while the second half gradually dismantles that myth as Hindus grows increasingly disillusioned and angry. Bourdieu cleverly encapsulates this shift via Hindus's perception and presentation of his own identity. When, near the beginning of the movie, Lucette tactfully asks whether he is Jewish – 'You are Jewish, aren't you?' ('Vous êtes juif n'est-ce pas?') – Hindus sidesteps the question by emphasizing his Americanness instead. In the last scene of the film, after Céline and Hindus's relationship has become strained, and a visibly upset and conflicted Hindus is leaving Krosol by bus, the tables are turned: he is politely asked by a friendly Danish sailor about his country of origin, 'Américain?' 'Non,' Hindus defiantly replies'; 'Juif!' Contrary to Roth, who, as we saw in the introduction, forces himself to suspend his 'Jewish conscience' so as to be able to celebrate Céline's literary genius, Hindus feels unable to disassociate the two.

Despite the undeniable artistic merits of Bourdieu's movie – which is especially evident in the strong performances of its two leads Denis Lavant and Philip Desmeules – we need to ask ourselves, how *accurate* is his reconstruction of the encounter? If we measure his movie against Hindus's own written account, we find some glaring discrepancies. His view that Hindus switches drastically from hero worship of Céline to utter revulsion is an over-simplification of the American's more morally nuanced account. He writes,

> He [Céline] rained the most hysterical abuse and accusations upon the heads of the Jews in *Bagatelles* and *L'École des cadavres* [. . .] He did not speak over the radio for the Germans or write in their newspapers, but the damage had been done. He had prepared the scapegoat though it was other hands than his that hurled it to destruction.[93]

In other words, Céline was a virulent antisemite, but not an active collaborator. He paved the way for the Holocaust, but did not participate in it: 'he was guilty, though not of the formal crime of collaboration of which he has been charged.'[94] Hindus gives Céline the benefit of the doubt regarding his support of Hitler and the Aryan theory: 'Their way, Céline saw, was not at all a good way. They were the same as in the days of the Kaiser, Pan-Germans with a new look. Their talk about the Aryan race was so much hogwash to camouflage their brutal hegemony.'[95] He even rushes to Céline's defence against Sartre for the 'slander' of having accused him of being paid by the Germans. And he refuses to concede that it was out of cowardice that he did not collaborate more with the Nazis, since 'he was a volunteer and his bravery was so conspicuous and important it was cited in the general order of the day to all the armies of France and was illustrated and glorified in the French magazines of the period.'[96]

Despite his Jewishness, Hindus is able to give a balanced, even generous, account of Céline, that praises qualities he possessed beyond his talents as a writer – namely, his bravery and honesty: 'I was impressed, throughout my stay, with his painstaking effort to be honest with me and I think he succeeded to a greater extent than he has ever done with anyone except members of his most immediate family.'[97] Indeed, like Philip Roth, Hindus is perfectly able to disassociate his revulsion at Céline's antisemitism from his intellectual and aesthetical attraction to his work:

> In the light of the most recent consequences of anti-Semitism [. . .] it is not perhaps entirely accidental for a writer to be fascinated by the minute particulars of the life, opinions, and work of a gifted man with whom he has much in common intellectually and aesthetically but who appears to be extremely antipathetic to the writer's people. Such fascination may be natural or even inevitable, and the result may be an inverse form of hagiography which itself constitutes a form of celebration.[98]

But Hindus goes even further than Roth by actually saying that it was not despite his Jewishness, but *because of it* that he was drawn to Céline:

> In my relations with Céline and in thinking about him I have sought consistently to understand him. To say that I have succeeded would be to say too much, but to say that I have completely failed would be too much also. My greatest handicap in the enterprise seems to be that I am American. To the Jew in me, massacred generation after generation, he was much more comprehensible than the American in me, for whom he was like a visitor from outer space.[99]

This quotation, and the fact that Hindus still felt able to write a highly favourable review of the English translation of *Castle to Castle* in 1969, completely contradicts Bourdieu's interpretation.[100] The director, as we have seen, portrays a Hindus who initially minimizes his Jewishness to emphasize his Americanness, only to do the very opposite at the end of the film. But Hindus's own account paradoxically illustrates the thesis that there is something about Céline's writing with which Jews feel an affinity. Jews

> feel at home with Céline because of his emotional intensity, his immense need for self-dramatization, his verbal gift, his operatic fears and anxieties, his excesses and exaggerations, and his apocalyptic sense of defeat, rooted in his feeling of being an outsider, a loser, a perpetual victim.

As for Céline's protagonists, 'they see themselves as marginal men, history's victims, who occupy their lives not with heroic, foolhardy acts but with stratagems of survival, the shifty, cunning manoeuvers of the powerless.'[101]

Bourdieu, then, portrays Hindus as deluded, rather than morally nuanced, in his assessment of Céline. And indeed, this confirms the underlying agenda to his movie. He has admitted that he wanted to show that these forms of 'intolerance, xenophobia and currents that ran against the rational and humanist' were still a threat.

> They are deeply anchored in our culture, our subconscious, our religion. And they can gain the upper hand because it's a very strong

> current of thought and confronted with it, reason can't do much. Because it's a discourse that refuses dialogue [. . .] I hope the film shows this monster and shows how it threatens us all in a way . . . even the most singular and extraordinary among us. We see that even someone like Céline can be seduced by this.[102]

Despite the well-intentioned artistic licence taken by Bourdieu, his film has incurred the wrath of extremist supporters of Céline. The website Égalité et réconciliation, run by Alain Soral, a former member of the Front national, accused the director of 'assassinating' Céline. It objected that Bourdieu and leading lady Géraldine Pailhas, who plays Céline's wife, Lucette Almenzor, were part of a 'champagne socialist' set who control French cinema and

> whose members can be found in almost all César-winning films. They are trophy collectors [. . .] A half century after the disappearance of the biggest French writer ever, it's not useful, that a film directed by the son of a self-righteous thinker . . . should reduce Céline to his antisemitism.[103]

Such attacks are clearly unjustified, motivated by political hatred and personal. By the same token, it is also true that Bourdieu has reappropriated both Hindus and Céline in order to make a political point, albeit from a far more morally acceptable standpoint than the far Right. In this respect, Bourdieu, despite his good intentions, is another unwitting participant in the Céline culture wars.

Within France itself, then, what can be done to diversify and nuance opinion on Céline? One strategy, as Henri Godard has suggested, is to look beyond traditional arbiters of cultural value such as academia, cultural institutions and artefacts to the economic sphere: in particular, auction houses. Céline manuscripts have reached high prices, even compared to other, less controversial literary giants such as Proust and Kafka. In 2001 a signed copy of *Journey* fetched 12,184,000 francs (1,857,439 euros) in the Drouot auction house. This was significantly more than the 7,000,000 francs (1,067,143 euros) fetched in 2000 by Christie's for volume I of Proust's *In Search of Lost Time*, or the 10,000,000 francs (1,524,490 euros) obtained at Sotheby's for Kafka's *The Trial* the same year.[104]

Those seeking to discredit Céline are quick to dismiss this economic value as entirely divorced from any artistic or literary merit: it merely reflects, in their view, the perverse attraction of Céline as a transgressive and taboo writer: 'If Céline is worth more than Proust, then that is because many of his texts are stamped with the seal of the forbidden, of exile, prison or prohibition.'[105]

Yet for those who consider Céline to be a great writer, literary auctions reflect a less conventional, but arguably more tangible, form of cultural consecration that is valuable precisely *because* it lies outside an officially sanctioned and institutional academic framework. Godard, one of the most probing and objective of Céline's biographers and critics, argues that such auctions actually provide a more reliable and accurate gauge of the esteem in which an author is held than specialist journals or publications, because non-specialist buyers at auction, who may or may not be readers of Céline, tend to follow an intuition that is uncluttered by the biased preconceptions that so often dog the critic:

> Consulting the value of [an author's] manuscripts in public auctions can prove to be more reliable than the number of articles devoted to him/her in specialist journals [. . .] The prices fetched by manuscripts in public auctions [. . .] give concrete expression in numerical terms to a widespread opinion forged by men and women, not all of whom would be able to discuss the author, but who have an intuition, supported by the amount they spend, that at times backs up their personal feeling as a reader.[106]

Literary auctions, then, have the advantage of accurately reflecting the general cultural esteem in which Céline continues to be held, even if they do not directly contribute to, or renew, intellectual debate on the author. At a psychological level, they are also a way of seducing the public with 'forbidden fruit' by offering them the opportunity to purchase something rare by a transgressive author.

A potentially effective way of reviving debate on Céline, but which risks exacerbating rather than resolving the Céline culture wars, is the proposed republication of his three antisemitic pamphlets. All hell broke loose when this very project was announced by Antoine Gallimard, the grandson of Gaston and current president of the prestigious French publishing house, in late 2017. The controversy this has generated exceeds even that of the 2011 debacle. At the time of writing, this project remains on hold, although permission has provisionally been granted, subject to certain stringent ethical and scholarly criteria being met. This latest polemic requires some understanding of the complex publication history of the pamphlets. Following their initial publication in the late 1930s and early 1940s, they were banned in France in 1951. But this ban was not imposed by the French government, as is often assumed, but at the express wishes of Céline and Lucette Destouches. In a 2001 interview, Lucette, who had continued to honour her late husband's wishes by filing lawsuits against anyone seeking their republication, reiterated their position: that from the early 1950s, Céline and she felt that the pamphlets had brought them nothing but trouble, belonged to a specific period of history and were thus no longer relevant. In this respect, she was backed by French law: the ban technically remains in force in France for a duration of seventy years, until January 2032. In 2012 Céline specialist Régis Tettamanzi, who had already published a stylistic study of his pamphlets as his doctoral thesis in 1999, was the first person to publish an annotated, critical edition of all four pamphlets, but he had to do so *outside France* with a Canadian publishing house (the duration of the ban is only fifty years in Quebec). This book remains unavailable in French libraries and bookshops.[107] Lucette Destouches' lawyer and close friend, the Céline biographer François Gibault, fiercely opposed this 2012 Canadian edition, even threatening to take the publishers to court, since it was in direct contradiction of his client's wishes.

However, when Gallimard made his announcement in late 2017, Lucette and Gibault did a complete U-turn. No doubt they were aware that Lucien Rebatet's fascist pamphlet *Les Décombres* was republished in 2015, without causing a major scandal. But the more pressing reason was financial: Lucette was, by then, aged 105 and in need of round the-clock medical care and three full-time assistants. The royalties she received from Céline's novels were simply not enough to cover her costs.

Even with Lucette's consent, there remained several major ethical and legal stumbling blocks. First, there were objections to the pamphlets' antisemitic content. The anti-racist organizations CRIF (Conseil représentatif des institutions juives de France) and LICRA (Ligue internationale contre le racisme et l'antisémitisme) were fiercely opposed to the republication and wrote a letter of complaint to Prime Minister Édouard Philippe. Knowing the legal difficulties of enforcing an outright ban, which would amount to censorship, the letter insisted that any new edition would have to meet very stringent conditions: specifically, the mandatory inclusion of a historically informed critical apparatus – one that was lacking in the existing Canadian edition – that would place the pamphlets in their ideological context and highlight their racist content and factual errors. In an unprecedented move, Philippe's direct representative, Frédéric Potier from the Ministry of the Interior, the délégué interministeriel à la lutte contre le racisme, l'anti-semitisme et la haine LGBT (DILCRAH), wrote a letter to Antoine Gallimard, the president of the Gallimard publishing house. The letter assured Gallimard that the government was not acting as a censor but as an 'early warning system' ('lanceur d'alerte'):

> In a context in which the scourge of anti-Semitism must be fought with greater purpose than ever, we need to consider very carefully the means by which these writings are made accessible to the wider public. The quality of the critical apparatus that accompanies them, and specifically its ability to shed light on the ideological and historical context that spawned them, and to reveal the author's biased positions and factual errors in the text, are henceforth decisive.[108]

The letter also sought assurances from Gallimard about the 'scholarly rigour and multidisciplinary nature' of his critical apparatus. The historian André Taguieff strongly backed this move, saying that it was out of the question to entrust the task of editing the new edition 'only to a specialist in literary history, however qualified he may be'. He added, 'It is not enough simply to have knowledge and admiration for Céline and his opus in order to undertake a work of this nature, which only a multidisciplinary team, principally made up of historians who specialize in the relevant areas, can carry out properly.'[109]

Céline critic Eric Mazet poured scorn on this initiative: '"Multidisciplinarity": the key word! The magic word! It will require at least a historian, a sociologist, a psychologist, a geographer, maybe even a linguist . . . otherwise nothing!'[110] The backlash, however, made Antoine Gallimard all the more determined to republish the pamphlets. On 4 March 2018, in *Journal du dimanche*, he relayed his decision to delay the project in order to 'take time to reflect, debate, find a way' and that he was contemplating 'associating my publishing house with a research institute to determine even more clearly the direction of our historical and pedagogical undertaking'.[111] But he was adamant that he would not back down: he expressed his outrage that this proposed new edition was being criticized even prior to its release and denounced 'the preachers who claim that Gallimard was a Nazi publishing house with an anti-Semitic catalogue', a thinly veiled swipe at Serge Klarsfeld, who, in 2009, had accused Antoine's grandfather, Gaston Gallimard, of publishing antisemitic works during the Occupation.[112]

But by now, the scale of the controversy was so big that even the French president, Emmanuel Macron, was dragged into it in his capacity as honorary guest at the annual dinner of CRIF, which took place in the Pyramide du Louvre in March 2018.[113] A brochure, entitled 'Céline contre les Juifs ou l'école de la haine' ('Céline against the Jews or the School of Hatred') was distributed to its nine hundred guests. Both the president of CRIF, Francis Khalifat, and Klarsfeld called on Gallimard to abandon the project to republish the pamphlets, the latter claiming that the involvement of a prestigious publisher would be a victory for all anti-Jewish authors. He implored Gallimard to 'have the decency to await our deaths before attempting once again to incorporate these pamphlets into the Pléaide, whose creator, your grandfather, dismissed by applying the Jewish statute.'[114] (This was an allusion to the fact that Gaston Gallimard had sacked Jacques Schiffrin, on 5 November 1940.)

In his speech, Macron was forced to steer a path between two diametrically opposed positions: that of his prime minister, Édouard Philippe, who had sanctioned the republication of the pamphlets, subject to an appropriate critical apparatus, and that of his dinner hosts, who were unambiguously opposed to their republication. Macron expressed his personal doubts that France needed the new edition of the pamphlets. He implied that he disapproved of the initiative to republish them, although he was pleased that 'in France there are still publishers able to ask this question without excusing it.' He concluded, however, with 'I do not think we need these pamphlets,' thereby contradicting his own prime minister.[115]

The salient questions asked about Céline in France today are strikingly reminiscent of those that were being asked about him in Israel in the mid-1990s: should he be published or not? Can he be admitted to the national cultural canon? Do these dilemmas warrant government intervention, and if so, what form should this intervention take? Israel's relationship to Céline is, of course, unique, given that nation's understandable sensitivity to the question of antisemitism. But in many ways, what happened there over two decades ago anticipates what is happening today in France. Israel's 'Céline controversy' was triggered by the publication of academic Ilana Hammerman's translation of *Journey* into Hebrew in 1994. Between February and April 1994, some 58 articles or items broached the topic in Israeli newspapers (many in the Left-wing newspaper *Haaretz*), as well as five radio broadcasts and five TV shows.[116] A motion to boycott the translation was initiated by two members of the Knesset (the Israeli parliament): Shaul Yahalom of the National Religious Party and Limor Livnat of the Likud, both Right-wing parties. However, the fiercest disagreements were within the Israeli Left. Representing both sides of the debate were historian and expert on fascism Zeev Sternhell and philosophy professor Yeshagahan Leibowitz. Sternhell, a Holocaust survivor, argued that when it comes to protest literature and the sociopolitical novel, we cannot separate the work from its author's political stance. This is especially true of Céline, because according to Sternhell he was not just a fascist, but a Nazi and supporter of racial theories. Contrary to the nineteenth-century composer Richard Wagner, or to the politician and journalist Édouard Drumont, Céline wrote in an era when antisemitism was no longer just theoretical. Stating his opposition to censorship, Leibowitz countered that one *should* separate an author from his or her work because these are two completely different things; Céline's personality is irrelevant. *Journey* is considered one of the most important works of the century; therefore, to translate it is the correct decision in the context of making world literature available in Hebrew. Others supporting Leibowitz, such as philosophy academic Adi Ophir, did so because of the 'literary, cultural and moral value' of Céline's novel. Not only was it a 'major work of world literature', they argued, but one 'that is crucial for understanding the nihilistic revolt conceived between the two world wars, and its destructive political consequences.'[117] Similar arguments have been advanced in France to justify republishing the pamphlets: provided they have a historically informed explanatory framework, they enhance our understanding of fascism and antisemitism in the 1930s. In a retrospective interview given in 2006, the Israeli translator admitted that her reasons for publishing the translation were not only 'to provide the audience with this reading experience (and deal with the challenge of translation)', but to 'try to undermine some cultural and ideological conventions here [in Israel]'.[118] In other words, Céline provoked a wider debate about what should be published in Israel, which tended to split opinion along ideological lines between Zionists and post-Zionists. As political scientist Michal Aharony concludes in her excellent summary of the 'Céline affair' in Israel, 'What are the borders, if any, of "what can be said" about Zionist and Israeli society and culture in the past and the present? [. . .] What is included in public and academic discourse in Israel, who is being excluded, and who has the power to decide?'[119]

As we have seen, the 'power to decide' about Céline specifically and the cultural canon more generally is just as difficult to determine in France and every bit as fiercely contested as it was in Israel in the 1990s. Exactly which power holds sway? Is it a dinner speech by President Macron? Or a legal decision by his prime minister that directly contradicts it? In such a highly charged and politicized forum, it is very hard to arrive at an objective decision that satisfies all parties. Remaining impartial is not an option.

On 3 July 2018 an illuminating debate was organized in a more neutral forum by the Société d'études céliniennes, at the prestigious research institute in Paris Sciences Po.[120] Of the half-dozen participants, only two were opposed to the republication of the pamphlets, although other opponents, such as Serge Klarsfeld, had been invited, but declined to attend. The start of the debate was delayed by a commotion caused by three young, uninvited guests from the organization Les Amis de la bienpensance (Friends of Political Correctness), who had already protested outside the Gallimard bookshop in December 2017. When the debate was eventually allowed to start, the first invited speaker, Gaston Gallimard, reiterated his desire to republish the pamphlets in *Cahiers Céline*, believing this to be an appropriate specialist outlet. He made it clear, however, that the Gallimard publishing house in no way endorsed the views of the pamphlets, as was demonstrated by its willingness over the years to publish numerous works on the Holocaust. His decision to delay the publication to an unspecified date stemmed primarily from a petition, published in many newspapers, that contained the names of 2,000 people who were opposed to the project. He concluded with a stern rebuttal of Klarsfeld's accusation that his grandfather had sacked Leo Schiffrin, once again emphasizing Gallimard's ethical integrity by publishing everything, without imposing moral censorship. The second speaker was historian Pascal Ory, who wrote the preface to the new edition of Lucien Rebatet's *Les Décombres*. He identified two reasons why this pamphlet, as opposed to Céline's, had successfully been republished without generating any scandal: the first was the thorough and scholarly explanatory notes; the second was that Rebatet was an inferior writer to Céline and hence less influential. Ory concluded that it was not morally inconsistent to denounce Rebatet's fascism while acknowledging his literary talent. (The editor of *Bulletin célinien*, Marc Laudelot, speculates that the success of this new edition of *Les Décombres* also stemmed from Klarsfeld's lack of opposition to it: Klarsfeld considers its antisemitism merely to be incidental.) The third speaker, Denis Salas, the only specialist in law present at the debate, opposed the republication on legal grounds. Céline, he recalled, explicitly opposed their republication, so his wishes are legally enforceable in France for seventy years. An author's decision to withdraw or express regret about his or her own work carries legal weight, which is exactly what Céline did in 1950, when he declared that he was 'not proud' of having allowed the republication of *School for Corpses*, in 1943. Salas warned that a new edition of the pamphlets would incite racial hatred. He cited the legal precedent of controversial comedian Dieudonné, whose racist rhetoric caused such public outrage, that the courts felt it necessary to intervene. Neo-Nazis and other racist groups could feel emboldened by this new edition to use Céline's racist writings for their own propaganda purposes. The memory of the Jewish victims of the Holocaust in France deserved to be honoured and respected. Quebec, where the pamphlets were published in 2012, was far less implicated in the Holocaust than France, where commemoration of its victims has become enshrined in official public discourse, such as when President Jacques Chirac issued a national apology for the role of the French state in the extermination of Jews. Written works had the power to cause genocide: like Camus' metaphor of the plague, what initially appears to be harmless, can quickly turn into a major threat to humanity. Next to speak was Régis Tettamanzi, who provided the critical notes to the 2012 Quebec edition, based on his 1993 doctorate. He defended the republication on the grounds of knowledge and elucidation: Céline could only fully be understood if proper light was shed on his opus. Neither Tettamanzi's doctorate, which he wrote without full access to the pamphlets, nor even the 2012 edition, which was limited to 1,000 pages, were able to go far enough. Tettamanzi added that the 2012 edition had been published without controversy and that the accusations of antisemitism levelled at Rémi Ferland – the head of Éditions 8, the Canadian publishing house in question and a respected academic – were completely unwarranted: such was Ferland's fondness for Jewish culture, that he had even learned Hebrew.

Céline critic and cultural historian Philippe Roussin was the most outspoken on the question of republication, highlighting genre and historical context as reasons to oppose it. He emphasized the intrinsic textual difference between the pamphlets, which Céline wrote very quickly, and his novels, over which he painstakingly laboured for years. The former need to be read according to a 'rhetorical logic', while the latter should be approached with a 'poetic logic'. Whereas this 'poetic logic' was morally acceptable back in the 1980s, thereby allowing Henri Godard to include more of Céline's works in the Pléiade collection, today the historical context has completely changed: xenophobia and antisemitism have come back with a vengeance, and therefore, political considerations should now be prioritized over literary ones. The present-day climate of intolerance has increased the capacity for Céline's incendiary language to reignite racial hatred, just as nineteenth-century racial theorist Édouard Drumont's antisemitic rhetoric did in the 1930s. Roussin also downplayed the supposedly comical aspects of Céline's pamphlets, as well as their contribution to his linguistic and stylistic revolution. While Céline's stylistic revolution needs to be recognized, it stems uniquely from his novels and not his pamphlets. Pascal Ory countered that it was precisely because of their present-day capacity to incite racial hatred that these texts should not be swept under the carpet, but brought out into the open and placed in a responsible critical framework that acknowledges, rather than silences, the threat that they pose. Since they are already available on the Internet anyway, with no critical apparatus, it is better to publish them in a more informed and responsible way. Roussin, however, expressed his doubts that a new critical apparatus, however intellectually rigorous, could defuse the danger of these texts and dispel people's prejudices: 25 per cent of North Americans, for example, claim that the Bible is right and Darwin is wrong.

The doyen of Céline studies, Henri Godard, leant towards Ory's position. A responsible and new publication is needed, precisely in order to lance the boil of antisemitism, as urgently as possible. Failure to do so would be tantamount to keeping the texts 'in the closet'. Moreover, the pamphlets are not only antisemitic, but contain numerous passages of significant literary merit. However, this literary aspect is frequently overlooked, owing to the widespread tendency, reinforced by far-Right websites, to pick out the most shockingly racist extracts and ignore the rest. Thus, a new edition would allow the pamphlets to be read in their entirety, rather than selectively. Nevertheless, it is vital, Godard stresses, that any new edition acknowledge, in full, the pain and hurt that these pamphlets can cause and not just focus on Céline himself and his writing style. Prominence should thus be given to the question of reader reception and the moral outrage elicited by the pamphlets among both Jews and non-Jews alike.

Finally, Pierre Assouline, the Céline critic enlisted by Antoine Gallimard to write the preface to the new edition, countered with the accusation of double standards: why should Céline's pamphlets not be republished, when approval has been given to republish with Fayard a new French edition of Hitler's notorious work *Mein Kampf*? Is Céline considered more dangerous than Hitler? Moreover, he disagreed with Roussin's assertion that Céline's language would incite racial hatred today. Nationalists already own copies of the pamphlets, either in their original editions or as illegal reprints. As for antisemitism today, its main source is from Islamic extremists who have no interest in French literature and would not read the pamphlets anyway. Assouline claims that it is *more* dangerous to suppress the pamphlets than to republish them, for two reasons: because this gives them a taboo status that paradoxically makes them an object of desire; and because it is worse if the only copies that are available (in libraries, on the black market or on extremist websites) have no critical framework that would place them in their proper context. There has never been an 'ideal' time to republish the pamphlets. Even in the 1930s, not everyone agreed with them (Ernst Jünger found them vulgar), and in the supposedly less antisemitic 1980s, a synagogue in the rue Copernic in Paris was blown up. Finally, the antisemitism of other writers from the 1930s was arguably *more* toxic – Paul Morand's antisemitism was straightforward and appealed to readers' logic, in contrast with Céline's satirical style, which was far too complicated and ambivalent to have the same rational impact. Assouline concluded by saying that if, and when, the go-ahead were given for the new edition, he would devote around twenty pages of his preface alone to the controversy their proposed republication had sparked.

What this latest polemic shows, once again, is the moral quagmire into which Céline continues to plunge France, not just within academia, but in all sections of the media and the highest corridors of political power. The Céline culture wars are far from over, but a sensible compromise would surely be to republish his pamphlets in a responsible way that also sheds important historical light on the antisemitism of the 1930s.

Epilogue

Although he died relatively young, Céline managed to cram several lifetimes into one, which, to a large extent, mirrored the turbulent times in which he lived. By the age of twenty, he was already a war invalid; aged thirty, he was a highly promising doctor, who conducted high-profile fact-finding missions for the League of Nations; fewer than two years shy of his fortieth birthday, he was heralded as a literary sensation, who was read by everyone, from André Gide to Joseph Stalin. He had the world at his feet and then decided to pull the rug from underneath them. Although not immediate, his fall from grace was spectacular when it came: exile, imprisonment and total ostracization. In both his early and late adulthood, he narrowly cheated death: first, when he was shot in the trenches in 1914, and second, during his incarceration in Denmark from 1945 to 1947, which almost certainly saved him from a firing squad back home. Aged 56, he was finally granted amnesty and began the long, painful process of rehabilitation. That he managed to regain the literary limelight at all in the last four years of his life is nothing short of a miracle and a testament to his huge talents as a writer.

Thanks to his multiple lives, Céline got to know human nature inside out. For a novelist, such intimate familiarity with his fellow man was both a huge asset and a heavy burden. On one hand, it significantly enhanced his powers of observation, which allowed him to create extraordinarily multifaceted characters with tremendous emotional range. But on the other, it served as a constant reminder of man's fragility and mortality, which weighed heavily on his conscience and left him with lingering mental scars. This is why, despite his strong work ethic and deep-rooted insecurities about money, Céline saw writing as far more than just a profession: it was the only means by which he could exorcize his demons. Not only did he write to live, but he lived to write. Insofar as writing was a form of catharsis, then his suffering was a good thing, because it gave his novels existential purpose and urgency.

Unfortunately, however, it is precisely this emphasis on suffering – not only his own, but that of man in general – that has led many to pigeonhole Céline as a nihilist. At first glance, the evidence to support this view is very compelling. Reading *Journey*, we recoil in horror from his harrowing, satirical accounts of the trench warfare that decimated an entire generation. Civilian life is no less grim, with its botched abortions, assassination attempts and even the horrific spectacle of child abuse, which the narrator fails to prevent. In his later works, especially *Fable for Another Time* and *Normance*, we shudder at Céline's relentless, hallucinatory depictions of aerial bombardment and wince at his excruciatingly scatological descriptions of his bowel movements in his Danish prison cell. Yet it would be mistaken to interpret Céline's black humour as evidence of a black heart. On the contrary, he uses it to shine a spotlight on the plight of the downtrodden and dispossessed: the malaria-ridden, alcoholic colonialists in far-flung corners of West Africa; the haggard, dehumanized workers in the Ford factories of Detroit; the penniless medical patients in Rancy; and the desperate refugees who scavenge for food in war-torn Germany.

In his novels, Céline's satire of man comes from a place of genuine empathy, rather than cynical disdain. René Schwob, as we saw earlier, was one of the very first writers to spot this distinction, which is why he rejected the notion that Céline was a nihilist. If he placed so much emphasis on suffering, Schwob maintained, this was proof, not of his antipathy towards humanity, but of the very opposite: namely, that he *loves* humanity too much. In fact, so great is his love for his fellow man (at least in his novels), that he is consistently frustrated by his inability to *alleviate* suffering. It is worth requoting Schwob's perceptive observation on *Journey*, which can be applied to Céline's fiction as a whole: 'Your [love] remains powerless to save those whose every defect you nevertheless know. This impossibility of being useful to anyone, this is one of the biggest lessons of your book.'[1]

This is key to understanding Céline's novels. They do not so much provide a damning indictment of mankind, as express *frustration* at his impotence in the face of suffering. And it is suffering, not evil, that Céline considers to be innate to man; his inability to tolerate this suffering is what usually brings out the worst in him, not malicious, premeditated intent. (Prime examples of this are Madelon's shooting of Robinson, or the colonel's cold indifference to the messenger who brings him news of Sergeant Barbusse's death.) Céline's natural inclination is thus to empathize, rather than condemn. Or rather, if he condemns anything at all, then it is the human *condition*, and not human nature per se. Were this not the case, then he would not write so movingly about individuals who remain stoical in the face of suffering, who somehow muster the courage to confront it head-on, despite knowing that it cannot be defeated. These occurrences remain etched in our minds, because they are so infrequent and unexpected. Thus, in *Death on Credit*, Ferdinand and his parents, who are usually at loggerheads, stand united at his grandmother's deathbed until the bitter end, in a rare display of emotional solidarity. Equally poignant, but even more out of the ordinary, are Bardamu's unusually proactive, yet futile, attempts to save the dying Bébert from the ravages of typhoid. But the truly unforgettable characters, those who most accurately embody Céline's frustrated idealism, as opposed to defeatist nihilism, are Molly and Alcide. Both are the salt of the earth and willing to sacrifice their own happiness for someone else's, without a murmur of complaint. Even though she loves him, the kind-hearted prostitute Molly tells the feckless Bardamu to go back to France; as for Sergeant Alcide, such is his devotion to his orphaned niece that he does not think twice about prolonging his posting in the harsh tropical climate, just to pay for her education.

Yet such altruistic characters are the exception, rather than the rule. Their willingness to tackle suffering head-on is admirable, but it is by far the road less travelled. The easier route is to escape it altogether. And the most prevalent source of escapism in Céline is humour, and specifically the humour and light-hearted atmosphere provided by popular culture. *Guignol's Band I and II*, *Death on Credit* and portions of the German trilogy are bathed in the nostalgic, exuberant ambience of Soho's music halls, Wapping's pubs in East London or the light operas, cabarets and early movie houses of the Opéra district in the Paris of the Belle Époque. Singing, music and dancing foster a communal spirit of laughter and celebration that offers escape from mortality and the troubles of the outside world. But this escape can only ever be temporary. Céline had read enough Freud to know that the death drive was a powerful instinct, which man can only keep at bay for so long. In the end, Céline's *anti*nihilist love of humanity invites us to choose between two diametrically opposed approaches to life: to embrace suffering, or to avoid it. Neither of these options is entirely satisfactory: the first entails too much self-sacrifice; the second means burying one's head in the sand.

It still remains a mystery, however, how such an acute observer of the human condition within his novels could get things so spectacularly wrong outside them. How can such penetrating insight and complete lack of judgement coexist in the same person? How do we reconcile the touching humanity of the fiction with the unspeakable cruelty of the pamphlets? Among major writers, very few – with the possible exception of Wyndham Lewis and Ezra Pound – have managed to sabotage their careers quite as comprehensively as Céline did when he unwisely decided to publish *Trifles for a Massacre* in 1937. Céline's legacy as a great writer will forever be tarnished by his antisemitism, as the present debate on the pamphlets reminds us. But this should not prevent us from acknowledging a more positive aspect of his legacy that is often overshadowed by his antisemitism: his wider impact on cultural forms beyond the novel itself. The gridlock created by the Céline culture wars has tended to obscure our awareness of a thriving Céline culture industry. Although it can be considered more marginal than mainstream, this industry has nonetheless left its mark, in ascending order of importance, on three different genres: cinema, theatre and the comic strip. Each of these genres has sought to adapt Céline's works to its own aesthetic form, but not always directly. Straight adaptations of his novels have alternated with more indirect allusions to his work, including his non-novelistic output: some theatre productions have focused exclusively on his lesser-known theoretical texts.

Let us start with the first of these genres: cinema. Céline and cinema should have been a match made in heaven. Surely, the dominant cultural medium, with the broadest popular appeal, must have welcomed with open arms an anti-elitist novelist who prided himself on writing for the common man? And yet things have not quite worked out this way: all attempts to bring his novels to the screen have come to nothing, even during his own lifetime, when he was able to have his say. How do we explain this failure? To begin with, there is Céline's own ambivalence about film. He quickly grew out of his early love of cinema as soon as he entered adulthood. This transition coincided with the replacement of silent movies with the talkies. In *Death on Credit*, the author recalls that, as a young boy, he loved to watch the silent films of George Meliès with his grandmother, which, according to Alain Cresciucci, 'aligns Céline's taste with fable, the fantastic, not with reality but illusion'.[2] Silent film thus had an enchanting, magical quality to it, which is implied by the title of Meliès' 1902 movie *Le Voyage dans la lune* (Journey to the Moon). Half a century later, in *Castle to Castle*, Céline nostalgically laments the loss of that sublime seductiveness of silent movie stars such as Suzanne Bianchetti:

> What a screen artist! And her vaporous negligees against a background of 'soft blue light!' of 'moonlight' . . . what a sublime artist, absolutely silent, no talkies in those days . . . it's the word that kills! . . . a woman that talks softens your pecker, ah, they came up hard at the silent pictures![3]

The talkies, Céline surmises, have forever trivialized cinema, with their trite dialogue, depriving us of the ability of its silent forebears to weave their subtle poetic magic.

Céline's sceptical attitude towards the talkies comes across in *Journey*. Bardamu, as we saw earlier, tries to escape the misery of his American sojourn by entering a movie house. But his hopes are swiftly dashed when he realizes that the 'Hollywood dream factory' is one big sham whose sole purpose is to dupe ordinary people into believing that the glamorous life they see on-screen is something to which they can personally aspire. Later, when Bardamu becomes an employee in Parapine's mental asylum, he regularly takes patients to the Tarapout cinema as part of their therapy. This is a likely satirical allusion to Georges Duhamel's snobbish perception of cinema as a source of intellectual impoverishment in *Scènes de la vie future*.[4] This equivalence between cinema and the 'dumbing down' of the masses is echoed later, in *Guignol's Band*, when Ferdinand enters the cinema, not for cultural enrichment, but purely in order to hide from the London police. He whiles away his time watching films starring the actress Pearl White. And as we saw in his attack on Hollywood as a vehicle of Jewish power and propaganda in *Trifles for a Massacre*, Céline's satire of the talkies also sometimes crossed the line from legitimate cultural critique to racist conspiracy theory.[5] With the exception of silent movies, then, Céline's novels (not to mention his pamphlets) are rather disparaging about film as a cultural form.

For all his aesthetic reservations about cinema, however, Céline knew that only a fool would choose to ignore its vast commercial potential. This is why he not only flirted with writing his own film scripts, but was prepared to liaise with several film directors who proposed to adapt his novel *Journey*. Altogether, he wrote four original film scripts and one very rough draft of a film adaptation of *Journey*. *Gangster's Holiday* was a mere synopsis of a few lines about a clown who becomes a failed gangster: this had the potential makings of a short film. More substantial and worthy of attention were the three film scripts he wrote between 1936 and 1948: *Secrets dans l'île* (Secrets in the Island), *Scandale aux abysses* (Scandal into the Abyss) and *Arletty: Jeune fille dauphinoise* (Arletty: Young Dauphinoise Woman), the latter written with his actress friend Arletty in mind for the starring role.[6] In both its theme and tone, this last script contains elements of the 'poetic realism' that was favoured by major film-makers of the time, such as Marcel Carné and Julien Duvivier. Céline combines an unhappy romance (between the beautiful Arletty and her weak husband Jérôme), with an adventure story (a young couple of pastors who travel around the world to preach to sinners and also escape from temptation) and film noir (the corruption of virtuous beauty by man's violence and vice). One notable figure who was frequently exploited by pre-war film-makers (such as in Carné's *The Devil's Envoys* and *Daybreak*) is the Devil as the real or symbolic figure of temptation. However, there is a certain *simplicity* to Céline's film scripts, which lack the originality and emotional complexity of his novels.[7]

If, in the end, Céline's own film scripts were never more than embryonic and speculative in their conception, several important directors were keen to adapt *Journey*. The most prominent of these were Abel Gance and Claude Autant-Lara during the author's lifetime, and Michel Audiard and Sergio Leone after his death. Gance took out an option on the novel in March 1933 with Robert Denoël for 300,000 francs. As a fan of Gance's film *Napoléon* and having got to know him personally while working for the journal *Eureka* in 1917, Céline was delighted. It was agreed between Céline and Gance to entrust the script to Francis Norman, a journalist from Bordeaux, who got as far as adapting the text of the New York episode. But Gance was overstretched with other film projects and underestimated the novel's difficulty.[8] When his interest in the project began to wane, fellow director Julien Duvivier, who had directed Céline's friend and actor Robert Le Vigan, was considered as a replacement, with the famous actor Jean Gabin proposed for the role of Bardamu, but this too fell through. A third director, Pierre Chenal, whose real name was Cohen, threw his hat into the ring, but was understandably put off when Céline made an antisemitic comment about Jews controlling French cinema.[9] Amid all these negotiations, Céline made a brief trip to Hollywood in the summer of 1934 to see if his director friend Jacques Deval, who was based there, could help him find an American producer, but to no avail. In any case, his efforts were only half-hearted, since his trip to Hollywood, as we saw earlier, was largely a pretext to try and win back his ex-lover Elizabeth Craig, who had, by then, moved to Los Angeles.

After the Gance project had eventually petered out, the last serious contender to try and adapt *Journey* during Céline's lifetime was Claude Autant-Lara, just one year before the latter's death, in 1960. Céline's interest in a film adaptation was revived for two reasons: he wanted to make money as a point of pride, since his books had yet to generate enough royalties to make up the generous advance given to him by Gallimard, and Autant-Lara's artistic credentials were impeccable.[10] Together with his co-writers, Jean Aurenche and Pierre Bost, he had successfully adapted three major literary works in an anarchical anti-bourgeois style that was well suited to a writer like Céline: *The Devil in the Flesh* (Raymon Radiguet), *Green Wheat* (Colette) and *The Red and the Black* (Stendhal).[11] Céline's hopes were sufficiently raised for him to write a scene that could act as a prologue for the film, once a screenwriter was found. Instead of including the conversation between Arthur Ganate and Bardamu that starts the novel, which is too philosophical in nature to be rendered visually, this scene is a dialogue between two society ladies near the Bois de Boulogne, who discuss the war (which they do not believe will happen) before heading off to drink a hot chocolate. Céline then suggests including views of Paris – the bus from Madeleine to Bastille, the passage Choiseul (where he grew up) and the barrage at Suresnes, on the river Seine – which constitute a visual backdrop that renders the peace and harmony of the Belle Époque that is about to disappear once Bardamu is mobilized and the war begins. Céline, in keeping with his literary aims, wishes to convey emotion, rather than to explain.[12] To this end, he also proposed some songs and military tunes from the era that would enhance this emotion musically, as well as visually.[13] But despite his efforts, the project, once again, never got off the ground.

However, in the almost sixty years since Céline's death, no adaptation has seen the light of day, despite the cooperation of his recently deceased widow, Lucette Destouches. The director who has probably come closest was Michel Audiard, in the late 1960s. Born in 1920, Audiard was a lifelong admirer of Céline who was known for his sharp feel for dialogue. Probably his most famous film remains the 1963 gangster classic *Crooks in Clover* (*Les Tontons flingueurs*), which itself gives a nod to Céline's *Guignol's Band* with its argot expression *mousse et pampre* ('moss and vine'). Lucette was enthusiastic about Audiard, who acquired the film rights in 1964 through his brother-in-law Jean-Paul Guibert's production company, Intermondia. A contract was signed with Gallimard in July that year, with a healthy advance of 200,000 francs. The overall budget was envisaged as around 15 million euros in today's money. On 20 September 1964, Agence France-Presse felt sufficiently confident in the project to announce that one of the major film stars of the day, Jean-Paul Belmondo, had expressed his enthusiasm for the main role of Bardamu, with Audiard hoping to get Shirley MacLaine to play Molly.[14] Indeed, Belmondo had made no secret of his love of Céline, to the extent that he would later call one of his racehorses Bardamu.[15] But there was a snag: the contract stipulated that the film would have to be shot by 1970. As the 1960s progressed, the script did not (despite the intervention of the film's putative producer, Maurice Bernard), and Audiard eventually had to admit defeat. He later confessed that both a lack of finance and the difficulty of doing justice to Céline's style were insurmountable obstacles: 'I was maybe scared with *Journey* that the style would get lost in the images.'[16] But all was not lost, or so it seemed. Italian director Sergio Leone, famous for his trilogy of spaghetti westerns, had long professed his admiration for Céline and was considered as the most likely candidate to take over the shooting of the film from Audiard, retaining Belmondo as Bardamu and Audiard to write the dialogue. But this too fell through, and Leone himself later admitted in his interviews with Noël Simsolo that it was probably better for a film-maker like him not to tamper with a masterpiece like *Journey*: 'I too am an "auteur", as a film-maker. My natural instinct would be to betray the essence of Céline's work. I would turn it into something else, and I am not sure if it is legitimate to do that.'[17] In the twenty-first century, François Dupeyron and Yann Moix are directors who have also expressed an interest in bringing *Journey* to the screen, but to no avail; and as recently as 2018, Canal+ was contemplating making a television series of the novel in eight episodes, but this has yet to materialize.[18]

Despite these repeated failures to transpose Céline's novels to the screen directly, many directors have quoted them *indirectly* in their own films via intertextual allusions and narrative clues. Not all of them can be listed here, but the earliest known example is from Julien Duvivier, whose 1946 film *Panic* features a *stand des nations* or shooting gallery.[19] This is a clear nod to the *stand des nations* in which Bardamu, accompanied by Lola, is haunted by flashbacks of the trenches. Of the more iconic directors, Jean-Luc Godard has been the one to reference Céline most extensively. In the fifth segment of his 1964 film *A Married Woman*, Charlotte's cleaning lady is called 'Madame Céline' and launches into a long monologue about her love life that Godard adapted from *Death on Credit*. Godard goes one step further in his famous film *Pierrot le fou*, which stars the darling of the French New Wave, Jean-Paul Belmondo. Marianne brings to her lover Pierrot (also called Ferdinand) a copy of Céline's book *London Bridge* (*Guignol's Band II*); this had been published by Gallimard in 1964, the year before the film's release. Marianne says, 'The writer has the same name as you [. . .] did you know him?' Moreover, in terms of its narrative structure, Godard's film echoes the same peripatetic and chaotic trajectory as Céline's novel: it tells the story of two conflicted lovers, locked in a passionate and unpredictable relationship, who have embarked on a utopian journey of escape to an unspecified destination. Thus Godard's Pierrot/Ferdinand and Marianne are reminiscent of Céline's Ferdinand and Virginie.[20] Two other film-makers from Godard's generation have also referenced Céline in their movies. The first is Jean-Pierre Melville, who begins his 1962 film *The Finger Man* (*Les Doulos*) with a maxim taken from Bardamu, when he contemplates the human condition in his New York hotel room: 'You have to choose. To die or to lie?' ('Il faut choisir. Mourir ou mentir?'). The second is Godard's fellow New Wave director Claude Chabrol, this time in a much later film, *The Ceremony* (1996).[21] Jeanne, the anarchical postal worker, 'borrows' *Journey* from the book collection of her friend Sophie's boss. This decision alludes to her anti-bourgeois subversiveness. To this list we can add political film-maker Costa-Gavras, whose 1965 film *The Sleeping Car Murders* shows a photograph of Céline in bed with his dog Bessy, taken during his Danish exile; the Godard-inspired film-maker Léo Carax, whose protagonist in his debut feature *Boy Meets Girl* (1984) recites passages from both *Journey* and *Death on Credit*; Bertrand Tavernier, whose 2002 film *Safe Conduct*, which is set during the Occupation, features the actor Denis Podalydes declaring that his favourite author is Céline; and more recently still, François Ozon's *In the House* (2012), in which Fabrice Luchini is knocked out by Kristin Scott Thomas using a copy of *Journey*.[22] If all of these directors are either French or based in France (Costa-Gavras), what Alain Cresciucci calls these 'Céline collages' are not exclusively confined to French-made films: one notable example is the American film-maker James McNaughton's *Wild Things* (1998), in which one of the main female characters reads a copy of *Death on Credit*, and expresses admiration for Céline's 'crazy vision of humanity'.[23]

All told, Céline has slipped into cinema via the back door, rather than through the main entrance. The theatre, however, has found it easier than the cinema to adapt his work: plays are less expensive and logistically complex to make than films, and unlike films, they tend to place more emphasis on the text and dialogue than on visual language. But the fortunes of these adaptations have been linked to his novels and other non-theatrical works, rather than his *own* plays, which have made little impact. This is especially noticeable in the case of *The Church*, the one play he published during his lifetime (and even then, only on the strength of his reputation with *Journey*). It was performed just once, on 2 December 1936, by an amateur troupe in the Théâtre des Célestins, in Lyon. Not even a strong publicity campaign could save it from falling into public and critical neglect.[24] The next performance was not until 1967, but in Rome, rather than Paris. It did not make it to the French capital until 1973, at the Théâtre des Mathurins, and was also shown on television.[25] But overall, *The Church* has proven to be a damp squib, exposing Céline's limitations as a playwright. A silk purse cannot be made out of a sow's ear.

This is why more astute theatre directors have turned to his novels for inspiration, because of their far greater dramatic potential. In 1968 – the year of the student uprisings – Alain Viala staged a montage of Céline's texts, in the American Centre in Paris, punningly entitled *Vers Céline et la nuit* (Towards Céline and the Night). In 1979, at the Lucernaire theatre in Paris, Stéphane Varegues sang *Une Heure avec L.-F. Céline* (An Hour with L.-F. Céline), essentially using extracts from *Journey* and *Guignol's Band*. The very same year, in Brussels, Daniel Peeters read extracts from the German trilogy. Pierre Marcabru of *Le Figaro* praised Peeters's rendition of the oral power of Céline's language.[26] The two French actors to have most frequently performed Céline onstage are Jean Rougerie and Fabrice Luchini. In 1975 Rougerie performed *Conversations with Professor Y*. So successful was the performance that it ran again in 1976, in 1981 under the title *Interviouve* and then again in 1986.[27] Rougerie anticipated a growing trend for adapting not Céline's novels, but some of his lesser-known, theoretical texts. A more recent example of this, albeit for CD and DVD, rather than for the stage, is Bernard Cavanna's 2018 musical adaptation, conducted by Philippe Nahon, of *À L'Agité du bocal*, Céline's virulent short pamphlet attacking Jean-Paul Sartre. Sung by three tenors, and accompanied by a documentary by Delphine de Blic, this recording was praised by Jacques Medina of *L'Obs* as 'a marvel of intelligence and inventiveness' ('une merveille d'intelligence, d'invention').[28] As for Fabrice Luchini, he is an avowed 'célinophile', who has given numerous stage performances, principally taken from *Journey* and *Death on Credit*. His first, in 1986, entitled *Journey to the End of the Night*, centred on Bardamu's medical practice in the *banlieue*, while in 2001, the year of the September attacks, in a play entitled *L'Arrivée à New York* (Arrival in New York), he switched his attentions to Bardamu's visit to America.[29] Apart from André Dussollier, who at the height of the coronavirus pandemic made a timely recording of Céline's medical thesis *Semmelweis* for the prestigious radio programme *France Culture*, Luchini is probably the best-known French actor to have become associated with Céline.[30] He became a regular visitor to Meudon, after he befriended Lucette Destouches.[31] The most successful stage, radio or musical adaptations share an ability to bring out the oral rhythm and musicality of Céline's language, something which the medium of film struggles to do.

When it comes to adapting Céline to other genres, we have seen that cinema has consistently flattered to deceive, and theatre has had mixed results. But a third genre has emerged as a true success story: the comic strip. This phenomenon is associated with the name of renowned illustrator and comic strip writer Jacques Tardi. Tardi has long been a Céline enthusiast, having discovered him at the age of seventeen. In the early 1980s, the project of a comic strip version of *Journey* was proposed to the publisher Futuropolis, but its main editor, Étienne Robial, was unenthusiastic.[32] This all changed when Futuropolis was taken over by Gallimard (Céline's publisher) a few years later. This smoothed the passage for Tardi to take the project forward, provided he got the consent of Lucette Destouches. He was put in touch with her by her friend and lawyer François Gibault, but Lucette initially refused. She was not keen on the idea of someone illustrating her husband's work with drawings and speech bubbles. Tardi, sensing that she and Gibault had negative preconceptions about the comic strip genre and were worried that he would produce something equivalent to the Smurfs, won them over when he showed them his illustrations for the first chapter, when Bardamu heads off to war. Having been given the green light, Tardi felt a tremendous burden had been lifted from his shoulders, but also a great sense of responsibility to do justice to the richness of Céline's text. As he later recalled, he knew that he had his work cut out:

> To illustrate Céline, it is not possible to do only two drawings per chapter! There are so many characters, so much action, complications . . . Céline's work is very dense. There's chaos everywhere . . . He goes for the jugular, he is prone to excess, he rambles, he exaggerates. It was essential that the drawings accompany the text.[33]

Tardi's monumental efforts were not in vain: as soon as it hit the bookshelves in the autumn of 1988, his illustrated adaptation of *Journey* became an immediate bestseller, proved a hit with the critics and has since been heralded as a classic of the comic strip genre. He was thus encouraged to illustrate both *Death on Credit* and *Cannon Fodder*, which were equally successful. So iconic have Tardi's illustrations of Céline now become, that no one else has dared to compete with him in trying to adapt the author to this genre.[34] However, just as in cinema, the influence Céline has exerted on the comic genre more generally is far bigger than is often realized. A recent book, for instance, has shown how Belgian author Hergé, the creator of famous comic book character Tintin, adapted elements of Céline's style to the depiction of his iconic hero.[35]

What this brief overview has shown is that, culturally speaking, Céline continues to be alive and well, not only in France, but in other countries. He will never be able to shake off the indelible stain of fascism and antisemitism, but his novels still rank among the very best ever written by a French author, whose powerful influence continues to be felt by writers and readers all over the world. It is perhaps worth concluding with a thoughtful comment by the acclaimed British actor Mark Rylance, who is set to bring to the stage the character of Ignace Philippe Semmelweis, the nineteenth-century Hungarian doctor who discovered that a lack of hygiene through basic hand-washing was the main cause of puerperal fever. During his time, Semmelweis's theory was dismissed, and he was ostracized by the medical community and society more widely. It was Rylance who brought Céline's biography of Semmelweis to Tom Morris, artistic director of the Bristol Old Vic, in order to turn it into a play, with the assistance of writer Stephen Brown. At the time of writing, performances of the play have been postponed because of the coronavirus pandemic. But the pandemic itself has brought the topicality of Céline's biography into sharp relief: the fate of Semmelweis anticipates the current COVID-19 crisis and the thorny ethical questions surrounding the dissemination of medical expertise in an emotionally charged political context. As Rylance aptly puts it,

> A pioneer like Semmelweis is like the sharpest knife in the cutlery drawer. It can cut through, but it is not the best thing for putting meat into your mouth. He could not get them to understand the rigour required with hand washing and he was constantly haunted by the ghosts of those he had seen die in the wards and who, in some cases, he himself had unwittingly killed [. . .] One thing that Céline did get right is that he was obsessive about his work. It was emotion that drove him. We praise rational behaviour so much, but it was heat or a fire that forged his brilliant mind. The lesson for me is that we should be allowed to be emotional. If we exclude people because they are emotional, we may well be missing things in our institutions.[36]

Emotion was central to Céline's writing, as was his belief in the necessity to challenge authority and moral hypocrisy. It often got him into trouble, but this is one instance in which he got it right.

REFERENCES

Introduction

1 Alphonse Juilland, *Elizabeth and Louis: Elizabeth Craig Talks about Louis-Ferdinand Céline* (Stanford, CA, 1991), p. 463.
2 Ibid., p. 464.
3 Louis-Ferdinand Céline, *Journey to the End of the Night*, trans. Ralph Manheim, foreword by John Banville (Richmond, 2012). Henceforth, this edition will be referred to as *Journey*.
4 Its topicality has benefitted this biography, since I was invited in October 2018 to participate in a BBC Radio 3 panel discussion on Céline's debut novel, to coincide with the centenary anniversary of the armistice: 'Landmark: *Journey to the End of the Night*', with Marie Darrieussecq, Andrew Hussey, Damian Catani and Tibor Fischer with Rana Mitter, *Arts and Ideas* (podcast), BBC Radio 3 (7 November 2018), www.bbc.co.uk.
5 Henri Godard, *Céline et Cie: Essai sur le roman français de l'entre-deux-guerres – Malraux, Guilloux, Cocteau, Genet, Queneau* (Paris, 2020), p. 76.
6 Henri Godard, 'Les Enjeux d'une autobiographie', in *Céline à l'épreuve: Réceptions, critiques, influences*, ed. Philippe Roussin, Alain Schaffner and Régis Tettamanzi (Paris, 2016), pp. 35–9.
7 Godard, *Céline et Cie*, pp. 81–90.
8 Ibid., p. 82.
9 'Rien ne leur paraît indispensable, rien ne leur paraît urgent', ibid., p. 83.
10 'L'orgueilleuse solitude de l'intellectuel fait place progressivement à une solidarité fraternelle le rattachant à tous les vivants comme lui en péril. Il ne s'agit plus d'un petit jeu d'appartement sans lendemain véritable, mais au contraire d'une mission essentielle dont chaque penseur, chaque homme d'esprit devient responsible', ibid.
11 Ibid., p. 84.
12 Philip Roth, *Entretien avec Jean-Pierre Salgas, La Quinzaine littéraire*, no. 419 (16 June 1984).
13 Two recent notable examples are Roman Polanski's past conviction for an illegal sex act with a minor, and a similar allegation against Woody Allen.

Both these famous directors have been boycotted and now struggle to find distributors for their movies.

14 Kevin Rawlinson, 'Cecil Rhodes Statue to Remain at Oxford after "Overwhelming Support"', *The Guardian* (29 January 2016), available at www.theguardian.com.

15 Henry Mance, 'The New Office Politics', FT Weekend, *Financial Times* (25 July 2020), p. 2.

16 A recent attempt to situate the controversial artist (including Céline) in relation to cancel culture has been made by Gisèle Sapiro, *Peut-on dissocier l'œuvre de l'artiste?* (Paris, 2020). For an interview of Sapiro on this work, see Élisabeth Philippe, 'Séparer l'homme de l'artiste: mode d'emploi', *L'Obs*, no. 2925 (19–25 November 2020), pp. 65–8.

17 Frederic Morton, 'The First to Mine Delirium', *Nation* (17 March 1969).

18 Dominick Abel, 'The Searing Black Humor of Celine', *Chicago News* (15 March 1969).

19 Erika Ostrovsky, 'Buffoons of the Apocalypse', *Saturday Review* (1 February 1969), pp. 31, 63.

20 Raymond A. Sokolov, 'Noodles and Hatred', *Newsweek* (27 January 1969), pp. 47–9.

21 Sarah Higginson Begley, 'Céline and His Three Dots', *Christian Science Monitor* (20 March 1969).

22 *Playboy* (April 1969), pp. 34b–c and 36b.

23 Milton Hindus, 'A Literary Event of the First Order', *Evening Globe* [Boston, MA] (9 February 1969).

24 Régis Tettamanzi, 'Bilans critiques', in *Céline à l'épreuve*, ed. Roussin et al., pp. 13–25.

25 Isabelle Blondiaux, *Céline: Portrait de l'artiste en psychiatre* (Paris, 2004).

26 I discuss this in Damian Catani, *Evil: A History in Modern Literature and Thought* (London, 2013), pp. 126–7.

27 Ibid., pp. 96–8.

28 Ibid., pp. 98–9.

29 Ibid., pp. 99–101.

30 Ibid., pp. 101–2.

31 Laurent Tatu, Odile Roynette and Julien Bogousslavsky, 'Louis-Ferdinand Céline: From First World War Neurological Wound to Mythomania', in *Neurological Disorders in Famous Artists: Part 4*, ed. J. Bogousslavsky and L. Tatu (Basel, 2018), pp. 23–37.

32 Ibid., p. 31.

33 Ibid., p. 33.

34 Céline, *Journey*, p. 48.

35 Ibid., p. 49.

36 Ibid., p. 50.

37 Ibid., p. 51.

38 Ibid.

39 Quoted in Blondiaux, *Céline*, p. 116.

40 Ibid., p. 118.

41 Ibid., pp. 118–19.

42 Ibid., p. 161.

43 Ibid., p. 156.
44 'On voulait faire de moi un acheteur! Un vendeur de grand magasin!', Jacques Darribehaude, 'Des Pays où personne ne va jamais', in Louis-Ferdinand Céline, *À l'Agité du bocal* (Paris, 2011), p. 54.
45 'Je voyais un type miraculeux, moi, qui guérissait, qui faisait des choses étonnantes avec un corps qui n'a pas envie de marcher. Je trouvais ça formidable. Il avait l'air très savant. Je trouvais ça, absolument, miraculeux, un magicien,' ibid., p. 50.
46 'Ma mère me disait toujours: "Petit malheureux, si tu n'avais pas les gens riches [. . .], s'il n'y avait pas les gens riches, nous n'aurions pas à manger. Ben, les gens riches ont des responsabilités . . .', ibid., p. 58.
47 'Quand le livre est sorti, j'ai été emmerdé. Céline est le nom de ma mère. Je croyais passer inaperçu. Je croyais faire l'argent de l'appartement, me retirer de l'affaire et continuer la médicine. Mais j'ai été découvert par un journal qui s'appelle Cyrano, qui a fini par me trouver après m'avoir cherché. À partir de ce moment là, la vie devient impossible. La vie médicale, je veux dire . . .', from an interview with Madeleine Chapsal, 'Voyage au Bout de la haine', *L'Express* (14 June 1957), Bibliothèque Nationale de France MICR-D-462 1957/01-1957/06.
48 'Quand les journalistes ont commencé à prendre le chemin de Meudon pour visiter le monstre, il en a rajouté, il leur en donnait pour leur argent. Il jouait un rôle, faisait de lui-même sa propre caricature. On le croyait, et il jubilait. Comme dans l'Antiquité romaine, dans la fosse aux lions, c'est du sang qu'on venait chercher. Alors il en donnait', in Véronique Robert avec Lucette Destouches, *Céline secret* (Paris, 2001), pp. 126–7.
49 'Le public s'intéresse à la voiture, à l'alcool, et aux vacances . . . Aujourd'hui on ne va pas lire Balzac pour apprendre ce que c'est qu'un médecin de campagne ou un avare. On trouve ça dans vos journaux, dans les hebdomadaires. Les jeunes filles aprennent la vie dans les hebdomadaires et au cinéma. Alors qu'est-ce que vient foutre un livre? Avant on y apprenait la vie dans un livre. Ces pourquoi on empechait les jeunes filles de lire des romans', ibid.
50 'Oui, là aussi, ils m'emmerdent. Dans le "Voyage", je fais encore certains sacrifices à la littérature, la "bonne littérature". On trouve encore de la phrase bien filée. A mon sens, au point de vue technique, c'est un peu attardé', ibid.
51 'Je n'écris pas pour quelqu'un. C'est la dernière des choses, s'abaisser à ça. On écrit pour la chose en elle-même', ibid.
52 'C'est un truc. En vérité je les méprise. Ce qu'ils pensent et ce qu'ils ne pensent pas. Si vous vous occupez de ce qu'ils pensent, vous avez affaire à des lecteurs, au lecteur, c'est tout dire! Non, pas besoin, il lit, tant mieux, il n'aime pas, tant pis!', ibid.
53 'J'en parle parce que je voudrais bien toucher une avance de Gallimard. J'en parle parce que c'est le commerce, qu'il faut que je paye cette maison horrible qui coûte horriblement cher, que je nettoie moi-même à l'aspirateur, dont je fais moi-même les carreaux, où je fais la cuisine et tout le bazar . . .', ibid.
54 'Je n'y tenais pas du tout à aller à Sigmaringen. Seulement, on voulait m'arracher les yeux à Paris. On voulait me tuer. Je me suis trouvé pris dans un tourbillon', ibid.

1 A Petit-bourgeois Childhood

1 Henri Godard, ed., *Romans I*, by Louis-Ferdinand Céline (Paris, 1981), p. 1365.
2 Louis-Ferdinand Céline, *Death on Credit*, trans. Ralph Manheim, preface by André Derval (Richmond, 2017), p. 37.
3 Henri Godard, *Céline* (Paris, 2011), pp. 14–15.
4 'C'était la misère . . . plus dure que la misère parce que la misère, on peut se laisser aller vautrer, mais là c'était la misère qui se tient, la misère digne, ça, c'est affreux', in Louis-Ferdinand Céline, *Cahiers Céline 2: Céline et l'actualité littéraire 2*, ed. Jean-Pierre Dauphine and Henri Godard (Paris, 1976), p. 162, quoted in François Gibault, *Céline I: Le Temps des espérances: 1894–1932* (Paris, 1977), p. 68.
5 Frédéric Vitoux, *La Vie de Céline* (Paris, 1988; rev. edn, 2005), p. 16.
6 David Alliot, *Le Paris de Céline* (Paris, 2017), p. 11.
7 'Je suis un indigène, un "Fellegh" de la banlieue . . .', from an interview with Gérard Jarlot, *France-Dimanche* (April 1956), quoted in Vitoux, *La Vie de Céline*, p. 14.
8 Céline, *Death on Credit*, p. 35.
9 Gaël Richard, Eric Mazet and Jean-Paul Louis, eds, *Dictionnaire de la correspondence de Louis-Ferdinand Céline, suivi d'une chronologie épistolaire*, vol. I (Paris, 2012), pp. 153–4.
10 Gibault, *Céline I*, p. 33.
11 Ibid., p.35.
12 Richard et al., *Dictionnaire*, p. 226.
13 On Céline's ancestry, see Eric Mazet, 'Un Poème d'Auguste Destouches', *Le Bulletin célinien*, no. 403 (January 2018), pp. 9–11.
14 Louis-Ferdinand Céline, *Guignol's Band*, trans. Bernard Frechtman and Jack Nile (Richmond, 2012), p. ix.
15 Ibid., pp. 153–4.
16 Ibid., p. 157.
17 Céline, *Death on Credit*, p. 42.
18 Céline, *Guignol's Band*, p. 152.
19 Ibid., pp. 151–2.
20 Godard, *Romans I*, p. 1362
21 Pierre Monnier, *Ferdinand Furieux* (Paris, 1979), pp. 23, 146, quoted in Godard, *Romans I*, p. 1362.
22 Godard, *Romans I*, p. 1362.
23 Ibid., p. 1396; Richard et al., *Dictionnaire*, p. 227.
24 Céline, *Cahiers Céline 2*, p. 191, quoted in Godard, *Romans I*, p. 1361.
25 David Alliot, *Madame Céline* (Paris, 2018), p. 63.
26 Henri Godard, *Un Autre Céline: De la fureur à la féerie* (Paris, 2008), pp. 45–8.
27 Michel Winock, *La Belle Epoque: La France de 1900 à 1914* (Paris, 2002), p. 21.
28 Charles Sowerwine, *France since 1870* (Basingstoke, 2009), p. 5.
29 Hugh Schofield, 'La Belle Epoque: Paris 1914', BBC News (7 January 2014), available at www.bbc.co.uk; on the influence of Renault's production methods on car manufacturer Henry Ford, see Dominique Lejeune, *La France de la Belle Époque: 1896–1914* (Paris, 2017), p. 129.
30 Maurice Crubellier, *Histoire culturelle de la France* (Paris, 1974), p. 18.

31 Colin Jones, *Paris: Biography of a City* (London, 2004), p. 429.
32 Céline, *Death on Credit*, p. 59.
33 Ibid., p. 60.
34 Ibid., p. 62.
35 Ibid.
36 Ibid., p. 61.
37 Ibid., p. 62.
38 Frédéric Vitoux, *Louis-Ferdinand Céline: Misère et parole* (Paris, 1973), pp. 71–89.
39 'Il est une minorité d'individus qui, dans les deux romans, savent se méfier justement du pouvoir illustre et blessant du langage. Ce sont les silencieux de cet univers romanesque, dont le mutisme choisi s'accorde bien à la lucidité. Ce sont les clairvoyants de ce monde de misère, les vrais malheureux peut-être par leur exacte vision des chagrins et des peines, mais en même temps les rares élus qui, prenant la mesure du monde, acquièrent, avec ses misères véritables, les éventuels remèdes à ses maux authentiques', ibid., p. 71.
40 Céline, *Death on Credit*, p. 229.
41 Godard, *Un Autre Céline*, p. 196.
42 Céline, *Death on Credit*, p. 229.
43 Ibid., p. 231.
44 Ibid., p. 234.
45 Henri Godard, *Mort à crédit de Louis-Ferdinand Céline* (Paris, 1996), pp. 20–22.
46 This is just a sample of the many synonyms from these lexical fields that are gathered in Henri Godard's glossary of Céline's slang terms, 'Vocabulaire populaire et argotique', in *Romans I*, pp. 1512–55.
47 Céline, *Death on Credit*, p. 214.
48 '[L]e silence de certains personnages, refusant d'imposer aux autres des mensonges ou même une parole bienvaillante mais contraignante et moralisatrice', 'un immense calme, un espace propice à la réflexion personnelle', in Vitoux, *Louis-Ferdinand Céline: Misère et parole*, p. 84.
49 Céline, *Death on Credit*, p. 49.
50 Céline, *Cahiers Céline 2*, p. 109.
51 Godard, *Un Autre Céline*, p. 101.
52 Céline, *Death on Credit*, p. 260.
53 Godard, *Romans I*, p. 1348.
54 Ibid., p. 1371.
55 'Tout en travaillant comme un nègre, chez mes parents, ou chez des patrons, je me procurais les programmes du lycée, les bouquins, avec mon argent de poche; je potassais dans les coins, me crevant les yeux que brulait le manque de sommeil. Tout se logeait dans ma tête, le latin, le grec, les maths, l'histoire. Cela dura des années. Personne ne m'encourageait, ni ne me disait où j'en étais', in Robert Poulet, *Mon Ami Bardamu: Entretiens familiers avec L. F. Celine* (Paris, 1971), p. 131, quoted in Godard, *Romans I*, p. 1374.
56 Godard, *Céline*, p. 35.
57 For the background to the style and content of Céline's childhood letters, see Sonia Anton, 'L'Apport des lettres d'enfance et de jeunesse', in *Céline à l'épreuve*, ed. Philippe Roussin, Alain Schaffner et Régis Tettamanzi (Paris, 2016), pp. 97–113.

58 Gibault, *Céline 1*, p. 73.
59 Ibid., p. 77.
60 'Je vous souhaite une bonne santé pour toujours, je vous remercie de tout mon Cœur des sacrifices que vous vous imposez pour mon avenir. Mais croyez moi que je ne serai pas un ingrat et que plus tard vous aurez tout lieu de vous contenter des grands sacrifices que vous faites pour moi Papa et Maman', from letter of 31 December 1907 in Henri Godard and Jean-Paul Louis, eds, *Lettres: Choix de lettres de Céline et de quelques correspondants (1907–1961)* (Paris, 2009), p. 30.
61 Letter of 4 September 1907, ibid., p. 6.
62 Letter of 11 September 1907, ibid., p. 8.
63 Letter from March 1908, ibid., p. 45.
64 Gibault, *Céline 1*, p. 85.
65 Ibid., p. 86.
66 Godard, *Mort à crédit*, p. 134.
67 '[L]e père Tonkin ne me plaît pas énormément, la mère Tonkin encore moins', in Letter from February 1909 in Godard and Louis, eds, *Lettres*, p. 50.
68 Gibault, *Céline 1*, pp. 105–6.
69 Ibid., p. 106.
70 Ibid., p. 107.
71 Céline, *Death on Credit*, p. 142.
72 Ibid., p. 147.
73 Ibid., p. 152.
74 Godard, *Céline*, p. 41.
75 Céline, *Death on Credit*, p. 203.
76 Ibid., p. 187.
77 Ibid., pp. 191–2.
78 Ibid., p. 203.
79 Ibid., p. 186.
80 Ibid., p. 99.
81 'Le vent a tout emporté sur la robe d'un clergyman', in Gibault, *Céline 1*, pp. 97–8; also quoted in Godard, *Romans 1*, p. 1371; '[U]ne jeune fille qui était à côté de moi me lâche une vraie sauce sur mes bottines jaunes', ibid. (Godard and Gibault).
82 Mikhail Bakhtin, *Rabelais and His World*, trans. Hélène Iswolsky (Bloomington, IN, 1984).
83 'En vérité Rabelais, il a raté son coup. Il a pas réussi. Ce qu'il voulait faire c'était un langage pour tout le monde, un vrai. Il voulait démocratiser la langue, une vraie bataille. La Sorbonne, il était contre, les docteurs et tout ça. Tout ce qui était établi, le roi, l'Eglise, le style, il était contre.' 'Rabelais il a raté son coup,' in 'Une Interview sur *Gargantua et Pantagruel* pour Le Meilleur Livre du Mois', in Louis-Ferdinand Céline, *Le Style contre les idées: Rabelais, Zola, Sartre et les autres* (Paris, 1987), pp. 119–25.
84 'Non, c'est pas lui qui a gagné. C'est Amyot. Le traducteur de Plutarque: il a eu, dans les siècles qui suivirent, beaucoup plus de succès que Rabelais. C'est sur lui, sur sa langue, qu'on vit encore aujourd'hui. Rabelais avait voulu faire passer la langue parlée dans la langue écrite: un échec. Tandis qu'Amyot, les gens maintenant veulent encore et toujours de l'Amyot, du style académique. Ça c'est écrire de la m. . . : du langage figé', ibid.

85 'Le français est une langue vulgaire, depuis toujours, depuis sa naissance au traité de Verdun. Seulement ça, on ne veut pas l'accepter et on continue de mépriser Rabelais. "Ah! c'est rabelaisien!" dit-on parfois. Ça va dire: attention, c'est pas délicat ce truc-là, ça manque de correction. Et le nom d'un de nos plus grands écrivains a ainsi servi à façonner un adjectif diffamatoire. Monstrueux!', ibid.
86 Céline, *Death on Credit*, pp. 102–3.
87 Ibid., p. 103.
88 Gibault, *Céline 1*, pp. 108–9.
89 '[P]our le choix des "élégantes"... des plus grandes cocottes de l'époque . . . aux lubies d'une clientèle "high life", la plus extravagante d'Europe, des "cercleux" les plus fantasques, des Reines du Boudoir. Dans mes poches, fermées par épingle de nourrice, je promenais dans une seule journée plus de richesse qu'un galion d'Espagne, retour du Perou', in Louis-Ferdinand Céline, *Bagatelles pour un massacre* (Paris, 1937), p. 370. Henceforth, referred to as *Trifles* (translations my own).
90 The task of delivering jewels is corroborated by his letter to Albert Paraz, 5 April 1951, and his spying is recounted in Claude Bonnefoy, 'L. F. Céline raconte sa jeunesse', in Céline, *Cahiers Céline 2*, p. 210, quoted in Gibault, *Céline 1*, pp. 109 and 113.
91 'Je connaissais tous les voleurs [...] je voyais venir ... À l'instant ... Pssss! Où ça filait dans le manchon. Je "toc-toc-toc"! trois petits coups à ma porte ... C'était entendu avec Ben Corème ... Ça s'arrangeait toujours très bien, jamais un scandale', in Céline, *Trifles*, pp. 370–71.
92 Ibid., p. 47.
93 Ibid.
94 'Faut pas que je pleurniche, y avait du plaisir dans mon rôle ... des compensations ... quand elles étaient belles les clientes ... assises ... froufroutantes ... je prenais des jetons terribles, je regardais les jambes. Je m'hypnotisais ... Ah! le moule des cuisses ... Ah! ce que je me suis bien branlé [...] J'ai eu une belle puberté, des rages de cul fantastique. Ça m'empêchait pas d'être honnête et d'une vigilance impeccable ...', ibid., p. 371. Gibault speculates that this 'voyeurism' may have inspired the episode in which Ferdinand spies on Madame Gorloge's sexual activities; see Gibault, *Céline 1*, pp. 109–10.
95 Letter 63 to Simone Saintu, 5 November 1916, in Louis-Ferdinand Céline, *Cahiers Céline 4: Lettres et premiers écrits d'Afrique, 1916–17*, ed. Jean-Pierre Dauphin (Paris, 1978), pp. 143–4.
96 Gibault, *Céline 1*, p. 114.
97 'Il faisait au moins deux mètres. C'est lui, cet immense, qu'a perdu la guerre en définitive et les armées russes. Ah! j'aurais pu leur annoncer déjà en 1910 qu'il allait tout perdre ... Il savait jamais ce qu'il voulait', in Céline, *Trifles*, p. 371.
98 'Il va rentrer dans la boutique ... Bamm! Il se refout un grand coup dans le chambranle! Il se tient la tête à deux mains ... Il recule ...', ibid., p. 372.
99 'Par l'effet des circonstances, son grand Palais sur la Neva, il est devenu depuis 18 "L'Institut pour le cerveau", l'Étude des Phénomènes Psychiques', ibid.
100 Gibault, *Céline 1*, p. 112.
101 Ibid., pp. 112–13.

102 Published by Charles Delagrave and the Société française de prophylaxie sanitaire et morale, 2nd edn (Paris, 1905), quoted ibid., p. 111.

103 '. . .[V]ous comprendrez facilement que ce ne soit point sans une très grande appréhension que je me sois résigné à abandonner complètement à lui-même et hors de tout contrôle un garçon de 17 ans déja très indépendent par caractère. Le danger m'apparaissait très nettement cependant de voir s'anéantir dans des fréquentations douteuses tout le bagage de santé d'instruction et d'éducation morale et physique que nous lui avions péniblement constitué dans notre modeste situation par de très lourds sacrifices d'argent', ibid., p. 110.

104 Ibid., pp. 116–18.

105 Ibid., p. 124.

106 Godard, *Céline*, pp. 53–5.

107 Ibid., p. 50.

108 Ibid., pp. 128–9.

109 '[C]e que je veux avant tout c'est vivre une vie remplie d'incidents que j'espère la Providence voudra placer sur ma route et ne pas finir comme beaucoup ayant placé un *seul* pôle de continuité amorphe sur une terre et dans une vie dont ils ne connaissent pas les détours qui vous permettent de se faire une éducation morale si je traverse de grandes crises que la vie me réserve peut-être je serai moins malheureux qu'un autre car je veux connaître et savoir en un mot je suis orgueilleux est-ce un défaut je ne le crois et il me créera des déboires ou peut-être la *Réussite*', in Louis-Ferdinand Céline, *Carnet du cuirassier Destouches*, reproduced in Appendice III of Henri Godard, ed., *Romans III* (Paris, 1988), p. 75.

110 'Vous n'avez pas besoin de cacher à Louis que c'est moi qui vous ai écrit mais il ignore que vous êtes venu. Je lui ai donné les 10 f. que vous m'aviez donnés, en lui disant que je les lui prêtais. Il doit encore à Bezard 5, Prunier 10, Clement 8,60. Je ne crois pas qu'il veuille vous le dire', in *Devenir Céline: Lettres inédites de Louis Destouches et de quelques autres, 1912–1919*, ed. Véronique Robert-Chovin (Paris, 2009), p. 23.

111 Letter of 12 August 1913, ibid., p. 29.

112 Letter of 5 August 1913, ibid., pp. 26–7.

113 '[N]ous, et particulièrement moi, avant été extrêmement bienveillants et patients pour votre fils! Jugeant que les coups de tête du début étaient dûs plutôt à de la jeunesse et à de l'impressionabilité de caractère qu'à un mauvais fonds, nous avons fermé les yeux et permis aux qualités réelles de percer et le voilà brigadier et le pied à l'étrier; je ne doute pas qu'il fasse maintenant tous ses efforts pour vous recompenser de l'éducation soignée que vous lui avez donnée et nous pour la confiance que nous avons eu en son avenir', in a letter of 9 August 1913, ibid., pp. 27–8.

114 'La leçon ayant été dure pour son amour-propre – je crois être l'interprète de ses bonnes resolutions', in a letter of 11/12 August 1913, ibid., p. 31.

115 '[L]e consentement du peuple à mener une vie de cochon. Les révolutionnaires étaient souvent traités de voyous, même par le peuple', quoted in Godard, *Céline*, pp. 55–6.

116 Godard, *Romans I*, pp. 1394–5.

117 Céline, *Death on Credit*, p. 77.

2 War and Colonialism

1 Véronique Robert-Chovin, ed., *Devenir Céline: Lettres inédites de Louis Destouches et de quelques autres, 1912–1919* (Paris, 2009), p. 168.
2 'Vous le savez j'écris un roman, quelques expériences personnelles qui doivent tenir sur le papier, la part de folie, la difficulté aussi, labeur énorme . . . D'abord la guerre, dont tout dépend, qu'il s'agit d'exorciser', in *Louis-Ferdinand Céline: Lettres à Joseph Garcin (1929–1938)*, ed. Pierre Lainé (Paris, 1987), p. 22.
3 Louis-Ferdinand Céline, *Journey to the End of the Night*, trans. Ralph Manheim, foreword by John Banville (Richmond, 2012), p. 9.
4 Ibid.
5 See Jean-Jacques Becker, *1914: Comment les Français sont entrés dans la guerre* (Paris, 1977). For a brief summary of Becker's position, see also David Stevenson, *Cataclysm: The First World War as Political Tragedy* (New York, 2004), p. 32.
6 Becker, *1914*, pp. 24–7.
7 Agathon, *Les Jeunes gens d'aujourd'hui* (Paris, 1913), quoted ibid., p. 31.
8 Ibid., quoted in Becker, *1914*, p. 28.
9 Robert-Chovin, *Devenir Céline*, p. 46.
10 'Le moral est bon, après les adieux déchirants à Rambouillet. Tout le monde s'en va vers l'inconnu avec cependant une petite barre sur l'estomac qui donne à la société une petite teinte d'exaltation qui masque l'appréhension d'ailleurs bien légitime. Cependant je suis persuadé que tout le monde fera son devoir. Jamais je n'ai eu le moral meilleur. L'avis de mobilisation générale doit être lancé à 12h', in letter of 1 August 1914, ibid., p. 36.
11 'Je crois que nous serons victorieux, ce serait très bien car seules les victoires indécises laissent des morts [. . .] Les officiers sont à la hauteur et le pitaine est épatant de sang-froid', ibid., p. 37.
12 'Enfin j'en tiens un !!!!!! Cette nuit nous avons revu les Allemands de près. (Nous en avons même tué un [. . .] J'en ai tombé un beau!) dont je t'envoie le livret militaire – tout son fourbi est dans le fourgon – ci-inclus. C'est un Dragon du Génie à Neustadt le pays du frère Schmitt. Il a été abattu d'un coup de pointe au cou. Nous marchons encore à peu près jour et nuit Presque sans arrêt, nous arrêtant une heure par-ci par-là [. . .] et surtout la traversée de la Meuse qui est le spectacle le plus horrible que j'aie jamais contemplé. Dans la nuit, j'ai vu des pontonniers allemands reconstruire quinze fois le même pont qu'engloutissait systématiquement notre artillerie. Je crois qu'une grande bataille est imminente où le sang ne sera pas marchandé. Allons-y !!!', in letter from Louis Destouches to his parents, received 17 September 1914, ibid., p. 52.
13 Stevenson, *Cataclysm*, pp. 42–50.
14 David Stevenson, *The Outbreak of the First World War: 1914 in Perspective* (London, 1997), p. 57.
15 'Au moment où je continue cette lettre, la bataille est engagé aux alentours de Bar-le-Duc. Nous sommes en réserve. Donnerons d'un moment à l'autre. Serai ce soir à cheval?!!!', in Robert-Chovin, *Devenir Céline*, p. 52.
16 Céline, *Journey*, p. 14.
17 Ibid., pp. 14–15.
18 Ibid., p. 15.

19 Ibid., pp. 14–15.
20 '[I]l est difficile de se nourrir, car moi qui n'aimais pas la viande je ne peux plus la sentir,' Robert-Chovin, *Devenir Céline*, p. 51.
21 Céline, *Journey*, p. 18.
22 Letter to Céline's parents, received 26 October 1914, in Robert-Chovin, *Devenir Céline*, p. 69.
23 François Gibault, *Céline 1: Le Temps des espérances: 1894–1932* (Paris, 1977), pp. 145–6; see also Gaël Richard, 'Le Cuirassier blessé et ses médecins,' *L'Année Céline* (2009), p. 187.
24 *Lettres*, 14-37c, in *Lettres: Choix de lettres de Céline et de quelques correspondants (1907–1961)*, ed. Henri Godard and Jean-Paul Louis (Paris, 2009), pp. 120–21, quoted in Richard, 'Le Cuirassier blessé,' p. 187.
25 Ibid., p. 192.
26 Ibid., p. 194.
27 *Lettres*, 14-37d, quoted in Richard, 'Le Cuirassier blessé,' p. 194.
28 Ibid.
29 Gibault, *Céline 1*, p. 154.
30 Richard, 'Le Cuirassier blessé,' p. 197.
31 Gibault, *Céline 1*, p. 155.
32 Richard, 'Le Cuirassier blessé,' p. 198.
33 Ibid., p. 200.
34 Gibault, *Céline 1*, pp. 158–9.
35 Dossier du Dr Gosset, Chancellerie de la Légion d'honneur, LH 1171/33, quoted in Richard, 'Le Cuirassier blessé,' p. 203.
36 Gibault, *Céline 1*, pp. 159–60.
37 '[J]e viens d'avoir une émotion qui fera date [. . .] nous sommes copieusement arrosés pendant 10 minutes par des obus de tout calibre [. . .] j'avais la main pleine de sang en arrivant,' in Robert-Chovin, *Devenir Céline*, p. 63.
38 Document provided by Helga Pedersen, quoted by Gibault, *Céline 1*, pp. 161–2.
39 Ibid.
40 Louis-Ferdinand Céline, *Death on Credit*, trans. Ralph Manheim, preface by André Derval (Richmond, 2017), p. 7.
41 Richard, 'Le Cuirassier blessé,' p. 203.
42 Gibault, *Céline 1*, p. 166.
43 Céline, *Journey*, p. 61.
44 Ibid.
45 Ibid., p. 60.
46 Ibid., p. 67.
47 Ibid.
48 Letter from Andrée Mégard to Louis Destouches, before May 1915, in Robert-Chovin, *Devenir Céline*, pp. 98–9.
49 'Et le major, hélas, ne resservirait pas. / En effet, la main pend, lamentable, brisée / Comme une fleur mourante à la tige écrasée'; 'Je puis tenir le sabre encore de la main gauche,' ibid., p. 99
50 Céline, *Journey*, p. 82.
51 Ibid., p. 83.
52 Ibid., p. 84.
53 Ibid., p. 89.
54 Ibid., p. 78.

55 Ibid., p. 43.
56 Ibid., p. 44.
57 The most detailed account of Céline's period in London, including his short-lived marriage to Suzanne Nebout, is Gaël Richard, 'Janine et Louis: Nouveaux documents sur Londres et Suzanne Nebout', *L'Année Céline* (2006), pp. 105–26.
58 Ibid., p. 106.
59 Louis-Ferdinand Céline, *Guignol's Band*, trans. Bernard Frechtman and Jack Nile (Richmond, 2012), p. 199.
60 Louis-Ferdinand Céline, *Cahiers Céline de l'Herne 1* and *2*, ed. Dominique de Roux, Michel Thélia et Michel Beaujour (Paris, 1963), p. 201; Frédéric Vitoux: *La Vie de Céline* (Paris, 1988; rev. edn, 2005), pp. 156–7.
61 Richard, 'Janine et Louis', pp. 106–7; Richard, 'Céline en Angleterre', *Cahiers de L'Herne*, nos 3 et 5: Celine (Paris, 2008), pp. 201–2.
62 Richard, 'Janine et Louis', p. 108.
63 Peter Dunwoodie, 'Des chinoiseries', Actes du Colloque international de Londres L.-F. Céline (5–7 July 1988), pp. 65–73; Laurent Simon, 'Une Source iconographique de *Guignol's Band*', *L'Année Céline* (2003), p. 86, quoted in Richard, 'Janine et Louis', p. 110.
64 Céline, *Guignol's Band*, p. 194.
65 Letter to Paul Marteau, 25 June 1949, in *Tout Céline, 2, Répertoire des livres, manuscrits et lettres de Céline passés en vente* (Paris, 1983), p. 111, quoted in Richard, 'Janine et Louis', p. 110.
66 See Eric Mazet, 'Céline et la Sirène', *Le Bulletin célinien*, 23 (July 1984), pp. 10–15; and André Derval, 'Édouard Bénédictus', Actes du Colloque international de Paris L.-F. Céline (2–4 July 1992), pp. 125–35; Richard, 'Janine et Louis', p. 111.
67 Céline, *Guignol's Band*, pp. 43, 56.
68 'J'avais tout pour être maquereau. Je refusais du monde à Londres. J'étais riche a 25 ans si j'avais voulu, et considéré – un monsieur aujourd'hui', in Henri Godard, 'Les Données de l'expérience – Londres', in *Romans III* (Paris, 1988), pp. 978–9; letter to Albert Paraz, 30 November 1948, *Cahier Céline 6: Lettres à Albert Paraz* (Paris, 1981), p. 202, quoted in Richard, 'Janine et Louis', p. 111.
69 '[B]lessé en 14, je me suis retrouvé à Londres, 2eme bureau . . . j'ai fait la connaissance d'une putain . . . je l'ai épousée . . . trois jours après je me barrais en Afrique, pleine forêt vierge . . . avis! . . .', extract from the first version of *La Brinquebale avec Céline* by Henri Mahé, in Louis-Ferdinand Céline, '31', *Cité d'Antin: états successifs du texte*, ed. Éric Mazet (Tusson, 1988), pp. 70–71, quoted in Richard, 'Janine et Louis', p. 112.
70 Louis-Ferdinand Céline, *Fable for Another Time* (*Féerie pour une autre fois 1*), trans. and intro. Mary Hudson, preface Henri Godard (Lincoln, NE, 2003), p. 93. Henceforth, referred to as *Fable*.
71 Richard, 'Janine et Louis', pp. 105–26.
72 Ibid., pp. 113–14.
73 Vitoux, *La Vie de Céline*, pp. 162–3, quoted in Richard, 'Janine et Louis', p. 112.
74 'Janine et Louis', p. 115.
75 Ibid.; Gibault, *Céline 1*, p. 222.

76 Céline, *Guignol's Band*, p. 97.
77 Richard, 'Janine et Louis', p. 116.
78 Cited by Henri Godard, *Romans III*, p. 979, note 4, based on Georges Geoffroy's testimony published in *Minute* (20 March 1964); quoted Richard, 'Janine et Louis', p. 116.
79 Richard cites as a possible inspiration Knut Hamsun's novel *La Faim* (1890, translated into French 1895), when the narrator is forced into exile from the prostitute Ylajali and boards the ship *Copegoro* (Richard, 'Janine et Louis', p. 116).
80 Céline, *Journey*, p. 195.
81 According to her sister Henriette, in a statement made to the High Court of Justice after Suzanne's death, 13 February 1923, quoted in Richard, 'Janine et Louis', Annexe 4, pp. 125–6.
82 Gibault, *Céline I*, p. 169.
83 Richard, 'Janine et Louis', p. 117.
84 Ibid., p. 119.
85 Letter of 27 October 1947, quoted in Richard, 'Janine et Louis', pp. 114, 120.
86 Céline, *Fable*, p. 92.
87 Henri Godard, *Céline* (Paris, 2011), p. 88.
88 Gibault, *Céline I*, p. 174.
89 Godard, *Céline*, p. 88.
90 Robert-Chovin, *Devenir Céline*, p. 178.
91 'Je suis un instant, absolument, exclusivement, parfaitement heureux. La brise m'arrive du large, saccaddée, rageuse, et saupoudre de sable doré les milles petites fleurs blanches qui se secouent aussitôt, toutes ensembles, en petites fleurs soigneuses de leurs corolles', letter to Céline's parents from Opi, 10 July 1916, ibid., p. 119.
92 Ibid., p. 121.
93 Godard, *Céline*, p. 89.
94 '[M]on fusil dans les bras pour toute éventualité', in *Devenir Céline*, p. 122.
95 'Je ne m'avais moi-même réalisé jusqu'ici que très imparfaitement ce que signifie l'isolement, les conditions de la vie civilisée le permettant mal et même pas du tout. Il est rationnel que dans la vie normale on compte pour une grande part les uns sur les autres. Même au feu, je n'avais éprouvé cette sensation si pénible au début, de se sentir seul, absolument seul et de savoir et se rendre parfaitement compte que quoi qu'il arrive, on ne devra compter exclusivement qu'avec et que sur soi-même. C'est une gêne qu'il faut vaincre au plus tôt, on n'en triomphe qu'avec une certaine énergie', letter from Bikomimbo to Céline's father, 13 October 1916, ibid. Robert-Chovin, *Devenir Céline*, p. 139.
96 Letter to Simone Saintu, 18 July 1916, 72, *Cahiers Céline 4: Lettres et premiers écrits d'Afrique, 1916–1917*, ed. Jean-Pierre Dauphin (Paris, 1978), pp. 54–8.
97 Letter from Louis Destouches to his father, Bikomimbo, 13 October 1916, in *Devenir Celine*, p. 140.
98 Ibid., pp. 140–41.
99 Ibid., p. 142.
100 Letter to Albert Milon, Campo, 15 September 1916, *Cahiers Céline 4*, pp. 89–93.
101 Letter to Simone Saintu, 12 October 1916, ibid., p. 117.
102 Letter to Simone Saintu, 17 January, ibid., p. 169.

103 Letter to Simone Saintu, 20 December 1916, ibid., pp. 161–2. The work in question is Bergson's thesis *Time and Free Will* (*Essai sur les données immédiates de la conscience*, 1889).
104 Céline, *Journey*, p. 111.
105 Ibid., p. 106.
106 Ibid., p. 112.
107 Ibid., p. 107.
108 For the contrast in tone between the letters and the novel, see Emmanuel Terray, 'Céline au bout de la nuit africaine', *Le Bulletin célinien*, 412 (November 2018), p. 16.
109 Céline, *Journey*, p. 118.
110 Ibid., pp. 111, 123.
111 '[E]n un langage violent et avec un accent portugais roulant', in letter from Batanga to Simone Saintu, July 1916, *Cahiers Céline 4*, pp. 45–7.
112 '"[D]epuis la guerre – il ne tuait plus jamais de singes, ils ressemblent trop aux hommes," dit-il,' ibid.
113 Céline, *Journey*, p. 118.
114 Letter to Céline's father, 30 August 1916, *Cahiers Céline 4*, p. 85.
115 '[L]a saignée pratiquée sur un rigoureux pied d'égalité n'aura pas épargné plus le docteur de science que les derniers des illettrés', ibid., p. 87.
116 Ibid.
117 Céline, *Journey*, p. 121.
118 Ibid., pp. 122–3.
119 Ibid., p. 127.
120 Ibid., p. 133.
121 Ibid., pp. 134–5.

3 Inventor and Doctor

1 Louis-Ferdinand Céline, *Journey to the End of the Night*, trans. Ralph Manheim, foreword by John Banville (Richmond, 2012), p. 190.
2 François Gibault, *Céline 1: Le Temps des espérances: 1894–1932* (Paris, 1977), p. 192.
3 Frédéric Vitoux, *La Vie de Céline* (Paris, 1988; revd edn, 2005), p. 120.
4 Pierre Monnier, *Ferdinand furieux* (Paris, 1979), p. 52, quoted ibid.
5 Céline's first translation from the English appeared in the February 1918 edition of the journal: *Des passages les plus saillants d'un message de l'éminent docteur Nutting à l'Associated Engineering Societies de Worcester. Mass. U.S.A.*, quoted in Gaël Richard, 'Henry de Graffigny', *L'Année Céline* (2009), p. 220.
6 'Bien sûr Courtial c'est de Graffigny grand inventeur et prince du rafistolage – génial imposteur à qui je dois beaucoup vous le savez', letter to Joseph Garcin, 21 April 1936, in Louis-Ferdinand Céline, *Lettres à Joseph Garcin (1929–1938)*, ed. Pierre Lainé (Paris, 1987).
7 Richard, 'Henry de Graffigny', p. 210.
8 Ibid., p. 212.
9 Louis Figuier, *L'Année scientifique et industrielle* (Paris, 1893), p. 1423; ibid., p. 214.
10 Richard, 'Henry de Graffigny', p. 208.
11 Ibid., p. 214.

12 Vitoux, *La Vie de Céline*, p. 121.
13 Louis-Ferdinand Céline, *Death on Credit*, trans. Ralph Manheim, preface by André Derval (Richmond, 2017), p. 298.
14 Ibid., pp. 303–4.
15 Ibid., p. 305.
16 Ibid., p. 306.
17 Ibid., p. 341.
18 Ibid., p. 414.
19 Richard, 'Henri de Graffigny', p. 227.
20 Céline, *Death on Credit*, p. 415.
21 Ibid.
22 Richard, 'Henri de Graffigny', pp. 224–5.
23 Ibid., p. 227.
24 Céline, *Death on Credit*, p. 425.
25 Ibid., p. 428.
26 Richard, 'Henri de Graffigny', p. 223.
27 Richard suggests the possibility of suicide, but there is no mention of this in the local press; see ibid., p. 228.
28 Robert Le Blanc, 'Le Choc de Breugel: Céline oublié à l'exposition de Vienne?', *Le Bulletin célinien*, 414 (January 2019), pp. 8–11.
29 Céline, *Death on Credit*, pp. 439–40.
30 Ibid., p. 466.
31 Ibid., p. 464.
32 Ibid., p. 468.
33 Julia Kristeva, *Powers of Horror: An Essay on Abjection* (New York, 1982), p. 3.
34 Ole Vinding, *Au Bout de la nuit* (Paris, 2001), pp. 39–40, quoted in Gaël Richard, *La Bretagne de Louis-Ferdinand Céline* (Tusson, 2013), pp. 41–2.
35 Charles Chassé, 'Choses vues: En visite chez L.-F. Céline', in *La Depêche de Brest et de l'ouest* (11 October 1933), pp. 1–2, repr. in Louis-Ferdinand Céline, *Cahiers Céline 1: Céline et l'actualité littéraire 1*, ed. Jean-Pierre Dauphine and Henri Godard (Paris, 1976), p. 87, quoted in Richard, *La Bretagne*, p. 40.
36 Godard, *Celine*, p. 102.
37 A phrase used by Alexandre Bruno in his medical doctorate, *Contre la Tuberculose, la mission Rockefeller en France et l'effort francais* (1925), p. 141, quoted in Richard, *La Bretagne*, p. 152.
38 Véronique Robert-Chovin, ed., *Devenir Céline: Lettres inédites de Louis Destouches et de quelques autres, 1912–1919* (Paris, 2009), pp. 151–8, quoted in Richard, *La Bretagne*, p. 46.
39 Charles Chassé, 'Choses vues', p. 87, quoted in Richard, *La Bretagne*, p. 46.
40 'Une grande science de la question et avec un art goûté des plus fins connaisseurs', in *L'Ouest-Éclair* (14 March 1918), p. 3, quoted in Richard, *La Bretagne*, p. 56.
41 *Le Nouvelliste* (19 March 1918), quoted in Richard, *La Bretagne*, pp. 56–7.
42 Although uncorroborated, this eyewitness account is found in P. G., 'Louis-Ferdinand Destouches dit Céline est mort', *Les Petites affiches de Bretagne* (7 July 1961), p. 6, quoted in Richard, *La Bretagne*, pp. 57–8.
43 Vitoux, *La Vie de Céline*, p. 126.
44 Ibid., p. 129.
45 Ibid., p. 133.

46 'C'est que la vocation médicale, je l'avais, tandis que la vocation littéraire, je ne l'avais pas du tout. Je considérais le métier littéraire comme une chose tout à fait grotesque, prétentieuse, imbécile, qu'était pas faite pour moi. Pas sérieux, quoi . . . Alors que j'avais toujours la vocation médicale . . . Oh, profonde . . . Ça, je ne trouvais rien de plus vénérable qu'un médecin des ma plus petite enfance . . .', from interviews with Jean Guénot and Jacques Darribehaude in Louis-Ferdinand Céline, *Cahiers Céline 2: Céline et l'actualité littéraire 2*, ed. Jean-Pierre Dauphine and Henri Godard (Paris, 1976), p. 147.
47 Richard, *La Bretagne*, p. 118.
48 Ibid., pp. 131–2.
49 Ibid., p. 208.
50 Interview by Eric Mazet with Colette Destouches, 3 October 1995, ibid., p. 203.
51 Ibid., pp 204–5; see also Vitoux, *La Vie de Céline*, p. 140.
52 'Le cœur des bourgeois est quelque chose d'inconcevablement terne et d'insensible à la misère des autres. Je ne dis pas cela pour Édith, quoique l'altruisme ne soit pas sa qualité dominante (où l'aurait-elle apprise?), mais par cette bande d'hideux égoïstes dont j'aperçois au hasard des rues les gueules rondes et fermées.' Letter to Albert Milon, 1920 [undated], in Henri Godard and Jean-Paul Louis, eds, *Lettres: Choix de lettres de Céline et de quelques correspondants (1907–1961)*, (Paris, 2009), p. 247, quoted in Richard, *La Bretagne*, pp. 206–7.
53 Philippe Alméras, *Dictionnaire Céline* (Paris, 2004), p. 192; Richard, *La Bretagne*, p. 131.
54 Richard, *La Bretagne*, p. 131.
55 Eric Mazet, interview of Colette Destouches, ibid.
56 Ibid.
57 Ibid., p. 149.
58 Ibid., pp. 144–50.
59 He would visit him between 1921 and 1924, when he also visited Marcel Brochard. Leduc was the charismatic discoverer of electronarcosis, and his publications *La Dynamique de la vie* (1913) and *L'Energétique de la vie* (1921) won him the Légion d'honneur; see ibid., pp. 151–2.
60 Ibid., pp. 206–7.
61 For a succinct account of Céline's thesis, as well as its non-conformist and literary tone, see Charles Coustille, *Antithèses: Mallarmé, Péguy, Paulhan, Céline, Barthes* (Paris, 2018), pp. 174–8.
62 Henri Godard, *Céline* (Paris, 2011), p. 115.
63 Ibid., pp. 117–19.
64 Vitoux, *La Vie de Céline*, p. 153.
65 'Vois-tu, c'est ici que se trouve ton vieux Louis. Ici, dans la rûche internationale. Entêté, je le suis, tu le sais. Me voilà. Cette fois, j'embrasse des problèmes d'hygiène de belles envergures, et mon Dieu, j'aime cela. Gunn évidemment fut mon père. Il sera dit que la Rockefeller remplira ma vie. Mais vois-tu, rien n'est mieux que la jeunesse. Tout le reste est vide et la beauté des jours est faite d'espérance,' letter to Albert Milon, Geneva, summer 1924, 24-5, in Godard and Louis, *Lettres*, p. 259.
66 For a detailed account of the conditions in the Ford factories, see Vincent Curcio, *Henry Ford* (New York, 2013), especially Chapters Nine and Eleven;

for an incisive summary of the socio-economic pros and cons of Fordism, see Ray Batchelor, *Henry Ford: Mass Production, Modernism and Design* (New York, 1994); for an analysis of Ford's treatment of the disabled, which corroborates Céline's account, see David Lacey, *Ford: The Men and the Machine* (London, 1986), p. 146.

67 'Cet état de chose à tout prendre au point de vue sanitaire, et même humain n'est point désastreux quant au présent, il permet à grand nombre de gens de vivre qui en seraient bien incapables en dehors de chez Ford. Mais Ford ne peut entretenir ce grand surplus d'inutiles qu'en raison de l'avance qu'il possède sur les autres en matière d'outillage standardisé. Cet outillage lui permet quelle que soit la qualité ridicule de son personnel de fabriquer à meilleur marché que tout autre', in *Louis-Ferdinand Céline (Docteur Destouches) à la Société des Nations, 1924–1927*, ed. Théodore Deltchev Dimitrov (Geneva, 2001), pp. 140–41.

68 Céline, *Journey*, p. 186.

69 'Le médecin chargé des admissions nous confiait d'ailleurs "ce qu'il leur fallait c'était des chimpanzés, que cela suffisait au travail auquel ils étaient destines", il prétendait d'ailleurs qu'on employait déjà ces animaux dans les plantations du Sud. [. . .] je m'étonnais un peu qu'il fît des remarques aussi désobligeantes d'une manière publique, toujours à haute voix, en m'assurant que les candidats non seulement étaient physiquement invalides mais mentalement aussi "complètement dépourvus d'imagination, dénués de sens critique, des crétins, voilà ce qu'il nous faut, pour nous l'ouvrier rêvé c'est le chimpanzé, . . .", in Dimitrov, *Louis-Ferdinand Céline*, p. 138.

70 Céline, *Journey*, p. 185.

71 '[S]'efforceront de prendre des mesures d'ordre international pour prévenir et combattre les maladies,' in Dimitrov, *Louis-Ferdinand Céline*, p. 445.

72 Ibid., pp. 445–6.

73 Ibid., p. 445.

74 'L'or en effet ruisselle à Cuba. A côté de cet Eden les États-Unis eux-mêmes ne sont que des ambitieux,' letter to Rajchman, 2 March 1925, ibid., Appendix doc. 43, p. 446.

75 'Le pays vous ne l'ignorez pas est sous une espèce de protectorat américain, et sa Constitution stipule que ceux-ci se réservent un droit d'ingérence dans le cas de"péril sanitaire"', ibid.

76 '[Les Cubains] ont peur de l'intervention américaine, toujours à prévoir en cas d'épidémie. Ils voudraient bien que nous les protégions à cet egard sanitairement', ibid.

77 'Un pan-americanisme effréné circule à Washington. L'industrie américaine a très besoin de débouchés. On courtise tres soigneusement nos échangistes. Je joue serré', ibid.

78 Dimitrov, *Louis-Ferdinand Céline*, pp. 446–7.

79 'Il s'agissait de faire, je l'ai compris, passer cette affaire pour strictement panamericaine. L'escamotage fut absolu', ibid., p. 101.

80 '[Q]ue nous faisons venir chaque année pour étudier notre organisation sanitaire', ibid.

81 Ibid.
82 'Ces gens sont si simplement orgueilleux que la grossièrté même leur paraît négligeable. Ils me rappellent dans leur manifestations politiques Les Allemands d'avant guerre', ibid., p. 101.
83 Ibid., p. 102.
84 Document 82, ibid., p. 102.
85 Document 114, ibid., pp. 152–3.
86 'La plainte de H. S. Cumming, Surgeon General des États-Unis, auprès de la Fondation Rockefeller brisera la carrière du docteur L. Destouches dès son debut', ibid., p. 447.
87 Ibid., pp. 159–67.
88 'Vu Gunn. Il m'a raconté la plainte de Cumming à mon sujet auprès de Rockefeller. Il me fait bien lâchement de l'honneur', ibid., p. 447.
89 Vitoux, *La Vie de Céline*, p. 160.
90 Ibid., p. 161.
91 Ibid., pp. 161–2.
92 Dimitrov, *Louis-Ferdinand Céline*, pp. 199–202.
93 Vitoux, *La Vie de Céline*, p. 162.
94 Ibid., p. 163.
95 Gibault, *Céline I*, p. 269.
96 'Il faut que tu découvres quelque chose pour te rendre indépendante à Paris. Quant à moi, il m'est impossible de vivre avec quelqu'un – Je ne veux pas te trainer pleurarde et miséreuse derrière moi, tu m'ennuies, voilà tout – ne te raccroche pas à moi. J'aimerais mieux me tuer que de vivre avec toi en continuité – cela sache-le bien et ne m'ennuie plus jamais avec l'attachement, la tendresse – mais bien plutôt arrange ta vie comme tu l'entends. J'ai envie d'être seul, seul, ni dominé, ni en tutelle, ni aimé, libre. Je déteste le mariage, je l'abhorre, je le crache; il me fait l'impression d'une prison ou je crêve', quoted (undated) in Vitoux, *La Vie de Céline*, p. 162.
97 Céline, *Journey*, p. 401.
98 Notes from an interview by Eric Mazet with Colette Destouches, 3 October 1995, quoted in Richard, *La Bretagne*, p. 213.
99 Alphonse Juilland, *Elizabeth and Louis: Elizabeth Craig Talks about Louis-Ferdinand Céline* (Stanford, CA, 1991), p. 60.
100 Godard, *Céline*, p. 123.
101 Ibid., pp. 123–4.
102 Vitoux, *La Vie de Céline*, pp. 275–6.
103 See, for instance, the report (Document 232) by Dr Lasnet, inspecteur général du Service de santé des colonies to Dr Rajchman of the final conference at Freetown (attended by Dr Destouches) on 27 May 1926, quoted in Dimitrov, *Louis-Ferdinand Céline*, p. 275.
104 Vitoux, *La Vie de Céline*, p. 173.
105 Ibid., pp. 169–70.
106 David Cannon, *The Paris Zone: A Cultural History, 1840–1944* (London, 2015), pp. 136–41.
107 Céline, *Journey*, p. 214.
108 Ibid.
109 Ibid., p. 220.
110 Ibid., p. 219.

111 Dimitrov, *Louis-Ferdinand Céline*, p. 27. 'Blennoragia' refers to excessive blennorrhea, or mucous discharge, especially as seen in gonorrhea.
112 Letter to Rajchman, Paris, 20 August 1929, ibid., pp. 29–30.
113 Letter to Frank Boudreau, 6 March 1929, ibid., p. 28.
114 '[A]daptée aux nécessités d'une population, *ouvrière, pauvre, mal logée*, sous un climat *pluvieux*, défavorable, et, de plus, à proximité des usines, dont les fumées ont encore une action nocive supplémentaire', ibid., p. 28.
115 Philippe Roussin, 'Getting Back from the Other World: From Doctor to Author', *South Atlantic Quarterly: Céline: USA*, XCIII/2 (Spring 1994), pp. 243–64.
116 Ibid., p. 247.
117 Ibid.
118 Céline, *Journey*, p. 200.
119 Ibid., p. 227.
120 Ibid., pp. 229–30.
121 Ibid., pp. 231–2.
122 Letter from Michel de Montaigne on 10 September 1570, quoted in Henri Godard, ed., *Romans I*, by Louis-Ferdinand Céline (Paris, 1981), pp. 1246–7.
123 Céline, *Journey*, p. 237.
124 Letter from Michel de Montaigne on 10 September 1570, quoted in Godard, *Romans I*, p. 1247.
125 Céline, *Journey*, p. 231.
126 '[A]près avoir eu l'impression que vous haïssiez tous les êtres, je me suis aperçu que ce dont vous souffriez au contraire – tant est grand votre amour des êtres – c'est qu'il ne soit pas plus grand encore; et qu'il reste impuissant à sauver ceux dont vous connaissez pourtant tous les tares. Cette impossibilité d'être utile à qui que ce soit, telle est une des plus grandes leçons de votre livre, et qui pousse au délire notre dégoût de nous-mêmes. Il faut, je crois, que vous ayez beaucoup souffert pour être capable de nous convoquer, sans en parler, à un si grand amour', in René Schwob, 'Lettre ouverte a L-F. Céline', *Esprit*, no. 6 (March 1933), pp. 1038–41, quoted in Louis-Ferdinand Céline, *Cahiers Céline de l'Herne 1* and *2*, ed. Dominique de Roux, Michel Thélia et Michel Beaujour (Paris, 1963), pp. 338–40.

4 Novelist and Pamphleteer

1 Louis-Ferdinand Céline, *Cahiers Céline 8: Progrès, suivi de Œuvres pour la scène et l'écran*, ed. Pascal Fouché (Paris, 1988), p. 8.
2 Henri Mahé's interview with Pierre Lainé, in *Louis-Ferdinand Céline: Lettres à Joseph Garcin (1929–1938)*, ed. Pierre Lainé (Paris, 2009), pp. 64–5.
3 Alphonse Juilland, *Elizabeth and Louis: Elizabeth Craig Talks about Louis-Ferdinand Céline* (Stanford, CA, 1991), p. 42.
4 Ibid., p. 503.
5 Ibid., pp. 460–61.
6 Frédéric Vitoux is unfairly dismissive of her input because of her limited French: see Frédéric Vitoux, *La Vie de Céline* [1988] (Paris, 2005), p. 207.
7 Juilland, *Elizabeth and Louis*, p. 481.
8 Ibid., p. 472.
9 Ibid., p. 186.

10 Henri Godard, *Céline* (Paris, 2011), p. 147.
11 Ibid., pp. 147–8; Vitoux; *La Vie de Céline*, pp. 188–9.
12 Lainé, *Lettres à Joseph Garcin*, p. 65.
13 Ibid., p. 69.
14 Ibid., p. 67.
15 See Denoël's account of this event, in 'Comment j'ai connu et lancé Louis-Ferdinand Céline', Institut Mémoires de l'édition contemporaine (IMEC), Collection Denoël, DNF 3.1, and also that of his wife, Cécile Denoël, 'Denoël jusqu'à Céline . . . qui lui ressemblait comme un frère', IMEC, Collection Denoël, DNF 3.2.
16 'Un livre promis à un retentissement exceptionnel. L'auteur débute en pleine maturité après une expérience de vie extrêmement riche et diverse', in Jean-Pierre Dauphin, 'Le Lancement de *Voyage* et la querelle du Prix Goncourt', *Le Bulletin célinien*, 413 (December 2018), p. 8.
17 Ibid.
18 'Vous aimerez ce livre ou vous le haïrez: il ne vous laissera pas indifférent. Une œuvre cruelle, mais si vraie, d'un accent si pleinement douloureux et si truculent à la fois, qu'elle s'imposera, sans délai, en dépit des révoltes,' ibid.
19 Philippe Roussin, 'Getting Back from the Other World: From Doctor to Author', *South Atlantic Quarterly:* Céline *USA*, XCIII/2 (Spring 1994), p. 251.
20 'Je suis médecin dans ce dispensaire municipal, c'est mon métier apres vingt autres,' in Philippe Roussin, *Misère de la littérature, terreur de l'histoire: Céline et la littérature contemporaine* (Paris, 2005), p. 29.
21 Ibid., p. 31.
22 Roussin, 'Getting Back from the Other World', p. 254.
23 Roussin, *Misère de la littérature*, pp. 34–5.
24 See his comments on literary prizes in 'Faut-il tuer les prix littéraires?: Réponse à une enquête du *Figaro*', *Le Figaro* (9 June 1934); Lucien Combelle, ed., *Louis-Ferdinand Céline: Le Style contre les idées: Rabelais, Zola, Sartre et les autres . . .* (Paris, 1987), pp. 117–18.
25 Louis-Ferdinand Céline, 'Hommage à Zola', in *Cahiers Céline de l'Herne 3*, ed. Dominique de Roux, Michel Thélia et Michel Beaujour (Paris, 1963), pp. 169–73.
26 Godard, *Céline*, pp. 128–9.
27 'On ne sortirait pas de prison si on racontait la vie telle qu'on la sait, à commencer par la sienne [. . .] La réalité aujourd'hui ne serait permise à personne. À nous, donc, les symboles et les rêves', in Céline, 'Hommage à Zola', p. 169.
28 '[N]ous sommes autorisés, certes, à nous demander si l'instinct de mort chez l'Homme, dans nos sociétés, ne domine pas déjà définitivement l'instinct de vie. Allemands, Français, Chinois, Valaques . . . Dictatures ou pas! Rien que des prétextes à jouer à la mort', ibid.
29 'Libéraux, marxistes, fascistes ne sont d'accord que sur un point: des soldats!', ibid., p. 171.
30 Ibid.
31 'Nous travaillons à présent par la sensibilité et non plus par l'analyse, en somme "du dedans"', ibid.
32 Blaise Cendrars, *Œuvres completes: t. IX: Correspondance 1924–59* (Paris, 1970), pp. 55, 66, quoted in Godard, *Céline*, p. 175.

33 Interview with E. Porquerol, in Louis-Ferdinand Céline, *Cahiers Céline 1: Céline et l'actualité littéraire 1*, ed. Jean-Pierre Dauphine and Henri Godard (Paris, 1976), pp. 46–7, quoted in Henri Godard, *Céline, Romans 1* (Paris, 1981), p. 1229.
34 See Godard, Notice to *Mort à credit, Romans 1*, pp. 1339–40.
35 Henri Godard, *Céline* (Paris, 2011), p. 177.
36 'Vous savez combien j'admire, je m'enthousiasme et vénère tout ce que vous avez donné, pensé, écrit', in *Cahiers Céline de L'Herne*, Letter 10, no. 5 (Paris, 1965), p. 52.
37 Ibid., Letter 3, p. 49.
38 'Je me refuse absolument, tout à fait à me ranger içi ou là. Je suis anarchiste, jusqu'aux poils. Je l'ai toujours été et ne serai rien d'autre [. . .] Tout système politique est une entreprise [. . .] hypocrite qui consiste à rejeter l'ignominie personnelle de ses adhérents sur un système ou sur les "autres". Je vois très bien, j'avoue, je proclame haut, émotivement et fort, toute notre degeulasserie commune, de droite et de gauche d'homme. Cela on me le pardonnera jamais', ibid., Letter 10, p. 52.
39 'Je suis anarchiste depuis toujours, je n'ai jamais voté, je ne voterai jamais pour rien, ni pour personne. Je ne crois pas aux hommes', ibid., Letter 13, p. 55.
40 'Vous n'êtes pas du peuple, vous n'êtes pas vulgaire, vous êtes aristocrate, vous le dites. Vous ne savez pas ce que je sais. Vous avez été au lycée. Vous n'avez pas gagné votre pain avant d'aller à l'école. Vous n'avez pas le droit de me juger. Vous ne savez pas tout ce que je sais – Vous ne savez pas ce que je veux – Vous ne savez pas ce que je fais. Vous ne savez pas quel horrible effort je suis obligé de faire chaque jour, chaque nuit surtout, pour tenir seulement debout, pour tenir une plume – Quand vous serez à l'agonie vous me comprendrez entièrement et là seulement. Je parle la langue de l'intimité des choses – Il a fallu que j'apprenne, que j'épelle d'abord. J'ai tout jaugé. Rien de ce que je dis n'est gratuit', ibid., Letter 13, p. 57.
41 '[M]on seul souci: toucher le maximum de lecteurs et à tout prendre je préfère ceux de droite. Ceux de gauche sont si certains de leur vérité marxiste qu'on ne peut rien leur apprendre. Ils sont bien plus fermés qu'à droite. Nul canard ne m'a plus abîmé que le *Populaire* au nom de "la valeur et de la dignité humaine"!!!', ibid., Letter 11, p. 53.
42 Vitoux, *La Vie de Céline*, p. 214.
43 '[P]as d'amour sans préservatif', in letter to Erika Irrgang, 22 June 1932, quoted ibid., p. 215.
44 Godard, *Céline*, p. 188.
45 Céline requests information on Bosch from Evelyn Pollet in a letter to her dated 20 November 1937, in Louis-Ferdinand Céline, *Cahiers Céline 5: Lettres à des amies*, ed. Colin W. Nettelbeck (Paris, 1979), p. 194, quoted in Henri Godard, *Un Autre Céline: De la Fureur à la féerie* (Paris, 2008), pp. 115, 117.
46 'Tout mon délire est dans ce sens et je n'ai guère d'autres délires' ('All my delirium is in that vein and I have no other deliriums'), in letter to Léon Daudet, 30 December 1932, in Appendix to Godard, *Romans 1*, p. 1108.
47 Godard, *Un Autre Céline*, p. 116.
48 'Elle m'a dit mille choses utiles et m'a rendu en quelques jours presque intelligent,' in Godard, *Céline*, pp. 190–91.

49 See, for instance, Céline's letter to Marks, 2 March 1934: 'It is necessary to fully indulge in carnal pleasures after such a puritanical period' ('Il convient aussi de vous précipiter dans les plaisirs charnels après une telle période puritaine'), in Henri Godard and Jean-Paul Louis, eds, *Lettres: Choix de lettres de Céline et de quelques correspondants (1907–1961)* (Paris, 2009), p. 414.
50 Hanging on the wall of the Boston Branch of Little, Brown was the telegram sent by the editor Herbert Jenkins listing the phrases that Marks had cut, as a reminder of the scandal the novel caused for the American reading public; Little, Brown & Company, *One Hundred and Fifty Years of Publishing: 1837–1987* (Boston, MA, 1987), p. 91, quoted in Alice Kaplan, 'The Céline Effect: A 1992 Survey of Contemporary American Writers', *Modernism/Modernity*, III/1 (January 1996), p. 119.
51 Georges Brassaï, *Henri Miller: Grandeur nature* (Paris, 1975), quoted in Godard, *Romans I*, p. 1279; and Kaplan, 'The Céline Effect', p. 118.
52 Robert Ferguson, *Henry Miller: A Life* (New York, 1991), pp. 307–8; François Gibault, *Céline I: Le Temps des espérances: 1894–1932* (Paris, 1977), vols II and III, quoted in Kaplan, 'The Céline Effect', p. 118.
53 Samuel Putnam, 'Prelude to the Revolution: Review of *Journey to the End of the Night*, by Louis-Ferdinand Céline', *Saturday Review of Literature* (28 April 1934), pp. 657–62.
54 Kaplan, 'The Céline Effect', p. 119.
55 Samuel Putnam, 'Review of *Voyage au bout de la nuit* by Louis-Ferdinand Céline', *Books Abroad*, VII/2 (April 1933), pp. 163–4.
56 Sterling North, 'Dr. Destouches Grants First Press Interview', *Chicago Daily News* (19 July 1934), p. 25.
57 Ibid.
58 Ibid.
59 Louis-Ferdinand Céline, *Journey to the End of the Night*, trans. Ralph Manheim, foreword by John Banville (Richmond, 2012), pp. 160–61.
60 Ibid., p. 159.
61 Ibid., p. 160.
62 Ibid., p. 167.
63 Ibid.
64 Ibid., p. 163.
65 Ibid., p. 164.
66 Ibid., p. 165 .
67 Ibid., p. 171.
68 Ibid., p. 174.
69 Ibid., p. 178.
70 Ibid., p. 180.
71 Quoted in Godard, Notice to *Romans I*, pp. 1234–5.
72 'Que vois-je? Dieu de mes pères! Que vois-je? Dix gaillards, accroupis dans de petites loges sans portes', in Georges Duhamel, *Scènes de la vie future* (Paris, 1930), pp. 210–11, see ibid., p. 1243.
73 Céline, *Journey*, p. 163.
74 Godard, *Céline*, p. 177.
75 'Question de film, des clous,' in letter to Henri Mahé, 4 July 1934, 34-27, in Godard and Louis, *Lettres*, pp. 429–30.

76 Godard, *Céline*, p. 177
77 Vitoux, *La Vie de Céline*, p. 268.
78 Letter to Junie Astor of 11 August 1934, in Godard and Louis, *Lettres*, p. 434.
79 Letter to Dabit, 14 July 1934, ibid., pp. 430–31.
80 Juilland, *Elizabeth and Louis*, pp. 382–3.
81 'Elizabeth s'est donnée aux gangsters,' letter to Mahé, 18 July 1934, 34-30, in Godard and Louis, *Lettres*, p. 431.
82 Godard, *Céline*, pp. 199–200.
83 'Elle s'exprime avec un lyrisme naturel. On peut compter sur ses doigts les virtuoses qui ne tuent pas la musique. La plupart d'entre eux ne savent pas ce qu'ils font: appris, forcés, la musique n'est pas leur langue,' statement made by Céline and transcribed (1935), quoted in Godard, *Un Autre Céline*, p. 138.
84 Godard, *Céline*, p. 201.
85 Letter to Lucienne Delforge, 2 June 1939, 39-17, in Céline, *Lettres*, p. 580.
86 'Mais la régularité de la vie, la réalité de la vie, m'écrase. Ce n'est pas tu sais que je veuille faire l'artiste, le fantasque, l'hystérique, le sujet-exceptionnel-qui-a-besoin-de-passer-ses-caprices. Dieu sait si j'ai cet affreux genre en horreur! Mais tu sais Lucienne que je ne peux pas, absolument pas être LÀ. Pour être un amant sérieux il faut être LÀ. Je suis bien plus avec les gens quand je les quitte [. . .] Je dois bien t'avouer que pour moi la réalité est un cauchemar continuel et Dieu sait si la vie m'a gâté en fait d'expérience! Si j'ai été servi par la réalité! [. . .] Ce qui m'affecte c'est d'avoir à m'occuper des choses qui ne sont pas transposées ni transposables si ce n'est qu'après des années, bien des années. Je ne voudrais pas mourir sans avoir transposé tout ce que j'ai dû subir des êtres et des choses. Là se bornent à peu près toutes mes ambitions', in letter to Lucienne Delforges, 26 August 1935, 35-27, ibid., p. 466.
87 'J'ai comme elle toujours sur ma table un énorme tas d'Horreurs en souffrance que je voudrais rafistoler avant d'en finir', ibid., p. 467.
88 David Alliot, *Madame Céline* (Paris, 2018), p. 44.
89 'Il avait aussi un côté Gatsby, nonchalant, habillé avec soin, décontracté, il était d'une beauté incroyable, les yeux bleus avec juste un petit rond noir à l'intérieur', ibid., p. 45.
90 'Je le regardais comme un être extraordinaire que l'on voit, qui ne parle pas, mais qui est là. Il était triste et absent. Tristement absent. On avait évidemment envie de savoir ce qu'il voulait, il avait l'air si malheureux', ibid., p. 20.
91 'Je voulais, mourir, je trouvais la vie si triste. Je n'avais pas d'amis, je ne parlais pas, j'étais entièrement tournée vers moi-même et sur la danse', in Godard, *Céline*, p. 223.
92 Alliot, *Madame Céline*, pp. 31–5.
93 Ibid., p. 21.
94 Ibid.
95 'Céline n'imaginait pas le sort que la critique allait faire à ce livre, qui lui avait coûté plusieurs années d'un effort horrible dans des conditions de santé effroyable', interview with André Roubaud, *Marianne* (10 May 1939), quoted in *Le Bulletin célinien*, no. 413 (December 2018), p. 8; and also IMEC, Collection Denoel, DNL, 3.3.
96 Godard, *Céline*, p. 220.
97 Quoted in Vitoux, *La Vie de Céline*, p. 494.

98 'C'est un médecin qui parle. Il n'a aucun motif de s'exprimer de la sorte', Marcel Lapierre, 'À travers les livres', in *Le Peuple* (3 June 1936), p. 5.
99 Ibid.
100 Louis-Ferdinand Céline, *Death on Credit*, trans. Ralph Manheim, preface by André Derval (Richmond, 2017), p. XI.
101 La Pierre, 'À travers les livres', p. 5.
102 André Rousseaux, 'Propos du samedi!', *Le Figaro* (23 May 1936), p. 5.
103 Louis-Ferdinand Céline, 'Lettre à André Rousseaux', *Le Figaro*, no. 151 (30 May 1936), p. 7.
104 'Je ne veux pas narrer, je veux faire RESSENTIR. Il est impossible de le faire avec le langage académique, usuel – le beau style', in 'Lettre à André Rousseaux', in Combelle, *Céline*.
105 '[C]apitale supériorite sur la langue dite pure, bien française, raffinnée, elle TOUJOURS MORTE, morte dès le debut, morte depuis Voltaire, cadavre, *dead as a door nail.* Tout le monde le sent, personne ne le dit, n'ose le dire. Une langue c'est comme le reste, ça meurt tout le temps, ça doit mourir', ibid.
106 Letter to Léon Daudet, May 1936, in Henri Godard and Jean-Paul Louis, eds, *Lettres: Choix de lettres de Céline et de quelques correspondants (1907–1961)* (Paris, 2009), pp. 493–95 (quoted in Combelle, pp. 57–60).
107 Ibid. *Lettres*, ed. Godard and Louis, p. 494.
108 'On apprend beaucoup par ce moyen. C'est peut-être ce qu'on me pardonnerait le moins facilement', p. 495.
109 *Cahiers Céline de l'Herne*, no. 5 (1965), pp. 236, 239.
110 Ibid., p. 240.
111 'L'auteur a voulu tout mettre dans son livre. Comme on met tout dans une cathédrale, la terre, le ciel, l'enfer, le purgatoire, les vertus, les pêchés, les saisons, la chair et l'esprit. Il n'y a pas que les piliers, les voûtes, les murs, les contreforts, tout l'appareil architectural. Il y a les statues, les miliers de statues, le pullulement inouï des statues. Et parmi ces statues s'il en est des édifiantes, il en est de fort inconvenantes aussi', in Robert Denoël, 'Apologie de Mort à crédit' (1936), reproduced in *Cahiers de L'Herne*, no. 5 (Paris, 1965), p. 243.
112 '[Il] occupera, j'en ai l'absolue certitude, une place de premier rang dans les lettres françaises', in A.-Charles Brun, 'Un Éditeur défend son auteur', *Le Petit Parisien* (4 August 1936), p. 4, repr. in *Le Bulletin célinien*, 420 (July–August 2019), pp. 7–8.
113 John Walcott, 'Confessions of a Novelist-Hero', *North American Review*, CCXLVI/2 (Winter 1938–9), pp. 390–93, IMEC ref. BI: BZ 590.
114 Ibid.
115 Norbert Guterman, *New Republic*, LXXXVI/1241 (14 September 1938), p. 165, IMEC ref. BI.Fol Z 1254.
116 Justin O'Brien, 'Autobiography of an Underdog', *The Nation* (27 August 1938), pp. 207–8 (review of Little, Brown and Company translation of *Death on the Instalment Plan*).
117 G. W. Stonier, 'Review of *Death on the Instalment Plan*, Chatto and Windus, Marks; and *L'École des cadavres*, Denoël', *New Statesman and The Nation* (14 January 1939).
118 'Daudet et Descaves se sont cette fois foireusement dégonflés', letter to Henri Mahé, 29 May 1936, Céline Godard and Louis, *Lettres*, p. 496; also quoted in Vitoux, *La Vie de Céline*, p. 293.

119 Godard, *Céline*, p. 21.
120 Ibid., p. 179.
121 *Cahiers Céline de l'Herne*, no. 5 (Paris, 1965), Letter 16, p. 57.
122 'Une nation de garagistes ivres, hurleurs et complètement Juifs', in Godard and Louis, *Lettres*, p. 450.
123 Godard, *Céline*, p. 196.
124 Ibid., pp. 229–30.
125 Vitoux, *La Vie de Céline*, p. 295.
126 Ibid., pp. 296–7.
127 Godard, *Céline*, pp. 232–3.
128 Vitoux, *La Vie de Céline*, p. 298.
129 Godard, *Céline*, p. 233.
130 Ibid., p. 234; see also Vitoux, *La Vie de Céline*, p. 298.
131 Godard, *Céline*, p. 234.
132 Vitoux, *La Vie de Céline*, p. 299.
133 *Mea Culpa and The Life and Work of Semmelweis . . .*, trans. Robert Allerton Parker (London, 1937). Henceforth, referred to as *Mea Culpa*.
134 Ibid., p. 21.
135 Ibid., pp. 30–31.
136 Ibid.
137 Ibid., p. 35.
138 Godard, *Céline*, pp. 236–8.
139 *Mea Culpa*, p. 13.
140 Ibid., p. 18.
141 Ibid., pp. 14–15.
142 Ibid.
143 'Ça les fait réfléchir à deux fois avant d'accuser *Mort à crédit* de n'être que sale érotisme etc. [. . .]', letter to the publisher MacIntyre (original in English), quoted in Godard, *Céline*, p. 239.
144 Céline, *Death on Credit*, preface, p. IV.
145 Véronique Flambard-Weisbart, 'Céline et Robert Allerton Parker', *Études céliniennes*, 5 (Winter 2009–10), pp. 5–25.
146 *Times Literary Supplement* (22 January 1938).
147 *The Statesman* (Calcutta) (27 February 1938).
148 Ibid.
149 John O'London, *Weekly* (4 February 1938).

5 Antisemite and Fascist Sympathizer

1 Frédéric Vitoux, *La Vie de Céline* (Paris, 1988, 2005), p. 545.
2 Henri Godard, *Céline* (Paris, 2011), p. 275.
3 Ibid., pp. 275–6.
4 Annick Duraffour and Pierre-André Taguieff, *Céline: La race, le Juif – Légende littéraire et vérité historique* (Paris, 2017); Nicholas Hewitt, *The Life of Céline: A Critical Biography* (Oxford, 1999), pp. 175–6.
5 Hewitt, *The Life of Céline*, p. 174.
6 Ibid., p. 175.
7 Godard points out that Céline's former mentor Élie Faure used Gobineau's theory to draw completely different conclusions, i.e. the progress of the

human race is assured and positively *enriched* by this hybridity. Godard, *Céline*, p. 259.

8 Hewitt, *The Life of Céline*, p. 170.

9 'Boniments que débitent les forains à l'entrée de leur porte pour inciter les gens à assister au spectacle', in *Trésor de la langue française*, quoted in Nicholas Hewitt, *The Golden Age of Louis-Ferdinand Céline* (Leamington Spa, 1987), p. 157.

10 Hewitt, *The Golden Age*, pp. 156–7.

11 André Derval, *L'Accueil critique de Bagatelles pour un massacre* (Montreal, 2010), pp. 19–36. On the reception of this pamphlet, see also Damian Catani, 'Louis-Ferdinand Céline: Literary Genius or National Pariah? Defining Moral Parameters for Influential Cultural Figures, Post-Charlie Hebdo', *French Cultural Studies Special Issue: Understanding Charlie*, XXVII/3 (August 2016), pp. 268–78.

12 Alain Badiou and Eric Hazan, *L'Antisémitisme partout aujourd'hui en France* (Paris, 2011), pp. 19–20.

13 André Derval, *L'Accueil critique*, p. 38.

14 Gisèle Sapiro, *La Responsabilité de l'écrivain: Littérature, droit et moral en France (XIXe–XXIe siècle)* (Paris, 2011), pp. 512–18.

15 'Quand Céline vient parler d'une conspiration du silence, d'une coalition pour empêcher la vente de ses livres, il est bien évident qu'il veut rire. Et quand il fait le juif responsible de la mévente, il va de soi que c'est une plaisanterie. Et si ce n'était pas une plaisanterie, alors il serait, lui, Céline, complètement maboul . . . Il fait de son mieux pour qu'on ne le prenne pas au sérieux . . . C'est un créateur. Il parle des juifs dans *Bagatelles* tout comme il parlait, dans *Mort à Crédit*, des asticots que sa force évocatrice venait de créer', in André Gide, 'Les Juifs, Céline et Maritain', *Nouvelle Revue française*, no. 295 (April 1938), pp. 630–36, quoted in André Derval, *L'Accueil critique*, pp. 63–4.

16 'Avant tout, il est un pamphlétaire. Cela se voyait dans les meilleures pages du *Voyage* . . . dans les meilleures pages de *Mort à crédit* . . . On lui demande un don, et un seul: savoir trouver la faille profonde de celui qu'il attaque, ne pas s'arrêter au ridicule, aux insignifiances; du premier coup atteindre à l'essentiel, au Cœur, à l'hypocrisie du problème . . . Ses "attaques" sont admirables . . .', in Jean Pierre Maxence, 'Louis-Ferdinand Céline: *Bagatelles pour un massacre*', *Gringoire* (4 March 1938), quoted in Derval, *L'Accueil critique*, pp. 234–5.

17 Marc Angenot, *La Parole pamphlétaire: Contribution à la typologie des discours modernes* (Paris, 1982), pp. 38–9.

18 Je n'ai pas aimé beaucoup *Mort à credit* . . .Tout était pourri, bourbeux, verdâtre et nauséabond . . . Dans *Bagatelles pour un massacre*, rien de sale, rien qui ne soit, au contraire, tres sain et aéré. Voici de la belle haine bien nette, bien propre, de la bonne violence à manche relevées . . . Ici le non-conformiste se débat avec vigueur, le solitaire s'affirme, montre les crocs, règle des comptes . . . je ne voudrais pas banaliser ce livre libérateur, torrentiel et irresistible du mot de chef-d'œuvre. C'est beaucoup plus grand que cela, et plus pur', in Jules Rivet, 'Bagatelles pour un massacre', *Le Canard enchaîné* (12 January 1938), p. 4.

19 Godard, *Céline*, p. 280.

20 Ibid., p. 281.

21 Véronique Flambard-Weisbart, 'Céline et Robert Allerton Parker', *Études céliniennes*, 5 (Winter 2009–10), p. 14. I am grateful to André Derval for alerting me to this article, which contains and examines the recently rediscovered correspondence between Céline and Parker.
22 'Je veux cependant essayer de trouver en Amérique un éditeur anti-Juif', ibid., p. 16.
23 Louis-Ferdinand Céline, *L'École des cadavres* (Paris, 1938), p. 164. All translations my own. Henceforth, referred to as *School*.
24 Ibid., p. 170.
25 Ibid., p. 28.
26 Ibid., p. 50.
27 Ibid., p. 253.
28 Ibid., p. 261.
29 Ibid., p. 141.
30 Ibid., p. 80.
31 Hewitt, *The Life of Céline*, p. 181.
32 Godard, *Céline*, p. 289.
33 Vitoux, *La Vie de Céline*, p. 562.
34 Godard, *Céline*, p. 290.
35 'Ferdinand jamais dégonfle. École Bagatelles retirés. Mesures Parquet Police. Votre journal rien à craindre,' in Pascal Fouché, *Céline 'Ça a débuté comme ça'* (Paris, 2001), p. 56.
36 Ibid., p. 57.
37 Duraffour and Taguieff, *Céline: La race, le Juif*, p. 31.
38 Ibid., p. 24.
39 Henri Godard, ed., *Romans III*, by Louis-Ferdinand Céline (Paris, 1988), pp. xx–xxi.
40 'Il me semblait avant le *Voyage*, observant (par comparaison) le trafic de la rue, si incohérent – ces voitures, ces gens qui se butent, culbutent, se battent pour avancer, tout ce zigzag, cette incohérence des démarches absurdes et si gaspilleuses, si imbéciles, qu'il devrait y avoir *tel le métro* un chemin plus net, plus *intime* pour se rendre en un point sans tout ce gaspillage, sans tout cette fastidieuse incohérence – dans la façon aussi de *raconter* mes histoires. Je vous énonce ainsi la difficulté simplement: passer dans *l'intimité même du langage*, à l'intérieur de l'émotion et du langage, à l'aveugle pour ainsi dire *comme le métro* sans se préoccuper des fastidieux incidents de l'extérieur. Une fois lancé de la sorte, *arriver* au bout d'émotion en émotion – au plus près toujours, au plus court, au plus juste, par le rythme et une sorte de musique intime une fois choisi, à *l'économie*, en évitant tout ce qui retombe dans l'objectif – le descriptif – et toujours dans la *transposition*', in letter of 28 September 1943, 43-36, in Henri Godard and Jean-Paul Louis, eds, *Lettres: Choix de lettres de Céline et de quelques correspondants (1907–1961)* (Paris, 2009), p. 739.
41 'Je vous admire mais je me permets un tout petit reproche – dans l'ensemble vous faites la part trop belle à la pensée et pas assez à l'émotion. Émotion dans le sens physiologique – le "Rendu émotif" C'est de *cela* bougre bordel de dieu dont notre race et notre langue a tant besoin, si ratatinée, si sèche, si calculière, si goujate, si mufle, si insensible derrière toutes ces facettes poétiques et raisonnables', in letter of June 1944, 44-21, ibid., pp. 756–7.

42 An example of this anti-militarist satire is Georges Courteline's 1886 novel (later adapted for the stage), *Les Gaîtés de l'escadron*, quoted by Godard, *Romans III*, p. XIV.
43 Letter of 24 July 1931, in Pierre Lainé, ed., *Louis-Ferdinand Céline: Lettres à Joseph Garcin (1929–1938)* (Paris, 1987), p. 31.
44 'Le roman célinien est toujours dans son fonds la reprise d'une expérience du passé transposé selon les voies d'un imaginaire. Quand il s'agit de personnes ou de lieux, l'histoire de ses œuvres montre que Céline a chaque fois besoin d'être séparé d'eux par les circonstances pour pouvoir les prendre comme matière a transposition', in Godard, *Romans III*, p. 879.
45 Vitoux, *La Vie de Céline*, pp. 573–4.
46 'Je me fais noter pour la discipline et le règlement', in Godard, *Céline*, p. 298.
47 Ibid., p. 299.
48 Fouché, *Céline*, p. 49.
49 Godard, *Céline*, pp. 300–301.
50 '[U]ne aventure qui ne doit se renouveler, j'imagine, que tous les trois ou quatre siècles', quoted in Godard, *Céline*, p. 302.
51 Ibid., p. 303.
52 Vitoux, *La Vie de Céline*, p. 592.
53 Godard, *Céline*, pp. 304–5.
54 'Elle coûtait cher l'Armée française, 400 milliards pour se sauver, 8 mois de belotes, un mois de déroute . . .', in Louis-Ferdinand Céline, *Les Beaux draps*, (Paris, 1941), p. 16, quoted in Charles-Antoine Cardot, 'Vichy face aux *Beaux draps*', *Le Bulletin célinien*, 420 (July–August 2019), p. 12. (Translations my own.)
55 '[E]xprime des sentiments personnels regrettables ou des critiques non justifiées à l'égard de l'armée et de ses chefs', ibid., p. 11.
56 Frank-Rutger Hausmann, 'L.-F. Céline et Karl Epting', *Le Bulletin célinien* (Brussels, 2008), p.39; quoted in Cardot, 'Vichy face aux *Beaux draps*', p. 13.
57 For a discussion of Bernhard Payr's role and that of the Amt Schrifttum, see Gérard Loiseaux, *La Littérature de la défaite et de la collaboration, d'après* Phönix oder Asches*? (Phénix ou cendres?) de Bernhard Payr* (Paris, 1995), pp. 29–49; '[U]n français populaire et ordurier inacceptable . . . abominable français de ruisseau', quoted in Charles-Antoine Cardot, 'Retour sur *Les Beaux draps*', *Le Bulletin célinien*, 423 (November 2019), p. 8.
58 'L'enfance notre seul salut [. . .] Sans création continuelle, artistique, et de tous, aucune société possible, durable, surtout aux jours d'aujourd'hui, ou tous n'est que mécanique autour de nous, agressif, abominable [. . .] Il faut un long et terrible effort de la part des maîtres armés du Programme pour tuer l'artiste chez l'enfant. Cela ne va pas tout seul. Les écoles fonctionnent dans ce but, ce sont les lieux de torture pour la parfaite innocence, la joie spontanée, la joie des oiseaux, la fabrication d'un deuil qui suinte déjà de tous les murs, la poisse sociale primitive, l'enduit qui pénètre partout, suffoque, estourbit pour toujours toute gaîté de vivre', in Céline, *Les Beaux draps*, pp. 170–71. Henceforth, referred to as *A Fine Mess*. (Translations my own.)
59 'Y a qu'à bouleverser les notions, donner la prime à la musique, aux chants en chœur, à la peinture, à la composition surtout, aux trouvailles des danses personnelles, aux rigodons particuliers, tout ce qui donne parfum à la vie,

guillerette jolie, porte l'esprit à fleurir, enjolive nos heures, nos tristesses, nous assure un peu de Bonheur d'enthousiasme, de chaleur qui nous élève, nous fait traverser l'existence, en somme sur un nuage', in *A Fine Mess*, pp. 171–2.

60 '[T]out imprégné de musique et de jolis rhythmes, d'exemples exaltants, tout ensorcelé de grandeur', ibid.

61 Frederic Spotts, *The Shameful Peace: How French Artists and Intellectuals survived the Nazi Occupation* (New Haven, CT, 2008).

62 Ibid., p. 19.

63 Ibid.

64 Ibid.

65 Philippe Burrin, *La France à l'heure allemande: 1940–1944* (Paris, 1995), p. 302.

66 Ibid., pp. 303, 307–9.

67 Spotts, *The Shameful Peace*, p. 65.

68 Hewitt, *The Life of Céline*, p. 176.

69 'L'homme était intéressant mais je haïssais la clique des petits maquereaux politiques qui l'entouraient et le P.P.F. me le rendait bien', in Vitoux, *La Vie de Céline*, p. 614.

70 Ibid., p. 604.

71 Ibid., p. 610.

72 Gerhard Heller, avec le concours de Jean Grand, *Un Allemand à Paris: 1940–1944* (Paris, 1981), pp. 152–4.

73 Burrin, *La France*, p. 332.

74 Godard, *Céline*, pp. 326–7.

75 The most comprehensive account of Karl Epting's role and that of the German Institute is to be found in Eckard Michels, *Das Deutsche Institut in Paris 1940–1944: Ein Beitrag zu den deutsch-französischen Kulturbeziehungen und zur auswärtigen Kulturpolitik des Dritten Reiches* (Stuttgart, 1993).

76 Spotts, *The Shameful Peace*, p. 141.

77 Ibid.

78 Vitoux, *La Vie de Céline*, pp. 644–5.

79 Barbara Lambauer, *Otto Abetz et les Français, ou L'Envers de la Collaboration*, préface de Jean-Pierre Azéma (Paris, 2001), p. 315.

80 Godard, *Céline*, pp. 352–3.

81 Paul Lay, 'The Beauty and Savagery of Ernst Jünger's Wartime Diaries', *New Statesman* (20 February 2019), available at www.newstatesman.com, accessed August 2020.

82 Vitoux, *La Vie de Céline*, pp. 651–2.

83 Ibid. See also Godard, *Céline*, p. 327; and Duraffour and Taguieff, *Céline: La race, le Juif*, pp. 593–6.

84 Ibid., p. 651.

85 Spotts, *The Shameful Peace*, p. 142.

86 Godard, *Céline*, p. 312.

87 Gérard Loiseaux, *La Littérature de la défaite*, p. 297.

88 Karl Epting, 'Céline, il ne nous aimait pas', in *Cahiers Céline de l'Herne 3*, ed. Dominique de Roux, Michel Thélia et Michel Beaujour (Paris, 1963), p. 56.

89 Céline requested 15 tonnes of paper from Epting on 15 April 1942, and another three or four tonnes on 4 May 1943. See Godard and Louis, *Lettres*, pp. 699 and 727; Godard, *Céline*, p. 332.

90 Godard, *Céline*, p. 518.
91 Ibid., pp. 309–10.
92 Ibid., pp. 312–13.
93 Spotts, *The Shameful Peace*, p. 226.
94 Godard speculates that Céline probably met Breker through Karl Epting and that his bust was based on photographs, rather than on life; see Godard, *Céline*, p. 325.
95 Spotts, *The Shameful Peace*, p. 227; and Godard, *Céline*, p. 315.
96 Vitoux, *La Vie de Céline*, p. 646; Spotts, *The Shameful Peace*, p. 227.
97 'Raison de Race surpasse chez moi Raison d'Art ou Raison d'Amitié. Êtes-vous mon cher Cocteau antisémite? Tout est là. Si vous l'êtes nom de dieu hurle-le et cela se saura,' in letter to Jean Cocteau of November/December 1941, in Godard and Louis, *Lettres*, 41-69, p. 662.
98 'Une classe privilégiée n'a plus d'utilité ni de sens, ni de vie, lorsqu'elle n'est plus capable de fournir des cadres à l'armée. C'est le critère, le seul. [...] – Du moment où elle n'est plus capable de fournir ce rôle, où elle ne fait plus enfants, ni officiers – elle n'est plus que parasitaire et donc désastreuse', in letter to Henri Poulain of 11 June 1943, 43-21, ibid., pp. 729–30.
99 'Je me souviens bien qu'un soir vous m'avez dit très franchement: "Vous en faites pas, Champfleury, je sais à peu près tout ce que vous faites, vous et votre femme, mais ne craignez rien de ma part . . . je vous en donne ma parole . . . et même, si je puis vous aider!" Il y avait un tel accent de sincérité dans votre affirmation que je me suis trouvé absolument rassuré. Mieux, un certain jour, je suis venu frapper à votre porte, accompagné d'un Résistant qui avait été torturé par la Gestapo. Vous m'avez ouvert, vous avez examiné la main meurtrie de mon compagnon et, sans poser aucune question, vous avez fait le pansement qu'il convenait, ayant parfaitement deviné les origines de la blessure', in Robert Champfleury, 'Céline ne nous a pas trahis' (March 1962), in Louis-Ferdinand Céline, *Cahiers Céline de l'Herne 3*, p. 65.
100 Louis-Ferdinand Céline, *Guignol's Band*, trans. Bernard Frechtman and Jack Nile (Richmond, 2012), pp. 27–8.
101 That five of the novel's characters – Ferdinand, Cascade, Borokrom, Clodovitz, Sosthène – are also exiles from Paris further reinforces, as Hewitt points out, its anti-Parisian quality. Hewitt, *The Golden Age*, p. 214.
102 Céline, *Guignol's Band*, p. VII.
103 Ibid.
104 Ibid., p. x.
105 Ibid., p. 4.
106 Ibid., p. 5.
107 Ibid., p. 6.
108 Ibid., p. 3.
109 Ibid., p. 4.
110 Ibid., p. 7.
111 Ibid.
112 Ibid.
113 Ibid., p. 10.
114 Hewitt, *The Golden Age*, p. 210.
115 Céline, *Guignol's Band*, p. 87.
116 Hewitt, *The Golden Age*, p. 210.

117 Ibid., p. 212.
118 See Regina Buccola, '"The Story Shall Be Changed": The Fairy Feminism of a *Midsummer Night's Dream*', in *William Shakespeare's A Midsummer Night's Dream, Bloom's Modern Critical Interpretations* (New York, 2010), pp. 146–7.
119 Introduction by Harold Bloom, ibid., pp. 4–5.
120 See, for example, Philip H. Solomon, *Understanding Céline* (Columbia, SC, 1992), p. 73.
121 Louis-Ferdinand Céline, *London Bridge (Guignol's Band II)*, trans. Dominic Di Bernardi (London, 2012), p. 193.
122 Ibid., p. 195.
123 'Il faudrait plus de musique [...] Tout devrait se rejoindre – voix et musique ne jamais oublier que l'homme *chantait* avant de parler. Le chant est naturel, la parole est *apprise*. Les sources à poésie sont au chant – pas au bavardage', in Godard and Louis, *Lettres*, 43-13, p. 725.
124 Vitoux, *La Vie de Céline*, pp. 636–7.
125 Godard, *Céline*, p. 357.
126 Vitoux, *La Vie de Céline*, p. 674.
127 Godard, *Céline*, p. 358.
128 Ibid., p. 359.
129 Ibid., pp. 359–60.
130 Vitoux, *La Vie de Céline*, p. 681.
131 Fouché, *Céline*, pp. 60–62.
132 Vitoux, *La Vie de Céline*, p. 682.
133 Godard, *Céline*, p. 360.
134 'Nous avons mis quelques jours à admettre la réalité de cet enchantement! à nous habituer à cette paix incroyable – Égoïstement l'on jouit hélàs de tant de bienfaits, heureusement pour l'inquiétude de nos âmes, nous sommes un peu survolés de temps en temps par la mort et la foudre! Tout est trop beau tout est trop bien', in letter to Karl Epting, July 1944, 44-24, in Godard and Louis, *Lettres*, p. 758.
135 Fouché, *Céline*, p. 61.
136 Louis-Ferdinand Celine, *North*, trans. Ralph Manheim (Urbana-Champaign, IL, 1996), p. 6. Henceforth, this edition will be referred to as *North*.
137 Ibid., p. 21.
138 Ibid., p. 442.

6 Prison and Exile

1 Frédéric Vitoux, *La Vie de Céline* (Paris, 1988, 2005), p. 753.
2 Louis-Ferdinand Céline, *Lettres de prison à Lucette Destouches et à Maître Mikkelsen: 1945–1947*, ed. François Gibault (Paris, 1998), p. 17.
3 David Alliot, *Madame Céline* (Paris, 2018), pp. 123–4.
4 Ibid., p. 124.
5 Louis-Ferdinand Céline, *Castle to Castle*, trans. Ralph Manheim, 3rd edn (Urbana-Champaign, IL, 2011), p. 43. Henceforth, this edition will be referred to as *Castle to Castle*. The original French quotations are in Henri Godard, ed., *Romans II*, by Louis-Ferdinand Céline (Paris, 1974), p. 38.

6 Céline, *Castle to Castle*, p. 24.

7 Godard, *Romans II*, p. 23.

8 Vitoux, *La Vie de Céline*, pp. 754–5.

9 'Combien sont nombreux les écrivains français qui à un moment ou l'autre ont du fuir leur Patrie! . . . *Presque tous furent exilés* . . . depuis *Villon* jusqu'à *Verlaine, Daudet* en passant par *Zola, Chateaubriand, Lamartine, Chenier* hélas guillotine . . . Bien entendu je ne vous apprends pas que la persécution est presque la règle dans l'Histoire de nos lettres et l'exil . . .', in Letter 1, May 1945, in Céline, *Lettres de prison*, p. 25.

10 See Céline, *Lettres de prison*, p. 12, and Henri Godard, *Céline* (Paris, 2011), p. 392, who argues that Céline's fourteen-month incarceration worked in his favour, by preventing his extradition back to France.

11 'J'étais évidemment le plus visé de Sigmaringen, si l'on m'y avait trouvé. J'aurais fait encore une fois de plus le bouc – Mais ni en Allemagne ni en France je n'ai jamais tenu d'emploi, de rôle, de semblant de rôle politique. J'étais libre l'employé, l'adhérent de rien ni de personne – C'est cela que ce trou du cul absolument salarié, <vendu> n'a jamais voulu admettre ni les autres – d'où furie totale. Je l'ai toujours hautement affirmé [. . .] Je l'ai hurlé sur tous les tons – L'histoire franco-allemande m'a semblé dès 1940, ridiculement conduit et engagé [. . .] et ne pouvait aboutir qu'aux catastrophes [. . .] – J'aurais été plus lâche et je serais parti en Espagne dès [19]40, puisque j'ai été absolument libre de tout profit de tout engagement [. . .]', in letter 135, 29 and 30 October 1945, in Céline, *Lettres de prison*, pp. 210–13.

12 'Abetz me détestait. Tous mes livres sont interdits en Allemagne depuis Hitler. L'on m'y trouvait anarchiste et insupportable – Si l'Allemagne avait gagné la guerre la Gestapo m'aurait fait supprimer [. . .]', ibid.

13 '[M]'a toujours détesté et était jaloux comme tous. Il déconne encore dans la mort même', ibid.

14 'J'ai fait a Sigmaringen de la médecine dans des conditions que je crois très héroïques – il y a mille témoins [. . .] D'ailleurs il n'était pas là, il était au Lac de Constance à se saouler et jouer aux cartes Ragot de petit fou de micro, furieux apres vingt tentatives pour sauver sa peau d'avoir fini par perdre. Idiot en tout – Tous ces gens ont pris de traits sur ma personne d'autorité et sur mes intentions – habitués qu'ils sont de se permettre pour la gueule n'importe quoi', ibid.

15 Vitoux, *La Vie de Céline*, p. 765.

16 Ibid., pp. 755–6.

17 'Notre seul espoir était votre retour! Mais aussi je m'accable de reproches j'ai du tournoyer autour de vous à l'état de fantôme pendant tout votre voyage! Vous qui entendiez vous amuser et vous reposer sans aucun souci!', in letter 25, 18 March 1946, in Céline, *Lettres de prison*, p. 67.

18 Godard, *Céline*, pp. 383–4.

19 Ibid., p. 384.

20 Céline, *Lettres de prison*, p. 12.

21 Ibid., p. 80.

22 Louis-Ferdinand Céline, *Cahiers Céline 13: Cahiers de prison: Février–octobre 1946*, ed. Jean-Paul Louis (Paris, 2019), p. 7.

23 Henri Godard, ed., *Romans IV*, by Louis-Ferdinand Céline (Paris, 1993), p. 565.

24 In order to differentiate between the two volumes, Gaston Gallimard persuaded a reluctant Céline to add *Normance*, the name of a character in his novel, as a subtitle to the second instalment: it thus became *Féerie pour une autre fois II: Normance*.

25 Louis-Ferdinand Céline, *Fable for Another Time (Féerie pour une autre fois I)*, ed. Henri Godard, trans. Mary Hudson (Lincoln, NE, 2003), pp. xiv–xv. Henceforth, this edition will be referred to as *Fable*.

26 Ibid.

27 Ibid., p. 4.

28 Ibid., p. xiii.

29 Ibid.

30 Ibid., p. xiv.

31 Ibid., p. 13.

32 Ibid., p. 148.

33 Ibid., p. 117.

34 'Laissera-t-on Bébert? Non on le prendra [. . .] Juste un petit tour au Danemark – le courage devant l'énormité du malheur manque . . . Encore longtemps à la fenêtre là – on pleure tous les deux . . . Toutes ces lignes-là, ces rues, ces verdures, ces toitures, la Seine son long sillon – l'Opéra – mon quartier – le Temple où j'allais avec grand-mère – la République,' in Céline, *Cahiers de prison*, Cahier 4, folio 6, p. 95.

35 Céline, *Fable*, p. 118.

36 Ibid.

37 Ibid.

38 Ibid., pp. 118–19, 121–2.

39 Ibid., p. 122.

40 Ibid., p. 47.

41 Ibid., pp. 47–8.

42 For an account of Céline and Gen Paul's 'love–hate' relationship, see Godard, *Romans IV*, pp. 1181–5.

43 Louis-Ferdinand Céline, *Normance*, trans. Marlon Jones (Urbana-Champaign, IL, 2009).

44 Ibid., p. 53.

45 'Le nouveau livre, *Féerie*, vous l'avez écrit par nécessité, pour satisfaire votre goût du style et vous avez eu raison. C'est une belle œuvre, réussie, que je suis fier d'avoir publiée. Mais ce n'est pas un livre commercial, de vente rapide. Il n'est pas écrit pour un grand public. Je ne m'en plains pas, mais ne vous en plaignez pas,' quoted Godard, *Céline*, p. 490.

46 Godard, *Céline*, p. 486.

47 'Votre humour n'est que de la rhétorique. Vous n'arrivez pas à me faire croire à votre violence. Vous mêlez tout – Exprès – [. . .] Vous voulez vendre, et bien donnez une marchandise facile! Et puis faites le polichinelle comme les bons vendeurs: radio – photos, interviews etc. . . . Ainsi vous attirerez l'attention sur vos livres. Vos diatribes contre votre éditeur sont inefficaces,' in letter 76, 14 December 1954, in Louis-Ferdinand Céline, *Lettres à la N.R.F.: Choix 1931–1961*, intro. Philippe Sollers, ed. Pascal Fouché (Paris, 1991), p. 142.

48 Louis-Ferdinand Céline, *Conversations with Professor Y*, trans. and ed. Stanford Luce (London, 1986, 2006), p. xxii.

49 Ibid., pp. 6–7.
50 Ibid., pp. 5, 11.
51 'Je suis l'objet d'une sorte d'interdit depuis un certain nombre d'années, et, en faisant paraître un ouvrage qui est malgré tout assez public, puisqu'il part de faits bien connus, et qui intéressent tout de même les Français, puisque c'est [. . .] une petite partie de l'histoire de la France, je parle de Pétain, je parle de Laval, je parle de Sigmaringen', interview with Albert Zbinden, quoted in Godard, *Romans II*, p. 936.
52 Louis Noguères, *La Dernière étape: Sigmaringen* (Paris, 1956); Céline, *Castle to Castle*, p. 158.
53 Henri Rousso, 'Sigmaringen, l'ultime trahison' (interview with Rachel Kahn and Laurent Perrin), France 3, *Cinétévé*, 9 March 1996.
54 Céline, *Castle to Castle*, p. 55.
55 'Est-il une histoire des bombardements qui puisse mieux faire éprouver au lecteur ce qui en constitue la gamme émotionnelle que leur évocation par Céline dans *Rigodon*', in Alain Corbin, 'Les Historiens et la fiction: Usages, tentation, nécessités . . .', *Le Débat*, 165 (May–August 2011), p. 61.
56 Henri Godard, *Romans III*, by Louis-Ferdinand Céline (Paris, 1988), pp. 980–85.
57 Christine Sautermeister, *Louis-Ferdinand Céline à Sigmaringen: Novembre 1944–mars 1945 – Chronique d'un séjour controversé* (Paris, 2013), p. 182.
58 Céline, *Castle to Castle*, p. 1.
59 Ibid., p. 10.
60 Ibid., p. 84.
61 Ibid., p. 83.
62 Ibid., p. 89.
63 Ibid., p. 90.
64 Ibid., p. 96.
65 Ibid., p. 101.
66 Ibid., p. 103.
67 Sautermeister, *Louis-Ferdinand Céline à Sigmaringen*, p. 105.
68 Fredric Jameson, 'Céline and innocence', in 'Céline USA', *South Atlantic Quarterly*, XCIII/2 (Spring 1994), ed. Alice Kaplan and Philippe Roussin, pp. 311–19.
69 Céline, *Castle to Castle*, p. 132.
70 Sautermeister, *Louis-Ferdinand Céline à Sigmaringen*, p. 105.
71 Céline, *Castle to Castle*, p. 148.
72 Ibid., pp. 130–31.
73 Ibid., p. 149.
74 Ibid.
75 Ibid., p. 158.
76 Ibid., p. 242.
77 Ibid., p. 243.
78 Ibid., p. 246.
79 Ibid.
80 Sautermeister, *Louis-Ferdinand Céline à Sigmaringen*, p. 204.
81 'Mes relations avec Laval furent en effet fort mauvaises tant qu'il fut au pouvoir, mais à Sigmaringen je n'ai jamais eu à me plaindre de lui. Je l'ai au contraire toujours trouvé dans l'infortune très digne, très patriote, et très pacifiste, toutes

qualitès qui sont faites pour me plaire', quoted by Marc Laudelot in 'Pierre Laval vu par Céline', *Le Bulletin célinien*, 412 (November 2018), p. 8.

82 Louis-Ferdinand Céline, *North*, trans. Ralph Manheim (Normal, IL, 1996), p. 36.
83 Ibid., pp. 36–7.
84 Ibid., p. 56.
85 Ibid., p. 57.
86 Ibid.
87 Ibid.
88 '[U]n patelin sinistre, des Boches timbrés, haïssant les Franzose [*sic*], la famine au milieu des troupeaux d'oies et de canards', Lucien Rebatet, 'D'un Céline l'autre', in *Cahiers Céline de l'Herne*, no. 3 (Paris, 1963), pp. 42–55 (p. 51), quoted in Godard, *Romans II*, pp. 1142–3.
89 'Je ne peux pas dire que nous en ayons conservé un très bon souvenir. C'était une famille de hobereaux pas sympathiques du tout. Des gens très durs. Les nazis avaient réquisitionné leur maison pour mettre des gens comme nous, étrangers à la politique. Nous y avons crevé de faim. Si finalement, nous sommes partis pour Sigmaringen, c'est que nous n'en pouvions plus', from an interview of Lucette Destouches by Christian Millau, *Le Nouveau Candide*, 58 (7–14 June 1962), p. 9, quoted in Alliot, *Madame Céline*, p. 216.
90 Céline, *North*, p. 115.
91 Vitoux, *La Vie de Céline*, p. 704.
92 Céline, *North*, p. 150.
93 Ibid.
94 Ibid., p. 151.
95 Ibid., p. 338.
96 Ibid., p. 346.
97 Ibid., p. 325.
98 Ibid., p. 326.
99 Ibid., p. 207.
100 Ibid., p. 193.
101 Ibid., pp. 124–5.
102 Ibid., p. 336.
103 Ibid., p. 338.
104 Ibid., p. 336.
105 Ibid., p. 389.
106 Ibid.
107 Godard, *Romans III*, pp. 1081–2.
108 Vitoux, *La Vie de Céline*, p. 859.
109 Details of the legal debacle surrounding *Nord* are provided by Godard, *Romans III*, pp. 1159–62.
110 Louis-Ferdinand Céline, *Rigadoon*, trans. Ralph Manheim, with an introduction by Kurt Vonnegut, Jr. (Urbana-Champaign, IL, 1997).
111 Vitoux, *La Vie de Céline*, p. 961.
112 Céline, *Rigadoon*, p. 43.
113 Ibid., pp. 45–6.
114 Ibid., pp. 152–3.
115 Ibid., p. 191.

116 Ibid., p. 187.
117 Ibid., p. 192.
118 Ibid., pp. 138–9.
119 Ibid., pp. 142–3.
120 Ibid., p. 143.
121 Ibid., p. 146.
122 Ibid., p. 79.
123 Ibid., p. 80.
124 Vitoux, *La Vie de Céline*, pp. 1187–8.
125 Céline, *Rigadoon*, p. 235.
126 Vitoux, *La Vie de Céline*, p. 774.
127 Godard, *Céline*, pp. 389–90.
128 Ibid., p. 390.
129 Ibid., p. 391.
130 'La masseuse juive nous renvoie à Bouchenwald [*sic*] – nous sommes accablés par les morts des camps de concentration – on étouffe', quoted in Godard, Céline, p. 397.
131 'Lorsque j'attaquais les Juifs, lorsque j'écrivais *Bagatelles pour un massacre* je ne voulais pas dire ou recommander qu'on massacre les Juifs. Eh foutre tout le contraire! Je demandais aux Juifs à ce qu'ils ne nous lancent pas par hystérie dans un autre massacre plus désastreux que celui de [19]14–18! C'est bien différent. On joue avec grande canaillerie sur le sens de mes pamphlets. On s'acharne à vouloir me considérer comme un massacreur de Juifs. Je suis un préservateur patriote acharné de français et d'aryens – et en même temps d'ailleurs de Juifs! Je n'ai pas voulu Auschwitz, Buchenwald', in letter to Jean Paulhan, 15 April 1948, in Henri Godard and Jean-Paul Louis, eds, *Lettres: Choix de lettres de Céline et de quelques correspondants (1907–1961)* (Paris, 2009), p. 1038.
132 Céline, *Castle to Castle*, p. 181.
133 Vitoux, *La Vie de Céline*, p. 801.
134 Ibid., p. 802–3; see also Godard, *Céline*, p. 407.
135 Vitoux, *La Vie de Céline*, pp. 815–16.
136 Louis-Ferdinand Céline, *Lettres à Denise Thomassen, 1949–51*, ed. Eric Mazet (Paris, 2003), pp. 1–15, 66.
137 Godard, *Céline*, pp. 421–2.
138 Vitoux, *La Vie de Céline*, p. 838.
139 This article is reproduced (English translations my own), together with a critical commentary of its background, by Marc Laudelot in 'L'Interview de Céline dans *Europe-Amérique*', *Le Bulletin célinien*, 422 (October 2019), pp. 7–23.
140 Ibid., p. 14.
141 Ibid.
142 Ibid., p. 16
143 Ibid., p. 18.
144 Ibid., p. 863
145 Ibid., p. 867.
146 Ibid., pp. 869–71.
147 Godard, *Céline*, pp. 457–8; Vitoux, *La Vie de Céline*, p. 874.
148 Ibid., p. 878.

149 Odile Roynette, *Un Long tourment: Louis-Ferdinand Céline entre deux guerres (1914–1945)* (Paris, 2015), pp. 223–7.
150 Alliot, *Madame Céline*, pp. 166–7.

7 Death, Legacy and the Céline Culture Wars

1 David Alliot, *Madame Céline* (Paris, 2018), p. 179.
2 Ibid., p. 180.
3 Ibid., p. 181.
4 Henri Godard, *Céline* (Paris, 2011), p. 498.
5 Ibid., pp. 181–3.
6 Ibid., pp. 190–91.
7 Godard, *Céline*, p. 515.
8 Alliot, *Madame Céline*, p. 185.
9 Ibid., p. 188.
10 Ibid., pp. 182–5.
11 Jérôme Dupuis, 'Le Grand amour d'Arletty', *Le Bulletin célinien*, 416 (March 2019), p. 21.
12 Ibid., p. 22.
13 Ibid., pp. 22–3. The film was never completed owing to production problems.
14 Marc Dambre, 'Autour de Céline: Roger Nimier, son ami et dernier interlocuteur chez Gallimard', Fondation Singer-Polignac-Paris, 9 November 2011, available at www.dailymotion.com.
15 Godard, *Céline*, pp. 499–500.
16 Pascal Fouché, *Céline*: *'Ça a débuté comme ça'* (Paris, 2001), p. 68.
17 Alliot, *Madame Céline*, p. 257.
18 '[Un certain] mépris haineux des petites gens qui est une attitude préfasciste', quoted in Henri Godard, ed., *Romans I*, by Louis-Ferdinand Céline (Paris, 1981), p. 1409.
19 Jean-Paul Sartre, Letter to Marie Ville, 12 September 1937, quoted by Robert Le Blanc, in 'Quand Sartre se référait à Céline', *Le Bulletin célinien*, 432 (September 2020), p. 23.
20 'Si Céline a pu soutenir les thèses socialistes des Nazis, c'est qu'il a été payé', ibid., p. 9.
21 Louis-Ferdinand Céline, *À l'Agité du bocal* (Paris, 2011), pp. 7–15.
22 'Toujours au lycée, ce J.-B. S.! toujours aux pastiches, aux "Lamanièredeux" . . . La manière de Céline aussi . . . et puis de bien d'autres . . .', ibid., p. 8.
23 'Voici donc ce qu'écrivait ce petit bousier pendant que j'étais en prison en plein péril qu'on me pende. Satanée petite saloperie gavé de merde, tu me sors de l'entre-fesses pour me salir au dehors', ibid., p. 9.
24 'Ténia, bien sur, ténia d'homme, situé où vous savez . . . et philosophe! . . .', ibid., p. 11.
25 'Il a délivré, paraît-il, Paris à bicyclette,' ibid.
26 'Mais les temps évoluent, et le voici qui croît, gonfle énormément, J.-B. S.!', ibid.
27 '[D']envoyer vos confrères détestés, dits "Collaborateurs" au bagne, au Poteau, en exil . . .', ibid., p. 13.
28 '[L]a hargne anti-sémite des petits-bourgeois français devint monstrueuse entre des mains allemandes – parfois des mains françaises', in 'Le Maréchal des logis

Céline', *Carrefour* (6 August 1952), quoted in Alain Cresciucci, 'Un Grand livre sur Roger Nimier', *Le Bulletin célinien*, 410 (September 2018), p. 21.
29 Roger Nimier, 'Donnez à Céline le prix Nobel!', *Les Nouvelles littéraires* (18 October 1956), quoted ibid., p. 23.
30 'Tout ça est pénible, et somme toute je vous aimais bien. Pourquoi diable avoir un si mauvais caractère?', in letter from Paulhan to Céline, 14 January 1955, ibid., p. 23.
31 Dambre, 'Autour de Céline: Roger Nimier, son ami et dernier interlocuteur chez Gallimard'.
32 The Allen Ginsberg Project, 'William Burroughs Conversation Continues – 3 (A Visit to Louis Ferdinand Céline)', 22 September 2020, https://allenginsberg.org.
33 Ibid.
34 Ibid.
35 Louis-Ferdinand Céline, *Lettres à la* N.R.F.*: Choix 1931–1961*, intro. Philippe Sollers, ed. Pascal Fouché (Paris, 1991), p. 220.
36 Letter 120, 20 November 1956, ibid., pp. 177–8.
37 Letter 160, 3 December 1957, ibid., pp. 209–10.
38 '[J]e vous serais très obligé de secouer cette Pléiade, et de m'y faire publier dès cette année, n'ayant pas à 67 ans, le loisir d'attendre je ne sais quel coup d'État . . .', in Letter 190, 7 February 1960, ibid.
39 Alliot, *Madame Céline*, pp. 205–6.
40 Frédéric Vitoux, *La Vie de Céline* (Paris, 1988, 2005), p. 951.
41 Fouché, *Céline: 'Ça a débuté comme ça'*, p. 73.
42 Godard, *Céline*, p. 529; Alliot, *Madame Céline*, pp. 208–9.
43 Alliot, *Madame Céline*, p. 210.
44 Ibid., p. 211.
45 Philippe Muray, *Céline* (1981; 2nd edn, Paris, 2001), pp. 12–15.
46 I address this controversy in more detail in Damian Catani, 'Louis-Ferdinand Céline, Literary Genius or National Pariah? Defining Moral Parameters for Influential Cultural Figures, Post-Charlie Hebdo', *French Cultural Studies Special Issue: Understanding Charlie*, XXVII/3 (August 2016), pp. 268–78.
47 'Quand au Ministre de la Culture, il est devenu le Ministre de la Censure – je le dis gentiment', quoted in Jules Vebret, *Céline l'infréquentable?*, préface de Jean-Marie Rouart de l'Académie française (Paris, 2011), pp. 163–4.
48 'Malheureusement, M. Mitterrand a préféré capituler (en un temps record!) devant une attitude communautariste, aussi estimable soit-elle,' ibid., p. 39.
49 'Ce recueil porte mal son nom [. . .] Si on parlait de "commémoration" plutôt que de "célébration", il n'y aurait plus d'ambiguïté', in A. Beuve-Méry and T Wieder, 'Frédéric Mitterrand fait volte-face et écarte Céline des célébrations de 2011', *Le Monde* (22 January 2011).
50 Antoine Peillon, *Céline, un anti-Sémite exceptionnel: Une histoire française* (Paris, 2011), p. 30.
51 Annick Duraffour and Pierre-André Taguieff: *Céline, la race, le Juif – Légende littéraire et vérité historique* (Paris, 2017), p. 23.
52 For a lucid discussion of this shift, see Patrick Baert, *The Existentialist Moment: The Rise of Sartre as Public Intellectual* (Cambridge, 2015), pp. 54–63.

53 Tristan Savin, 'Céline: Les derniers secrets', *Lire*: Céline, les derniers secrets, hors série 7 (May 2008), p. 82, repr. in David Alliot, *D'un Céline l'autre*, pp. 1008–11. Interview with Madeleine Chapsal, 'Voyage au bout de la haine', *L'Express*, no. 312 (14 June 1957), pp. 15–18, 22–3, Bibliothèque Nationale de France, micr d-462 1957/01-1957/06.

54 'J'ai écrit des choses sur des Juifs. J'ai dit qu'ils magnigançaient une guerre, qu'ils voulaient se venger de Hitler. Bon. Ça ne nous regardait pas (le secrétaire de rédaction ne mettra pas ça non plus)', in an interview with *L'Express* (14 juin 1957). Bibliothèque Nationale de France (MICR D-462 1957/01-1957/06).

55 'Vous disparaissez, vous race blanche [. . .] le fond est jaune. Ce n'est pas une couleur, le blanc, c'est un fond de teint. La vraie couleur, c'est le jaune. Le Jaune a toutes les qualités qu'il faut pour devenir le roi de la terre.' Ibid.

56 '[P]as une ligne de l'œuvre de Céline ne relève d'autre chose que d'une faculté toute physique de tenir une plume et de la tremper dans la fange', published in *L'Express* (28 June 1957), p. 31.

57 '[E]t s'étonne que nous accordions de la place: "à l'infamie et à la crasse intellectuelle du monsieur en question"', ibid.

58 See 'Sur la réponse d'un préfet', *L'Humanité*, 13 September 1957, p. 2, BNF:MICR D-30 L1.15 – MFM, which announces its support of the ban of Céline's TV interview; *Télé-Magazine*, 192 (28 June–4 July 1957), p. 25; and *Télé-Magazine*, 193 (5–11 July 1957), p. 21. Both issues of *Télé-Magazine* discuss the suspension of the newsreader for pronouncing Céline's name; the second (July issue) includes the government denial of capitulation to pressure (BNF: DN2-702 L4 19-B).

59 Jean-Louis Bory, 'Que faire avec Céline?', *Le Nouvel Observateur* (25 February 1965), pp. 26–8, (BNF: Fol-Z-15751964/11/19-1965/02/25).

60 'Je continue à croire que *Voyage* et *Mort à crédit* sont des livres remarquables. Mais les derniers Céline ne sont pas intéressants. Voyez-vous, je suis un homme engagé, alors, moi, le Céline de *Bagatelles*, non, absolument non. Céline allant se loger dans un château allemand, Céline partant derrière les troupes allemandes, non et non. Cela ne me plaît pas', ibid.

61 'Céline appartient à tout le monde. Il s'est trompé seulement parce qu'il portait un regard littéraire sur la réalité. Il transformait la réalité avec son langage. Beaucoup d'écrivains viennent de lui. À commencer par Sartre. L'écriture de Sartre, ou si l'on veut sa 'vision verbalisée' vibre un peu de la même façon que celle de Céline [. . .] Et puis, qu'est-ce que l'engagement aujourd'hui? Pendant la guerre d'Algérie, les écrivains ont pu s'engager politiquement à fond et parallèlement écrire des œuvres tout à fait désengagées', ibid.

62 Philippe Sollers, 'Stratégie de Céline', *Le Magazine littéraire*, no. 292 (October 1991), pp. 30–37, repr. in Philippe Sollers, *Céline* (Paris, 2009), p. 23.

63 Muray, *Céline*, pp. 192–4.

64 Philip Watts, *Allegories of the Purge: How Literature Responded to the Postwar Trials of Writers and Intellectuals in France* (Stanford, CA, 1998), pp. 140–63.

65 Louis-Ferdinand Céline, *Bagatelles pour un massacre* (Paris, 1937), p. 192, quoted in Duraffour and Taguieff, *Céline, la race, le Juif*, p. 28.

66 Duraffour and Taguieff, *Céline, la race, le Juif*, pp. 269–75. On Céline's integration of racial politics into his style, see also David Carroll's chapter 'Literary Anti-Semitism: The Poetics of Race in Drumont and Céline', in his *French Literary Fascism: Nationalism, Anti-Semitism and the Ideology of Culture* (Princeton, NJ, 1995), pp. 171–95; and Sandrine Sanos's chapter 'Negroid Jews against White Men: Louis-Ferdinand Céline and the Politics of Literature', in her *The Aesthetics of Hate: Far-Right Intellectuals, Antisemitism, and Gender in 1930s France* (Stanford, CA, 2013), pp. 158–93. Sanos also considers gender to be an important attribute of Céline's racialized style.

67 Pierre Antoine Cousteau, 'M. Lefumier doré du intitulé Céline rallie système', *Rivarol* (20 June 1957).

68 Many of these polemical opinions from the far Right were gathered in the summer of 1957 by Roger Capgras, the former socialist militant and editor of the non-sectarian newspaper *Dimanche-Matin* (which ran from 1953 to 1957); see Marc Laudelot, 'La Polémique de l'été 1957 dans l'hebdomadaire *Dimanche-Matin*', *Le Bulletin célinien*, 421 (septembre 2019), pp. 7–15.

69 '[F]aveurs exceptionnelles dont aucun autre n'a bénéficié [...] le martyr d'une cause ensevelie dans l'Histoire et baignée dans le sang de ses victims', ibid., p. 9.

70 '[P]romesse de fidélité à l'immonde dans l'œuvre de Céline, qui commence à la première ligne du *Voyage*', ibid., p. 13.

71 Ibid., p. 14.

72 '[I]l y a quelque excès à parler de reniement pour un homme qui n'a jamais connu ni principes ni drapeau', ibid., p. 10.

73 On the Nazis' reservations about enlisting Céline to their cause, see Marie-Christine Bellosta, 'Rééditer les pamphlets?', *Magazine littéraire: Nouveaux regards: Louis-Ferdinand Céline*, hors série (2012), p. 97.

74 Louis-Ferdinand Céline's letter to Milton Hindus, 11 June 1947, in Milton Hindus, *The Crippled Giant: A Literary Relationship with Louis-Ferdinand Céline* (new and expanded edn, Hanover, NH, 1986), pp. 97–9.

75 Letter from Louis-Ferdinand Céline to Milton Hindus, 15 May 1947, ibid., p. 92.

76 Jean-Pierre Richard, *Nausée de Céline* (Paris, 1980), pp. 66–7; Muray, *Céline*, p. 195.

77 Alice Kaplan and Philippe Roussin, 'Céline's Modernity', *South Atlantic Quarterly: Céline: USA*, XCIII/2, pp. 421–43 (p. 427).

78 Ibid., p. 428.

79 See Pascale Gaitet, *Political Stylistics: Popular Language as Literary Artifact* (London, 1992), pp. 146–7. Gaitet compares the 'emotive subway', to 'the reader's submission to a constant movement forward', in which she has a 'physical consistency that has to be overcome by the power of the novel, a power that operates in a manner either violent or seductive'. Roussin similarly invokes the rhetorical trope of *captatio* to describe the seductive hold Céline's oral prose exercises on his reader, by 'trapping' him into listening to his speaking voice: see Philippe Roussin, *Misère de la littérature, terreur de l'histoire: Céline et la littérature contemporaine* (Paris, 2005), pp. 431–2.

80 Louis-Ferdinand Céline, *Conversations with Professor Y*, trans. Stanford Luce (bilingual edn, Hanover and London, 1986), p. 97.

81 Louis-Ferdinand Céline, *Death on Credit*, trans. Ralph Manheim (Richmond, 2017), pp. 299–300.

82 Céline, *Bagatelles pour un massacre*, p. 38.
83 Ibid., p. 39.
84 Ibid.
85 Ibid., p. 40.
86 Kaplan and Roussin, 'Céline's modernity', p. 429.
87 Louis-Ferdinand Céline, *London Bridge (Guignol's Band II)*, trans. Dominic Di Bernardi (London, 2012), p. 401.
88 'On a l'impression d'un Rabelais qui n'a rien à dire, mais qui aurait toujours à sa disposition des cascades d'adjectifs extraordinaires', André Malraux in Frédéric J. Grover, *Six entretiens avec André Malraux sur les écrivains de son temps (1959–1975)* (Paris, 1978), p. 86, quoted in Duraffour and Taguieff, *Céline, la race, le Juif*, p. 29.
89 Louis-Ferdinand Céline, *Normance*, trans., Marlon Jones (Urbana-Champaign, IL, 2009), p. 18.
90 Ibid., p. 8.
91 Ibid., p. 15.
92 Alice Kaplan, 'The Céline Effect: A 1992 Survey of Contemporary American Writers', *Modernism/Modernity*, III/1 (January 1996), pp. 117–36.
93 Hindus, *The Crippled Giant*, p. 56.
94 Ibid., p. 55.
95 Ibid., p. 54.
96 Ibid., p. 61.
97 Ibid., p. 55.
98 Ibid., p. 2.
99 Ibid.
100 Milton Hindus, 'A Literary Event of the First Order', *Evening Globe* (Boston, MA) (9 February 1969).
101 Morris Dickstein, 'Sea Change: Céline and the Problem of Cultural Transmission', *South Atlantic Quarterly: Céline USA*, XCIII/2 (Spring 1994), p. 217.
102 Bourdieu is quoted in Kim Willsher's article on the film, 'Céline: French Literary Genius or Repellent Antisemite? New Film Rekindles an Old Conflict', *The Guardian* (13 March 2016), available at www.theguardian.com.
103 Ibid.
104 These figures are quoted and denounced by Antoine Peillon in *Céline: Un Anti-Sémite exceptionnel: Une Histoire française* (Paris, 2011), p. 28.
105 'Si Céline vaut plus cher que Proust, c'est que nombreux sont ses textes qui sont frappés du sceau de l'interdit, de l'exil, de la prison ou de la proscription', Maxime Rovere, 'Chez les bibliophiles, le soufre se fait or', *Le Magazine Littéraire*, 505 (February 2011), p. 80.
106 '[L]a consultation de la côte de ses manuscrits en ventes publiques peut se révéler plus sûre que le nombre des articles qui lui sont consacrés dans des revues specialisées [. . .] Les prix qu'atteignent en vente publiques les manuscrits [. . .] concrétisent sous forme chiffrée une opinion diffuse captée par des hommes et des femmes qui ne seraient pas tous capables de parler de l'auteur, mais chez qui une intuition, gagé par la dépense qu'ils font, est venue quelquefois étayer un sentiment personnel de lecteur', in Henri Godard, *À Travers Céline: La Littérature* (Paris, 2014), pp. 96–8.

107 On the question of the ban, as well as the Canadian edition of the pamphlets (Louis-Ferdinand Céline, *Écrits polémiques*, édition critique établie, présentée et annotée par Régis Tettamanzi (Quebec, 2012), see the interview with Régis Tettamanzi by Matthias Gadret, 'Les Entretiens du *Petit Célinien* (VII): Régis Tettamanzi', *Le Petit célinien* (23 September 2012), www.lepetitcelinien.com.

108 '[D]ans un contexte où le fléau de l'antisemitisme doit être plus que jamais combattu avec force, les modalités de mise à disposition du grand public de ces écrits doivent être réfléchis avec soin. La qualité de l'appareillage critique qui les accompagne, et notamment sa capacité à éclairer le contexte idéologique et historique de leur production ainsi que le décryptage des biais de l'auteur et des erreurs factuelles dans le texte sont des lors déterminants', quoted in Marc Laudelot, 'Une Réédition sous surveillance', *Le Bulletin célinien*, 403 (January 2018), p. 5.

109 '[I]l ne suffit pas de connaître et d'admirer Céline et son œuvre pour pouvoir entreprendre ce travail que seule une équipe pluridisciplinaire, composée notamment d'historiens spécialisés dans l'étude des domaines concernés, peut mener à bien', ibid., p. 7.

110 'Pluridisciplinarité': le mot clef! le mot magique! Il faudra au moins un historien, un sociologue, un psychologue, un géographe, peut-être aussi un linguiste . . . sinon rien!', ibid., p. 6.

111 See Marc Laudelot, 'Le Bras de fer entre Gallimard et le CRIF continue', *Le Bulletin célinien*, 406 (April 2018), pp. 13–17.

112 Ibid., p. 15.

113 Ibid., p. 13.

114 '[A]yez la décence d'attendre notre mort pour tenter à nouveau d'inscrire ces pamphlets dans le catalogue de la Pléiade dont votre grand-père a renvoyé le créateur en application au statut des juifs', ibid., p. 13.

115 Ibid., p. 14.

116 Michael Aharony, 'Nihilism and Anti-Semitism: The Reception of Céline's *Journey to the End of the Night* in Israel', *Rethinking History*, XIX/1 (June 2015), p. 128, fn 9.

117 Ibid., p. 119.

118 Ibid., p. 122.

119 Ibid., p. 124.

120 Marc Laudelot, 'Un Débat sur la réédition des pamphlets', *Le Bulletin célinien*, 410 (September 2018), pp. 5–10.

Epilogue

1 René Schwob, 'Lettre ouverte a L-F. Céline', *Esprit*, 1/6 (1 March 1933), pp. 1038–41, quoted in Louis-Ferdinand Céline, *Cahiers Céline de l'Herne 1* and *2*, ed. Dominique de Roux, Michel Thélia et Michel Beaujour (Paris, 1963/1965), pp. 338–40.

2 '[S]itue le goût célinien du côté de la féerie, du fantastique, non du côté du réel mais de l'illusion,' in Alain Cresciucci, 'Céline et le ciné', in *Céline à l'épreuve: Réceptions, critiques, influences*, ed. Philippe Roussin, Alain Schaffner and Régis Tettamanzi (Paris, 2016), p. 276.

3 Louis-Ferdinand Céline, *Castle to Castle*, trans. Ralph Manheim, 3rd edn (Urbana-Champaign, IL, 2011), pp. 49–50.
4 Cresciucci, 'Céline et le ciné', p. 277.
5 Ibid., pp. 277–8.
6 Ibid., pp. 280–81.
7 Ibid., pp. 282–3.
8 David Alliot, *Madame Céline* (Paris, 2018), pp. 262–3.
9 Ibid., p. 263.
10 Godard, *Céline* (Paris, 2011), p. 525.
11 Cresciucci, 'Céline et le ciné', p. 283.
12 Ibid., p. 284.
13 Godard, *Céline*, p. 525.
14 Alliot, *Madame Céline*, p. 268.
15 Ibid., p. 366.
16 'J'ai peut-être eu peur avec le *Voyage* que le style se perde dans les images', ibid., p. 269.
17 'Je suis aussi un auteur, en tant que cinéaste. Spontanément, je trahirai l'œuvre de base de Céline. J'en ferai quelque chose d'autre, et je ne sais pas s'il faut le faire', in Cresciucci, 'Céline et le ciné', p. 289 fn. 46.
18 Alliot, *Madame Céline*, pp. 270–71.
19 Ibid., p. 271; Cresciucci, 'Céline et le ciné', p. 285.
20 Cresciucci, 'Céline et le ciné', pp. 287–8.
21 Ibid., p. 285.
22 Alliot, *Madame Céline*, pp. 271–2.
23 Ibid., p. 272.
24 Pascal Fouché, *Céline: 'Ça a débuté comme ça'* (Paris, 2001), p. 90.
25 Ibid., pp. 91–2.
26 Ibid., p. 92.
27 Ibid.
28 Jacques Medina, 'Céline en musique: *À l'Agité du bocal*, de Bernard Cavanna, par *Ars Nova*, Direction Philippe Nahon (CD + DVD, empreinte digitale)', Le Choix de L'Obs, *L'Obs*, 2816 (25–31 October 2018).
29 Fouché, *Céline: 'Ça a débuté comme ça'*, p. 93.
30 '"Semmelweis" de Louis-Ferdinand Céline, choisi et lu par André Dussollier', 15 April 2020 www.franceculture.fr.
31 Alliot, *Madame Céline*, p. 295.
32 Ibid.
33 'Pour illuster Céline ce n'est pas possible de faire deux dessins par chapitre! Il y a tellement de personnages, d'actions, d'emmerdes . . . L'œuvre de Céline est très dense. C'est un foisonnement bordélique . . . Il charge, il en rajoute, il radote, il exaggère. Il fallait que les dessins accompagnent le texte,' ibid., p. 296.
34 Ibid.
35 Bastien Bertine, *Céline Comix: Louis-Ferdinand Céline et la bande dessinée* (Paris, 2021).
36 Vanessa Thorpe, 'Why I Had to Tell the Story of the Genius Who Invented Hospital Hygiene' (interview with Mark Rylance on *Doctor Semmelweis*), *The Guardian* (13 June 2020), www.theguardian.com.

BIBLIOGRAPHY

Works by Céline

Novels

Céline's novels and selected other works are edited and annotated by Henri Godard in the Bibliothèque de la Pléiade collection:

Henri Godard, ed., *Romans I: Voyage au bout de la nuit, Mort à credit* (Paris, 1981)

—, ed., *Romans II: D'un Château l'autre, Nord, Rigodon* (Paris, 1974)

—, ed., *Romans III: Guignol's Band 1 et 2 (Le Pont de Londres), Casse-pipe* (Paris, 1988)

—, ed., *Romans IV: Féerie pour une autre fois 1 et 2 (Normance), Entretiens avec le professeur Y* (Paris, 1993)

English-language Editions:

Castle to Castle, trans. Ralph Manheim, 3rd edn (Urbana-Champaign, IL, 2011)

Death on Credit, trans. Ralph Manheim, preface by André Derval (Richmond, 2009)

Fable for Another Time (Féerie pour une Autre Fois 1), with explanatory notes and preface by Henri Godard, trans. and intro. Mary Hudson (Lincoln, NE, 2003)

Guignol's Band, trans. Bernard Frechtman and Jack Nile (Richmond, 2012)

Journey to the end of the Night, trans. Ralph Manheim, foreword by John Banville (London, 2012)

London Bridge (Guignol's Band II), trans. Dominic Di Bernardi (London, 2012)

Normance, trans. Marlon Jones (Urbana-Champaign, IL, 2009)

North, trans. Ralph Manheim (Urbana-Champaign, IL, 1996)

Rigadoon, trans. Ralph Manheim, intro. Kurt Vonnegut, Jr. (Urbana-Champaign, IL, 1997)

Pamphlets

Mea Culpa [1937], in *Cahiers Céline 1: Céline et l'actualité littéraire 1932–1957* (Paris, 2003)

Bagatelles pour un massacre (Paris, 1937)

L'École des cadavres (Paris, 1938)
Les Beaux draps (Paris, 1941)
À L'Agité du bocal (Paris, 2011)
Écrits polémiques, ed. Régis Tettamanzi (Québec, 2012)

English-language Editions

Mea Culpa and the Life and Work of Semmelweis, trans. Robert Allerton Parker (London, 1937)

Other

Cahiers Céline 8: Progrès, suivi de Œuvres pour la scène et l'écran, ed. Pascal Fouché (Paris, 1988)
Cahiers Céline 13: Cahiers de prison: Février–octobre 1946, ed. Jean-Paul Louis (Paris, 2019)
'Hommage à Zola', in *Cahiers Céline de l'Herne 3*, ed. Dominique de Roux, Michel Thélia et Michel Beaujour (Paris, 1963), pp. 169–73
L'Église (Paris, 1952)

English-language editions

The Church: A Comedy in Five Acts, trans. Mark Spitzer (Los Angeles, CA, 2003)
Conversations with Professor Y, trans. and intro. Stanford Luce (Hanover, NH, 1986; 2nd edn, London, 2006)
Semmelweis, trans. John Harman (London, 2008)

Correspondence

Cahiers Céline 4: Lettres et premiers écrits d'Afrique, 1916–17, ed. Jean-Pierre Dauphin (Paris, 1978)
Devenir Céline: Lettres inédites de Louis Destouches et de quelques autres, 1912–1919, ed. Véronique Robert-Chovin (Paris, 2009)
Dictionnaire de la correspondence de Louis-Ferdinand Céline, suivi d'une chronologie épistolaire, ed. Gaël Richard, Eric Mazet and Jean-Paul Louis, 2 vols (Paris, 2012)
Lettres à Albert Paraz, 1947–1957, ed. Jean-Paul Louis (Paris, 2009)
Lettres à Denise Thomassen, 1949–51, ed. Eric Mazet (Paris, 2003)
Lettres à Henri Mondor, ed. Cécile Leblanc (Paris, 2009)
Lettres à Marie Canavaggia 1936–1960, ed. Jean-Paul Louis (Paris, 2007)
Lettres à la N.R.F.: Choix 1931–1961, ed. Pascal Fouché, preface by Philippe Sollers (Paris, 1991)
Lettres: Choix de lettres de Céline et de quelques correspondants (1907–1961), notes by Henri-Godard and Jean-Paul Louis (Paris, 2009)
Lettres de prison à Lucette Destouches et à Maître Mikkelsen: 1945–1947, ed. François Gibault (Paris, 1998)
Louis-Ferdinand Céline: Lettres à Joseph Garcin (1929–1938), ed. Pierre Lainé (Paris, 1987)

Interviews and Surveys

Céline, Louis-Ferdinand, 'Rabelais il a raté son coup: Une Interview sur *Gargantua* et *Pantagruel* pour Le Meilleur Livre du Mois', in Louis-Ferdinand Céline, *Le Style contre les idées: Rabelais, Zola, Sartre et les autres* (Paris, 1987), pp. 119–25
Interview with Elisabeth Porquerol, in *Cahiers Céline 1 et 2*, pp. 46–7
Interviews with Jean Guénot and Jacques Darribehaude, in *Cahiers Céline 1 et 2: Céline et l'actualité littéraire 1 et 2* (1976; 2nd edn, Paris, 1993), pp. 145–68
Interview with Louis-Albert Zbinden, *Radio Suisse Romande* (25 July 1957), transcribed in Godard, *Romans IV*, pp. 936–45
Interview with Madeleine Chapsal, 'Voyage au bout de la haine', *L'Express* (14 June 1957), Bibliothèque Nationale de France, MICR D-462 1957/01-1957/06
Interview with Robert Stromberg, 'A Talk with Louis-Ferdinand Céline', *Evergreen Review* (New York), V/19 (July–August 1961), pp. 102–7, reprod. in part in *Cahiers Céline 2*, pp. 172–7
North, Sterling, 'Dr. Destouches Grants First Press Interview', *Chicago Daily News* (19 July 1934), p. 25
Rousseaux, André, 'Faut-il tuer les prix littéraires?: Réponse à une enquête du *Figaro*', *Le Figaro* (9 June 1934), p. 4

Biographies of Céline

Fouché, Pascal, *Céline: 'Ça a débuté comme ça'* (Paris, 2001)
Gibault, François, *Céline I: Le Temps des espérances: 1894–1932* (Paris, 1977)
—, *Céline II: Délires et persécutions: 1932–1944* (Paris, 1985)
—, *Céline III: Cavalier de l'Apocalypse: 1944–1961* (Paris, 1981)
Godard, Henri, *Céline* (Paris, 2011)
Hewitt, Nicholas, *The Life of Céline: A Critical Biography* (Oxford, 1999)
McCarthy, Patrick, *Céline* (London, 1975)
Vitoux, Frédéric, *La Vie de Céline* (Paris, 1988; revd edn, Paris, 2005)

Other Biographical Sources

Alliot, David, *L'Affaire Louis-Ferdinand Céline: Les Archives de l'ambassade de France à Copenhague 1945–1951* (Paris, 2007)
—, and François Marchetti, *Céline au Danemark* (Paris, 2008)
Alméras, Philippe, *Dictionnaire Céline* (Paris, 2004)
Dimitrov, Théodore Deltchev, ed., *Louis-Ferdinand Céline (Docteur Destouches) à la Société des Nations, 1924–1927* (Geneva, 2001)
Richard, Gaël, 'Le Cuirassier blessé et ses médecins', *L'Année Céline* (2009), pp. 185–204
—, 'Janine et Louis: Nouveaux documents sur Londres et Suzanne Nebout', *L'Année Céline* (2006), pp. 105–26
—, 'Henry de Graffigny', *L'Année Céline* (2009), pp. 205–38
—, Eric Mazet and Jean-Paul Louis, eds, *Dictionnaire des personnages, des noms de personnes, figures et référents culturels dans l'œuvre romanesque de Céline*, 2 vols (Tusson, 2008)

Roux, Dominique de, Michel Thélia and Michel Beaujour, eds, *Cahiers Céline de l'Herne* (Paris, 1963, 1965, 1972, 1981, 2008)

Witness Accounts of Céline

Denoël, Cécile, 'Denoël jusqu'à Céline . . . qui lui ressemblait comme un frère', IMEC, Collection Denoël, DNL 3.2
Denoël, Robert, 'Comment j'ai connu et lancé Louis-Ferdinand Céline', Insitut Mémoires de l'édition contemporaine (IMEC), Collection Denoël, DNF 3.1
—, Interview with André Roubaud, *Marianne* (May 1939), quoted in *Le Bulletin célinien*, 420 (July–August 2019), p. 8
Juilland, Alphonse, *Elizabeth and Louis: Elizabeth Craig Talks about Louis-Ferdinand Céline* (Stanford, CA, 1991)
Millau, Christian, interview with Lucette Destouches, *Le Nouveau Candide*, 58 (7–14 June 1962), p. 9
Robert, Véronique, interview with Lucette Destouches, *Céline Secret* (Paris, 2001)

Biography of Lucette Destouches (Céline's Third Wife)

Alliot, David, *Madame Céline* (Paris, 2018)

Secondary Works Exclusively or Partly Devoted to Céline

Alliot, David, *Céline: Idées reçues sur un auteur sulfureux* (Paris, 2011)
—, *Le Paris de Céline* (Paris, 2017)
Anton, Sonia, *Céline épistolier: Écriture épistolaire et écriture littéraire* (Paris, 2006)
Blondiaux, Isabelle, *Céline, Portrait de l'artiste en psychiatre* (Paris, 2004)
de Bonneville, Pierre, *Céline et les femmes* (Paris, 2015)
Carroll, David, 'Literary Anti-Semitism: The Poetics of Race in Drumont and Céline', in *French Literary Fascism: Nationalism, Anti-Semitism and the Ideology of Culture* (Princeton, NJ, 1995), pp. 171–95
Combelle, Lucien, ed., *Louis-Ferdinand Céline: Le Style contre les idées: Rabelais, Zola, Sartre et les autres . . .* (Paris, 1987)
Coustille, Charles, *Antithèses: Mallarmé, Péguy, Paulhan, Céline, Barthes* (Paris, 2018)
Dauphin, Jean-Pierre, *Bibliographie des articles de presse et des études en langue française consacrés* à *Louis-Ferdinand Céline, 1914–1961* (Tusson, 2011)
Derval, André, 'L'Accueil critique de *Bagatelles pour un massacre*' (Montreal, 2010)
Duraffour, Annick, and Pierre-André Taguieff, *Céline: La race, le Juif – Légende littéraire et vérité historique* (Paris, 2017)
Gaitet, Pascale, *Political Stylistics: Popular Language as Literary Artifact* (London, 1992)
Germinario, Francesco, *Céline – Letteratura politica e antisemitismo* (Milan, 2011)
Godard, Henri, *À Travers Céline: La Littérature* (Paris, 2014)
—, *Un Autre Céline: De la fureur à la féerie* (Paris, 2008)
—, *Céline et Cie: Essai sur le roman français de l'entre-deux-guerres – Malraux, Guilloux, Cocteau, Genet, Queneau* (Paris, 2020)

—, *Céline scandale* (Paris, 1998)
—, *Mort à crédit de Louis-Ferdinand Céline* (Paris, 1996)
Hausmann, Frank-Rutger, *L.-F. Céline et Karl Epting*, ed. Arina Istratova (Brussels, 2008)
Hewitt, Nicholas, *The Golden Age of Louis-Ferdinand Céline* (Leamington Spa, 1987)
Hindus, Milton, *The Crippled Giant: A Literary Relationship with Louis-Ferdinand Céline*, new and expanded edn, with selections from the Céline–Hindus correspondence (Hanover, NH, 1986)
Kaplan, Alice Yaeger, 'The Céline Effect: A 1992 Survey of Contemporary American Writers', *Modernism/Modernity*, III/1 (January 1996), pp. 117–36
—, *Relevé des sources et citations dans 'Bagatelles pour un massacre'* (Tusson, 1987)
Kristeva, Julia, *Powers of Horror: An Essay on Abjection* (New York, 1982)
Monnier, Pierre, *Ferdinand Furieux* (Paris, 1979)
Muray, Philippe, *Céline* (1981; 2nd edn, Paris, 2001)
Pagès, Yves, *L.-F. Céline: Fictions du politique* (1994; 2nd edn Paris, 2010)
Peillon, Antoine, *Céline, un anti-Sémite exceptionnel: Une Histoire française* (Paris, 2011).
Richard, Gaël, *La Bretagne de Louis-Ferdinand Céline* (Tusson, 2013)
Richard, Jean-Pierre, *Nausée de Céline* (Paris, 1980)
Roussin, Philippe, *Misère de la littérature, terreur de l'histoire: Céline et la littérature contemporaine* (Paris, 2005)
—, ed. Alice Kaplan and Philippe Roussin, *South Atlantic Quarterly: Céline: USA*, XCIII/2 (Spring 1994)
—, *Céline à l'épreuve: Réceptions, critiques, influences*, ed. Philippe Roussin, Alain Schaffner and Régis Tettamanzi (Paris, 2016)
Roynette, Odile, *Un Long tourment: Louis-Ferdinand Céline entre deux guerres (1914–1945)* (Paris, 2015)
Sanos, Sandrine, 'Negroid Jews against White men': Louis-Ferdinand Céline and the Politics of Literature', in *The Aesthetics of Hate: Far-Right Intellectuals, Antisemitism, and Gender in 1930s France* (Stanford, CA, 2013), pp. 158–93
Sautermeister, Christine, *Louis-Ferdinand Céline à Sigmaringen: Novembre 1944–mars 1945: Chronique d'un séjour controversé* (Paris, 2013)
Sollers, Philippe, *Céline* (Paris, 2009)
Solomon, Philip H., *Understanding Céline* (Columbia, SC, 1992)
Thomas, Merlin, *Louis-Ferdinand Céline* (London and Boston, MA, 1979)
Vebret, Jules, *Céline l'infréquentable?*, preface by Jean-Marie Rouart (Paris, 2011)
Vitoux, Frédéric, *Louis-Ferdinand Céline: Misère et parole* (Paris, 1973)
Watts, Philip, *Allegories of the Purge: How Literature Responded to the Postwar Trials of Writers and Intellectuals in France* (Stanford, CA, 1998), pp. 140–63

Articles on Céline

Aharony, Michal, 'Nihilism and Anti-Semitism: The Reception of Céline's *Journey to the End of the Night* in Israel', *Rethinking History*, XIX/1 (2015), pp. 111–32
Beuve-Méry, Alain., and Thomas Wieder, 'Frédéric Mitterand fait volte-face et écarte Céline des célébrations de 2011', *Le Monde* (22 January 2011)

Bory, Jean-Louis, 'Que faire avec Céline?', *Le Nouvel Observateur* (25 February 1965), Bibliothèque Nationale de France (BNF), Fol-Z-15751964/11/19-1965/02/25

Tatu, Laurent, Odile Roynette and Julien Bogousslavsky, 'Louis-Ferdinand Céline: From First World War Neurological Wound to Mythomania', in *Neurological Disorders in Famous Artists, Part 4*, ed. Julien Bogousslavsky and Laurent Tatu (Basel, 2018), pp. 23–37

In *Le Bulletin célinien*

Brun, A.-Charles, 'Un Éditeur défend son auteur', *Le Petit Parisien* (4 August 1936), repr. in *Le Bulletin célinien*, 420 (July–August 2019), pp. 7–8

Cardot, Charles-Antoine, 'Vichy face aux *Beaux draps*', *Le Bulletin célinien*, 420 (July–August 2019), pp. 11–14

Cresciucci, Alain, 'Un Grand livre sur Roger Nimier', *Le Bulletin célinien*, 410 (September 2018), pp. 21–3

—, 'Retour sur *Les Beaux draps*', *Le Bulletin célinien*, 423 (November 2019), pp. 5–9

Dauphin, Jean-Pierre, 'Le Lancement de *Voyage* et la querelle du Prix Goncourt', *Le Bulletin célinien*, 413 (December 2018), pp. 7–18

Laudelot, Marc, 'Le Bras de fer entre Gallimard et le CRIF continue', *Le Bulletin célinien*, 406 (April 2018), pp. 13–17

—, 'Un Débat sur la réédition des pamphlets', *Le Bulletin célinien*, 410 (September 2018), pp. 5–10

—, 'L'Interview de Céline dans *Europe-Amérique*', *Le Bulletin célinien*, 422 (October 2019), pp. 7–23

—, 'Pierre Laval vu par Céline', *Le Bulletin célinien*, 412 (November 2018), pp. 7–8

—, 'La Polémique de l'été 1957 dans l'hebdomadaire *Dimanche-Matin*', *Le Bulletin célinien*, 421 (September 2019), pp. 7–15

—, 'Une Réédition sous surveillance', *Le Bulletin célinien*, 403 (January 2018), pp. 5–8

Le Blanc, Robert, 'Le Choc de Breugel: Céline oublié à l'exposition de Vienne?', *Le Bulletin célinien*, 414 (January 2019), pp. 8–11

Mazet, Eric, 'Céline et la Sirène', *Le Bulletin célinien*, 23 (July 1984), pp. 10–15

—, 'Un Poème d'Auguste Destouches', *Le Bulletin célinien*, 403 (January 2018), pp. 9–11

Terray, Emmanuel, 'Céline au bout de la nuit africaine', *Le Bulletin célinien*, 412 (November 2018), pp. 13–23

The Polemical Background to Céline

Announcements in favour of banning Céline's TV interview, *Télémagazine*, 193 (5–11 July 1957), p. 21, BNF, DN2-702L4 19-B

Bellosta, Marie-Christine, 'Rééditer les pamphlets?', *Magazine littéraire, Nouveaux regards: Louis-Ferdinand Céline*, hors série (2012), p. 97

Catani, Damian: 'Louis-Ferdinand Céline, Literary Genius or National Pariah? Defining Moral Parameters for Influential Cultural Figures, Post-Charlie

Hebdo', *French Cultural Studies Special Issue: Understanding Charlie*, XXVII/3 (August 2016), pp. 268–78
Cousteau, Pierre-Antoine, 'M. Céline rallie le fumier (doré) du système', *Rivarol* (20 juin 1957)
Flambard-Weisbart, Véronique, 'Céline et Robert Allerton Parker', *Études céliniennes*, 5 (Winter 2009–10), pp. 5–25
Gadret, Matthias, 'Les Entretiens du *Petit Célinien* (VII): Régis Tettamanzi', *Le Petit célinien* (23 September 2012), www.lepetitcelinien.com
'Pour et contre', *L'Express* (28 June 1957), p. 31, BNF, MICR D-462 1957/01-1957/06
Savin, Tristan, 'Le Making of par Madeleine Chapsal', in *Lire*: Céline, les derniers secrets, hors série 7 (May 2008), p. 82
'Sur la réponse d'un préfet', *L'Humanité* (13 September 1957), p. 2, BNF, MICR D-30 L1.15-MFM
Télémagazine, 192 (28 June–4 July), p. 25
Willsher, Kim, 'Céline: French Literary Genius or Repellent Antisemite? New Film Rekindles an Old Conflict', *The Guardian* (13 March 2016)

Lectures and Podcasts on Céline

Dambre, Marc, 'Roger Nimier, son ami et dernier interlocuteur chez Gallimard', Autour de Céline, Fondation Singer-Polignac-Paris, 9 November 2011, www.dailymotion.com/video/xmeqba

Reviews of Céline's Novels and Pamphlets

Abel, Dominick, 'The Searing Black Humour of Celine' (review of *Castle to Castle*, Ralph Manheim's translation of *D'un château l'autre*, 1969), *Chicago News* (15 March 1969)
Guterman, Norbert, 'Dirt for Art's Sake', *New Republic*, XCVI/1241 (14 September 1938), p. 165, IMEC, BI. Fol Z 1254
Higginson Begley, Sarah, Review of *Castle to Castle*, 'Céline and His Three Dots . . .', *Christian Science Monitor* (20 March 1969)
Hindus, Milton, 'A Literary Event of the First Order', *Evening Globe* (Boston, MA) (9 February 1969)
Morton, Frederic, 'The First to Mine Delirium' (review of *Castle to Castle*), *Nation* (17 March 1969)
O'Brien, Justin, 'Autobiography of an Underdog' (review of John H. P. Marks's translation of *Death on the Instalment Plan*, 1938), *The Nation* (27 August 1938), pp. 207–8
O'London, John, Review of *Mea Culpa* and *The Life and Work of Semmelweis* (trans. Robert Allerton Parker), *Weekly* (4 February 1938)
Ostrovsky, Erika, 'Buffoons of the Apocalypse' (review of *Castle to Castle*), *Saturday Review* (1 February 1969), pp. 31, 63
Putnam, Samuel, 'Prelude to the Revolution' (review of *Journey to the End of the Night*, trans. John H. P. Marks, 1934), *Saturday Review of Literature* (28 April 1934), pp. 657–62
—, Review of *Voyage au bout de la nuit* by Louis-Ferdinand Céline (Paris, 1932), *Books Abroad*, VII/2 (April 1933), pp. 163–4
Review of *Castle to Castle*, *Playboy* (April 1969), pp. 34b–c and 36b.

Review of *Mea Culpa* and *The Life and Work of Semmelweis*, *The Statesman* (Calcutta) (27 February 1938)
Review of *Mea Culpa* and *The Life and Work of Semmelweis*, *Times Literary Supplement* (22 January 1938)
Rousseaux, André, 'Maintenant aux querelles!' (review of *D'un château l'autre*, 1936), *Le Figaro* (23 May 1936)
Sokolov, Raymond, 'Noodles and Hatred' (review of *Castle to Castle*), *Newsweek* (27 January 1969), pp. 47–9
Stonier, G. W., 'Review of *Death on the Instalment Plan*, Chatto and Windus, Marks; and *L'École des cadavres*, Denoël', *New Statesman and The Nation* (14 January 1939)
Walcott, John: 'Confessions of a Novelist-Hero' (review of *Death on the Instalment Plan*), *North American Review*, CCXLVI/2 (Winter 1938–9), pp. 390–3, IMEC, BI:BZ 590

Reviews of Theatrical and Musical Adaptations of Céline

Medina, Jacques, 'Céline en musique: *À l'Agité du bocal*, de Bernard Cavanna, par *Ars Nova*, Direction Philippe Nahon (CD + DVD, empreinte digitale)', Le Choix de L'Obs, *L'Obs*, 2816 (25–31 October 2018)
Thorpe, Vanessa, 'Why I Had to Tell the Story of the Genius Who Invented Hospital Hygiene' (interview with Mark Rylance on *Doctor Semmelweis*), *The Guardian*, 13 June 2020, www.theguardian.com

Literary and Cultural Background

Angenot, Marc, *La Parole pamphlétaire: Contribution à la typologie des discours modernes* (Paris, 1982)
Baert, Patrick, *The Existentialist Moment: The Rise of Sartre as Public Intellectual* (Cambridge, 2015)
Brassai, Georges, *Henry Miller: Grandeur nature* (Paris, 1975)
Buccola, Regina, '"The Story Shall Be Changed": The Fairy Feminism of a *Midsummer Night's Dream*', in *William Shakespeare's* A Midsummer Night's Dream, Bloom's Modern Critical Interpretations (New York, 2010), pp. 146–7
Cannon, David, *The Paris Zone: A Cultural History, 1840–1944* (London, 2015)
Catani, Damian, *Evil: A History in Modern Literature and Thought* (London, 2013)
Crubellier, Maurice, *Histoire culturelle de la France* (Paris, 1974)
Duhamel, Georges, *Scènes de la vie future* (Paris, 1930)
Ferguson, Robert, *Henry Miller: A Life* (New York, 1991)
Grover, Frédéric J., *Six entretiens avec André Malraux sur les écrivains de son temps (1959–1975)* (Paris, 1978)
Lane, Véronique, *The French Genealogy of the Beat Generation: Burroughs, Ginsberg and Kerouac's Appropriations of Modern Literature, from Rimbaud to Michaux* (New York, 2017)
Loiseaux, Gérard, *La Littérature de la défaite et de la collaboration, d'après Phönix oder Asche? (Phénix ou cendres?) de Bernhard Payr* (Paris, 1995)

Mance, Henry, 'The New Office Politics', FT Weekend, *Financial Times* (25 July 2020), p. 2
Philippe, Élisabeth, 'Séparer l'homme de l'artiste: Mode d'emploi', *L'Obs*, no. 2925 (19–25 November 2020), pp. 65–8
Rawlinson, Kevin, 'Cecil Rhodes Statue to Remain at Oxford after "Overwhelming Support"', *The Guardian* (29 January 2016), available at www.theguardian.com
Sapiro, Gisèle, *La Responsabilité de l'écrivain: Littérature, droit et moral en France (XIXe–XXIe siècle)* (Paris, 2011)
—, *Peut-on dissocier l'œuvre de l'auteur?* (Paris, 2020)
Spotts, Frederic, *The Shameful Peace: How French Artists and Intellectuals Survived the Nazi Occupation* (New Haven, CT, 2008)

Historical Background

Badiou, Alain and Eric Hazan, *L'Antisémitisme partout aujourd'hui en France* (Paris, 2011)
Batchelor, Ray, *Henry Ford: Mass Production, Modernism and Design* (New York, 1994)
Becker, Jean-Jacques, *1914: Comment les Français sont entrés dans la guerre* (Paris, 1977)
Burrin, Philippe, *La France à l'heure allemande: 1940–1944* (Paris, 1995)
Corbin, Alain, 'Les Historiens et la fiction: Usages, tentation, nécessités . . .', *Le Débat*, 165 (May–August 2011), pp. 57–61
Curcio, Vincent, *Henry Ford* (New York, 2013)
Heller, Gerhard, *Un Allemand à Paris: 1940–1944*, with the help of Jean Grand (Paris, 1981)
Jones, Colin, *Paris: Biography of a City* (London, 2004)
Lacey, David, *Ford: The Men and the Machine* (London, 1986)
Lambauer, Barbara, *Otto Abetz et les Français, ou l'envers de la collaboration*, preface by Jean-Pierre Azéma (Paris, 2001)
Lay, Paul, 'The Beauty and Savagery of Ernst Jünger's Wartime Diaries', *New Statesman* (20 February 2019), available at www.newstatesman.com
Lejeune, Dominique, *La France de la Belle Époque: 1896–1914* (Paris, 2017)
Michels, Eckard, *Das Deutsche Institut in Paris 1940–1944: Ein Beitrag zu den deutsch–französischen Kulturbeziehungen und zur auswärtigen Kulturpolitik des dritten Reiches* (Stuttgart, 1993)
Noguères, Louis, *La Dernière étape: Sigmaringen* (Paris, 1956)
Ory, Pascal, *Les Collaborateurs, 1940–1945* (Paris, 1980)
Rousso, Henri, 'Sigmaringen, l'ultime trahison' (interview with Rachel Kahn and Laurent Perrin), France 3, *Cinétévé*, 9 March 1996
Schofield, Hugh, 'La Belle Epoque: Paris 1914', *BBC News*, www.bbc.co.uk
Sowerwine, Charles, *France since 1870* (Basingstoke, 2009)
Stevenson, David, *Cataclysm: The First World War as Political Tragedy* (New York, 2004)
—, *The Outbreak of the First World War: 1914 in Perspective* (London, 1997)
Winock, Michel, *La Belle Époque: La France de 1900 à 1914* (Paris, 2002)
—, *Nationalisme, antisemitisme, fascisme en France* (Paris, 1990)

ACKNOWLEDGEMENTS

This book has taken me on my own journey, sometimes into the night, but with some welcome shafts of daylight. I am particularly grateful to Vivian Constantinopoulos, my editor at Reaktion Books, for commissioning this biography and ably guiding me towards its completion with her patience, attention to detail and sound advice on both its style and content. Amy Salter and the editorial team at Reaktion Books have been similarly helpful, efficient and conscientious when preparing the proofs. I am much indebted to my Birkbeck colleague and friend Eckard Michels, for his careful reading of the entire manuscript and sharing his historical expertise on the chapters that discuss Vichy France and Collaborationism. My heartfelt thanks go to the librarians and archive team at IMEC, in the beautiful Abbaye D'Ardenne in Normandy, especially André Derval, Julie Le Men and Mélina Reynaud, for granting me image rights and for their generous assistance during both my visit in August 2019 and the many challenging months that followed. I would like to thank François Gibault for permission to reproduce images from his private collection, Marc Laudelot, editor of *Le Bulletin célinien*, for his invaluable pointers on the latest Céline scholarship and François Marchetti for the nuggets of information on Céline's exile in Denmark that he shared with me by telephone in March 2019. To Margaret McCormack for her meticulous compiling of the Index and Kit Yee Wong for publishing tips, I also extend my sincere thanks. I am grateful to Rana Mitter and Zahid Worley at BBC Radio 3 for inviting me to a stimulating panel discussion on Céline in October 2018 and to Robert Barsky and Yvonne Boyer for asking me to present my work on the author to the Bandy Center at Vanderbilt University in April 2021. Over the last few years, I have benefitted from the input of colleagues and students at Birkbeck, who have acted as a valuable sounding-board for many of the ideas in this book. Financial assistance from the School of Arts at Birkbeck for the images, Index and production costs has also greatly been appreciated.

Since Céline is both the most appropriate and ill-advised author on whom to write during a global pandemic, I would like to take this opportunity to acknowledge the moral support of the following people: Patrick Baert, Emily Baker, Nicole Catani, Mario, Linda and Remo Catani, Dennis Clarke, Martin Crowley, Zahid Durrani, Memet Erdemgil, Ceri Evans, Rian Evans, Carlos Galvis, George Guida, Jonathan Hosgood, John Kraniauskas, Olivia Kesselring, Julien and Patrice Laloye,

David Lehman, Bertrand Marchal, Caroline Micaelia, Clare Mulholland, Emma Murray, Ollie Nelkin, Jonathan Shih, Patrick Theriault, Luis Trindade, Marielle Van der Meer, Peter Williams, Stacy Williams and Greg Zinger.

PHOTO ACKNOWLEDGEMENTS

The editors and publishers wish to express their thanks to the below sources of illustrative material and/or permission to reproduce it.

Alamy Stock Photo: pp. 6 (Everett Collection Inc), 273 (Photo 12/Luc Fournol); Archives Louis-Ferdinand Céline/courtesy IMEC (Institut Mémoires de l'édition contemporaine), Saint-Germain-la-Blanche-Herbe: pp. 50 and 51 (photos Burrow), 157, 260, 261; Archives Louis-Ferdinand Céline – Collection Lucie Destouches et François Gibault/courtesy IMEC: pp. 29, 31, 62, 79, 109, 110, 112, 133, 183; Archives Robert Denoël/courtesy IMEC: p. 135; Fonds Louis-Ferdinand Céline/courtesy IMEC: pp. 70, 121, 138, 148, 261; Getty Images: pp. 65 (adoc-photos/Corbis), 264 (AFP), 271 and 272 (Roger Viollet/Lipnitzki); LPLT (CC BY-SA 3.0): p. 279.

INDEX

Page numbers for illustrations are in *italics*